MEMOIRS

OF

THE LIFE

OF THE

RIGHT HON. WARREN HASTINGS

MEMOIRS

OF

THE LIFE

OF THE

RIGHT HON. WARREN HASTINGS,

FIRST GOVERNOR-GENERAL OF BENGAL.

COMPILED FROM ORIGINAL PAPERS.

BY THE REV. GEORGE ROBERT GLEIG, M.A.

IN THREE VOLUMES

VOL. III.

GYAN

Published by

GYAN

Gyan Publishing House
5, Ansari Road
Daryaganj, New Delhi-110002
Phone: 011-47034999, 9811692060
E-mail: books@gyanbooks.com

Distribution Network
gyanbooks.com
India, USA, Canada, UK, Australia, France

ISBN: 978-81-212-7345-9 (Set)
978-81-212-7342-8 (PB)
First Published, 1841

2nd Impression 2023

Printed at: Gyan Press, Delhi.

MEMOIRS OF THE LIFE OF THE RIGHT HON. WARREN HASTINGS (VOL. III.)
Author: GEORGE ROBERT GLEIG

MEMOIRS

OF

THE LIFE

OF THE

RIGHT HON. WARREN HASTINGS,

FIRST GOVERNOR-GENERAL OF BENGAL.

COMPILED FROM ORIGINAL PAPERS.

BY THE REV. G. R. GLEIG, M.A.

CHAPLAIN TO THE ROYAL HOSPITAL AT CHELSEA, AND RECTOR OF IVYCHURCH, IN KENT.

AUTHOR OF

THE LIFE OF SIR THOMAS MUNRO.

VOL. III.

LONDON:

RICHARD BENTLEY, NEW BURLINGTON STREET,

Publisher in Ordinary to Her Majesty.

1841.

CONTENTS OF VOL. III.

MEMOIRS,

&c. &c.

CHAPTER I.

State of Affairs in Carnatic and at the different Native Courts—Correspondence with different Functionaries.

WHILE these things were going on elsewhere, the important business of the war, including the immediate defence of the Carnatic, and the conduct of a variety of subsidiary operations, was not neglected. Of the mission of Sir Eyre Coote to assume the command of the army at Madras, as well as of the march of a large detachment of troops overland from Bengal, notice has elsewhere been taken. Sir Eyre found, on reaching the scene of action, that everything was there in confusion. The Sepoys, dispirited by recent reverses, could scarcely be brought to look the enemy in the face. The Europeans, few in number, were dispersed and broken up into petty garrisons. There was neither unity of purpose, nor vigour of design, among those whose business it was to direct in the field. There was wrangling and mismanagement, and extreme jealousy of foreign interference among the persons composing the cabinet. Moreover money, stores, cattle, provisions, every thing on which the efficiency of an army depends, was wanting. And while the Nabob, from whom the means of supporting the war was expected, declared himself unable to furnish a single rupee, and complained bitterly of the insults that were offered to him, Hyder, the common enemy of him and of the English, ranged over the open country at pleasure. Nevertheless, Sir Eyre Coote, though he reported these things to the Supreme Council with the acrimony and querulousness that characterised his temper, spared no personal exertions to repair the evils which they were eminently calculated to produce. The troops were paid a portion of their arrears. Cattle for draught and carriage were, as far as possible, provided, a bold face was put upon affairs in general, and the army took the field. I need not follow it in its career of drawn battles, and somewhat profitless victories. Whatever could be done to work a machine so imperfectly mounted as to defy the ingenuity of man to work it effectually, Sir Eyre Coote accomplished; and he had the satisfaction, at the close of the campaign to perceive, that, though the Carnatic was not free, his own troops had recovered their confidence, while Hyder, dispirited by the results of various encounters, was become proportionably deficient in enterprise.

Sir Eyre Coote complained that from the Governor and Council of Fort St. George he did not receive the support to which he was entitled. They would neither supply his wants by their own efforts, nor permit him to find supplies for himself, and he sought from the Supreme Council such an enlargement of powers, as would render him in the conduct of the war quite independent. Lord Macartney, on the other hand, accused Sir Eyre Coote of acting towards himself and his colleagues with intolerable insolence. He would pay no attention to advice, far less obey an order in matters purely military; yet he was for ever interfering with civil affairs, which no wise concerned him. Neither were these gentlemen content to make their appeals by letter. Each sent his agent to Calcutta,—Mr. Graham, Sir Eyre Coote's Persian interpreter, coming on behalf of the General, and Mr. Staunton, private secretary to Lord Macartney, offering himself as the representative of the Governor. Mr. Hastings could not but feel that he was thrown by these proceedings into a difficult situation. He therefore strove, as the best and wisest course, to reconcile the complainants one to another; and wrote with this view the following letters:—

To the Right Honourable Lord Macartney.

Fort William, 21st March, 1782.

My Lord,—I have derived the highest satisfaction from the receipt of your letter of the 2d ultimo, by the hands of Mr. Staunton. I am truly sensible of the force of your Lordship's sentiments in my favour when I consider that, in the most arduous and critical situation of affairs under your Government, you have deprived yourself of the able assistance of your confidential secretary for my ease and information. The impression which so flattering a mark of your Lordship's attention has made upon my mind, I will not attempt to describe, persuaded that Mr. Staunton has observed, and will do justice to them. I will content myself with simply making you my warmest acknowledgments. I have endeavoured to give effect to your Lordship's design in this ingenuous proceeding by the most free and unreserved communication of my sentiments to Mr. Staunton upon every subject which you have charged him with, and I trust that they are such as will convince your Lordship of the anxious desire which I have to co-operate with you firmly and liberally for the security of the Carnatic, for the support of your authority, and for the honour of your administration, by every aid which this Government and my personal influence can afford.

I refer your Lordship to Mr. Staunton for the detail and result of the long and frequent conversations which we have had; he will give you complete information, and I hope as complete satisfaction on every point which has been in discussion.

I am persuaded that, after those clear explanations which have now taken place, no future interruption will happen to that mutual good understanding and cordiality with which our correspondence commenced, and I beg leave to assure your Lordship that few things are more the objects of my wishes than to preserve and improve this harmony for the protection and advancement of the important interests committed to our charge. I have the honour to be, with the highest esteem, my Lord, your Lordship's most obedient and most faithful humble servant.

To Lieut.-Gen. Sir EYRE COOTE, K.B.

Fort William, 21st March, 1782.

Dear Sir,—The public letters which you will have received from this Government since Mr. Graham's arrival will have convinced you of my particular and ready desire to afford you every support which could be given to you by the influence of this Government, nor has that of the other members of it been less zealous for the same effect. You will have perceived that we have confined our interposition to influence only. The reason, and that which operated with greatest force on my mind was, that the tone of authority would but have given offence, and perhaps excited defiance, and though the Court of Directors have empowered us to issue our orders to the other presidencies, and have commanded them to obey us, yet as they have given us no power to enforce our orders, the obedience which may be paid to them remains as optional as the compliance which they might have given to our advice, before we were invested with this extraordinary charge. The president and select committee are possessed of our full sentiments on the points which you have specifically referred to us, and it is at their peril if they refuse to conform to them.

Notwithstanding your pointed reference to us of the subject of cattle, and its essential consequence to every movement of your army, I own that I felt a repugnance at the interference of this Government in a point of such inferior detail; but this sensation was much removed by Lord Macartney himself, who had instructed Mr. Staunton to consult me upon the subject. From the charges of oppression and venality which have been publicly and universally thrown on some of his predecessors, great allowances must be made for his Lordship's apprehensions of the consequences which every act of apparent violence may produce on his reputation, and I have no doubt that he will be equally pleased and relieved by the opinion which we have given upon this subject, for it is impossible that he should have any other doubt or scruple respecting it. If the service should require the appropriation of every bullock in the Carnatic to save it from impending destruction, none but a visionary casuist, and he must be far removed from any interest in it, would seriously object to it. The same principle will equally apply to every other exigency of the war, and more especially to your particular command, which we have said ought to be unlimited both in its place and operations. We have exacted from the select committee, as far as we could exact it, their fullest confidence in your conduct, and their assured sanction to all your acts.

That liberal allowance which we have recommended to them to give, I should recommend to you to assume in every case which falls under our description of the necessity requiring it; that is, to repeat the words of our letter, the conciliation of the dependant chiefs of the Carnatic, the acceptance of terms offered by those of the enemy, and in general such other acts as do not fall within the express line of military command, but which may contribute to the success of its operations, either by adding strength to our arms, or weakening those which may be opposed to them. And I believe I may venture to say that such would have been the terms of our letter to you, dictated for the purpose of removing the restraints which your late difference with the government of Fort St. George might induce you to impose on your conduct, but for our apprehension that both its construction and operation, if our sentiments were conveyed in an official form, would contradict and defeat the conciliatory spirit which has dictated the mode of interference which we have adopted.

I can readily believe that it must be foreign from your wishes to add to your unavoidable vexations any grounds of contest with the government of Fort St. George, to which you are not compelled by some very strong necessity. But in a service of such hazard as yours, many cases must occur to which the regular powers of your command may not be competent, for which no provision has been made, which will not wait for express instructions, or which may be defeated of their objects by communication. These may be of the most important consequence, and perhaps such as may decide on the existence of the Company's interests in the Carnatic. In every such case I must suppose that you would act by the inherent authority of your general trust, and that the Government under which you act would ratify it. I understand that opportunities have occurred, and it is sufficient for the application of the principle which I have recommended that such may occur, of reconciling and binding the Polygars and other dependant chiefs of the Carnatic to our interest by concessions pledged to them under a guarantee in which they could confide; of offers made by men of high command in the service or dependant on the enemy, of engagements for money or provisions on specified conditions; of districts either newly recovered or unprovided of agents, for the security of their revenue, and too remote for their timely appointment in the regular mode. These are instances which occur to my recollection, of such a necessity as I have supposed would warrant your acting without express instructions, and bind the Government of Madras to ratify and confirm it. But even these may require for your complete justification, both that they should be combined with such other circumstances as will form the necessity of a discretionary latitude, and that the mode in which it is exercised should be in itself unexceptionable. Neither could this Government prescribe on points of such nice distinction, nor will they admit of a specification. They are in their nature contingent and indefinite.

I feel that I write under a check that will not allow me the free expression of my decided judgment, for I am imperceptibly led to advise caution, where I had intended to excite confidence and decision. I will therefore close the subject by assuring you that you cannot possess the confidence of this Government in a greater degree than that which it is already disposed to give you; but you immediately depend upon another Government, whose actions we have no power to control, and whose confidence we should wish, even if we had that power, to flow spontaneously to you, rather than that it should be yielded to our authority, or to the compulsion of necessity. I am afraid I must speak plainer to be clearly understood. In a word, if I myself stood alone in the charge of the government of Fort St. George, I would give you an unbounded liberty of action, or if I had not given it, and you had assumed it, I would approve or ratify your assumption of it. But in the application of this doctrine to others who will judge for themselves, and have a right to judge for themselves, I am fearful of saying what they should give, or you should take, lest my opinion, which cannot operate as authority, should prove the occasion of fresh differences, and draw on me the imputation of having excited them, in contradiction of my professed desire of reconciling those which have already arisen.

I have but a word to say upon the allusion which you make in the beginning of your letter to the long intermission which has happened in our correspondence. I will own that I could not but regret that while I was labouring to afford you all the aids of this Government, my intentions, even in the very instances in which I had been impelled by the most friendly consideration for your reputation, scarce less than for the public service, were either misrepresented or misconstrued as injurious to you. How you could credit such a suggestion I cannot conceive. But I have made allowances. Its impression on my feelings, though not slight, was transient, and you have done me justice in the conviction which you express that it has produced no cessation in my zealous endeavours for the general success of our affairs; for perhaps you are the only man now on earth from whom I could sustain personal grievances, and not only forgive them, but allow him to extort from me my applause, and even my esteem for his public virtues. Your exertions and sacrifices have been such as exceed any credit which could have been given you for them, or could have been expected from any man.

You are already so fully informed on other points by the letters of the Board, that I will not add to the length of this by repeating them, further than to refer you to Mr. Graham, to whom, considering him as your confidential agent, I have explained my sentiments in the fullest manner upon every point relative to the public affairs, and our objects in them upon which you can desire to be informed, and I trust to his comprehension and judgment for the faithful repetition of them. I have the honour to be, dear Sir, &c.

The results of this reference to the Supreme Government were so far advantageous, that Lord Macartney and his colleagues in office gave way; and the General was enabled, so soon as the return of dry weather would allow, to take the field again with powers considerably enlarged. It cannot be said, however, that the campaign of 1782 was in any respect a glorious one. The British army still laboured to a fearful extent under the disadvantage of inadequate means of transport, while the whole country within which its operations lay, was a desert. Perhaps, too, Admiral Souffrein, however inferior to Sir Edward Hughes in seamanship, at least equalled his gallant adversary in activity and mental resources; by which means large reinforcements of French troops made good their landing, and the important fortress of Trincomalee was lost. The English, on the other hand, were not successful in an attempt to surprise Arnee, within which a large amount of Hyder's treasure was deposited. They fought but a doubtful battle in its neighbourhood, and sustained the loss of a regiment of European cavalry, which was drawn into an ambuscade and destroyed, on the march back to Madras. Moreover it was at this juncture that the General, made aware of the treaty into which the Bengal government had entered with the Mahrattas, endeavoured, by threatening Hyder with an attack from that quarter, to lead him into negociations for peace; a proceeding which was greatly blamed by the civil authorities as an encroachment on their privileges; and which, not, as was insinuated, without some secret interference on their parts, led to nothing. Finally, after various encounters at sea, and marches and countermarches on shore, the former in no instance decisive, the latter harassing and unsatisfactory to those engaged in them, the army returned in September to its cantonments at Madras; where the General, having sustained two shocks of paralysis, gave up the command, and set out soon afterwards for Bengal.

And now, before I proceed to describe the consequences of this unfortunate event, or to follow up the progress of the war to its termination, it may be well if I insert one or two specimens of the sort of correspondence which the Governor-general kept up all this while with his public and private agents in various parts of the world. Let it be borne in mind that India was not then, as it is now, subject, either directly or indirectly, throughout its length and breadth, to British influence. Native powers there were in every quarter independent, and jealous one of another; to preserve peace among whom was a point of scarcely less importance to the Company than to hinder them from combining for the destruction of the English. Accordingly, residents were stationed at the courts of Hyderabad, Naugpoor, and Poonah, not less, as a matter of course, than at Lucknow; while Delhi itself, in spite of the decay of the Mogul power, was not overlooked. For the King's great supporter, Nudjeff Cawn, was dead; many powerful chiefs were intriguing to receive the vacant honour, while the Mahrattas strove to wring from the King's weakness a grant of territory, which would have brought them into dangerous and inconvenient proximity with the English. At Delhi, therefore, as well as at the other capitals, Mr. Hastings was determined to establish a resident, through whom he might be informed of events as from day to day they befel, and to whom he might trust for the proper maintenance of British interests.

I subjoin a few specimens of the manner in which this important species of correspondence was carried on. Mr. Hastings's letters are never, as will be seen, formal or stately. They are, on the contrary, open, frank, and friendly; indeed, it was a marked feature in his character that no man ever served under him, and did his duty, but that he succeeded ere long in establishing a strong claim on his personal regard. Mr. Holland, to whom the following are addressed, was the gentleman whom the Madras government thought fit to remove; but who was continued at Hyderabad by the authority of the Supreme Court, and did good service there.

To John Holland, Esq.

Fort William, 6th March, 1782.

Sir,—A letter which I had the pleasure to receive from you, dated, as I believe, the 5th of December, 1780, or written about that time, contained the detail of a conversation which you had with the Nabob

Nizam-ul-Moolk upon the subject of the confederacy which had been formed against our nation, and of which in the conversation he acknowledged himself to have been the author, justifying it on the principles of self-defence, and charging Sir Thomas Rumbold with having compelled him to it by his threats, and actual infringements of the treaty subsisting between him and the Company. Your letter was laid before the Board, but by some accident has been mislaid, as neither the original nor duplicate after a long search can be found in the office. I shall esteem myself greatly obliged to you if you will send me an attested copy of it in duplicate, as it is of the utmost consequence to the defence of my public character against the attempts which have been made in England to charge me with having been the occasion of the present war in the Carnatic. What I recollect of the Nizam's declarations is so full and absolute a confutation of that aspersion, that I believe it will require no other. I am, with great esteem, Sir, yours, &c.

To the same.

Calcutta, 14th March, 1782.

Sir,—I have just received your favour of the 8th instant, and all the preceding in their order, with (as I believe) all their duplicates. The reports of the Berar agents are absolutely false, and appear to be as contrary to the policy of their master, who is himself no less anxious than your Nabob to obtain possession of the person of Ragonaut Row.

Having committed the charge of the treaty for peace with the Peishwa to Mr. Anderson with full powers, and Mahdajee Sindia having also received full powers for the same purpose from the Peishwa, it is unnecessary, and might tend to impede the effect of their commissions, were we to make his highness acquainted with any of the points of our positive instructions, or to give him an effective participation in the negociation. Yet I think it may be of use to undeceive him upon the points which he has supposed us disposed to yield, whether the supposition be his own, or the suggestion of others. You may therefore affirm on the surest authority that we never will consent to deliver up Ragonaut Row to any one, or to do any act that shall abridge his personal liberty; that we will not surrender Salsette; that we will not pay a single rupee either as an indemnification for the expenses of the war, as a restitution of revenue, or on any other ground; nor that we will subject the Company to the chout or any other tax or tribute. With respect to the last article, you may qualify the assertion, by supposing a bare possibility of it in the event of his abandoning us, and compelling us to purchase an alliance as a counterpoise to his power if opposed to us. Though I express such a supposition, it is so inconsistent with his wisdom, his interest, and his good faith, that the improbability of it places it almost beyond the bounds of possibility.

You will be pleased to observe that I have confined these negative assertions to the three points contained in your letter, it being unnecessary to add what resolutions have been formed on others which are not objects with the Nabob Nizam Ally Cawn.

Mr. Holland was as yet comparatively a stranger to Mr. Hastings; Mr. Chapman was not; and hence the difference of tone observable in the letters addressed to each. Yet in the former instance, not less than in the latter, a spirit of kindness and personal interest is shown, which could hardly fail of insuring the zealous co-operation of the individual who was its object. It was Mr. Chapman's duty, on the other hand, to conciliate and manage the Court of Berar, which the interference of Sindia, in adjusting the Mahratta peace, had considerably disconcerted. Let the subjoined tell their own tale; for they are selected at random from many more which relate to the same subject.

To Charles Chapman, Esq.

Fort William, 9th March, 1783.

Sir,—I have received yours of the 15th and 16th ultimo. I have but one answer to the Rajah's message, and that he has repeatedly received with full replies to all his letters.

I made advances to Mahdajee Sindia by the advice of Moodajee. It produced an immediate treaty of peace with Sindia separately, and a general cessation of hostilities. It has since produced a treaty with the Peishwa, which has been ratified on both sides, and is doubtless by this time interchanged, as the 24th of the last month was appointed for that final ceremony. On what grounds can I now depart from it, or Moodajee require it? I have declared him to be the prime mover of this negociation. Is it his wish that I should break the treaty with which it has terminated, and say that this also was by his advice? If I could submit to practise so weak and faithless a policy, what credit would he give to my professions of friendship towards himself? Besides, you may assure him that the consequences would be fatal to myself in the punishment which the justice of my country would inflict on me for the violation of its faith.

In a word, I shall ever consider Moodajee as the friend of the English nation, to whom I first made him known, and in whose favour have exacted its gratitude for the instances which I have experienced of his attachment to its interests. But as I never depart from the path which I have once chosen, and as I have never yet committed or countenanced a breach of engagement, I must adhere to those which I have concluded with the Peishwa and Mahdajee Sindia, and as he was the original author of both, I expect his support of both. I am, Sir, your most obedient servant.

To the same.

Fort William, 9th March, 1783.

My dear Chapman,—I am sorry to perceive the great alteration which has taken place in the disposition of the Naugpoor government to ours, and that you have experienced the effects of it so sensibly in its present treatment of you. Be patient: pay no unbecoming court or submission to any; nor seem to perceive any cause for resentment, unless the provocation be such as you cannot pass without notice. If they talk of your leaving them, acquiesce; and rather demand your dismission than stay with indignity: but do not, I repeat, too precipitately construe it. I cannot account for the present appearances, either in this change of temper in Moodajee nor in the uncommon spirit of procrastination which has prevailed in obstructing the ratification of the treaty, although the Mahrattas are more noted for this quality than any other nation on earth. Endeavour to discover the grounds of it at your court.

One specimen more I feel myself called upon to give, of the style, rather than of the matter, of Mr. Hastings's Indian correspondence. The following is addressed to a gentleman who, in consequence of certain changes introduced into the manner of providing the Company's investments, had complained to the Governor-general of the heavy losses to which he was exposed.

To Simeon Droze, Esq.

Wednesday.

Sir,—I am sorry that I have kept you so long in suspense; but I have had more to say in answer to your letter than could be comprised in a written reply, solicited as I am by the incessant and present calls of other affairs. I am, I know not how, the only responsible man to individuals, as I am, of course, principally responsible to the Company for the success of this undertaking. Every person whose interest is affected by it looks with resentment to me as the author, and I fear none make distinctions of times or of circumstances, but all claim as a right the same emoluments to be drawn out of the new investment, as they privately and unconfessedly drew from the regular investment, without regard to the public distress, to the Company's wants, or to the personal hazard to which the members of this Government, and myself especially, are exposed, by so daring an innovation. When the produce of the investment yielded the proprietors of India stock their dividends, the intermediate profits which it afforded were subjects of envy to many, of mere speculation to others, but of real concern to none. The produce of the present investment must go wholly to the payment of the bills which were granted for the money which was raised to provide it, (wholly, I say, for little of the little surplus will go to the proprietors.) Their dividends will be stopped, and the whole body will be in arms upon so trying an occasion. They will be told, and, true or not, it is universally believed, that every article of the investment is provided for the Company at 30 or 40, and even 50 per cent. beyond its real cost; this difference will be stated (not true) as a clear profit to the Board of Trade, and a comparison will be drawn between their situation and that of their principals. The advantages of the plan will be overlooked; it will be imputed to the worst motives, and myself and my colleagues shall be charged with the whole guilt, because we were the authors of it. Punishments for collective acts generally stop at the most conspicuous actors, and I shall probably be sacrificed for the sake of example, and my name and fortune blasted and ruined.

After this statement I leave the application to your candour. If you reply, that all your hopes after twenty years' service must end in disappointment, and the prospects of irretrievable indigence, you may hurt me by the reproach, but I cannot reply to it. I cannot affirm, though on the strongest conviction, that you have yet a fair prospect of a reasonable subsistence; that much more moderate rates will leave you still a profit of which our employers in England would grudge you the attainment. You may have years of service yet to come, which will yield you a compensation for a present and temporary forbearance; and a forbearance of what? of advantages which were unknown to the service till lately, though now become the rights of office. I have passed some years on the spot of which you have now the first charge, and in my younger days held for some time the charge of the chiefship, though not the name; and I can safely swear, that I neither gained, nor looked to gain, a rupee from the investment itself. My profits arose from a different source. I do not mean to express a wish that the service should return exactly to the same situation, and I am aware that the change of circumstances has made it difficult to draw a comparison between the means of profit which were offered at that time and those of the present; but I affirm that a wide difference ought to be made between a time of distress and a season of prosperity; between an unpopular and desperate expedient, which nothing but success can prevent from falling, with the most dreadful vengeance, on the heads of its projector, (I will no longer use the plural number,) and the ordinary process and return of a trade which, in the worst management of it, gratified all the expectations of its proprietors. Let me add something in my own behalf. I think I have not shown myself an enemy to the Company's servants. My enemies charge the reverse to me as a crime; I hope you have never found me adverse to your interests or wishes. Place a slight and temporary difference of private interest in one scale, and my ruin and disgrace in the other, and let your own justice determine whether you shall add or diminish the weight of the first.

I now answer particular points of your letter. I doubt whether I can honourably tell you the specific rates of the proposals which were tendered to me, since they were entrusted to me for the use of the proposers, and it would be an abuse of confidence to make the conditions the ground of your own defeat, nor, I apprehend, will it be necessary. I have seen others yet much below these, and I know the general estimate of them. You have better opportunities of attaining the same knowledge.

You have the Board's general opinion of the preference which ought to be given to the Company's servants; and especially members of the Board of Trade.

I have but one word more. If you propose such terms as will warrant their acceptance, and such I meant when I gave you similar assurances in our last conversation, I am myself disposed, and have no doubt of the like disposition in my colleagues, to give my assent unhesitatingly, and without looking too nearly to comparisons for their instant acceptance.

I have said but a very small part of what I feel on this subject. I wish that you may see what I have said through its proper medium. If you do not, a volume of reasonings will pass discoloured to your judgment of it.—I am, &c.

CHAPTER II.

Intelligence of the proceedings at Home reaches Calcutta—Correspondence with Lord Shelburne and Major Scott.

In the midst of cares and anxieties such as these, when every thought of his heart was devoted to the public service, Mr. Hastings received from home intelligence of the proceedings which had been taken, as well in the House of Commons as in the Court of Directors, against himself. The news was not very gratifying, neither had it the effect of encouraging him to further exertions in so thankless a cause: yet there was a principle within which enabled him to bear up against it; and he determined to persevere in his own course, because he knew that it was the best. It was impossible, however, that he should refrain from giving vent to his indignation in the letters which noticed these attacks, and set his own conduct in its proper light. Nevertheless the most vehement of them all proves, that motives infinitely superior to those of personal feeling swayed him; and that if ambition were in any degree the cause of his adherence to office, it was ambition of the purest and noblest kind. He desired to win a lofty reputation for himself, by bestowing important benefits on his country. Lord Shelburne's accession to power had just been communicated to him when the following was written.

To the Right Honourable the Earl of SHELBURNE.

Fort William, 12th December, 1782.

My Lord,—I have had the honour to receive a letter from your Lordship by the hands of Mr. Dunkin, to whom I have given such assurances of my desire to promote his interests as my great respect for your Lordship's recommendation required; and I shall be happy if I can afford him a more substantial proof of it.

I return your Lordship many thanks for the professions of esteem which you have done me the honour to make to me. I read them with a pleasure not, I own, unmixed, and should at this time feel less embarrassment in my acknowledgment of them were your Lordship's situation now the same as it was when they were written. You are in a condition too elevated, and my relation to it is too dependant, to allow me to distinguish between the sensations excited by my own interest and the pride of being so honourably noticed by a person of your Lordship's eminent talents and virtues. Yet I think that my veneration for your Lordship's character has not always been accompanied by the same grounds for imputing it to an unbecoming bias, if a wish to obtain the support of your authority in my public station can be ranked under such a construction. I think not; for I can truly declare that I do not wish to hold my place longer than the duration of the present scene of multiplied warfare; and so far I am most perfectly disinterested.

Permit me, my Lord, to add, that I shall be most happy if I may profit by the favourable sentiments which you have entertained of me, so far as to be honoured with your friendship, when all my views of ambition and fortune are closed; and in the mean time I will promise you that you shall see nothing in my conduct that shall discredit your present opinion of it.

I shall now address your Lordship in your ministerial character.

It is now more than two months since the news arrived of the severe censures passed upon my conduct by the Secret Committee of the House of Commons, and this was speedily followed by the intelligence of the subsequent resolution of the House of Commons for my dismission from office. It is unfortunate for the public welfare that this act, if it is to prove effectual, did not reach us in its complete state, and that my removal and the effective succession could not take place in the same instant with the denunciation of the former. This Government subsists more by the influence of public opinion than by its real power or resources; and it never required the support of that credit (I had almost said delusion) so much as at this time, in which all its exertions are required for the desperate support of the Carnatic. A more important negociation, likewise, has been for some months depending for a new connexion with the Mahratta state, and for its alliance against the invader of the Carnatic. I had entertained the most sanguine expectations of the event, which has only been retarded by the mutual jealousy of the different powers who are interested in it, each aspiring to be the principal, and opposing it as the act of a rival. I now greatly fear the reverse. Think, my Lord, of the English newspapers and Leyden gazettes circulating through every state in Europe, and every European colony in Asia, the suspension of the powers of the first British Government in India, at a period such as the present, in the express words of the resolution of the House of Commons; and a French emissary at Poona in possession of such an instrument to work on the procrastinating spirit of the Mahrattas!

I have not seen the reports of the Secret Committee, but I have read the resolutions which closed them, and boldly venture to assure your Lordship that either the former consist of partial selections, or they are most positive and direct evidences of the opposite of every resolution which was professed to be formed upon them, and which contains my condemnation. As your Lordship must be in possession of the reports, and has been minutely informed of the train of events and measures which have passed since the commencement of my Government, I will avail myself of the credit which I believe I possess with your Lordship for veracity, and of the sure means which you have of detecting me if I part from it, by affirming, without reference to a long train of argument to prove it, that I have never in a single instance broken the faith of a treaty, or deserted or injured the interests of the Company; that I have never sacrificed the honour of my nation; that I had no more concern in the origin and commencement of the Mahratta war than the Lord Advocate of Scotland; that it began without my knowledge; that it was resumed not only without my knowledge, but on principles as adverse to me as the Mahrattas; that I supported the government of Bombay in the prosecution of their first plan with money, with a powerful military aid, and (I confess) with encouragement; and I believe it is generally understood that if the detachment sent from Bengal had not seasonably arrived for their salvation, that presidency was lost; its credit, and with it our military reputation, were utterly ruined. We retrieved both; we in our turn reduced the Mahratta state to a condition which, but for the calamities which ensued in the Carnatic would have enabled us to command a peace on our own terms, and that was the only issue of the war that I looked for. I affirm also, my Lord, that the invasion of the Carnatic was not caused by the Mahratta war, but by the known weakness of the Carnatic, the dissipation of its forces, its poverty, caused by private embezzlement, and by a great confederacy formed against all the British governments in India, a confederacy which was the avowed act of the Nabob Nizam Ally Cawn, and declared by him to have been prompted by a consideration for his own security against the menaced hostilities of the presidency of Fort St. George; that his reliance on the faith and justice of this Government had induced him to withhold his support of the confederacy; that my influence with the government of Berar withdrew that member of it; and that a diversion, projected by me, opposed by Mr. Francis, and enforced by violence, both deprived it of its most active member (Hyder excepted), and produced a general peace with the Mahrattas. In a word, my Lord, the Mahratta war was the war of the presidency of Bombay and of the Court of Directors. The prosecution of it was mine, and the Mahratta peace is exclusively mine. Forgive me the boast when I add that I have been the instrument of rescuing one presidency from infamy, and both from annihilation; and desperate as the affairs of the Carnatic are, if my hands are not tied or enfeebled, I will yet be a contributor to its ultimate preservation.

I fear to load your Lordship with papers, but I may presume to refer you to such as are material in the despatches which will come officially into your possession, and therefore I beg leave to recommend to your Lordship's attention as a part of the means by which the great aids have been furnished which we have been enabled to afford to Bombay and Fort St. George, an account and explanation of the extraordinary resources of this Government which were created in the course of the last two years, consisting in an increase of revenue, a diminution of charges of collection, a reduction in the cost of the investment, and above all, a new fund, which my colleagues, against their declared judgments, permitted me to form on my own separate responsibility, which, without territory, the eclat of conquest, or the addition of military establishments, already yields more than fifty lacs of rupees. I have an infinite pleasure in testifying to your Lordship that I owe the success of this plan to the incomparable industry and ability of the person whom I chose as an essential part of it for its execution, the son of my late and most valued friend, Mr. Vansittart.

Your Lordship will hear that we have waited these six months for the ratification of the Mahratta treaty, and probably that the Mahrattas were forming designs to invade us, for such reports are always fabricated on the eve of every despatch. I will assure your Lordship that no such designs exist in any known foundation, and that peace is as durably established with the Mahrattas as if it had received every possible sanction that the most powerful guarantees, or all the obligations of religion, could give it. The principal, Mahdajee Sindia, is bound by interest to support it, and the state exists by his power. The chief of Berar complains that he is not a party, and has written to me that he will obtain the instant accomplishment of the treaty, if I will constitute him the guarantee in the place of Mahdajee Sindia. The Nabob Nizam Ally Cawn, in all the pride of a descendant of the great Nizam Al Moolk, indignantly resents the neglect shown to the sovereign of Deccan, who alone has authority to regulate all its interests, still professing, but with more reserve, the same conciliating disposition; and

Nanna Furneess, though the titular ruler of the Mahrattas, yet possessing no support in himself, hesitates through fear of the other parties. In the mean time, the presidency of Bombay is in the actual collection of a revenue yielding, by their account, fifty lacs of rupees, which they must restore when the treaty is ratified; and to balance this advantage, we are deprived, by the indecision of the minister, of the assistance of the Mahrattas against Hyder, who has usurped a territory of near eighty lacs from them, and they are as impatient to reclaim it as we are to gain their co-operation.

I forbear to speak of the affairs of the Carnatic; Sir Eyre Coote is with us, but his constitution is so broken that I fear for his existence. Yet infirm as he is, he is our only resource, and his presence would yet retrieve the miserable state of the Carnatic, even though he should be deprived of the powers of motion. He is willing and sometimes impetuous in his resolution to return thither. He has infinite merit for his exertions, and he cannot have a better testimony than mine, for he has never been over-partial to me.

I know not in what direction the tide of popular prejudices may have run when the news arrived in England of my transactions during the last year at Benares; but in the fear of misrepresentation and of misconstruction, I made out an early report of it for the immediate information of this Council, and joined to the report all the vouchers and attestations which could confirm the truth of it. For the same reason I have caused a number of printed copies to be made of it, and one of these I have directed my agent, Major Scott, to present to your Lordship. I entreat that you will honour it with your acceptance, and that you will bestow an early half hour of your leisure to read it. Allow, my Lord, this kind indulgence to the solicitude which I feel to preserve your good opinion; for even your Lordship's candour may not be proof against suggestions fortified by the general opinions which are entertained against great revolutions. I trust to my narrative for my clear acquittal of any criminal imputation; and I solemnly asure your Lordship that I neither added a rupee to my fortune by the excursion, nor ever intended it. I could in truth add that I am a sufferer by it.

It may perhaps prove a gratification of curiosity to your Lordship to receive a book which is in every process of it the manufacture of this country.

While I am writing this, I have received a letter from Major Scott, dated the 30th June, in which he mentions it to be the expressed injunction of your Lordship's friends, communicated to mine, that I should continue to exert myself for the public service, without suffering myself to be influenced by any discouraging reports, of whatever authority, from England. While I offer my grateful acknowledgments for this fresh instance of your Lordship's favourable disposition, I beg leave to assure you that I shall most literally fulfil your commands, which have added to my confidenee, but not to my determination, to persevere consistently in one line of conduct, from which I have never suffered myself to deviate under the worst denunciations of public disgrace and dismission, nor ever shall, while I am not disabled by them from the power of discharging my duty with effect to the Company and my country. I am certain that I shall be honoured with your Lordship's most strenuous and effectual support, if you can give it without a sacrifice of more important interests; but I can well conceive situations of things which may compel even your judgment, however repugnant to your inclinations, to make the little interest which the public may have in my continuance in office yield to higher acquisitions. In such a case I shall submit to my lot with cheerfulness, and still retain the due sense of your Lordship's goodness. This only I beg of your Lordship, that you will not suffer my character to be blackened by criminal accusations, nor joined with the names of others with whom it never had a connexion, nor my peace of mind wounded, and my influence blasted with official reproaches and invectives, by those who may seek my removal. These indignities I have borne during a long period of time, because the state over which I preside could bear it. It is no longer in a condition to sustain the depreciation of its executive member, and in such a case I should consider myself as a noxious incumbent on it. I will further declare that I cannot act effectually with a mere negative sufferance; I stand in need of the confidence and support of those under whose authority I act, most publicly bestowed. If on these conditions I cannot remain, I declare it to be my wish to be honourably relieved; and if such be your Lordship's commands, I thus formally and previously assure your Lordship that they now have, and shall receive, my most willing submission, acquiescence, and concurrence.

I most heartily congratulate your Lordship on the new and elevated dignity which I hear his Majesty has been pleased to confer upon you, and unite my wishes to those of thousands who feel for the prosperity of the British nation, that it may long enjoy the benefit of your Lordship's administration. I have the honour to be, with the greatest respect, my Lord, your Lordship's most obliged and faithful servant.

P.S.—I cannot close this letter without expressing to your Lordship the great satisfaction which I feel in my colleagues, men of unexampled benevolence and equality of temper, of uncommon but different talents, and all warmed with a cordial affection to each other, and a confidence in mine to them, and in my experience and integrity. Of these your Lordship will be pleased to know that I place a particular confidence in Mr. Macpherson, from whose activity of mind and pleasantness of manners, no less than in an exact concurrence of sentiment formed perhaps on a mutual communication of some years, I have derived the most useful assistance when I was in a state of health which very much required it, and which might have proved fatal had it reduced me to leave the administration in the hands of men adverse to each other, or to my own general line of conduct. To the effects of the same cause and continual interruption, I beg your Lordship to attribute the length of this letter, which with more leisure I should have endeavoured to comprise within a more reasonable compass, and to have given it the same materials of information.

The same ship which carried the above conveyed to Major Scott a long letter, in which most of the topics touched upon in Mr. Hastings's communications to Lord Shelburne are noticed at length. In this he speaks bitterly of the probable effects of the circulation through India of the resolutions hostile to himself, and makes no secret of his contempt for the qualifications of the individuals by whom it was proposed to supersede him. He then goes on to notice the existing state of the Mahratta negociations, and says, "I am impatient for the ratification of the Mahratta treaty, only because others are so. War may be made by one party only, and best when the other is averse to it.

Peace must be the work of both. The clamours for peace have not influenced my conduct, which has been formed on my own principles. I have never discovered an impatience, but sometimes affected an indifference about it. Let new negociators come, and avow peace to be their determination and sole object, and they will revive every claim that the composed insolence of Mahratta presumption can devise; namely, Chout, Ragoba, Salsette, collection of Guzerat, indemnification for expenses of war, acknowledgment of being aggressors, restoration of Cheyt Sing, Tanjore, tribute to Nizam, surrender of Northern Circars."

In like manner he refers to the arrangements which had been made for ensuring a continuance of the Company's investments; the addition secured to the permanent revenue by the salt monopoly; the large reductions of expenditure which he or his colleagues had been effecting; "but which will now," he adds, "be suspended till I am more certain of my fate; for I will not create enemies in order to ease the burthens of my successors." Then passing on to the affairs of Oude, he says, "I have sent Mr. Bristow to Lucknow. This is due to the authority of the Directors when not inconsistent with my own; if he does his duty, the superior advantages he possesses will enable him to restore the officers of the Nabob. He cannot make them worse than they were made by Mr. Middleton and Mr. Johnson." So also in reference to the Carnatic, he explains, that all is in confusion there. "Lord Macartney has quarrelled with Sir Edward Hughes, driven away the old General, writes insolent letters without information, and has treated the Nabob with unparalleled indignities." But it is unnecessary to go on, inasmuch as the reader will find in the following ample information respecting the political aspect of affairs at the moment. It also is addressed to Major Scott.

Fort William, 1st February, 1783.

My dear Scott,—Mr. Berrie is arrived with your remaining despatches. Nothing could be more satisfactory. You have far exceeded my most confident hopes, and bound me yours for ever. I beg that you will make my grateful acknowledgments to Mr. G. Johnstone. You cannot express them in terms stronger than the sense which I entertain of what I owe to his support. This is the second time that he has been the essential and effectual champion of my reputation. I shall write to him by the Fox now under despatch. I send you a copy of our general letter of intelligence. The great events which it reports are, 1st, the death of Hyder; 2d, that of his only political emissary Nersing; 3d, the defeat of Tippoo; three fortunate coincidences; 4th, the ratification of our treaty with the Mahrattas; 5th, Sir Eyre Coote's intention to return to the coast on the instant of the Medea's arrival; 6th, the appearance of the French squadron and its departure, I think, to the islands; it has done little mischief and the last; 7th, arrival of our squadron at Bombay, to be expected back early in March;

8th, the Bengal detachment now at Guzerat, ordered to return to our own dependencies; 9th, the departure of General Matthews to Angengo. His force united will be 1,500 Europeans and Company's battalions of sepoys; 10th, Tippoo's return to his main army; and 11th, its junction with the French from Cuddalore. The rest must be more detailed. The Nabob Wallah Jaw has preferred a long list of charges against Lord Macartney. One that he has granted sunnuds to the collectors in his own name, and without the Nabob's confirmation, in violation of the condition on which the assignment was granted, and the only mark of sovereignty reserved to the Nabob. This is avowed, and on the weakest grounds. We have pronounced it a breach of our treaty, have ordered the Nabob to be replaced in charge of the revenue, and of his entire authority, and accepted his engagements to deliver one-third more of money (with Soucar security) of cattle and of grain, than the amount received under Lord Macartney's administration of the province. If Lord Macartney refuses, I will move for his suspension, and expect the Board's concurrence. Nizam Ally Cawn detests the Nabob, yet exclaims against our treatment of him, and Hyder has used it as an argument to deter others from a connexion with us.

By Bassalut Jung's death, Guntoor reverted to the Company. Lord Macartney proposed to reclaim it; sent forces to the frontier, and entered into a negociation with the son of Fazil Beg, in actual rebellion against his master Nizam Ally Cawn. We have peremptorily forbidden the select committee to proceed. We have availed ourselves of the Company's orders of the 11th April, 1781, to invest Sir Eyre Coote with an absolute command of the forces, and the war in the Carnatic. His unexampled zeal and past exertions warrant this: their inactivity requires it. On his departure they disbanded the army, dismissed or separated all its followers, and when Hyder died, they could not assemble it. What an advantage lost! If Sir Eyre arrives safe, our success is morally certain. We shall give him ten lacs. Tippoo's funds are exhausted, the crops have failed in Mysore. The Carnatic is destitute both of grain and plunder. His troops discontented, his army reduced, his authority unsettled, and intrigues suspected. The French have no resource, if he abandons them, and if they follow him, are lost to their national service for ever. The Mahrattas will certainly attempt to recover the possessions wrested from them by Hyder, and have probably begun their operations. Bussy was sick at Mauritius in September, and all his people sick. Nizam Ally Cawn and Moodajee profess friendship to us. Nizam Ally is engaged in quelling the rebellion of Elesham Jung, the son of Fazil Beg, and Moodajee sick. Mahdajee Sindia is firm and consistent. *He will prove the best ally we ever had.* Remember this. Our revenue increases: the demands on it are still large; but we will answer them. Early last year I projected the revision and correction of our establishment. Mr. Macpherson's illness prevented it. We began, and I fell sick. Since my recovery, the arrears of business and Mr. Wheler's indisposition hindered its renewal. I shall propose to resume it as soon as the Fox is gone, and hope with hard working to accomplish it in two months. A great reduction may be made, and shall. If I am confirmed and trusted, I know myself able to restore to this Government its former abundance, and pay all its debts in two years of peace; but if I am to be still threatened with dismission, my acts reprobated, the whole responsibility thrown on me with only an equal voice in the Council, I cannot discharge my trust with credit or effect, and will relinquish it; for the season of contention is past. Write frequently, and by the post; direct your letters to Mr. Latouche, at Bussora. Send no gentlemen emissaries. They arrive late, and become a perpetual charge upon me. Present my most grateful respects to Lord Mansfield. I am in better health than for many years past, and Mrs. Hastings's is much mended. She joins in compliments and good wishes. Adieu. Yours ever most affectionately.

Let Mr. Sulivan know that his son and grandson are well. May God bless him.

There was no proceeding on the part of his superiors which more effectually roused the indignation of Mr. Hastings, than their eagerness to condemn his line of policy in reference to Benares, of which their own despatches proved that they were not competent to judge. I subjoin a letter to Mr. Scott on this head, because it is both clear in its reasoning, and singularly characteristic of the writer.

Fort William, 5th February, 1783.

My dear Scott,—Again accept my thanks for your incessant labours in my cause, and, more than all, for the affection which prompted them. I cannot express the sense which I have of them, but be assured that they have made an impression on my mind which never can be effaced while I have life.

You have justly observed that it is for my reputation, and not for my office, that I am solicitous, or for the latter only as the first is involved in it. To this let me add another consideration, which has ever operated, and shall to the last operate, as a fixed principle on my conduct; viz., that if I am at length driven to the mortifying necessity of throwing up the service, it shall not proceed from personal disgust or resentment, but solely from the united conviction that I cannot retain it without public ruin and private ignominy.

A late occasion had nearly warmed me into a resolution of this kind. As I make it a rule to allow my first impulses to cool, I have recovered my correct judgment upon it, and will wait the issue without any predetermination. The circumstance to which I allude is this:—

Three days ago I received a letter from Mr. Hornby, with a copy of the resolutions of the Court of Directors in July last, condemning my conduct in the affairs of Benares as a breach of treaty, &c., and justifying Cheit Sing. Are these men aware that, in their eagerness to vilify me, they sow the seeds of distrust and rebellion among their own subjects, and that a declaration so authentic in the favour of a rebel, now residing under the protection of the chief of the Mahratta State at the crisis of our negociations with him, might tempt the former to resume his pretensions, and the latter to espouse them; that the present Rajah might be terrified into measures as desperate from despondency as those which ambition and ingratitude dictated to his predecessor, and that a slight spark would be sufficient to blow up our possessions and those of the Vizier, if it fell on so combustible a ground? What is to follow these resolutions? An order to restore Cheit Sing? The conclusion is inevitable; for if we were bound by treaty with him, if he faithfully performed all his conditions of it, and we have broken our engagements with him, and the Court of Directors solemnly pronounce this as their judgment, they must render him justice, or they are the violators of public faith by their own avowal.

It will not be expected that I should obey such an order, and how can I oppose it without exposing my person, fortune, and reputation to the most fatal extremities? And how can I elude it but by resigning the trust which imposes on me so infamous a duty?

I had written a letter upon this occasion to the Court of Directors, and another to Lord Shelburne; but on mature reflection I have suppressed both. The former you shall see. I trust to Lord Shelburne's assurances, and to the injunctions of Lord Ashburton and Sir Robert Palk. In the meantime I hope that my narrative, which I find must have arrived in England within a few days of the passing of these resolutions, will have completely defeated them; for if there ever was a demonstration produced by argument, I have demonstrated the falsehood of Cheit Sing's pretences to independency, and those of his advocates who assert that we were bound by any treaty, or any engagement differing from that of a common zemindarry sunnud. While the Court of Directors assume the style and form of the late Parliamentary resolutions, they may affirm what they please with the preface that "*It appears to this Court,*" for who can contradict them whilst they have the dishonest discretion to conceal the grounds of the assertion? I fight with an invisible enemy when I attempt to repel such an assault, for if I suppose the quarter from which it came, I may be assailed from another, and after all my defence comes too late to evade the blow. I have looked over the original minutes of the Council which relate to the first settlement with Cheit Sing, and these (if they can be copied in time,) shall be sent to you. My own proposition, which was the ground of the treaty, though most liberal to Cheit Sing, amounted to no more than this; that a temporary settlement should be formed with Cheit Sing, subject to the correction of the Court of Directors, with a revenue fixed, that he might not be made the tool of private rapacity, or, in other words, as Mr. Barwell will well remember, of Philip Francis's; and therefore, that no demand should be made on him, nor any authority permitted to interfere in the management of his zemindarry, while he paid his rents punctually, and was obedient to our Government. These concessions were never proposed to be made engagements, but optional indulgences, or rather obligations, which we might choose to impose on ourselves, not which he should claim. Attend to the words, *settlement, management, revenue,* and *zemindarry,* and to the reference made to the pleasure of the Court of Directors for a final arrangement, and you will find that my plan, had it been adopted, would have bound this Government to no other conditions than those which are granted to any other zemindar. But my plan was not adopted; so there is an end of it. The second authority which I meet with in our proceedings is the letter of instructions given to Francis Fowke, dated 24th August. In this his tenure is styled a *zemindarry;* the agreement, a *settlement;* the Company's relation to him, a *sovereignty;* his, a *vassalage;* his charge, *management, collection, and regulation of the revenues.* The word *tribute* is twice used to express *revenue,* and an assurance is added that *we do not mean to increase his tribute; and so long as he adheres to the terms of his engagement, will never demand any augmentation of the annual tribute which may be fixed.*

But these instructions (which by the bye are very ambiguous in the two clauses which I have last quoted; viz., *we do not mean,* and *we will not*) are the surest rules of Fowke's commission; they are not an engagement, but the directions by which an engagement, or more properly a *settlement,* was to be formed. These, therefore, whatever the author of them meant, impose no obligation; but they evidently show that neither Mr. Francis nor his colleagues considered Cheit Sing in any other light then but that of a zemindar, a dependant, and a vassal. This authority, therefore, is out of the question.

The third authority is by no means equivocal. It is a letter written on the same day by the Board in my name to Cheit Sng. In this he is informed that Mr. Fowke is ordered to take *possession* of the *zemindarry* which he held; and to grant the zemindarry to him on the footing of his former tenure, with a reservation twice expressed of the Company's sovereignty; and a denunciation of forfeiture if he ever proved unfaithful to the Company.

The sum of the revenue is fixed, and is called a *tribute*, but no assurance is given that it should not be exceeded, nor was such assurance intended.

But even this authority, weak as it is, conveyed no rights. It only announced to him the outlines of the settlement which was to be made with him, and was in effect Francis Fowke's credentials. In effect, none of these are authorities. The only authorities are the interchanged deeds of the settlement, that is to say, the sunnud and cabuleeat. I never conceived myself bound by any other, nor had a thought of any other, and these are clearly and absolutely against every pretension of his independency, and as clear a justification of my conduct towards him. If the loose and desultory passages of our consultations are to be accepted as national obligations affecting our public faith, no man in office can be secure from error, for no man can know by what obligations he is bound. I have now before me a great volume, as much as I can lift, which comprises the business of the settlement made with the Rajah of Benares, and it contains no more than three months' consultations. All the books of our secret department only from October, 1774, to the present time, I suppose, amount to fifty great folios. But even on this ground I dare rest my vindication. If the subject is not already obsolete, you will gather from this loose discussion sufficient argument to refute all that can be alleged against me.

I shall bear with patience and forbearance every article of abuse that is yet to come; but the right of judging when I ought to quit the service, because I can no longer retain it with effect or with credit, I shall certainly exercise; and at all events I shall stay till I know the result of the present deliberation in Parliament concerning India. I wish to see the war closed in the Carnatic, by the dispersion of Tippoo's followers, and the defeat and capture of the French; and this, I trust, will be effected before the month of October, if Coote gets safe to the coast and lives. When this work is accomplished, I care not what they do with me in England.

I can write few other letters, and those must be very short; but you must supply them with my friends, and remember that the moment you have received and read any of my letters, and can afford an hour's leisure, you must carry them to Mr. Sulivan, and read them to him. Adieu. Yours most affectionately.

The following refers to the state of the Carnatic, whither Sir Eyre Coote, though still an invalid, was preparing to return. The agreement alluded to was that into which the Supreme Government had entered with the Nabob, during the anarchy of Sir Thomas Rumbold and Mr. Whitehill's administrations. It had always been a thorn in Lord Macartney's side, and he laboured incessantly to dissolve it. But to this Mr. Hastings would not consent.

To the same.

Fort William, 6th February, 1783.

My dear Scott,—The accompanying extracts from our proceedings fully explain both their objects and motives. You will perceive that they had been the subjects of our private discussions, by the question put to Mr. Holland, before they were formally debated. The presence of the General enabled me to bring them to a termination. The behaviour of Lord Macartney has been unpardonable to the Nabob, and has certainly proved of great injury to our credit. As it manifestly proceeded from personal indisposition, and that originated with our agreement with the Nabob, of which it is a direct infringement, I at least could not refuse to afford the Nabob such redress as it might be in the power of our Government to afford him; and if his Lordship refuses to submit to our decision, I am determined to propose, though I should stand alone, to proceed to the last extremity with him. Mr. Wheler stands on the same ground with me, having been joined with me in forming the agreement, and Sir Eyre Coote will support and enforce our resolutions. It is not pleasing to pass judgment on the conduct of the gentlemen of Fort St. George, or to interfere in the detail of their affairs; but our own faith is concerned; our revenues are exhausted to defend the Carnatic, our grain feeds it, our forces have constituted the principal strength of their army, and we gave them the man who has saved it from destruction. They were unable to face the enemy till Sir Eyre Coote commanded their army, and it was reduced to a state of inaction and inability the instant that he quitted it. If he had remained there, the death of Hyder would have been instantly followed by the dispersion of his followers. This is morally certain, as certain as that no movement has been made since, and that none will till he resumes the command. His zeal and spirit are without example. His constitution is irrecoverably gone; yet he has enough left to bear him through one campaign, which, I trust, will be a short one, and may God grant him life to enjoy at home the reputation, rewards, and honours that are due to his virtues. I am resolved to give him all the support of this Government, though I am certain that he will quarrel with me the moment we are separated. I will forgive his private failings while his public merit entitles him to my respect.

Read these proceedings with attention. Believe me that I never will interfere in the concerns of the other presidencies, but where the faith and interests of our own are at stake; and assert this for me. An opinion prevails that we may lawfully suspend the members of the other presidencies for making treaties without our sanction, but that our control does not extend to the breach of treaties, which the Act of Parliament allows with impunity. I maintain that the power in the second instance is implied in the first, or the first is nugatory. I will put it to the test if I am forced to it; and whatever consequences may personally befal me, I am certain that it will be attended with one public benefit, in bringing the absurdity of the law before the notice of Parliament, and exacting from it a more effectual or better defined provision. I am, my dear Scott, most warmly and most affectionately yours.

Many more letters, all in the same strain, though addressed to different persons, and therefore differing in the minutiæ of style and expression, are now before me, but I do not think it necessary to insert them. It will be more to the purpose if I state, that of the effects which Mr. Hastings anticipated from the temper displayed in the Court's despatches, one, and that not the least inconvenient, began immediately to be felt. The support which his colleagues had heretofore freely rendered became lukewarm and doubtful. They saw difficulties before them where none had previously appeared, and distrusted even their own judgment in more than one important transaction which was passed. Perhaps there was nothing unnatural in this, yet Mr. Hastings felt it acutely, and expressed himself, as will be seen, like a wounded man as often as he found occasion to notice it. On the other hand, the recommendations conveyed to him by many of his most influential friends in London, neither to answer nor obey the ill-judged instructions from home, staggered him. He knew that obedience would in many instances prove fatal, but he knew at the same time that its opposite must exasperate the anger if it did not add to the number of his enemies. Take the following as a specimen of the state of his mind at this juncture.

To the same.

Fort William, 22d March, 1783.

My dear Scott,—I am much distressed. You press me to pay no regard to the orders of the Court of Directors, nor suffer them to influence my resolutions.

You tell me that this is the advice of Lord Mansfield, and for his opinions I feel an almost religious veneration. Mr. Bensley goes further in what you quote of his declaration to the Court of Directors, and says that I ought not to obey them. I judge from this expression that the state of my influence in this Government was very much misconceived in England. I was very feebly supported, if supported, before the late letters from the Court of Directors arrived. Since that period my colleagues have wholly withdrawn their support, and seem anxious to show that they have withdrawn it. This is all that I will allow myself to say of them. But, as a specimen of their present disposition towards me, I will send you the minutes delivered on a proposal made by me for the appointment of Mr. Richard Sulivan to be our agent at Hyderabad. You will judge whether the objections are candid or ostensible, and will form your own conclusions on the reference made to orders of the Court of Directors not in being, but in possibility. I must yet except Mr. Wheler from the preceding reflections. He has acted honourably towards me, and I believe wishes to support me both from principle and affection.

The order for the recall of Markham and the re-appointment of Francis Fowke has passed. I do not know what will be the effect of the order if the Court of Directors shall pass it for the restoration of Cheit Sing; but I am certain that it will be supported by Macpherson and Stables.

Our treaty with the Nabob Wallah Jaw has drawn on him such a load of misery and infamy as he has never experienced, ill as he has been ever treated. We have annulled his assignment, and the Court of Directors have cancelled the treaty of which it was a part. Lord Macartney will probably, I am convinced he will, retain the assignment against all justice and faith, against the authority of the Company too ambiguously expressed, and in defiance of our engagements. Our Board will be unanimous in passing the severest censures on him, but I fear will proceed no further. They will probably protest, but leave their own acts unsupported, and the Nabob the victim of them. I will do my duty, and if I can do no more I will protest against them.

I have been the principal instrument of prevailing on Sir Eyre Coote to return to the coast. He avows his dependance on me, and though I have at no time received his support, he shall have mine if all the other members of the Council should withhold; for in his public character he merits it, aye, and every sacrifice that can be made with it. He is gone: we have given ten lacs with him, though we have passed orders on the treasury for near eighty lacs undischarged. This sum is consigned to him, and we have exercised the authority given us by the Court of Directors, to order the Governor of Fort St. George to allow him the uncontrolled command and conduct of the army. The rest will depend materially upon him. If he is not counteracted by Lord Macartney, he will assuredly finish the war in the Carnatic, the troubles of which now require nothing but opposition to end them. If Lord Macartney shall refuse to allow him the command of the army and conduct of the war, if he shall refuse to part with the revenue and sovereignty of the Carnatic, and shall withhold its resources of treasure, grain, and cattle from the army, I know not what may be the consequences.

In the mean time I will do my utmost to maintain the credit and influence of the Superior Government, and to provide resources for all its wants. Great exertions I cannot make, for we want decision; we want vigour and unanimity; and I possess but a single voice, though I am charged in all obnoxious measures with the sole responsibility. I dread the effects of such a state at such a season; but I must bear my part in it until I can be properly relieved from it, and for that purpose I have written a letter to the Court of Directors declaratory of my resolution to resign. My friends, who do not know the disability to which I am reduced, will be apt to impute this to impatience and precipitation. I cannot describe my condition even to you, but it will be self apparent ere long, and you may trust me, when I declare to you that I feel it more distressing than even the vexations which I suffered in 1775; for then I was free from responsibility, though disarmed of power. I am now without power, with a thousand urgent calls for it, and am alone responsible. Can I, in such a situation, wish to retain an office which may involve me in everlasting infamy? for if any great calamity shall befal us, and I can see many openings through which calamity may come, the world, which never waits to listen to long stories, and which wants the understanding to discern the nice points of discrimination between acts done under a collective authority, and those which spring from divided powers and different opinions, will fix the guilt of it on me alone, and my reputation will be the victim of others' misconduct.

For the rest I refer you to the letter itself; it speaks my real feelings and describes my real situation. Pray Lord Mansfield to read it. I would rather retire to indigence and obscurity, which may be my lot, possessed of his esteem, than remain as I am, and waste years yet to come in reproach, shame, and fruitless expectation. The person for whose sake alone I wish for wealth has expressed the same sentiment, and for myself I can live on a bare competence.

I wish you to print and publish the forty-four and following paragraphs of the letter of the Court of Directors of the 28th of August, 1782, the fourth, fifth, and sixth paragraphs of the same letter, my minute of the 7th of March, and my letter to the Court of Directors, but not without the approbation of Lord Mansfield and Mr. Sulivan. These form my justification to the proprietors. Those to whom my letter is addressed will probably suppress it, or use it only for a subject of resentment, although I think I have given no cause for this; for surely I have not exceeded the bounds which the necessary defence of my own character prescribed, and I have even weakened that defence in the endeavour to preserve that respect which under every provocation is due from me to them, while I remain subject to their authority. I own that it would be more pleasing to me could the publication be made the act of authority. I think it ought, for if I have received the most flattering support from the Proprietors of the East India Company, I have served them with fidelity, zeal, and gratitude; and, however I may complain, I wish to mark the distinction which I make and feel between them and thirteen of their representatives, to retain their approbation even of my departure from their service.

The papers to which I allude shall be copied and enclosed with this. Adieu, my dear Scott, yours ever affectionately.

The following will, I think, be read with an almost melancholy interest. It describes the condition of a noble spirit torn and agitated with the sense of wrongs endured; yet nowise forgetful of the respect due to itself, even in the utterance of complaint. For on all sides, and by all parties with whom he was officially connected, Mr. Hastings seems at this moment to have been betrayed. The Court of

Directors, that is to say a majority in that body, rendered furious by their lack of power to remove him, adopted every imaginable expedient to harass and annoy. They condemned his general policy without understanding it, and stooped so low as to take from him and from his Council, for he never acted except with the authority of the Council, the right of nominating individual servants to particular offices in the country. The obvious effect of such hostility was, that his colleagues ceased to trust either him or themselves, and wavered and hesitated, not because they saw just ground of hesitation in the measures that were proposed, but because they were taught to believe that they could not more gratify their superiors at home than by opposing the views of their Governor abroad. Moreover Lord Macartney, of whom Hastings's best friends had entertained the highest opinion, and in whom Hastings himself had expected to find a steady and an able coadjutor, took, as has been shown, an early opportunity of acting for himself. It is necessary that this matter should be placed in a proper point of view, and a few words will suffice for that purpose.

When it was first proposed to recommend Lord Macartney as a fit person to succeed Sir Thomas Rumbold in the government of Madras, there were many sensible and influential proprietors, who felt that a step was about to be taken of grave importence. Hitherto the individuals advanced to offices of trust under the Company had all been trained in the Company's service; the nomination of Lord Macartney, if carried into effect, would entirely innovate upon this practice. And independently of the wound thus about to be inflicted on the immediate interests and ambition of an influential class of persons, there was at least some danger lest the absence of local knowledge, on the part of those to whom the field would thus be thrown open, might prove of serious hurt both to their employers, and to the people whose destinies they should be appointed to control. For though it was admitted on all hands that there had been of late extreme mismanagement, and worse than mismanagement, at Fort St. George, men were not quite prepared to avow, that the evil could be cured only by seeking elsewhere than among the Company's experienced servants, for one to whom the functions of government might be entrusted. Accordingly the proposition, when first brought forward, was received by many with disapprobation; by almost all with the sort of misgiving, which a little address from one side or the other would have at once converted either into approval or its opposite.

Mr. Hastings's friends were then, as they continued to be throughout, very powerful in the Court of Proprietors. It was, therefore, an object of the first importance with Lord Macartney, and his patrons, to secure their support, while they again desired nothing so much, as to have at the head of affairs in the Carnatic one who should approve of Mr. Hastings's policy, and be prepared to go heartily along with him. Lord Macartney was thus taught, that he could not better serve his own interests, than by appearing to hold Mr. Hastings and his system of administration in respect, and he omitted no opportunity, so long as the question remained undecided, of professing an ardent admiration of both. Accordingly his nomination, after a feeble resistance, was carried; and he took office, morally pledged to carry out Mr. Hastings's measures, as far as his influence, at the head of a subordinate government, would enable him to do so.

Mr. Hastings's friends lost no time in communicating to the Governor-general, both the fact of Lord Macartney's appointment, and the grounds on which they had themselves sanctioned it. Indeed there is now lying before me a letter from Mr. Pechell, in which the writer not only congratulates Mr. Hastings on an event which could not fail of proving as satisfactory to him as it would without doubt be beneficial to the Company, but entreats his correspondent to communicate with Lord Macartney as with one towards whom not even the appearance of reserve would be necessary. Therefore the new Governor was no sooner established at Madras, than Mr. Hastings proceeded to lay before him, not formally and officially, but with all the openness of private confidence, his own views and opinions on every subject connected with the interests of the presidency. He explained to him the reasons why such ample powers had been conferred on Sir Eyre Coote; and showed him that to withdraw them now would be fatal. He stated his own opinions as to the course which it would be judicious to follow in dealing with the Nizam, with the Nabob, and with the Rajah of Tanjore. He explained the nature of the agreement which the Supreme Government, superseding that of his Lordship's predecessor, had entered into for the management of the Nabob's revenues during the continuance of the war. He advised Lord Macartney to consider well, whether it would not be judicious to absorb Tanjore in the general government of the Carnatic. He urged him to purchase the alliance of the Nizam, and to turn his arms against Hyder, even by restoring to him the Northern Circars, should such a sacrifice be necessary; and last of all he gave the surest proof of a generous spirit of confidence, by telling his Lordship that, as some of these measures would in all probability prove distasteful both at home and on the spot, he was free to speak of them as emanating from the Governor-general, to whose experience he had been taught to bow, and by whose advice he acted. I confess that I do not know how any man in Mr. Hastings's situation could have gone further to prove his perfect reliance on the good feelings of a colleague, and his assurance that the good feeling was mutual. For he issued no orders, he assumed none of the bearing of a superior. He merely offered suggestions to be acted upon, or not, according to the dictation of Lord Macartney's judgment, while at the same time he professed his willingness to relieve an inexperienced functionary from odium, by taking upon himself the responsibility of certain acts, should they be carried into effect.

Lord Macartney left his friends in London, fully impressed with the belief, that he intended to make Mr. Hastings his great master in the science of Indian politics. His first proceedings, so soon as he had established himself in his government, contradicted that belief. There was not one of all Mr. Hastings's suggestions of which he approved. There was not one step taken by the Supreme Government, previous to his arrival, which he did not condemn. Unquestionably he had a perfect right to do all this if he chose, and to argue each question on its own merits, in his correspondence with Bengal. But he had no right first to reject Mr. Hastings's propositions, and then to communicate the substance of them to the Court of Directors, as furnishing ground of censure against their Governor-general. Yet such was the nature of his proceeding; and it is of this that Mr. Hastings complains. Who can be surprised to find that, from that hour, everything like friendship or cordiality between them ceased?

To Laurence Sulivan, Esq.

Fort William, 27th March, 1783.

My dear Friend,—I am very apprehensive that my friends, not aware of my situation, will blame me for a resolution which I have lately taken and notified in form to the Court of Directors by these despatches. After eleven years that I have held my station under discouragements unknown to my predecessors, opposed and thwarted by my colleagues in office, counteracted and reviled by my superiors, and never possessing any but accidental and temporary power, you, my good friend, will not impute to me the imbecility of sacrificing my place and all my hopes to a momentary impatience and the petulancy of disappointment. No, my dear Sir; you may believe me when I assure you that I cannot retain it with any hope of credit, nor without the hazard of losing all the little which I have acquired. The advice which has been repeated to me in all my letters from England is, that I shall not regard the late orders of the Court of Directors. They were not aware of the effect of those orders in depriving me of my influence abroad, and of support at home. They considered these orders but as an empty sound, which would produce the terror of a moment and pass without consequence. In truth, they have as effectually disarmed me as if they had reduced me to the state of a mere secretary of the Board. My authority is not only taken from me at a time when I most require it, but proclamation of my deprivation is made to all the world; and the men who were supposed to be my firm and determined supporters, and to whose appointment many were induced on that consideration only to yield their consent, at least I was told so, object to the most trivial matters if I propose them, and in their minutes affectedly join their professions of submission to the Company's orders, with their opposition to me in such a manner as if they were afraid of being suspected of any thing like a leaning towards me. I may injure them by this construction of their intentions, but the effect is the same from whatever cause it proceeds. With Mr. Wheler I am every way satisfied.

If there is any department of Government which is exclusively mine, or which would be left to my absolute choice by men disposed to act with me cordially, it is the appointment of my own representatives in foreign courts. We wanted one at Hyderabad. Richard Sulivan, whose brother had been destined to that appointment from home, who was recently removed from a similar office with the Nabob Wallah Jaw, but without any expression of displeasure which was aimed at him, appeared to me a proper person for it, and surely well qualified, for (David Anderson always excepted) I do not know his equal. I mentioned it privately to Sir Eyre Coote, who eagerly approved it. I did the same to Mr. Stables, who hesitated and I postponed it. After an interval of near a fortnight, the Nabob, Ally Cawn, having extricated himself from a war in which he had been some time engaged with one of his own vassals, I thought it wrong to leave him longer without some minister attending him from this Government, especially as he was sore on the Mahratta treaty, and that was just concluded. I proposed the appointment and recommended Richard Sulivan for it, having in the mean time written to him and learnt that it would be agreeable to him. It was opposed on the grounds that Nizam Ally Cawn would be averse to it on account of Sulivan's connexion with the Nabob Wallah Jaw, and that it would displease the Court of Directors. Mr. Wheler assented. The old General was warm for it, but minuted no opinion as I could not prevail on the other members to minute theirs. These were afterwards delivered to the secretary, but Mr. Graham, the General's secretary, has since told me that the General would give no opinion upon the question, because he thought it liable to the objection of being disagreeable to Nizam Ally Cawn. For these reasons, though the question stands determined, I have resolved to write to Nizam Ally Cawn, and state the doubt which has been suggested, leaving it to him to decide on the issue of this business.

Some time ago, when Richard Sulivan and Assum Cawn, the Nabob Wallah Jaw's Dewan, were here, I had concerted a plan with the latter for effecting a reconciliation between the two Nabobs. Assum Cawn was to go first from his master to Hyderabad, and secretly persuade Nizam Ally Cawn to propose a meeting with me, which he was assured the Nabob would eagerly solicit, and it was planned that the Nabob Wallah Jaw should be a party. We have many points depending with Nizam Ally Cawn which we must settle, and with the support and confidence of my council I think that I could have settled them better than any other could, and have transferred the terms of his alliance from a partial to a general connexion, and added some advantages to it. As soon as the late advices arrived from England, I saw that the design was no longer practicable, and let Assum Cawn know that I had dropped it. I had flattered myself with closing my service with a measure which would have reflected a lasting credit on me. Mr. Macpherson only was privy to it, and this makes me the more distrustful of his motives in the objections which he has since made to Richard Sulivan's appointment.

Major Scott will show you the minutes of this transaction, I mean of my proposal respecting Richard Sulivan.

I cannot hope to be allowed independent powers, nor other colleagues. Neither do I wish to remove these, though I foresee that I shall be less able to act with them, than I now am. It would relieve me if I could engage the decided support of Mr. Wheler; but I cannot exact it, nor would he give it beyond certain lines.

Perhaps even you, my respectable friend, while you feel for my difficulties, may yet entertain so favourable a sense of the source from which they have originated, as to be more inclined to reprove my opposition to it, than to wish it removed. It is natural, and whenever a man of business like you shall be at the head of the direction, every man like myself will be glad and proud to obey him. No man has ever manifested the principle of obedience in substantial acts equally with me. The orders which I have opposed were all personal and vindictive. I have no doubt that a different conduct will be observed with my successor; and of this I am certain, that the veriest stock with a human form, and a share of animation equal to the ordinary functions of life, will perform more service to the Company, with proper powers and confidence reposed in him, than I can do with neither.

In the resolutions in the Court of Directors concerning my transactions at Benares, what a dreadful lesson have they formed for their service! A subject of their sovereignty rebels against the representative of their authority, massacres 200 of his attendants, and attempts his life. It is not pretended, nor suspected that I had any motive for the provocation which drew on me so infamous a vengeance, but to relieve the Company's distresses. The Court of Directors, who ought to have set the first example in punishing this first instance of revolt in their subjects, who ought to have considered it as a precedent which may hereafter operate to their own destruction,—they take the part of the murderer, complain that *I disgraced him in the eyes of his subjects and others, and that it may have a tendency to weaken the confidence which the "native princes" of India ought to have in the justice and moderation of our Government.*

Infinitely worse will the example prove, if their conduct should teach their vassals that the sure means of acquiring the protection of the Court of Directors, and to become princes of India, will be to throw off the authority of the Company and assassinate their servants; and if it should have a tendency to weaken the confidence which their servants in India ought to have in the justice, truth, and common policy of their rulers.

I could have guarded myself most effectually against their censures, by avoiding all responsibility, and covering myself with their orders in whatever I did. I could have kept their troops and treasure at home, when the Presidency of Bombay was engaged in schemes to which it was confessedly unequal. I could have suffered the disgrace of the unhappy affair of Worgaum to remain an indelible stain on the British name. It was no concern of mine. I could have suffered the Carnatic to fall an easy prey to Hyder, when Francis opposed the measures which I suggested for its preservation, and I could have justified it on the principle of self preservation; the prior care due to the first possessions of the Company; the want of authority from home; the season of the year, which would render it an act of madness to send their troops to perish by sea; and by a fair estimate of ways and means, which would prove that we had not assets for such an enterprise. I could have acquiesced in the violations of faith, which the Government of Madras were guilty of towards Nizam Ally, and contented myself with protesting against it. I could have seen Chimnajee lay Bengal waste, for it was scarce in his power to avoid it, and nothing but my private aid prevented it.

I could have sat quietly down when our ordinary resources would yield no more supplies for the war, and ruin threatened. What business had I at Benares?

But if I had observed this discreet and safe conduct, let me ask, not you, my friend—but my most rancorous enemies, what would have been the state of the Company, or whether it is likely that it would at this time have existence?

In the mean time I could have provided an ample fortune for myself, by means which no one could have assumed to hurt or discredit me. Their salt manufacture, under a proper management, would have yielded me many lacs; and the Court of Directors, with their appointment of young Gregory to be chief of the Council of Patna, have declared that the Court ought not to monopolize the opium, that is, that it should be the free trade of those whose superior advantages of place and power could appropriate it. In this arrangement, I certainly could have had my share, and allowably. I have done neither. I originally converted these funds to the Company's use. When the Company's orders and General Clavering's mismanagement had reduced the first to a loss, I, against the will and judgment of all my colleagues, and at my own risk, restored and improved it.

It now yields a clear net income, by a process the most easy and simple, of Cs.Rs. 57,25,673 15 0

The opium, under all the discouragements of war .	6,06,428	14	3
Both together . .	63,32,101	13	3

To these add the annual increase of the land revenue seventy lacs; the increase of the revenue of Benares and its security, which I rate at forty; the payments made by the Nabob Vizier; and upwards of thirty lacs of rupees designed for my own private use and converted to the relief of the Company's wants, and let the sum total speak what I have done for the Company by departing from the beaten tracks, and exploring the wilds of peril and reproach, and what I might have done for myself, had I quietly plodded in the former, as any other man possessing my place, and the same means, might and probably would have done.

A Mr. Dunkin tells me that at the time in which the most violent attacks were made upon me, and a number of candidates stood for my place, you made interest with Lord North to allow me to remain with the fullest support, while I chose it, and to make choice of Lord Macartney to succeed me. This I think is the substance of a long detail. If in any point I have misrepresented it, impute it to my inattention in combining the facts of which I have composed it. I credit the information, and perhaps the more readily as it affords me a fresh instance of your watchful regard for my reputation and interests; but it is right to undeceive you with respect to the man on whom you placed so uncommon a dependence; I mean Lord Macartney. Yielding implicitly to the warm and earnest recommendation of my first friends, viz., yourself, Mr. Pechell, whom I never remember but with an aching heart, and General Caillaud, I set aside all reserve, and began a correspondence with his Lordship on a footing of unbounded confidence. His Lordship confirmed me in this disposition, and invited me to continue in it.

Read in the enclosures the fruits of my candour, and

the evidence of his treachery and dishonour. His motive I cannot guess; for when my letters were written, and many months after, (for I did not return to Calcutta, nor concern myself in any acts of the Council, till the February following,) nothing had passed between us, that could have given him the most distant cause of offence; nothing in effect but professions and proofs on my part of a most cordial regard. He cannot even invent a ground of suspicion against me. Yet it appears that at this very time, when he professed himself my friend, and solicited my advice, he made use of my letters as criminal charges against me. What a man!

It is true that in giving my opinion concerning Tanjore, I gave him a liberty to avail himself of it; that is, to use it as authority to strengthen his own, if he meant to conform to it. Surely he will not say that this latitude extended to his applying it only as an instrument to injure me. I am ashamed of the Court of Directors for countenancing such a shameful departure from one of the first principles of society. How meanly did I think of them and of their censures, drawn from so miserable a source!

Adieu, my dear friend. This is the last long letter which I am likely to give you the trouble of reading from me; for I shall henceforth only look to my speedy release from this scene of discredit, and to the happiness of meeting you in England. May God grant it!

I subjoin a letter to Lord Macartney himself, having reference to the same subject. I cannot find that it led either to a satisfactory explanation of his Lordship's proceeding, or to a renewal of confidence and friendship between them.

To the Right Honourable Lord MACARTNEY.

Fort William, 13th April, 1783.

My Lord,—I was greatly surprised to read in the late general letters from the Court of Directors, very severe expressions of their displeasure, grounded on my private and confidential letters to your Lordship. It is true that I gave you an express permission to avail yourself of my opinions in any manner that you pleased, but your Lordship will recollect the relation in which I had then the honour to stand to your Lordship. I was not writing to a man against whom I was to guard my words, and to prescribe the exact and precise use which I might allow him to make of them, but I submitted them unreservedly to his honour, faith, and generosity on such liberal grounds as the severest discretion might warrant. Our common friends, amongst whom were some whose faintest wishes were a law to me, had assured me that you desired my confidence and advice; that you sought to make the line of my conduct the rule of your own; and they enjoined me to begin a free and unreserved communication of sentiments with you; without waiting for any advances on your part to dispense with the usual cautions of a new acquaintance. I did so. I not only addressed your Lordship with the familiarity of an old friendship, but afforded a very early, and what I deemed a most substantial proof of my desire to cultivate a good understanding with your Lordship in the first letter which I wrote to you after my knowledge of your arrival at Madras, which was also my first knowledge of your appointment to the government of that presidency. I afterwards received, and felt a sincere pleasure in receiving, a letter from you which corresponded with the declarations of my friends. I have not the letter at hand, but I well remember the purport of it. It professed such sentiments as my own heart, already prepossessed in your Lordship's favour, received with pleasure. It professed a deference for my judgment and solicited my advice. This I freely gave, but as I gave it with the view of rendering it serviceable to your Lordship, and to the public, I told you that you might avail yourself of it publicly, and in any way that your Lordship pleased. In legal acceptation, such a licence might perhaps be construed into the allowance of converting the advice and opinions offered for your service to be instruments of my own ruin, if "you were pleased" to make that use of it. But I should have falsified my opinion both of your understanding and honour, if I could have descended to make such an exception. I meant it, and I knew that you would so understand it, as a permission to apply my advice to the construction of your public measures, if it was conformable to your own sentiments, and in that event to quote it as mine, and to lessen your own responsibility by the weight which the public, and perhaps the Court of Directors, might attribute to my experience. If you disapproved my advice, if my opinions appeared erroneous in your judgment of them, there could be no use in communicating them; and as the communication of them might injure me, it would have been an ill requital of confidence to make it without consideration of the consequences; it would have been criminal to make it in such a manner as might expose me to the resentment of my superiors; but if used for the purpose of drawing a criminal accusation from it, or of contrasting your own integrity with mine,—your Lordship will forgive me for supposing the possibility of such a case, and to your justice I refer the sentence due to the perpetration of the act which I have stated, and which I have only stated for the purpose of viewing the subject in every possible application of it.

I will frankly own that when I first met these passages of the general letters, I yielded to that natural impression which they would have made on your Lordship's mind in a similar case; but as it seemed, on a more temperate reflection, too severe to pronounce, on appearances which I was not able to reconcile to any justifiable grounds, a conclusion derogatory from the principles of honour, and as nothing had passed between your Lordship and myself at the time in which your letters to the Court of Directors were written which could have furnished the remotest plea for hostility, if any provocation can be pleaded for a breach of private confidence, I checked my first suspicion, and in the hope that what your Lordship had written, perhaps with other views, and with candid intentions, had been perverted by a false construction to a purpose unforeseen by your Lordship; I resolved to lay this full exposition of the subject, and my own feelings excited by it, before your view, that if you please you may afford me such an explanation of it as you may judge due to me for the apparent injury which I have suffered, and even to yourself, if you conceive the estimation of a man so inconsiderable as I am deserving of your attention. This satisfaction I leave entirely to your Lordship's option, myself neither claiming nor soliciting it. But you will allow me to claim as a right, that you will impart to me what you have written to the Court of Directors, on the ground of my letters; I mean the extract of your letters on the subject of the Northern Circars, and the Rajah of Tanjore, to which the 31st, 34th, and 35th paragraphs of their letter to your presidency, dated 12th July 1782, refer.

I need not inform your Lordship that this letter is not intended as a private communication; nor, of course, that I shall deem myself exempt from every kind of reflection in the use which I may make of your reply.

CHAPTER III.

Progress of Affairs in the Carnatic—Death of Sir Eyre Coote—Letter to Lord Macartney—Peace with Tippoo—Letter to the Court of Directors.

While the heads of the two governments were thus passing into a state of open hostility, the affairs of the subordinate province, so far from retrieving themselves, appeared from day to day to become only more complicated. There was no cordiality between the civil and the military authorities; there was no good understanding between the Nabob and the Governor. Indeed the very elements themselves seemed to war against the English; for a furious storm fell upon the coast, and almost all the vessels in which grain for the supply of the presidency had been kept, were driven from their moorings and destroyed. Meanwhile the death of Hyder, though communicated both to the Governor and the General, was permitted to pass unimproved. The former, to do him justice, urged an advance; the latter declared that the army was not in a condition to move; and he moved at last only to find, that the opportunity of striking a great blow had escaped him. In a word, the spirit of faction seemed to have taken entire possession of men's minds; insomuch that at a moment when the horrors of famine were around them; when the Carnatic was everywhere a desert, and Fort St. George itself was saved, only through the ignorance of the French and of Tippoo touching the helpless state into which it had fallen; they whose duty it was to labour for the public good wasted their time in profitless disputes concerning questions of personal dignity and personal power.

Once more the master spirit of Warren Hastings devised and carried into execution plans for the preservation of India. Fresh supplies of men, of money, and of provisions were ordered to be transported to Madras; fresh negociations were opened with the Mahrattas and the Nizam for the invasion of Mysore. But the measure on which, more than on all the rest, the Governor-general depended, was the resumption, with dictatorial powers, of the general command of the troops by Sir Eyre Coote. Feeble as he was in body, and somewhat weakened in mind, that veteran officer still bore a name, which as both friends and foes had been taught to think highly of it in other days, so they were not now likely to treat it otherwise than with respect. At the same time Mr. Hastings well knew that the General was not in any respect what he once was. He therefore endeavoured, as much as possible, to screen him from the annoyance of angry discussions, and wrote, with this view, the following letter, to a member of Council at Fort St. George.

To Alexander Davidson, Esq.

Fort William, 11th January, 1783.

Dear Sir,—I address myself to you upon a subject in which I am exceedingly interested, because you are the only person capable by situation of affording me the assistance which I require, and from whom I can at the same time confidently solicit it.

Sir Eyre Coote, notwithstanding his very broken constitution, has declared his resolution of returning to the coast, and will take his passage in the Medea frigate immediately after her arrival. In this determination he has been in a great measure influenced by his knowledge of the wishes of the members of this Government; and, I fear, much against those of his own family. I, for my own part, consider him as the only instrument capable of converting the present crisis to the security of the Carnatic, and the exclusion of our European enemies on the event of the dispersion or departure of the army of Mysore. This may prove the easy work of a few months if the General is allowed the full and undisturbed direction of all the military operations, and such aids as your Government can afford him. We shall renew our solicitations for that effect, and I have no doubt of your acquiescence in them. But I will own to you, that my fears for his success arise from another cause, which will not bear an ostensible discussion. I have read with infinite concern the letters which were addressed to him by the Select Committee in the course of the late campaign. The language of these, and more especially their implied sentiments, were often such as must have affected him severely, and the more so because of his inability, from the incessant calls of duty, and the debility of his constitution, to enter into a train of discussion in reply to them.

His temper, which is naturally too subject to irritation, has acquired an increased sensibility from the distempers which oppress him; and if, under the weight of these, he will again adventure on so arduous and fatiguing a service, he merits at least the return of personal attention and tenderness. He cannot bear the provocations of official letters written in the spirit of reproach and hostility. I have studied him, and find him capable of the most connected and perfect exercise of his understanding when his spirits are composed. But if they are agitated, and a slight cause will agitate them, it weakens his recollection, and sometimes throws him into sudden and dangerous fits of sickness.

I cannot prescribe to you as a member of Government either the style or subjects of your public correspondence, because I must suppose that every letter, and every act of your government, is dictated by a sense of unimpassioned duty. Yet allow me, my dear Sir, to recommend and request without other explanation, that you will, as much as it may be in your power, prevent any correspondence of such a nature as that to which I have alluded, and be the conciliator between him and the committee. I know not how far you might consider it as incompatible with the obligations of personal connexion, but so far as you may, with consistency of character, I would wish to engage your support of the General in his operations. I am sure that, in expressing this wish, I desire nothing which the strictest principle of honour may not avow, and that it is conformable to what I have known of your general character, which I have ever believed to be mild, reasonable, and conciliating.

It is unnecessary to add my motive for the uncommon

solicitude which I show on this occasion. I might, perhaps with equal propriety and truth, declare that I have an interest in it equal at least to any private concern of my own; but I will assure you that I shall receive and remember your compliance with my wishes in the instances to which I have applied them as a personal obligation requiring from me an equal return.

I wish you to consider this as a confidential letter. That, however, must depend on your option. I have the honour to be, with a very sincere esteem, dear Sir, your most obedient and faithful servant.

The career of Sir Eyre Coote was on this occasion a brief one. He died, as is well known, four days after being carried ashore, and left behind him a name second only to that of Clive in the history of Indian warfare. Nevertheless the bare act of despatching him was not without its uses, in introducing a better spirit into the military councils of the province. There was no renewed cordiality, indeed, between Lord Macartney and Mr. Hastings; whose estrangement became, on the contrary, from day to day more complete. But his Lordship ceased to interfere so much as at one time he seemed anxious to do in the movements of the troops, and the army took the field in good order. I cannot say much of its successes. After destroying the fortifications at Wadewash and Carungoly, and throwing supplies into Vellore, from the siege of which Tippoo withdrew, General Stuart retired to Madras, where, till the end of April, he remained inactive, waiting for the arrival of Sir Edward

Hughes on the coast, that together they might attack Cuddalore.

I should go far beyond the proper limits of this work, if I were to describe the further progress of a war, in the conduct of which Mr. Hastings had no direct share, and which was often waged upon a plan of which he did not approve. My purpose will be sufficiently served when I state, that the French, having received large reinforcements, took up a fortified position in front of Cuddalore; while the fleet, mustering sixteen sail, kept open their communications by sea. Having waited till these lines were completed, General Stuart set out from Madras; and on the 13th of July a general assault was given. It was not successful; yet the enemy, distrusting their own capability of sustaining a second, withdrew in the night, and, shutting themselves up within the walls of the town, were immediately invested. Meanwhile the hostile fleets met, and a fierce encounter took place, more to the detriment of the French than the English; though the latter were so much crippled that Sir Edward Hughes found himself obliged to bear up for Madras roads that he might refit. But no decisive consequences followed. Souffrein indeed made good his point of communicating with the besieged, to whom he sent supplies both of men and material. Nevertheless, ere Bussy could turn his advantages to account, intelligence of peace between Great Britain and France was received. As a matter of course hostilities ceased on the instant; while the French general sent off peremptory orders for the return of the detachment which accompanied Tippoo, and earnestly invited Tippoo himself to become a party to the proposed pacification.

Tippoo Saib now stood alone as the enemy of England; and had Mr. Hastings been absolute in India, the war against him would have been prosecuted to extermination. For the Nizam and the Mahrattas were both engaged to invade Mysore, and a single campaign rightly managed must have led to his total overthrow. But peace with Tippoo was Lord Macartney's favourite project, and he hastened, without pausing to consult the Supreme Government on the subject, to pave the way for its accomplishment. Lord Macartney had no grounds of justification in this proceeding. As the head of a subordinate presidency, it might be his duty to suggest,—but he had no right to act, except by explicit orders from Calcutta; while his mode of acting proved to be as impolitic as the assumption of powers which did not belong to him was offensive. Lord Macartney's treaty, when at length drawn up, took no notice of the Nabob, the principal in the war, nor made the slightest mention of the Mahrattas, without whose co-operation Tippoo never could have been induced to listen to his proposals. Nor is this all. In his eagerness for peace, he went so far as to propose the surrender of certain districts near the ghauts, which would have been to Tippoo of extraordinary value, because more than ever opening for him a road, at any moment, into the heart of Carnatic. Mr. Hastings has the merit of having put a direct stop to so discreditable an arrangement. He forbade it at every hazard, justly declaring that such an acknowledgment of inferiority would be more injurious to the interests of Carnatic than a continuance of the war for any conceivable length of time. Neither did he permit the Nabob to be slighted, or the Mahrattas exasperated by a display of indifference to their interests. As will be shown by and bye, a proceeding which was charged against him as a crime, namely, his refusal to sign a treaty which the Supreme Council had ratified, and the substitution of a new one drawn up by his own hand, was in point of fact an act of justice, of which the inconveniences, whatever they might be, were attributable not to him, but to the over-weening self-conceit and prejudices of the Governor of Madras.

All this while Mr. Hastings had the twofold burthen to bear, of wanton and groundless censure cast upon him by his superiors at home, and a great deal of annoyance through the misconduct and timidity of the Company's servants abroad.

In Oude, affairs, so far from adjusting themselves, became day by day more entangled. Mr. Bristow blamed the Vizier and his minister, the Vizier and his minister threw the blame on Mr. Bristow, and they were not contradicted by the reports which Major Palmer communicated, while passing to and fro on his mission to Rohilcund. Of the effect produced on his own mind by the Court's censure, I have in my selection from Mr. Hastings's private correspondence endeavoured to convey a correct idea. I do not think that the reader will blame me for inserting here, in illustration of the same, a single public document. It is his reply to the Court's letter, a powerful and well written paper, which, though more than once printed elsewhere by fragments, has never, as far as I know, been offered to general perusal, as a whole. I think it entirely overthrows the dotage of Cheyt Sing's right of sovereignty, and exculpates the Governor-general from all just blame for having dealt with him as with a traitor.

To the Honourable Court of Directors of the Honourable United East India Company.

Fort William, 20th March, 1783.

Honourable Sirs,—In your letter to the Governor-general and Council, dated 28th August, 1782, you have been pleased to enter into a large discussion of my proceedings at Benares, and to apprize the Board of certain resolutions comprehending your judgment upon them. These resolutions, as the immediate cause and subject of my present address, I shall, to avoid the perplexity of frequent and remote reference, hereto subjoin.

"That it appears to this Court, that on the death of Sujah Dowlah, 1775, a treaty was made with his successor, by which the zemindarry of Benares, with its dependencies, was ceded in perpetuity to the East India Company.

"That it appears to this Court, that Rajah Cheyt Sing was confirmed by the Governor-general and Council of Bengal in the management of the said zemindarry (subject to the sovereignty of the Company) on his paying a certain tribute which was settled at Sicca rupees 22,66,180; and that the Bengal Government pledged itself that the free and uncontrolled possession of the zemindarry of Benares and its dependencies should be confirmed and guaranteed to the Rajah and his heirs for ever, subject to such tribute, and that no other demand should be made upon him nor any kind of authority or jurisdiction exercised within the dominions assigned him, so long as he adhered to the terms of his engagement.

"That it appears to this Court, that the Governor-general and Council did, on the 5th July, 1775, recommend to Rajah Cheyt Sing, to keep up a body of 2,000 horse, but at the same time declared there should be no obligation on him to do it.

"That it appears to this Court, that Rajah Cheyt Sing performed his engagements with the Company in the regular payment of his tribute of Sicca rupees 22,66,180.

"That it appears to this Court, that the conduct of the Governor-general towards the Rajah, whilst he was at Benares, was improper, and the imprisonment of his person, thereby disgracing him in the eyes of his subjects and others, was unwarrantable and highly impolitic, and may tend to weaken the confidence which the native princes of India ought to have in the justice and moderation of the Company's government."

I understand that these resolutions were either published or intended for publication. As they have proceeded from an authority so respectable, any reader of them will naturally, and without hesitation, believe, that the facts on which they necessarily and indispensably depend, have been fully established. And who are the readers? not the proprietors alone, whose interests is immediately concerned in them, and whose approbation I am impelled by every motive of pride and gratitude to solicit; but the whole body of the people of England, whose passions have been excited on the general subject of the conduct of their servants in India; and before them I am arraigned and prejudged of a violation of the national faith in acts of such complicated aggravation, that if they were true, no punishment short of death could atone for the injury which the interest and credit of the public had sustained in them.

I hope, therefore, I shall not be thought to give unnecessary trouble in calling your attention to a subject not wholly personal, nor to fail in the respect, in which I have never yet failed, to your honourable Court, in the mode of my vindication, which will not admit of the common delicacies of expression; for I cannot admit facts, however affirmed, which I know to have no existence, and by which my character has been blamed, nor will a simple denial or refutation of them be sufficient against such a charge, if I can at the same time appeal to your own knowledge, prove by the evidence of your own arguments, and to what your honourable Court possesses in candour, for my first justification and acquittal.

The facts affirmed, or expressed in terms equal to affirmation, in your resolutions are as follows:

1st. That the Bengal Government pledged itself

that the free and uncontrolled possession of the zemindarry of Benares and its dependencies should be confirmed and guaranteed to the Rajah and his heirs for ever.

2d. That it pledged itself that no other demand should be made upon him, nor any kind of authority or jurisdiction exercised within the dominions assigned him, so long as he adhered to the terms of his engagement.

3d. That the Governor-general required him to keep up a body of 2,000 horse, contrary to the declaration made to him by the Governor-general and Council on the 5th July, 1775, that there should be no obligation on him to do it.

4th. That Rajah Cheyt Sing was bound by no other engagements to the Company, than for the payment of his tribute of Sicca rupees 22,66,180.

5th. That Rajah Cheyt Sing was a native prince of India.

6th. The judgment passed on my conduct, as deducible from the facts, is, that it was "improper, unwarrantable, and highly impolitic, and may tend to weaken the confidence which the native princes of India ought to have in the justice and moderation of the Company's Government." I must crave leave to say, that the terms "improper, unwarrantable, and highly impolitic," are much too gentle as deductions from such premises, and as every reader of the latter will obviously feel as he reads the deductions which inevitably belong to them. I will add, that the strict performance of solemn engagements on one part followed by acts directly subversive of them, and by total dispossession on the other, stamps on the perpetrators of the latter the guilt of the greatest possible violation of faith and justice.

But this and every other conclusion from the facts

advanced in proof of them, will fail, if the facts themselves have no existence. I do, therefore, most positively and solemnly deny their existence.

I deny that the Bengal Government pledged itself that the free and uncontrolled possession of the zemindarry of Benares and its dependencies should be confirmed and guaranteed to the Rajah and his heirs for ever.

I deny that the Bengal Government pledged itself that no other demand should be made upon him, nor any kind of authority or jurisdiction exercised within the dominions assigned him, so long as he adhered to the terms of his engagement.

I deny that I ever required him to keep up a body of 2,000 horse contrary to the declaration made to him by the Governor-general and Council on the 5th July, 1775, that there should be no obligation on him to do it.

My demand (that is, the demand of the Board) was not that he should maintain any specific number of horse, but that the number which he did maintain should be employed for the defence of the general state.

I deny that Rajah Cheyt Sing was bound by no other engagement to the Company than for the payment of the tribute of Sicca rupees 22,66,180.

He was bound by the engagements of fealty, and absolute obedience to every order of the Government which he served. The various and repeated professions of his letters are proofs and acknowledgments of this construction of his vassalage; and his own cabulceat, or instrument by which he engaged to perform the duties of his zemindarry, expresses it in the acknowledgment of the Company's sovereignty.

I deny that Rajah Cheyt Sing was a native prince of India.

Cheyt Sing is the son of a collector of the revenue of that province which his acts, and the misfortunes of his master enabled him to convert to a permanent and hereditary possession. This man, whom you have thus ranked among the princes of India, will be astonished when he hears it, at an elevation so unlooked for; nor less at the independent rights which your commands have assigned him; rights which are so foreign from his conceptions, that I doubt whether he will know in what language to assert them, unless the example which you have thought it consistent with justice, however opposite to policy, to show, of becoming his advocates against your own interests, should inspire any of your own servants to be his advisers and instructors.

I forbear to detail the proofs of these denials. In legal propriety I might perhaps claim a dispensation from it, and require the charges to be proved, not myself disprove. But I have already disproved them in my narrative of my proceedings at Benares which has been long since in your hands, and is, I hope, in the hands of the public. So that I think it sufficient to refer, and to point out the ninth and following pages of the copy which was printed in Calcutta, for a complete explanation, and I presume as complete a demonstration of the mutual relation of Rajah Cheyt Sing the vassal and subject of the Company, and of the Company his sovereign.

The subject to which I now proceed, and on which I rest my fullest acquittal, is too delicate to admit of my entering upon it without requesting your indulgence and pardon for whatever may appear offensive in it, and declaring that I should have submitted in silence to the severest expressions of censure which you could pass upon me, had they been no more than expressions and applied to real facts; but when the censures are not applied to real facts, and are such as substantially affect my moral character, I should be myself an accomplice in the injury, if I suffered the slightest imputation to remain, which it was in my power wholly to efface.

A breach of faith necessarily inplies antecedent and existing engagements, and can only be construed such by the express terms of those engagements. I have been guilty of this crime in my treatment of Cheyt Sing, or of none, and may be allowed to regret that while you stated such facts as implied it, you did not in terms declare it. There is an appearance of tenderness in this deviation from plain construction, of which, however meant, I have a right to complain, because it imposes on me the necessity of framing the terms of the accusation against myself, which you have only not made, but have stated the leading arguments so strongly, that no one who reads these can avoid making it, or not know to have been intended.

But permit me to ask: May I not presume that this deviation arose from something more than a tenderness for my character and feelings? that it was dictated by a consciousness that no such engagement existed? for if any such did exist, why were not the terms of the engagement produced in support of the charges.

But even the facts which are affirmed in the resolutions are such as must depend upon some evidences, for they cannot exist independently. If the Bengal Government "pledged itself," its pledge must be contained in the written instruments which were expressly formed and declared to define the reciprocal relation and obligation of the Rajah and the Company. The resolutions of your honourable Court, as they stand unconnected in their original state, must be accepted as the conclusions from certain and established evidence, and this evidence, I must presume, you meant to produce in the long process of detailed argument, which precedes them in your general letter. This consists of pieced extracts from opinions delivered by me in the debates of Council, which not only preceded the settlement made with the Rajah Cheyt Sing, when his zemindarry became the property of the Company; but, strange as it will appear, which passed on an occasion wholly foreign from it, and at a time when the Company had not obtained the cession of the zemindarry. At the point of the settlement, your detail stops. Had it proceeded, it must have exhibited the conditions of the settlement, which would have contradicted every fact which you have asserted; and every man of candour will believe that this was the only reason why it did not proceed. For why are my speculative opinions on the claim made upon the Nabob Assof ul Dowlah for the cession of the zemindarry of Benares, which I thought an infringement of a treaty already subsisting with him, and upon the mode by which we should allow Rajah Cheyt Sing to exercise the management of his zemindarry when it had become the property of the Company, quoted in evidence against me; when the actual deeds which conveyed to Cheyt Sing his possession of the zemindarry, and all the conditions by which he had it, were the only criteria by which my conduct towards him could be tried? The debates from which my opinions are extracted are so voluminous, and my share in them bears so large a proportion, that it would take up much time and argument to prove, what I could prove, that in their collective and relative sense they are perfectly consistent, so far as they can apply at all, to my subsequent conduct; but were it otherwise, they are not to be made the rules of my conduct; and God forbid that every expression, dictated by the impulse of present emergency, and unpremeditatedly uttered in the heat of party contention, should impose upon me the obligation of a fixed principle, and be applied to every variable occasion.

The wisdom of the legislature has declared that the whole collective body of the Governor-general and Council shall be bound by the opinions of the majority; but the doctrine implied in your quotation of my opinions is the reverse of that obligation, if my opinions were not conformable to those of a majority of the Board; and if they were, the acts of the Board, formed on such concurrent opinions, ought to be quoted as the rules of my conduct, not the opinions which only led to them.

Having solemnly pronounced that Rajah Cheyt Sing had performed his engagements with the Company, and that my conduct towards him was "improper and unwarrantable," you proceed to say that, "such further resolutions as you may think proper to come to on this very important subject will be communicated to us by a future conveyance." This I cannot otherwise understand than as an indication of your intention to order the restoration of Rajah Cheyt Sing to the zemindarry of Benares. It will be expected after the judgment which you have passed as an act of indispensable justice; and whenever this promissory declaration is made public, as it must be, if not already known, what may have been expected will be regarded as a certainty. If anything were wanting but the express notification of your intention to confirm it, the recall of Mr. Markham, who was known to be the public agent of my own nomination at Benares, and the reappointment of Mr. Francis Fowke by your order, contained in the same letter, would place it beyond a doubt. This order has been obeyed, and whenever you shall be pleased to order the restoration of Cheyt Sing, I will venture to promise the same ready and exact submission in the members of your Council.

Of the consequence of such a policy I forbear to speak. Most happily the wretch whose hopes may be excited by the appearances in his favour is ill qualified to avail himself of them; and the force which is stationed in the provice of Benares is sufficient to suppress any symptoms of internal sedition; but it cannot fail to create distrust and suspense in the minds both of the rulers and of the people; and such a state is always productive of disorder.

But it is not in this particular consideration that I dread the effects of your commands. It is in your proclaimed indisposition against the first executive member of your first Government in India. It is as well known to the Indian world as to the Court of English proprietors, that the first declaratory instruments of the dissolution of my influence in the year 1774 were Mr. John Bristow and Mr. Francis Fowke. By your ancient and known constitution, the Governor has been ever held forth and understood to possess the ostensible powers of Government. All the correspondence with foreign ministers is conducted in his name: and every person resident with them for the management of your political concerns is understood to be more especially his representatives, and of his choice, and such ought to be the rule; for how otherwise can they trust an agent nominated against the will of his principal; or how, knowing him to act under the variable instructions of a temporary influence or the casual dictates of a majority, can they rely on the measures which he may propose, and which a sudden change of influence, always expected in a deviation from constitutional forms, may undo, and subject, in every instance of their connexion, to a continual fluctuation of affairs?

When the state of this administration was such as seemed to admit of the appointment of Mr. Bristow to the residency of Lucknow without much diminution of my own influence, I gladly seized the occasion to show my readiness to submit to your commands. I proposed his nomination; he was nominated and declared to be the agent of my own choice. Even this effect of my caution is defeated by your absolute command for his reappointment, independent of me, and with the supposition that I should be adverse to it. I am now wholly deprived of my official powers, both in the province of Oude, and in the zemindarry of Benares.

Nor will the evil stop at these lines. My general influence, the effects of which have been happily manifested for the support of your interests, is now wholly lost, or what may remain of it sustained only by the prescription of long possession, and something perhaps of personal attachment, impressed by habits of frequent intercourse.

I almost shudder at the reflection of what might have happened had these denunciations against your own minister in favour of a man universally considered in this part of the world as justly attainted for his crimes, the murderer of your servants and soldiers, and the rebel of your authority, arrived two months earlier. You will learn by our common despatches what difficulties Mhadajee Scindia has had to surmount in reconciling the different members of the Mahratta state to the ratification, and even, when ratified, to the interchange of the treaty concluded by him in May last with this Government. I dare to appeal even to your judgment for the reply, and to ask, whether the ministers of the Peishwa, possessing the knowledge of such a circumstance, would not have availed themselves of it to withhold their consent to the treaty, either by claiming to include Cheyt Sing as a party in it, or either overtly or secretly supporting his pretensions, with the view of multiplying our difficulties; or, which is most probable, waiting for the event of that change in the superior Government of Bengal, which such symptoms portended, before they precipitated their interests in a connexion with a declining influence, which they might obviously conclude would render this, with all its other acts, obnoxous to that which succeeded it.

Their counter part of the treaty is ratified, and in our actual possession; and such is the character of the man whom we have made our principal and guarantee of it, that it will ensure us against any change of sentiment which might arise from any cause in the breasts of his countrymen. I am happy in having been the sole instrument in the accomplishment of so happy an event. It originated in a scene of universal revolt, encompassing my own person; it began with the immediate separation of the first power of the Mahratta state from the general war, and was followed by the instant and general cessation of hostilities,—in effect by a permanent peace: for I have a right now to affirm this, having positively assured you that it would prove such while the formal confirmation of it remained so long in a state of suspense. In every progressive state of it, it has met with obstructions which might have discouraged even the most determined perseverance:—in the known indisposition of the presidency of Bombay; in the calamities of the Carnatic; in the alarming interference of the President and Select Committee of Fort St. George, by the exaggerated portrait of their affairs in a letter addressed to our minister, and sent in circulation through the midst of the Decan and Indostan, entreating him at all events, and with whatever sacrifices, to precipitate the conclusion of the treaty, and save them from destruction but above all, in the vehement exclamations for peace from men of every description in Great Britain.

To all those counteractions I have apposed the principles of firmness and defiance, and, aided by the peculiar talents and wariness of Mr. David Anderson, I have at length brought my wishes and yours to their destined point. Perhaps with a less able minister I might yet have failed; but even the merits of his services I claim as my own, for it was my choice which called his mind into action, and my confidence that gave it its best exertions. Pardon me, honourable Sirs, this digressive exultation. I cannot suppress the pride which I feel in this successful achievement of a measure so fortunate for your interests and the national honour; for that pride is the source of my zeal so frequently exerted in your support, and never more happily than in those instances in which I have departed from the prescribed and beaten path of action, and assumed a responsibility which has too frequently drawn on me the most pointed effects of your displeasure. But however I may yield to my private feelings in thus enlarging on the subject, my motive in introducing it was immediately connected with its context, and was to contrast the actual state of your political affairs, derived from a happier influence, with that which might have attended an earlier dissolution of it.

It is now a complete period of eleven years since I first received the first nominal charge of your affairs. In the course of it, I have invariably had to contend, not with the ordinary difficulties of office, but with such as most unnaturally arose from the opposition of those very powers, from which I primarily derived my authority, and which were required for the support of it. My exertions, though applied to an unvaried and consistent line of action, have been occasional and desultory; yet I please myself with the hope that in the annals of your dominion which shall be written after the extinction of recent prejudices, this term of its administration will appear not the least conducive to the interests of the Company, nor the least reflective of the honour of the British name; and allow me to suggest the instructive reflection of what good might have been done, and what evil prevented, had due support been given to that administration which has performed such eminent and substantial services without it.

You, honourable Sirs, can attest the patience and temper with which I have submitted to all the indignities which have been heaped upon me in this long service. It was the duty of fidelity which I essentially owed to it. It was the return of gratitude which I owed, even with the sacrifice of life, had that been exacted, to the Company, my original masters, and most indulgent patrons. To these principles have I devoted every private feeling and persevered in the violent maintenance of my office; because I was conscious that I possessed in my integrity, and in the advantages of local knowledge, those means of discharging the functions of it with credit to myself and with advantage to my employers, which might be wanting in more splendid talents; and because I had always a ground of hope that my long sufferance would disarm the prejudices of my adversaries, or the rotation of time produce that concurrence in the crisis of your fortune with my own, which might place me in the situation to which I aspired. In the mean time there was nothing in any actual state of your affairs which could discourage me from the prosecution of this plan. There was, indeed, an interval, and that of some duration, in which my authority was wholly destroyed; but another was substituted in its place, and that, though irregular, was armed with the public belief of an influence invisibly upholding it, which gave it a vigour scarce less effectual than that of a constitutional power. Besides, your Government had no external dangers to agitate, and discover the looseness of its composition.

The case is now most widely different: while your existence was threatened by wars with the most formidable powers of Europe, added to your Indian enemies, and while you confessedly owed its preservation to the seasonable and vigorous exertions of this Government, you chose that season to annihilate its constitutional powers. You annihilated the influence of its executive member. You proclaimed its annihilation. You virtually called on his associates to withdraw their support from him; and they have withdrawn it; but you have substituted no other instrument of rule in his stead, unless you suppose it may exist, and can be effectually exercised, in the body of your Council at large, possessing no power of motion but an inert submission to the letter of your command, which, however necessary in the wise intention of the Legislature, has never yet been applied to the establishment of any original plan or system of measures, and seldom felt but in instances of personal favour or personal displeasure.

Under such a situation I feel myself impelled, by the same spirit which has hitherto animated me to retain my post against all the attempts made to extrude me from it, to adopt the contrary line. The season for contention is past, the present state of affairs is not able to bear it. I am morally certain that my successor in this Government, whoever he may be, will be allowed to possess and exercise the powers of his station, with the confidence and support of those who, by their choice of him, will be interested in his success.

I am become a burthen to the service, and would instantly relieve it from the incumbrance, were I not apprehensive of creating worse consequences by my abrupt removal from it. Such an act would probably be considered by Mhadajee Scindia as a desertion of him in the instant of his accomplishment of his treaty and defeat the purposes of it which yet remain to be effected by his agency. I am also persuaded that it would be attended with the loss of the Commander-in-Chief, in whose presence alone I look for the restoration of peace in the Carnatic, which he, perhaps, would think too hazardous an undertaking with no other support than a broken Government. I have no wish remaining, but to see the close of this calamitous scene, and for that I hope a few months will be sufficient. My services may afterwards be safely withdrawn; but will be still due, in my conception of what I owe to my first constituents, until they can be regularly superseded by those of my appointed successor, or until his succession shall have been made known, and the period of his arrival near at hand.

It therefore remains to perform the duty which I had assigned to myself as the final purpose of this letter, to declare, as I now most formally do, that it is my desire that you will be pleased to obtain the early nomination of a person to succeed me in the Government of Fort William; to declare, that it is my intention to resign your service as soon as I can do it without prejudice to your affairs, after the allowance of a competent time for your choice of a person to succeed me; and to declare, that if in the intermediate time you shall proceed to order the restoration of Cheyt Sing to the zemindarry from which, by the powers which I legally possessed, and conceive myself legally bound to assert against any subsequent authority to the contrary, derived from the same common source, he was for crimes of the greatest enormity dispossessed, and your Council shall resolve to execute the order, I will instantly give up my station and the service

To these declarations suffer me to add this reservation; that if in the mean time the acts of which I complain shall, on a mature revision of them, be revoked, and I shall find myself possessed of such a degree of your confidence as shall enable me to discharge the duties of my station, I will continue in it until the peace of all your possessions shall be restored, or it shall be your pleasure to allow me to resign it.—I have the honour to be, honourable Sirs, your most obedient and faithful servant.

P.S.—Upon a careful revisal of what I have written, I fear that an expression which I have used, respecting the probable conduct of the Board in the event of orders being received for the restoration of Cheyt Sing, may be construed as intimating a sense of dissatisfaction applied to transactions already passed. It is not my intention to complain of any one, but to vindicate my own character, and to state the difficulties of my situation. Neither do I mean, by excepting one person, to cast a censure on any others. Yet I feel in my esteem for Mr. Wheler, and in my solicitude to avoid even the imputation of reflecting unjustly on his conduct, a duty impelling me to declare, that in my experience of it since the time that we were first in the habits of mutual confidence, it has been fair and honourable to myself, and zealous to the public, equally free from profession and subterfuge, and his support given to me in every instance equal to whatever claim I might have to it.

CHAPTER IV.

State of Parties at Home—Overthrow of the Coalition—Unsatisfactory condition of things in India—Lord Macartney's Treaty with Hyder—Famine—Mrs. Hastings's Illness and return to England—Letters on various subjects.

It will be necessary once more to advert to the state of parties at home, to which Mr. Hastings's good name, as well as the fate of the East India Company, continued to furnish ample ground of discussion. I alluded in a former chapter to the formation of a Cabinet, which, because of the incongruous materials out of which it was built up, has ever since been designated the Coalition. I spoke also of the abortive issues to the India debates which marked its first entrance upon office, and of the assurance of Mr. Fox that, early in the following session, a broad and sweeping measure would be brought forward, and the question settled for ever. With this promise on the part of the minister, and this expectation raised in the country, and among the proprietors of India stock, the houses of parliament separated, and for several months the public, at least, was relieved from the consideration of a subject which had begun in some measure to weary rather than to interest.

Meanwhile throughout the recess, events were

continually occurring, all of them more or less connected with the personal fortunes of the subject of this memoir. In the month of August, for example, the Fox packet arrived from Calcutta, bringing official intelligence of the peace with the Mahrattas. The triumph of Mr. Hastings's friends was, as might have been anticipated, extreme; for up to the latest moment a contrary persuasion had prevailed; and the majority in the Direction made no scruple both to act and to speak, as if in every point he had shown himself the dupe of Mahratta cunning. They were of course compelled, on such evidence, to alter their tone; yet in Lord Macartney's angry letters they found some salve to their mortification, and they hastened to deal out blame as usual, where they ought to have administered praise. They met, coldly expressed their pleasure that the war had come to an end, and instantly went on to censure the Governor-general, because he had made choice of Sindia as his agent in the negociation. Nor was this all; the subject of presents was again brought forward. Mr. Hastings was charged with rapacity in accepting them; and a resolution was passed, that the ten lacs furnished by the Vizier should be credited to his public account. Nothing could be more illiberal than all this, unless indeed it be another paragraph in that memorable despatch, which required the Governor-general to account for every gift received by him since his first acceptance of office. For Mr. Hastings had repeatedly forestalled the Directors on this point, by first applying the sums advanced personally to himself to the public service, and then explaining to the Court how, and for what purpose, he had done so. But the majority were by this time furious with rage. They felt that they had placed themselves in a false position, and, like obstinate men who have gone far astray, they chose rather to flounder on, than by an honest effort of self-denial to acknowledge their mistake, and endeavour to make amends for it.

It was at this juncture, that Mr. Hastings's letters, announcing his intention on certain conditions to resign, arrived in London. No event could have occurred more satisfactory to the Government, which thus enjoyed the prospect of attaining without a struggle the great object of their ambition—the Indian patronage. So delighted indeed was Mr. Fox, that he spoke of Hastings as having removed from his shoulders an intolerable burthen; even while his hostility, and that of Mr. Burke, continued unabated. Mr. Hastings's best friends likewise congratulated themselves on the determination at which he had arrived, though for reasons widely different from those by which the Cabinet were swayed. They rejoiced, because so decisive an act on his part entirely refuted the calumnies of such as spoke of him in the light of one who could not be removed from office except by violence. Yet there was one personage in the realm who made no concealment of his regret on the occasion. The King everywhere avowed his belief, that the retirement of Warren Hastings at such a juncture would be perilous in the extreme to the English interests in India; and the fact of his doing so had no tendency to conciliate for the Governor-general the good will of a Cabinet which their royal master was well known equally to distrust and dislike.

It was now the month of October, and the Court of Proprietors, where his merits were still liberally acknowledged, resolved to anticipate any censure which might be cast on Mr. Hastings, by voting him, ere the session of Parliament opened, their formal thanks for his long and invaluable services. The business was well managed by Major Scott, Mr. Sulivan, and others, if indeed the expression be allowable in a case where no management appears to have been necessary; for the body of the Proprietors were of themselves steadily his friends. Accordingly while men's minds were filled with anticipations of what might happen—for the India question, it was well known, would be one of the first brought on for discussion—the Court met, and proceeded to business. I cannot refuse to my reader the satisfaction of deriving from one who was personally present a knowledge of the principal events which occurred at this meeting. The following is Major Scott's report to Mr. Hastings.

London, Queen-square, 10th November, 1783.

Thank God, my dear Sir, I can now congratulate you most sincerely upon the completest triumph that ever man received, who, from his exalted station has been so much the object of admiration on the one hand, and of envy on the other; but I will regularly detail the business from the date of my last letter. In that I informed you we meant to call a General Court. After several meetings with our friends, and those of the other members of the Supreme Council, Mr. Macpherson and Mr. Stables, in order to settle the mode of our proceeding, it was Governor Johnstone's opinion that the thanks of the Court should only be given to you; but that if the friends of the other gentlemen wished a vote of thanks, it ought to be a separate motion. This however they would not consent to, and Lord Mansfield observed to me, that it was not a point worth splitting upon, adding, with a peculiar archness, "You know the story, I and Doctor Radcliffe cured the fever." We thought it right to defer the meeting of the General Court as long as it could be done previous to the opening of the session, that what I have invariably contended for might happen, namely, that the sense of the East India Company upon your conduct might be taken in the fullest and fairest manner—trick and chicane being necessary in the common intercourse of politicians with each other, but totally useless to Mr. Hastings, and unworthy the justice of his cause.

Our letter for calling the General Court was given in on Wednesday the 39th of October, and appointed for Friday the 7th instant. Not long after the Court was summoned, Lord Loughborough and a Mr. Anstruther (who so strenuously supported us last year) paid a visit to Johnstone in order to persuade him to give up the business, and to permit you quietly to retire, as you wished to do. That after you had written for a successor, it was absurd to say anything more on the subject. His lordship added, that he heard we proposed voting you a continuation of Lord Clive's jaghire; and then he went into a long detail of the Mahratta war, insisting upon it that you were the author of it. "In a word (he added), you will be disgraced and defeated, and I advise you to give up the cause at once."

Johnstone made a very just and a very sarcastical reply: "As to giving away jaghires of £30,000 a year, I have hitherto invariably opposed such extravagant grants; however, when I alter my opinion upon that subject, I will apply to your lordship for assistance, who had so considerable a share in conferring that reward on Lord Clive. Whenever I propose a reward for Mr. Hastings, it shall be such a reward as is suited to the moderation of that gentleman's character, not to the greatness of his merits. As to our being disgraced, it is impossible, and I scarcely think it possible we should be defeated, but at all events I am determined to proceed, and I leave it to your friend Anstruther to instruct you on the subject of the Mahratta war. Last year, my lord, when you wished to distress Lord Shelburne, my support of Hastings was laudable, and would you really wish me to accommodate my conduct to your politics? Be assured I will not." Loughborough went away in despair of persuading Johnstone, but every engine was set at work to overset us. I received a note from Lord Mansfield last week, to tell me to be active, "as there were indefatigable machinations against us," I saw his lordship the next day at Caen Wood, who told me that if the ministers persisted in their absurdities as to India, they must break to pieces; and added, that two days before, the first draft of the King's speech was produced to the Cabinet. In that his Majesty was to recommend the consideration of India affairs to Parliament, and to adopt all the nonsense of the select committee, as to our having lost the confidence of the natives, &c. &c. He told me Lord Stormont would do all he could, but that if he did not succeed, there would be a division amongst the ministers on the first day of the sessions. He much approved of our motion, and desired we would not relax a moment. We got all our friends together, and on Friday the Court was as full as at the important debates of the last year, and consisted of the most respectable characters in the kingdom. Amongst them was the Archbishop of York, General Oglethorpe (now ninety-six years of age), the honourable Mr. Greville, General Caillaud, Sir Francis Sykes, Mr. Barwell, &c. &c. In short, gentlemen of all parties,

The business was exceedingly well conducted, as the printed debate will show you, and your enemies were so confounded by the impression which the oratory of Johnstone and young Dallas had upon the Court, that they were afraid to divide, lest the opposition should appear most thoroughly contemptible, but a Mr. Edward Moore, the most stupid of men, brother of Peter Moore, was the single negative to the motion.

The Fox I hope will be delayed a few days, and then I shall be able to tell you what effect our meetings will have upon his Majesty's ministers. I hear, and from authority too, that they very much approve of the moderate language we adopted, both in the motion and in the debate. One circumstance I confess pleases me beyond expression—that although the members of the Supreme Council are thanked, the debate entirely turned, as it ought to do, on the merits of the Governor general.

The next morning early I called on Lord Mansfield, who was greatly pleased with the happy conclusion of a business in which so many of his Majesty's ministers opposed us, till they saw the torrent too strong to be resisted, and that the well earned popularity of your character would bear down every opposition.

The ideas of Mr. John Robinson differed materially from ours, and the motion he wanted us to bring forward, was of a most curious nature, being in fact a panegyric upon the two youngest members of the Supreme Council. It ran:—That Macpherson arrived at Madras in August, 1781, reconciled contending parties, and performed most essential services. That he came to Bengal, found all in confusion; was zealous and active in the public cause. That from the time of his arrival, such and such supplies were sent to Bombay and Madras; that at such a time Stables arrived, and from that period great things had also been done. We rejected this motion unanimously, and at last it was agreed, as I have before said, simply to include them in the vote of thanks, upon the principle of Lord Mansfield, "that I and Doctor Radcliffe cured the fever." If we may judge from present appearances, no man in England will dare in future to attack your public conduct, and volunteers daily and hourly start up.

I am so pleased with a pamphlet of the Earl of Stair's, (which I shall send you,) that I transcribe an extract from it in this part of my letter.

"Our title to our acquisitions in India has now got stability from long possession; and however much private vices, or private injustice may have stained the administration of the Company's servants, their system of government appears solid, and has on trial resisted and triumphed over all the attacks which Europe and Asia combined have made upon it. This being the case, the frequent, trifling, partial, peevish interferences of Parliament in the Company's affairs, cannot but be hurtful to them, and are derogatory, in some sort, to the dignity of Parliament. Above all, the late attempts in Parliament to dismiss from his government with disgrace, the Company's great minister, the powerful Chatham of the East, who has shaded with laurels every dubious part of his former conduct, were proceedings of a most absurd ingratitude, for which no reason can be assigned but a detestable one, viz. his possessing what many men covet to possess. I never saw, probably never shall see, Mr. Hastings. What I write are the unbiassed effusions of impartial justice, charmed to find a fit subject for panegyric. I neither have, nor never had any connexion with him, or with the East India Company or their affairs ; yet I think it strange to see all the force of reform bent towards that quarter of the globe, in which alone our affairs have been conducted with success."

You will observe, my dear Sir, notwithstanding the warm and glowing terms which my Lord Stair uses, that he talks of the dubious parts, and Johnstone, in his speech, admits, for the sake of argument, that such there may be: I have, however, provoked the attack, and it has been shrunk from. Upon this subject too I am sure you will admire the energetic and animated language of young Dallas. Lord Mansfield says our Court is the school of oratory, and that Dallas goes far beyond Mr. Dunning as a public speaker.

I never saw the effect of oratory more strikingly displayed! Baber thinks him beyond, and I think him equal to Mr. William Pitt.

I have now but this wish, that whenever the situation of public affairs and your own inclination lead you to return home, I may have the happiness to meet you and Mrs. Hastings in the most perfect health, with your constitution recovered from the shock it received by that rascally fever last year.

11th November, 10 at night.—I have been in the House of Commons to-day to hear the debate upon the speech. It passed without a division, after some smart conversation between Mr. Fox, Mr. Pitt, and Governor Johnstone. The King's speech recommends the notice of India to the House, in general terms. Lord Ossory, who moved, and Sir Francis Bassett who seconded the address of thanks, said that, as India was our great stake, it became a subject of the utmost importance. Mr. Pitt agreed with them, but hoped that ministers would bring forward their plan fully and completely, and that it would be fairly and impartially considered. Fox gave notice that this day week he would make a motion on India business; but he spoke with the utmost mildness and caution. No personal reflections; no illiberal abuse as heretofore: no declaration that the proprietors had acted illegally or indecently, in opposing the wishes of Parliament. All he said was, that he would propose his plan, and leave it to the wisdom of the House to adopt or to reject it.

Johnstone complimented Fox upon his moderation, but confessed he was disappointed not to hear a syllable uttered in praise of Mr. Hastings, when India was the subject under the discussion of the House. Did not the members know, he added, what great things Mr. Hastings had done—that he had concluded the Mahratta peace, had saved Madras, and conquered Bednore and Mangalore?

Mr. T. Pitt said he should wait till Mr. Fox brought forward his plan; that however he expected to see the whole at once, and not that the ministers should bring it forward scrap by scrap. Mr. Burke did not venture to speak a syllable, and thus this day's business went off.

From what Lord Mansfield told me, I should suppose their plan is so exceedingly absurd, that it will be thrown out. But at all events, my dear sir, your business is now fully accomplished, and whatever they do, it will tend to set your character in a fairer point of view, if possible, than it now is, in the opinion of every honest man in this nation.

I dare say I shall write again before the ship goes; but I close this to prevent accidents.

I am ever, my dear Sir, most faithfully and gratefully yours.

The following brief account of the results of Mr. Fox's India Bill, and the breaking up of the Coalition cabinet, is full of interest. I give it, because it connects these events with the personal history of Mr. Hastings.

From Major Scott.

London, Queen-square, 20th December, 1783.

My dear Sir,—I have written to you several times, both overland and by the ships that have sailed since the 11th of November, which is the date of the last letter that I have had time to take a copy of. The events since that period to the present day are wonderful indeed; and I may say, as Lord Mansfield said of your proceedings at Benares, that this month contains changes and chances of importance enough to make the history of an age.

Agreeably to Mr. Fox's notice the first day of the Sessions, he brought in his motion for the India Bill on the 19th of November, which was prefaced by a very long speech, on which, as it has been printed, and as my answer to it has also been printed, I shall here make no remarks. The Bill was read for the first time two days after; and on the second reading, the 1st of

December, in spite of the very sound arguments offered against it, it was carried for commitment by a majority of two to one. It was again debated most powerfully at the third reading, but carried, the numbers being 208 to 106. Thus this important Bill, founded on injustice and supported by the most glaring falsities, passed one branch of the legislature. The East India Company made every possible stand, and no efforts were untried to turn the tide in the House of Commons; but unfortunately the very arguments we offered to avert the mischief were the arguments which carried the Bill through, namely, that it was in the first place a violation of every thing we should hold sacred in this country, and in the next place that it would extend the power of the minister and increase his patronage beyond all reasonable bounds by giving him entire possession of the East India Company. Our next resource was the House of Lords, and here we hoped to make a firm stand. Lord Thurlow sent for me the day before the Bill had finally passed the Commons; he took very great pains to obtain complete information on the subject, and he lamented very sincerely that I had been so long in England at so critical a period without obtaining a seat in the House of Commons, where such bold and infamous assertions had passed uncontradicted, merely for want of some person to speak to matters of fact. I had the pleasure to meet Lord Thurlow and Lord Temple several times before the business came on in the House of Peers. They both expressed the highest regard for you, and the firmest conviction of the importance of your services to the public. Lord Temple, in particular, made use of the following remarkable expressions:—"You must know, Major Scott, perfectly well, that if the present Bill should be lost in our House, we shall turn out the Ministry; in that case we wish most cordially to support

Mr. Hastings, and I hope to God he will not think of quitting Bengal. I have taken great pains to make myself acquainted with the transactions in Bengal during his administration, and I find the deeper I go the more reason I have to admire the conduct of Mr. Hastings."

On the 9th instant the Bill was read for the first time in the House of Peers, when Lord Thurlow made one of the finest speeches ever uttered in Parliament, to which I have attempted, though in vain, to do justice in the printed account of debates which will accompany this letter. I sent the speeches to the press, as they were so miserably given in the newspapers. The King was certainly very much alarmed when he thoroughly understood the drift of Mr. Fox in bringing in his Bill. Lord Temple had a conference with His Majesty on the 11th, and the consequences which have resulted from it are most important. All those noblemen who are denominated the friends of the constitution, and who have strenuously defended the King's prerogative, came up to town, and when the Bill was read a second time on the 15th, the House of Lords was fuller than it has been known during the present reign. Our counsel opened the business with wonderful ability, and defended the Company with great success. The Minister lost the question that night at twelve o'clock by a majority of eight. The counsel went on the next day, and young Dallas made one of the finest speeches ever pronounced at that bar. It will be printed immediately. No part was more approved of than that in which he mentioned your services and the treatment you had met with. The debate was put off for that night by consent, and the next day, the 17th, it came on. Lord Loughborough was afraid to rise, and the Bill was very feebly supported, indeed, by Lords Carlisle, Sandwich, and Derby; and their arguments completely refuted by Lords Gower, Walsingham, Coventry, Rawdon, Camden, and the Duke of Richmond. Many others meant to have taken a part for us, and amongst the rest Lords Mansfield and Stormont; but the opposition was so contemptible that neither they, nor Lord Thurlow, spoke. At eleven at night the House divided, and the Bill was rejected by a majority of nineteen. Thus fell this famous Bill, and with it the Coalition. Lord Mansfield stopped and talked to me for ten minutes as he went into the body of the House of Lords. I was at the bar. "Well, Major," said his Lordship, as he shook me by the hand, "it is all over; the Bill is lost. This is an important victory for Hastings, and another proof of the wonderful ascendancy of his fortune; it will make a dreadful confusion, but you are neither of you responsible for that. It is the fault of the man who would bring in such a Bill." Lords Mansfield and Stormont voted against the Bill. That night it was known the Ministry would be changed, and the next day the King sent a message to Lord North and Mr. Fox, requiring them to surrender the seals as Secretaries of State. The public papers will tell you the confusion that is likely to ensue upon this great change. Parliament will be dissolved in two or three days, and both Lord Thurlow, now Chancellor, and Lord Temple, one of the Secretaries, say I *must come in*, as they want information exceedingly in the House of Commons upon India business. I shall write to you more fully upon the subject hereafter. I dined yesterday with Lord Mansfield, who had just parted with Lord Gower, the new Lord President, who declared that he did not intend ever again to become a public man; but the same principle which would take from the Company their charter, might have deprived him of his estate; it therefore behoved him to stand forth in support both of the King and the people. He added, this Mr. Hastings is a most extraordinary man, for it is he who has turned out the Ministry. Lord Mansfield said he had declared to some of them long ago, that if they attempted to crush Hastings they would suffer for it.

I am sure, my dear Sir, it will give you infinite pleasure to hear that the warm and animated expressions of Lords Thurlow and Walsingham (when you was the subject of their praise) were received by the House of Peers with the utmost attention and pleasure, and that no one Peer, not even Lord Loughborough, attempted to cast the smallest censure upon you. On the contrary, though he misrepresented the acts of your government, he most earnestly entreated the House to put Mr. Hastings entirely out of the question ; that it was the system he wished to correct, and no man had blamed the system more than Mr. Hastings.

But the conduct of Mr. Fox throughout this business is surely the most extraordinary of any other. Before he brought in his Bill, he waited upon Lord Mansfield, who told him that he disliked the measure exceedingly, but if Mr. Fox wished to carry it, he would advise him by all means not to say a syllable about Mr. Hastings ; for that his character was so high, and his friends so active, he would involve himself in very great difficulties if he attempted anything against him. Mr. Fox promised he would not, and he sent his friend Sheridan to Halhed to bespeak our neutrality the very day he moved for leave to bring in the Bill. Sheridan wished to see me, but I refused to meet him. After this I was very much astonished, indeed, to find that Mr. Fox went fully into all the scandalous stories related in those execrable libels (as Lord Temple calls them), the Ninth and Eleventh Reports of the Select Committee, and at the close of his speech to hear him declare that he meant not to be personal against Mr. Hastings. I believe, indeed, he now most heartily repents his conduct.

I have persuaded Mr. Sulivan to push the departure of the Surprise as much as possible, and I hope she will be despatched early in the week. Enclosed is a letter from Lord Mansfield to Sir Thomas Mills. His Lordship desires you to be prepared for every thing. If the new Parliament is against the Ministry, there will be another change in six months; if not, we may hope to see a stable administration, which will support you most heartily. Lord Thurlow and Lord Temple are much alarmed lest you should quit Bengal, but I hope there is not the smallest reason to apprehend that; though I wish they would send you a proper successor who may take possession whenever you have an inclination to come away.

The opinion expressed by Lord Mansfield, that the overthrow of the administration was in great measure the work of Mr. Hastings, was nowhere more warmly taken up than among the ex-ministers themselves. If, therefore, they had previously regarded him with disfavour, disfavour degenerated henceforth into rancorous hatred, which nothing could appease except the total ruin of the man, to whose firmness they attributed their own political overthrow. On the other hand, the new ministers, Mr. Pitt, Lord Temple, and Lord Thurlow, spoke of him in terms of the highest admiration, and every where avowed their design of supporting him to the uttermost. In the Court of Directors, likewise, a somewhat flexible body, a marked change in his favour took place; while the Proprietors more and more found cause to congratulate themselves on the part which they had played throughout. Still Mr. Pitt's government was as yet weak. It had, indeed, the support of the King and of the country; and in spite of Lord Temple's unexpected resignation, the rest determined to stand their ground. But a majority in the House of Commons was against them, and matters were not, as was believed, ripe for a dissolution. Accordingly, the same letters which conveyed to Hastings accounts of his growing triumphs, and of the estimation in which he was held in high quarters, warned him to be prepared for a sudden reverse, and urgently pressed upon him the necessity of attending more than he had heretofore done to his private fortunes. The following is a curious and an important document:—

From the same.

London, Queen-square, 11th January, 1784.

My dear Sir,—I sent you copies of all my late letters by the Valentine Indiaman, and an account of our political situation, at the close of the year. I will bring up my relation of our late transactions, although there is no immediate prospect of despatching this letter, except by the post over land.

I have already informed you of the interviews I had been honoured with by the Lord Chancellor; since the date of my last I have seen him every day. He is very firmly and sincerely attached to you, and every one of his Majesty's present ministers profess the utmost esteem and respect for you. The ministry is completely fixed, and if they will not desert the King (of which I trust there is no danger), I am sure the King will not desert them. Mr. Pitt, our present minister, has communicated to the Court of Proprietors the propositions he means to move in Parliament, and they have been approved of by a majority of five to one. What will be their fate to-morrow we cannot say, or whether the ministers will be able to conduct any business with the present House of Commons. I must refer you, my dear Sir, to the newspapers, and the daily publications which I will send to you, for an account of the great and extraordinary violences to which our enemies have been driven, by the virtue of the House of Lords, in throwing out that abominable India Bill, and, in consequence, breaking up the Coalition ministry. You will hardly believe that the brother of your amiable and worthy deceased friend, Elliot, should now be one of your avowed enemies; or the Lord Advocate Dundas, your steady friend and supporter, yet both these facts are strictly true,

I was at Court on the day the House of Commons presented their bold address to the King, and Sir Gilbert then told me that, had the India Bill passed, it was the intention to have removed you immediately on the charge of peculation, contained in the eleventh Report of the Select Committee. I hear also, from undoubted authority, that in the event of your removal, Lord Macartney, or Mr. Eden, Sir Gilbert Elliot's brother in law, would have been Governor-general, and Smith Commander-in-Chief. Thank God so rascally an arrangement is for ever defeated. I told Sir Gilbert my opinion very plainly of the conduct of your persecutors; but it is strange indeed, my dear Sir, that the very circumstance which tends of all others to display your character as a disinterested man, in the fairest point of view, should, in spite of all we can say, have been used as the strongest ground of crimination against you—I mean your bringing to the credit of the East India Company so large a sum as 200,000*l.*, which every other man almost would have appropriated to his own use. Even Lord Thurlow condemns you here; not that he has a shadow of doubt of your being able completely to explain every circumstance to his perfect satisfaction; but he says, you are to blame in not having considered the wretches you have to deal with here, and that if, by the utmost stretch of human ingenuity, it is possible to misrepresent any act of yours, Mr. Burke and his committee will take the advantage of every thing. You ought, says Lord Thurlow, to have been aware of this, and to have explained every part of a transaction (which he is convinced will redound to your honour) in such a manner, as to have confounded the malice of your enemies.

Mr. Dundas and I are now on the best of terms. The first time I met him was at Lord Thurlow's, when he told me that I must do him the justice to say he had never doubted the honour, the integrity, or the abilities of Mr. Hastings, though he had differed from him as to some of his political opinions; that these differences were at an end, for the Mahratta war was at an end, and every part of your conduct of late years appeared to him highly meritorious. Dundas is now Treasurer of the Navy, and will be one of the principal managers of the House of Commons on the side of administration. He is absolutely to come forward in your support, against Burke, and I am now furnishing him with materials to make use of in your defence. His argument is, "I never doubted the honour or integrity of Mr. Hastings; I blamed his politics of 1778; I thought he could not make peace with the Mahrattas, but I have been mistaken. His relief and support of the Carnatic, his improvement of the revenues of Bengal, his spirit and activity, claim every degree of praise that I can bestow upon him, and every support that his Majesty's ministers can afford him." This, my dear Sir, is Mr. Dundas's present language; and if the ministry stand (of which I have no doubt), and carry the present bill through, you will be appointed *His Majesty's Governor-general of Bengal.* Lord Thurlow does not entirely approve of the intended bill, by which the Governor-general and Commander-in-Chief are to be appointed by the King, and the other two by the Company. He sent me yesterday to put the following question to Mr. Dundas:—"If the bill should pass, his Majesty means to appoint Mr. Hastings the Governor-general of Bengal: suppose the House of Commons should then be mad enough to address the King to remove him, what is to be done?" Mr. Dundas answered, "The King will appoint Mr. Hastings Governor-general of Bengal: most assuredly, if such an address should be proposed, we shall resist it; should it be carried against us, we must dissolve the Parliament, so that you need be under no apprehensions: if we have strength enough to carry the bill, be assured we shall have strength enough, and more than enough, to preserve Hastings." Thus we stand, my dear Sir, with ministers. The King speaks of you in the warmest terms, and a prodigious majority through the kingdom espouse your cause and execrate your opponents.

In my last letter I told you that Lord Bathurst had interested himself exceedingly to procure me a seat in Parliament, and that every thing was settled for my coming in for West Looe, in the room of Sir William James. Lord Mansfield thought I should be better out of the House; but the Lord Chancellor was exceedingly anxious for my coming in, and pushed it all he could. However, as party has run very high, Mr. Pitt was afraid that Mr. Fox and Mr. Burke would represent it in an invidious light; and though he and his friends wished most earnestly that I should be in the House, they rather were inclined to defer my appearance for the first week, and Mr. Buller is to quit for me at any time. The Chancellor is exceedingly displeased at this, and says they will live to repent their timidity, and that he would be answerable that neither Mr. Fox nor Mr. Burke should browbeat me. I am sure, my dear Sir, you will highly approve of my being entirely guided by the Chancellor in this affair, and therefore I shall keep myself prepared to be elected whenever he thinks the time proper, or rather, when he can persuade others to think so, for he says, they will live to repent my not being at this moment in Parliament. He argues thus:—"I have seen the greatest orators in the House of Commons struck dumb by a fact. The boldest assertions are hazarded there, because there is no one who has knowledge or resolution enough to contradict Mr. Fox; you would do it; and I am sure when the bill was depending, you would have turned the House, by stating to them what you have done off hand to me in conversation." Mr. Dundas told me yesterday that there was nothing they wished more anxiously than to have me in the House of Commons, but that it had been thought more prudent to bring in Mr. Buller for a few days, till the first tumult had subsided.

Before this letter is concluded, I shall be able to tell you much more of the real state of our affairs. In my last I told you that Lord Gower calls this, "Hastings's administration;" and many of the party give me the credit of having contributed more than any one amongst them to overturn the late ministry. Addresses to the King are preparing from all parts of the kingdom, urging his Majesty to preserve the constitution inviolate, and promising to support him. The faction on the other side is composed of bold, needy, and desperate men; but as the City of London and the kingdom in general place implicit confidence in young Pitt, one of the wonders of this age, I think Lord North and Mr. Fox will be completely defeated. The former is infinitely a more base and contemptible character than the latter. What a wonderful public life is yours, my dear Sir, both in England and in India! Almost every man despaired in July, 1782, when the death of the Marquis of Rockingham kept you in Bengal and saved India. Again, in October, when ministers and a majority of Directors had determined upon your removal, your constituents at that time preserved you. Whatever Lord Shelburne's private opinion may be, a bill was brought into Parliament in his administration, or ready to be brought, which had for one object your removal, though perhaps upon more honourable terms than that wretch Mr. Burke approved of. Shelburne's overthrow changed the face of affairs, and Lord Stormont's opposition prevented the Coalition from doing anything the last session; but, at the commencement of the present, Mr. Fox came forward with a vengeance, and your cause was forgotten for the time, in attempts to preserve the constitution and the Company. Fox failed in his attempt, and failing, fell with all his connexions.

We have had two conferences with Mr. Pitt, which gave us great satisfaction. His propositions, I think, are very fair, considering the madness and the prejudices of men in general with respect to India. Lord Thurlow thinks Mr. Pitt has taken too much; that all appointments whatsoever ought to be in the Company, subject to his Majesty's approval, and that the Crown should have a control as strong as possible at home. However, we readily acquiesced in Mr. Pitt's schemes, in order to show our sense of the services he had rendered the Company, by opposing a man who grasped at all we possessed.

James Macpherson has acted very steadily with us

throughout this business; and I assure you, my dear Sir, I am at a loss for words sufficiently forcible to do justice to the merit, application, and constancy of Governor Johnstone, both towards you and the East India Company. I trust we shall elect him a Director on Wednesday next in the room of that traitor, Sir Henry Fletcher.

You will excuse me, my dear Sir, if many important events have passed unnoticed in my late letters to you. Twenty times have I sat down to write to you in the last ten days, and as often been called away on material business. Lord Thurlow asked me the other day if I ever eat or slept? Thank God, I have enjoyed an uninterrupted share of health, and, having a good cause, did not despond even when our affairs wore the most gloomy aspect. The Chancellor is a firm, intrepid man, so is Dundas, but I wish the other ministers possessed as much courage as they do honour and industry. I am only afraid of their timidity, though they certainly acquire more and more courage every day.

We have now a decided majority in the Court of Directors, and I am upon the most friendly terms of communication with our present Chairman, Mr. Nathaniel Smith,

You will receive, as I understand, a paragraph of disapprobation, couched, however, in decent language, for having arraigned the conduct of the Directors, and you will, with this, receive their warmest thanks for the wonderful exertions by which you have saved India and improved the revenues of Bengal.

17th January. I sent a copy of this over land last night: I shall now close it and begin another to-morrow. I am ever, my dear Sir, most faithfully and gratefully yours, JOHN SCOTT.

All this while Mr. Hastings, to whom these changes in his favour could not for many long months be communicated, was labouring under the effects of the ill-judged and unjust censures, which both the House of Commons and the Court of Directors had passed upon him. His colleagues in the Supreme Council, from being lukewarm supporters of his policy, became, in consequence of these censures, positively hostile. With Lord Macartney his disputes assumed, day by day, a more bitter tone; while both Oude and Benares, for the right management of which he had rendered himself in a marked degree responsible, fell, in the hands of Messrs. Fowke and Bristow, into terrible confusion. The latter of these gentlemen, indeed, seems, like the Governor of Madras, to have aimed at nothing less than the total annihilation of the Nabob Vizier's authority. Of this, as was natural, the Nabob Vizier complained, while, at the same time, he made it appear that so long as the system of oppression and interference continued, it was impossible that he should be in a condition to discharge with punctuality his debts to the Company. Moreover, as if fate had determined to vex Mr. Hastings with all its storms, a failure in the periodical rains threatened to produce a famine; while Mrs. Hastings's health, which had long been declining, laid him under the stern necessity of sending her to England. Now

Mr. Hastings was to a remarkable degree devoted to the wife of his bosom. She was his friend, his confidant, his solace, his supreme delight; and the prospect of a separation from her, as it would have been at any moment grievous, so it seems to have affected him, at this juncture, with positive anguish. Mr. Hastings, however, was not the sort of man to make any unbecoming display, either of mortified ambition or of lacerated feelings. He did not scruple, indeed, as has been shown elsewhere, to cast back on his accusers their unmerited rebukes, while his private communications to those to whom he believed he could unburthen himself are all tinged, both now and afterwards, with a deep shade of melancholy. Nevertheless his energies forsook him not. "I will resign this thankless office," said he, "on the first favourable opportunity; but I will not be driven from it, either by the folly of my subordinates, or the injustice of my superiors. I have saved India in spite of them all from foreign conquest, neither will I quit my post until the internal affairs of this great country shall have been restored to something like order." Accordingly, with a marvellous command of temper, he applied the energies of his mind to the ungracious task of retrenchment and reform, endeavouring to persuade where he felt that he ought to have had authority to command, and yielding many a point to the weakness of others, which his own better judgment disapproved.

The external relations of British India were at this time satisfactory enough. With France and Holland there was peace; and if at the outset some soreness continued, especially on the side of the former nation, even of this the good sense of the Governor-general got rid. He set at nought the punctilious obstinacy of the Governor of Madras; and, taking more account of the substance than of the shadow of things, gave up at once, and with a good grace, what must have been given up with a bad grace in the end. With the Mahrattas again, the best understanding prevailed. They were now the allies of the English, and, engaging themselves as such to put an end, either by negociation or force of arms, to the war with Tippoo Saib, they extricated Mr. Hastings out of what he felt to be an embarrassing dilemma. For it was consonant to his general policy, that in a war affecting the Carnatic, the English should appear in the light of allies, or subsidiaries only. Carnatic was the realm not of the East India Company, but of the Nabob of Arcot. It was against Carnatic that the sovereign of Mysore had carried on hostilities, and if on that field the English happened to oppose him, they did so, ostensibly at least, because they were bound by treaty to defend and support a prince with whom the King of England was in alliance. In a word, Mr. Hastings knew that among the native powers there was a rooted jealousy of the encroachments of the English, not unnatural to men who beheld principality after principality first taken into alliance, and then absorbed by these strangers; and he was exceedingly anxious, just at that moment, to show, that the English were not wholly regardless of the faith of treaties, nor bent on aggrandising themselves at the expense of violated engagements and outraged decency.

It was Mr. Hastings's anxious wish, that the Mahrattas should stand forward as mediators between the hostile powers of Mysore and Carnatic. This, however, he could bring about only by recognizing the Nabob as the principal in the quarrel, and his views being eagerly embraced both by the Nizam and the Mahratta chiefs, Mr. Hastings conceived that nothing remained for him, or for the presidency of Madras, except to carry on hostilities boldly, and with vigour, till it should be announced to them that the rival princes were in treaty. Lord Macartney took in this, as he did in all the rest of his dealing with the Nabob, a view diametrically opposed to that of the Governor-general. Having seized the Nabob's revenues in order to maintain the war, and deprived him of all authority over his own subjects, he could not see the smallest necessity for consulting him in the management of a peace; to purchase which, indeed, his Lordship was prepared to give up a portion of territory, over which he could claim no other right of sovereignty than that of the sword. Accordingly Commissioners were by him appointed who repaired to Tippoo's camp, and there negociated a treaty into which the name of the Nabob was not so much as introduced, nor any notice taken either of the Nizam or the Mahrattas. Mr. Hastings was justly indignant at this proceeding. He could not, indeed, interfere to stop the negociation, because peace, on almost any terms, the Company were eager to obtain; and had the accomplishment of that wish been deferred for a single season, to his ambition, not to his sense of right, the circumstance would have been attributed. But he did his best to lessen the appearance of wrong in the eyes of the powers whom the Madras Government was insulting, and to repair the injury which had been heaped upon them. For this, prejudiced historians have blamed him, but it is not the only act of his with which prejudiced historians have dealt unfairly.

There is no carrying on war in any country of the world without a heavy expenditure of money; and in India the costs of keeping armies in the field are fearful. Throughout six years, the Bengal states had been called upon to maintain, at different points in the theatre of operations, not fewer than 70,000 fighting men: besides supplying the wants both of Madras and Bombay out of their own resources. The inevitable consequences were the accumulation of a debt, to provide means for the payment of which—I do not say in its capital, but in its interest—sorely perplexed those at the heads of departments. It was vain to speak of reducing their establishments, and so acquiring, by degrees, the funds of which they stood in need. Not a sepoy could be discharged with six months pay due to him; while the idea of paying up the disbanded troops, while the claims of those with arms in their hands remained unsatisfied, was not to be entertained for a moment. Besides, you cannot borrow in India, as you can in England or France, upon public credit, and trust to the management of future years for the means of wiping out the loan. Neither might the local government venture to draw upon the home authorities to such an amount as could in any material degree assist them in their difficulties. There remained, therefore, but one resource. The payments from Oude and Benares were to a large extent in arrear; while the rulers of both countries importuned the Governor-general to take the management of their respective affairs into his own hands. I have had occasion, in a previous chapter, to show that with the proceedings of the residents at both durbars Mr. Hastings had long been dissatisfied. He now, therefore, brought the subject formally before the Supreme Council, and after a good deal of argument, prevailed upon a majority to commit the arrangement of the business to his care.

The following long letter will best explain both the nature of the difficulties under which he laboured, and the measures which he proposed to adopt for the purpose of surmounting them. I have read it myself with great interest, and cannot therefore doubt that it will be read with interest by others.

To Major Scott.

Fort William, 15th October, 1783.

My dear Scott,—The principal occasion of these despatches is to convey to the Court of Directors an early information of the state of their affairs at Lucknow, and I have made an appeal to them of greater length than any that I ever wrote in my contest with General Clavering and his party.

The sum of the story is this: As Mr. Middleton pleaded the opposition of the Nabob Vizier for the non-performance of the arrangements formed between us, at his own solicitation, when we were at Chunar, and represented the Nabob as reduced to a state of extreme affliction and despondency by my repeated and strong instances concerning them, the inconsistency seemed to me so strange and unnatural, and I was so solicitous of undeceiving the Nabob, that I resolved to depute Major Palmer to him for the purposes of convincing him that in what I had required I had never exceeded the points of his own most urgent solicitation; of inquiring into the causes of the dissatisfaction which he was said to have conceived at my acts; and to assure him that I never would interfere in his affairs but at his own request, nor make any demand upon him but for the sums which he owed to the Company.

Major Palmer went off with this message, and found Mr. Richard Johnson in actual possession of the powers of the residency, which Mr. Middleton quitted soon after to escort his wife to the borders of Bengal. Johnson abused his trust, or was charged with it, and kept the Board and myself in total ignorance of his acts, though unauthorized, and of the state of the country, which was in universal revolt. For this he was recalled; and soon after, Mr. Middleton, for his neglects; and Mr. Bristow appointed in his stead; but not till I had made him write to the Nabob for his consent, and had obtained it. I thought that I had secured Bristow's fidelity by his gratitude, and Mr. Macpherson pledged himself to me for his good behaviour. I never give great trust without confidence, nor confidence by halves. I gave Bristow instructions on every possible case that I could suppose, or he require them; and spoke my sentiments very freely of Hyder Beg, the minister, whom I suspected of a collusion with Middleton and Johnson, and blamed equally with them for acts which I have since had reason to believe were imposed on him by their ascendant over him. On this ground, and on no better, Mr. Bristow, after an ineffectual attempt to draw Hyder Beg into a confederacy with him to usurp all the powers of the Government, proceeded to an open assumption of them to himself. Major Palmer, who had been deputed to Fyzoolla Cawn, found matters on his return in this train; and, at the solicitation of the Nabob and his minister, transmitted their complaints of it to me. I laid them before the Board, first in a private, and next in a public manner. After many shifts and delays, they were sent to Mr. Bristow for his reply to them. After longer delays, he replied. The Board acquitted him of every charge without any evidence but his denial of them; and I have adjudged him guilty of every one, even on the same evidence of his own defence. And I have appealed from their sentence to the Court of Directors. My letter of appeal, my minute containing the examination of Bristow's defence, and all the papers of reference, have been copied in their order, and will be sent to you with this. It is my earnest desire that they may be published, if the Court of Directors hesitate to punish the authors of these oppressions, and to relieve the Nabob of Oude. It is not Mr. Bristow nor Mr. Cowper against whom I complain, but the members of the Board, and Mr. Macpherson especially, whose instruments they are, and the puppets of his direction. These have dared to affirm that they have acted by my instructions; than which nothing can be more false, nor more opposite to my principles or to my nature. As a bad cause requires extraneous helps, I expect that this will be defended by recrimination. Major Palmer, having been on intimacy with Cowper, wrote to him some familiar notes, which contained an allusion to the dissensions at Lucknow, and he having obtained Palmer's permission to show them to Bristow, they both took copies of them, and sent them to Calcutta, where they were artfully shown to two or three men who were known to have a quick feeling for my interests, and by them reported to me as containing some indiscreet avowals of Major Palmer, which would hurt him and me. I apprised Palmer of it, and have got the copies from him, he himself having been obliged to apply to Cowper for them. These I will send you, because I suspect that they will be surreptitiously sent home for the same defamatory purpose. To prevent this, I formally made a demand of Messrs. Stables and Macpherson, that they would produce the papers on record if they had them, and thought them of consequence. They refused it, and Mr. Macpherson on a principle of honour *most dishonourable;* for he says that those who have them ought not to publish them without the consent of the parties, though they have been already produced by one of the parties to vilify the other; and I have protested against the refusal as a denial of common justice. I refer you to the correspondence and my own marginal notes for those passages of which I suspect an advantage will be taken; and if you hear of this correspondence in England, publish it with the rest of this general subject, or make such other use of it as will best refute the calumnies that may be built upon it. You will find it a specimen of the candour of Palmer's mind, and the unsuspecting honesty and generosity of his heart.

There is not living a man of more candour; and had he, a witness of acts which reflected infamy on my character, remained a tacit spectator of them, he would have been the basest of all men. He has knowingly sacrificed all his hopes by the part which he has acted; and they whose villanies have been brought to light through his means have nothing left but to brand him with the names of incendiary and informer, and so they might a man who should awaken me when an assassin had a dagger at my throat and I sleeping.

You will wonder that all my Council should oppose me. So do I. But the fact is this: Macpherson and Stables have intimidated Wheler, whom they hate, and he them most cordially. Macpherson, who is himself all sweetness, attaches himself everlastingly to Stables, blows him up into a continual tumour, which he takes care to prevent from subsiding; and Stables, from no other cause that I know, opposes me with a rancour so uncommon, that it extends even to his own friends, if my wishes chance to precede his own in any proposal to serve them. In Council he sits sulky and silent, waiting to declare his opinion when mine is recorded; or if he speaks, it is to ask questions of cavil, or to contradict, in language not very guarded, and with a tone of insolence which I should ill bear from an equal, and which often throws me off the guard of my prudence; for, my dear Scott, I have not that collected firmness of mind which I once possessed, and which gave me such a superiority in my contests with Clavering and his associates. My last year's sickness has left a debility upon my constitution which I cannot remove, nor shall till I try a colder climate. One thing let me add to close the subject: I early remonstrated with Stables on his conduct, and asked him if, in my personal behaviour to him, I had given him any cause of offence. He declared that I had not, but treated him with an attention and confidence which had always given him the greatest pleasure, or words to that effect; but talked of his situation, Company's orders, and expenses.

The preceding will be a preface or clue to the subject of my minute on Bristow's defence, which I desire you to read with attention, and oblige my good old friend to read it. It is of too great length for Lord Mansfield; yet I value his good opinion so much that I wish he could see it. I have written it with a view to make it complete in itself, and not to depend on its relative materials for the comprehension of it; so that it is probable most readers will content themselves with that and Bristow's defence, which is a curious production.

I expect an answer from Macpherson when the packet is closed; but it shall not for that reason fail of a reply. I shall deal with him as I have ever done with others, openly and fairly. He will aim his most weighty strokes at me through the medium of his letters to England. Be sure to avail yourself of this intimation, and claim the right of discrediting every information so insidiously offered, whether to the public, to the Company, or to higher powers.

The next subject of importance is the business of the Nabob Walla Jah's assignment. In this, as in the last, Mr. Wheler's conduct has made me ashamed of him. He readily entered into the treaty of the 2nd of April, 1781, with the Nabob, which has thrown the Nabob into the merciless hands of Lord Macartney. He equally condemns Lord Macartney's conduct, and affects an equal pity for the Nabob with myself; and I have told him, with all the delicacy that I could, that, as a gentleman, independently of public considerations, he ought to support and redress the Nabob. The Lord Macartney and his Committee refused to part with the assignment, and I urged the members of the Board to suspend them for it. I urged it in conversation, not officially. They agreed, against my advice, to write again to the Committee, and to write also to the Council to command the restitution of the assignment in more peremptory terms. I did not like, as I said in the words of my old and wise friend Dupré, to show my teeth without the power of biting; but, not choosing to break upon such a subject, and glad to gain the second point, if the first was unattainable, I submitted. The letters were written, and met the reception they deserved. I summoned a meeting of the Board *specially* to read the letter; but I could not get them to decide upon it. Stables, as usual, was inflexibly silent, and Macpherson talked, but said nothing. When I found that nothing could be done, either for or against, I said that I would take the letter home, and propose my own opinion upon it. You shall have a copy of it, with my opinion delivered on the first refusal.

It will be curious to observe the similarity in style and substance of the letters of the Nabob Walla Jah and the Nabob Assof o' Dowla. They both suffer the same deprivation and personal insults; and both feeling alike, have expressed the same feelings, not only in the same words, but almost in the same turn of sentiment.

Many friends and many foes will ask alike, what interest have I in the concerns of the Nabob Walla Jah? I answer, none. I am not a creditor of the Nabob, nor connected with any. I never received from him any pecuniary bounty, except a thousand rupees, or pagodas (I forget which), which he gave to each member of the Council when I was one at Madras, on some public occasion, for a ring; and if he had offered me crores, lacs, or less gratuities, I should have rejected them, not less from a scruple of honour which would render it a crime deserving of infamy to receive gifts from those who have appeals to my justice, faith, or integrity, than because I should deem it equally infamous to plunder a plundered man. He knew me too well even to suggest the remotest proposal of the kind; nor, poor man! has he for some years past had either present means or credit to raise them. Possibly the emissaries of the Rajah of Tanjore will have insinuated the reverse, and therefore I furnish you with an answer to them. But for the late support which I have given to the Nabob, I have the following inducements:—

1st. The faith of a public treaty binding me publicly as the head of the Government which made it.

2nd. The faith and honour of a gentleman, who made the treaty.

3rd. The conviction with which I am impressed that

the public credit of our faith is necessary to our future existence; and that we have shown such a contempt of it in so many other instances, that, with this crowning the whole, nobody will trust us.

4th. That this defect of our political character was the cause of the late confederacy against us, and the consequent invasion of the Carnatic.

5th. The authority and dignity of this Government, which required present reparation for the restoration of both.

6th. That the defects of our alliance with the Nabob of the Carnatic may be forced on the notice of the public, and defined by specific declarations or engagements.

7th. The indignation which, as a man, I feel against acts of tyranny and insolence.

What reception my minute will meet you will know before the close of this letter. I suspect it will be a rejection in terms, a proposal to wait the Company's orders, and perhaps a protest.

The President and Select Committee of Fort St. George have repeatedly called on us for powers and instructions to treat with Tippoo. We have peremptorily refused to do either, affirming that we had no claim on Tippoo but to his acceptance of the article of the treaty with the Peishwa which included him, and which required no other written engagement; that for this the Mahrattas were accountable, and had engaged to compel him by force of arms, if he refused; that the Mahrattas had an interest to fulfil this part of the engagement, and that we forfeited our right to it by engaging with him in a separate and direct treaty.

But Lord Macartney wishes to yield portions of the Carnatic to Tippoo, which he says are of no note, but lie *convenient* for Tippoo, and *therefore* we have objected to it. He has also demanded our consent to demand from Tippoo the reimbursement of all the sums which we have expended in the war, and a compensation for all the losses and devastations of the Carnatic, reproaching us for having neglected them in our treaty with the Peishwa—an example of folly, impudence, and inconsistency to which we have scarce made a reply, but have referred the proposition to the Court of Directors, with a copy of the letter which Lord Macartney and his Committee wrote to Mr. Anderson and circulated through the Courts of Hydrabad and Poona in its route to him, petitioning him, for mercy's sake. to conclude the treaty at all events, and instantly, though with the sacrifice of every ally that we had, and save Fort St. George from a ruin inevitably impending without it.

I have the pleasure to add, that I have a letter from David Anderson, advising me that letters have been received both by the Peishwa and Mahdajee Sindia from Tippoo, declaring his acquiescence in the article of the treaty which includes him. Yet I think that his Lordship will, if he can, still prevent the effect of this declaration; and if he does, he will quote the orders of the Company for his authority.

We are here under great apprehensions of a famine. The solstitial rains have failed in all the western parts of Hindostan, from beyond Lahore to the Carrumnassa. It has raged most violently in the countries most remote; our province of Bahar has suffered greatly by the failure of the last harvest, and by the artificial want caused by the apprehensions of greater. The complaints and fears of it have already extended to Bengal, where we have great plenty. I have recommended the appointment of a committee to provide against the growing evil, and the other members have agreed to the plan. It remains to appoint the members, who, I fear, will not be of my choice.

Soon after Nedjif Cawn's death, I, at the pressing instance of the King and Vizier, deputed Major Browne to Delhi with private instructions, approved by Wheler and Macpherson, the only members of the Council. He was detained by Mirza Sheffy Cawn, who succeeded Nedjif Cawn in the command of the army; and the King again pressingly requiring his presence, and writing to me to assist him, I recommended to the Board to assist him, a very small force being sufficient to give or take the lead in his administration, and more likely to prove a defence to the Nabob Vizier's northern dominions than our scattered regiments quartered over them against his will. The two members of the Board have opposed it, and Mr. Stables moved for Major Browne's recall.

But this is of little moment. Many other matters I pass which would be of consequence in an ordinary train of affairs, but are lost in the magnitude of those which mark the total imbecility of this Government or reflect infamy on our national character.

I regret that I never gave you a detailed explanation of our salt department; I believe I left it to S. Sulivan to write it to his father, and I know that he did write it. But he has other cares; I find at least that it is unnoticed, and in a printed report of a Committee of the Proprietors, I read it with astonishment stated as a mere transfer of the profits of the land revenue to the salt. The fact is, that it now yields a clear net income of more than fifty lacs, unincumbered with official charges, unexposed to invasion, a rich dominion without garrisons or a military establishment, and all of my own creation; for you will remember that I extorted the Board's consent to the first trial of it on my own responsibility, every member of the Board opposing it, and even my friend Mr. Barwell not daring to take his share in the hazard of it. Yet no sooner was it found to answer, than a scramble was made for the patronage of the salt agencies; of which I ought not to complain since the first comptroller was left to my choice, and he has amply repaid my confidence. My dear Scott, do not suffer this acquisition to be overlooked, when I am charged with profusion of expense. The charge is wickedly false, but were it true, what are the most exaggerated excesses of our disbursements, compared to such an accumulation of revenue, as fifty lacs in a single article? I will send you the account. That of the two first years, abridged, is as follows:—

	Rupees.		
Net produce of 1187 or 1780-1 . . .	25,83,129	7	8
Net produce of 1188 or 1781-2, from the account closed 30th April, 1783 . .	50,00,105	3	9
Estimate of ditto, 1189 or 1782-3 . . .	50,96,883	2	0

The produce of the last year can only be estimated. The two first sums are actually realized, and Rs. 47,77,086 2 1 of the latter. The rest is certain.

I shall leave this letter open for new matter to the last. In the mean time, I inform you of an event likely to happen in my own family, to which I already look, though yet distant, with anguish. Had affairs gone on but indifferently, it was my resolution to leave India in January next. But as my presence may be a kind of check on Macpherson, who I am convinced would observe no bounds with the Nabob Vizier, were I out of the way, I cannot in honour depart till I receive either an answer to my letter of March last, or till my successor is nominated, and either arrived, or so near that my departure, if pressed by the season, may produce no intermediate ill consequence: that is to say, I will wait, if necessary, till the next season, which is at least one year longer. In the mean time, as Mrs.

Hastings's constitution visibly declines, though not subject to the severe attacks which she used to experience, she will depart at the time which I had fixed for mine with her, and I shall do all that I can at this early period to make the resolution irrevocable. I stay most reluctantly on every account, for my hands are as effectually bound as they were in the year 1775, but with this difference, that there is no lead substituted to mine: and my constitution is, I fear, broken beyond the power of any aid in this climate to repair it. I have held a court of conscience in my own breast, which has determined the duration of my service, and beyond that no consideration upon earth shall induce or compel me to act longer with such associates.

> "These wicked creatures yet do look well favored
> When others are more wicked: not being worse
> Stands in some rank of praise."

I in my heart forgive General Clavering for all the injuries he did me. He was my avowed enemy. These are my dear friends, whom Mr. Sulivan pronounced incapable of being moved from me by any consideration on earth. I thought so too, though a ray of inspiration very early flitted across my imagination more than once, and showed me the naked character of Macpherson, with his borrowed robes lying by him; but I either treated the warning as an illusion; or it escaped me while some more pressing object called off my attention; or I chose rather to be deceived than to yield to doubtful suspicion.

Have you seen what the Court of Directors have written about the ten lacs, and the Begums of Fyzabad?

The first subject is contained in the 54th and 55th paragraphs of their general letter dated the 15th January, 1783—the last in the ten first paragraphs of the letter of the 14th of February.

The first is written in harsh, and almost rude language. The last is insolent, for they ascribe to the Begums of Fyzabad a motive for their conduct which they themselves never thought of, and suggest that they armed themselves for defence against my oppressions, suspecting that I should treat them as I had treated Cheyt Sing. Are these men the rulers of India?

These paragraphs have furnished the malevolence of Stables, with a plea for proposing a new inquiry into their conduct; but his friend has ill-supported him; and as he loves the crooked better than the straight path, he has confined himself to the apparently gentle proposition of informing the Begums, that the Court of Directors have ordered our Government to prevent their suffering oppression from the Nabob, and to allow "*those ladies an asylum* (the words of the general letter) in our own provinces." The fact is, that the Nabob and his mother are at this time on very good terms, and in my heart I believe that this motion is made to set them again at variance, as they are at present confederates against Mr. Bristow. I have opposed both, and both questions remain yet undetermined. I fancy they will drop.

I am more hurt by the manner in which you tell me Lord North professes his kindness to me, than I should be were he to declare himself against me; and I conclude from it, more than from every other symptom, that it is full time for me to quit, and that I ought to have given place a twelvemonth ago; for what credit can I gain, how indeed can I avoid losing credit, when I am barely suffered, and the man whose power and dignity of character had equally drawn my hopes of support towards him above all others, says, he will befriend me, but expresses his impatience at my stay? I want not such friendship, nor shall I thank him for it. I thank those only who support me because they think me fit for my office. If I am not fit, let his Lordship give his friendship to a fitter; but that I see is not the merit for which my successor is to be elected. However, let him be who he will, if he has but common honesty, and something even less than common sense, he may do more good than I can, because he will be supported, and I hope he will have the powers of his station. This Government may yet subsist for a few years of peace on the resources of its own constitution, but every year of vicious or neglected administration will accelerate its ruin, and you and I, Scott, will both live to see it, if it is not totally reformed in its principles.

I am glad that I gave up the ten lacs. My subsequent letters, and the accounts accompanying them, will have informed you, as I have informed the Court of Directors, that I have provided altogether by private means, intended for my own use, but appropriated wholly to the Company's, twenty-eight lacs instead of ten; and had it not been for Mr. Richard Johnson's ingratitude, I should have increased the sum to forty lacs. The whole of this sum might have been mine; and what a lesson have the Directors preached to others, by telling me that I had no right to do otherwise than I have done! You say that you have no doubt that the proprietors will allow me the interest of the first sum for life. I hope rather that no more notice will be taken of it; for if I have but 100*l.* a year to live on, I will not accept it. I have many reasons for this resolution, but I cannot assign them all in writing; but if it should be ever proposed, my dear Scott, in my name forbid, and if done, reject it. I will have no annuity from the Company, not even for a double life, and were it not that I cannot bear to see Mrs. Hastings reduced to a state of poverty, I would not solicit even the principal; for I could with ease accommodate myself to a very little more than nothing. I am happier in my reputation, if that remains, and it must, unsullied, and in the hopes of being received with friendship by the most virtuous and respectable characters of my country, than I should be with the enjoyment of crores without them.

20th October. The Commissioners for regulating the price and distribution of grain were sworn in this day. I will send you a copy of the plan. I am confident of its effect. The members are T. Graham, George Cuming, Thoms Law, and George Templer. To prevent a subject of such importance from becoming a point of contention, I drew up the rough sketch of the plan privately with Auriol, and made him carry it to Macpherson and Stables, proposing it as an act of the Board, not as a suggestion of mine. With some little difficulties it was agreed to, and they left me the choice of the members, who are all well inclined to each other. It had the instant effect of opening the Galas in Calcutta, where an artificial want had already prevailed. I shall see their daily proceedings, and you may swear in my name that the famine of India shall not invade the provinces of our dominion. I hope it will draw the emigrants of other countries into our own, and be the means of establishing a scheme which I have laboured to bring to pass these eleven years, a chain of granaries on the banks of the two great rivers, built of solid masonry, to be filled in times of superabundance, which always hurts our revenue, with a provision of three months and closed. I have begun such a provision in the fort, where we have *bottled up* 70,000 maunds, and I do not intend to *uncork it* till it has stood twenty years. The plan is simple. It consists of an arched building of six feet in thickness of an indefinite length, with partitions, an opening left over each, which, when the partitions are filled, is closed with masonry, so that the external air is totally excluded. I have made a fair trial of the design, and found it to answer, in so much that I am certain the grain would remain in a sound state for fifty years so deposited. Grain purchased when it is in such plenty that the raiats want a sale for it will aid the revenue. In effect it will cost nothing but the first cost of the buildings.

I have written a long letter to Mr. Darell, which I wish you to see, and to urge him to make public use of it. It relates wholly to augmentations made by me to the revenue, and particularly in the salt, of which I have given him a history. It ought not to be lost.

Mr. Macpherson publicly takes to himself the merit of having abstained from all exercise of his right of patronage. He unluckily assumed the same modest merit one day to me, and I reminded him of the following, which were all instances in direct contradiction to it:—

1. Colonel Morgan, appointed to the command in chief of the army at Surat, given to make room for

2. Lieutenant-colonel Allan Macpherson, quarter-master-general.

3. Lieutenant-colonel A. Macpherson, contractor of the cantonments of Barrackpoor.

4. Mr. Bristow, resident at Lucknow.

5. Sir John Cuming commands a detachment at Futtey Ghur, and Colonel Muir, an officer of the first merit, depressed to make room for him.

6. Colonel McLeod to the command of the resident's body guard at Lucknow, done when I was sick ; a breach of treaty.

7. Mr. Wordsworth, custom-master at Buxar.

8. Francis Muir, a very recent appointment, secretary to the committee of grain.

9. Mr. J. Hanney, a commissioner of customs.

10. Mr. Farquharson, paymaster to the 3d brigade. I omit other little ones, of which I have not a correct remembrance. But these include the command of almost the whole service.

Mr. Stables made a claim for a provision for two relations, or dependants of his, before he had been a month here—Messrs. Dent and Addison, two obscure men whose faces I yet scarcely know. I am not sure that I have seen the former. Mr. Dent has one of the salt agencies, and Mr. Addison is commissioner for the sale of opium. These are two of the most lucrative offices at the presidency, and I was compelled to accommodate a prior engagement to poor Belli to make room for Mr. Dent. Belli, however, has an office with which he is satisfied, though much inferior to the other. Now I hear that Mr. Stables complains that a young man in his own family holds a place more lucrative than his own, which he quotes as a proof of the shameful dissipation of the Company's money; and he is constantly ready to oppose every appointment proposed by me on that ground. Even two that were gratuitous he opposed.

I. The Nuddea collections had fallen very much in decline, and the Rajah was overwhelmed with debts contracted to pay it. I desired Harry Vansittart to undertake the reformation of it, without any salary or other emolument; for there were numbers of competitors soliciting it as a collectorship, and I wished to save the last (one more excepted) of the old zemindarry families from annihilation. He cheerfully accepted the trust. I proposed it to the Board, and Mr. Stables objected, because he was already provided for; and there were other servants out of employment, and without salaries. Vansittart has restored the Jumma, and put the revenues on a footing that will prove as advantageous as it has ever been to the Company, and retrieve the Rajah from insolvency.

2. The revenue of Bahar had fallen thirteen lacs in balance, and was otherwise in a state of great disorder. The committee, at my instigation, proposed to send Shore, the acting chief, to make the new settlement, recover the arrears, and correct the defect of the administration. Mr. Stables objected, because Mr. Shore's *abilities* were wanted in the committee, and because there were other men of *equal abilities* out of employment; as if the reformation of a province was to be provided for by appointment in routine.

What I have said on this subject, I do not wish to be made public, unless those gentlemen shall, by publicly contrasting their moderation with my profusion, render it necessary, merely in my defence.

I desired the Board, when our differences respecting Mr. Bristow first broke out, to take up the Britannia for an express upon that subject and the affairs of Madras. Mr. Stables objected to the expense, but the other members agreed. I added to the proposal, as an alleviation of the expense, to give her 400 tons of fine goods. I soon after heard that it was industriously published that I was attempting the ruin of the shipping interest at home; and Mr. Dacres and his council (though he and I had together adjusted the assortment of her cargo) wrote a formal letter, desiring that we would rescind the resolution on that ground. Unable to contend with my own colleagues. and with the Board of Trade, who could prevent her despatch, I gave her up. Indeed another objection presented itself, which was, that she did not arrive in time, and that of course she would make too long a passage. She in consequence went on another account to Madras, where she arrived on the 18th October, in three days and one night from her quitting the pilot, an instance of expedition unknown at any time of the year. If she had gone on her first destination, she would in all probability have reached England in February.

I close my letter. My last minute of the 1st November remains unanswered, and I have little inclination, and less ability for a reply, if they should answer it.

I referred Governor Johnstone, Mr. Bensley, and Mr. Darell to you particularly for the sight of my papers in your possession. My other friends will see them of course. Among these *desire* Mr. G. Vansittart to read them. Governor Johnstone, if he desires it, I wish you to allow an early perusal of them. You and Halhed must study them. The rest I leave to you. This letter must be communicated with some caution, for I know not what I have written, and it may not be fit in all the parts of it for the perusal of more than yourself.

I desire you to present my kind compliments, with Mrs. Hastings's, to Mrs. Scott, and our love to Lizzy, who must not forget us. Mrs. Hastings will be offended with me if I do not mention her especial good wishes for yourself. Adieu, my dear Scott, yours ever most affectionately.

P.S.—I have written to Mr. Johnstone that he cannot defend me without the sacrifice of his friend Mr. Macpherson, and therefore desired him only to be silent. *Quamquam O!* I do not willingly resign my claim to his eloquence. I also depend on Baber, because the defection, not to say baseness, of his kinsman, will irritate him to a greater exertion of his zeal rather than diminish it.

All the measures alluded to here were pressed forward to their accomplishment. Mrs. Hastings quitted her home, and left her husband desolate.

Mr. Hastings vigorously exerted himself to avert from Bengal the famine with which it was threatened; and, laying an embargo on all the ships in the river, prevented the exportation to other ports of the grain which speculators had collected. Meanwhile the business of the Lucknow expedition was brought to a point; and opened out the way for new calls upon the discretion and firmness of the Governor-general. But why should I go on? Let Mr. Hastings speak for himself.

To Major SCOTT.

Sangur Roads, 10th January, 1784.

My dear Scott,—I have thus far attended Mrs. Hastings, and shall see her embarked this evening in the Atlas, which is a little distance from us. I shall write to no one, and have written to no one but yourself, and no one will be so unreasonable as to be offended at it. I had begun a letter to the Court of Directors, but it contained too much of myself, and I dislike the subject. What I should have written you may say, if you see occasion for it,—not else.

In my letter to the Court of Directors by the Surprise, I told them that it was my fixed determination to resign the service as soon as a reasonable time should have elapsed from their receipt of that notice, to admit of their nomination of my successor, and to expect his near approach, and I accordingly entreated them to make the nomination. I at the same time laid my plan in my own mind to leave Bengal in one of the ships of this season; for I had good grounds to expect that the Surprise, which left her pilot the 7th of April, would arrive in England at farthest by the end of August, and afford time for the new appointment to take place by the end of March. In the meantime the charge, though temporary, would be as safely lodged in the hands of Mr. Wheler as my own; for he has talents for business, and lacks only a confidence in himself, which the next in succession, wanting his talents, possesses most abundantly. But a short interval compelled me to relinquish my purpose. Mr. Bristow's conduct, and the consequent distraction which I saw gathering in Oude, left that country and its government without a resource, but in my exertions to retrieve it, and my departure would have rendered the Nabob and his minister desperate. While I remained, I knew that they would place a reliance on me even for more than I could effect for their relief; and I foresaw, or thought I foresaw, in the timid and indecisive opposition of my colleagues, and in the frantic perseverance of Mr. Bristow, a growing remedy in the very evils which he himself created, and which his own folly would lead him to exaggerate. I felt, too, for the wretched Nabob Walla Jah, who seemed to catch at me, for he had not a straw left besides, as his last resource; and for his preservation I myself had some, though but a faint dependence on my colleagues, whose inclinations tended the same way with mine, though they were cautious of proceeding to extremities.

On these combined inducements I resolved to wait the arrival of my successor, or to allow another year to the possible indecision of my superiors. I can expect no thanks for this sacrifice, for there are few who will comprehend the degree of it, but I have yielded to a sense of duty, of honour, and consistency; and in the reflection of having fulfilled the part allotted to me by each of these obligations, I shall seek my consolation.

Mrs. Hastings's declining health required her instant departure. She was not afflicted with any severe attack of sickness in the last rainy season, but I was alarmed with daily symptoms, and could only attribute her escape to the weakness, not to the strength of her constitution. I was told too, that another season might prove fatal to her. I consented to part from her, nay, I urged her departure, nor even in the painful hour of trial do I repent it. I will follow her within the present year, nor shall any consideration detain me beyond it. Indeed, my own constitution is much impaired, and I shall expect another attack in the next rains, though I shall be as much as possible upon my guard against it.

Possibly there may be among those who have laboured to work my removal, some whose disappointment may construe the change of my resolution into a breach of engagement, and impute my former declaration to deception: or they may charge me with the presumption of attempting to intimidate. My friends will require no justification, for they will not be able to devise any other motives for my present plan than those which I have assigned. I shall suffer materially in my fortune by it, and lose by it every domestic comfort, besides something of my public influence in the too well established belief that my affection will not suffer me to remain in the long endurance of a state of separation.

I dwell too long on the subject of my private feelings; but you will pick out of this display of them what may be requisite for the satisfaction of my friends, the information of the public, should the public require it, and the refutation of false suggestions. I now proceed to matters of more importance.

In the packet which I have delivered to the care of Mrs. Hastings, you will find the sequel of our proceedings on the subject of the affairs of Oude, continued in a series of numbers, beginning where I left off in my despatches.

The sum of these is, that, after a long state of indecision, Mr. Wheler's return to the presidency afforded me an occasion to force the business to a crisis. Mr. Wheler was not pleased at Bristow's conduct; he was in a party with men whom he did not like, nor they him. Many of Mr. Bristow's letters lay before the Board unanswered, all filled with invectives against Hyder Beg Cawn, the avowed detail of acts of authority done by himself, and complaints that nobody would obey him. It appeared evident that, though he was absolute at the capital, nobody regarded him at a distance from it, where all seemed prepared to scramble for themselves. I stated the consequence of this state of affairs at a meeting of the Board on the 16th of last month, at which Mr. Bristow's letters were read; I stated the necessity of going further, if they meant to support Mr. Bristow, or of restoring the Nabob Vizier's authority, since the present state was anarchy, and declared them solely responsible for the consequences, since they would neither enforce my instructions, nor give Mr. Bristow others. But why need I detail it? The other members were greatly alarmed, and held many consultations together, desirous of an accommodation, but unable to determine on the mode of it. I was desired to state in writing the points which I required (not a public but confidential communication) that, knowing my sentiments, they might propose what I was not likely to reject. This was Mr. Macpherson's proposition in a conversation which I had with him on the subject, and I accordingly wrote and gave to Mr. Wheler a paper containing in substance the requisitions offered as an alternative, viz., that Mr. Bristow and Mr. Cowper should be recalled, and the resident's office withdrawn, and the Nabob Vizier restored to his authority, or that new instructions should be given to Mr. Bristow by the other members of the Board, prescribing his conduct, and that I myself should be freed from any longer responsibility.

This produced, after a discussion of twelve days, their joint minute of the 28th of December, to which I on the instant replied, and, as they ought to have expected, rejected the offer. I had the satisfaction to find one of their body, Mr. Wheler, ashamed of it. They met again, composed another minute, explanatory of the last. We assembled on the 31st to read it. I acquiesced, and orders have been actually despatched to Mr. Bristow to depart from Lucknow as soon as Mr. Wombwell, the accomptant of the residency, whose office alone remains, shall have received from the Vizier the written securities or shroffs of credit for the Company's arrears and growing debt: and for this act I have agreed to take upon myself the responsibility; if that is a charge which I can exclusively take, or they yield. Thus this affair at present rests. I have indeed conquered, but I feel little inclination to triumph in my victory; for my hands are yet fettered; and such is the wretched state of the Vizier's affairs, that nothing can be more discouraging than the prospect before me. If the Nabob Vizier shall desire me to come to his assistance, I shall offer it to the Board, and shall be better pleased if they refuse than if they assent to it. Yet I will do what I can to gain their assent. You will observe that my minute of the 31st December, accepting of the proffer of the other members. is not among the papers which I send you. Get it if you can. The numbers forty and forty-two are for private inspection only. The latter might alarm if it were made public.

Mr. Macpherson is going to sea for his health, and Mr. Stables to Mongheer. I hope that with Mr. Wheler's help I shall make a good use of their absence in bringing up all the arrears of business, in which we are dreadfully tardy. Adieu, my dear friend, yours ever most affectionately.

P. S.—I have received your overland advices to the 1st of August, and was made most happy by them.

To the same.

Fort William, 18th January, 1784.

My dear Scott,—I left the Atlas under sail on the morning of the 10th, and may God prosper her on her voyage!

Nothing remarkable has since happened. Mr. Macpherson sailed on the same day a passenger in the Belmont for Ganjam, for the recovery of his health. Mr. Stables is preparing to make an excursion to Mongheer. I have written a minute, of which I will send you a copy, tendering my services to go to Lucknow. Mr. Wheler wishes it, but he is of too feeble a mind to join with his friends against the opposition of his enemies, even to the accomplishment of his own wishes; and Mr. Stables, whom he has in vain attempted to influence to assent to the measure, has, as I understand, positively refused it, although they all three, when they resigned to me the separate charge of the concerns in Oude, promised me their support, and Mr. Macpherson himself dictated the clause of my last minute of the 31st, in which I have expressed my reliance on that assurance. Nevertheless I shall make the proposition, and let it take its course. Possibly Mr. Stables will suffer it to lie after his fashion, and go away without making a reply to it. If he does, I will avail myself of my own casting voice, and trust to their irresolution for the confirmation of the measure after it has taken place. I can hardly say what is my motive for precipitating myself into such a scene of difficulty. I know that I can do much more if I am myself the immediate agent, than I can by distant influence and a delegated authority; but I may fail, for most wretched is the state of the Vizier's dominions, and I may lose my reputation in the consequences of it. On the other hand, I may be the instrument of retrieving it and of paying the debt which is due from the Nabob to the Company; and if I do, I shall close my service with glory and leave a lasting good name behind me, whatever reproaches the inventive malice of my countrymen may cast upon me for having saved the national interests and honour from the ruin which, but for my exertions, would have fallen on both.

By late intelligence from Madras, I find that Lord Macartney's conduct has been disapproved in England, and that our Government has been even censured for its forbearance. I am told that Mr. James Macpherson has expressed much displeasure on this account, and that Lord North has said that the only relief can proceed from us, and that we shall be culpable if we withhold it. Let me not be involved in this reproach, for I have laboured with all my might, both in public remonstrances and in private conferences, to persuade my colleagues to take a decided part. They are sufficiently severe in their judgment, but cannot be brought to pass sentence, and thus the affair rests. Lord Macartney treats our opinions and orders with equal contempt, exercises his vengeance on the Nabob, who lies at his mercy without hope, and our decision waits for the next Company's despatches. You are long since in possession of the materials which will justify me in this business, and I trust to your vigilance and admirable recollection for their production in my vindication, whenever this shall require it.

My object in pointing these references to you at this time is to show that I have not been wanting in my endeavours to incite my own Board to do justice to the

Nabob. It is true that I did not in direct terms propose the suspension of Lord Macartney for his violation of one engagement and contempt of our orders; but it will evidently appear that I judged it necessary. While I saw in the members of the Board a disposition to support the Nabob, and that withheld from its effect but by the fear of the consequences arising from Lord Macartney's supposed interest at home, and the manifest determination of the people in power in England to condemn every act of this Government which could be attributed in a more especial manner to me than to my colleagues in office, I was unwilling to propose the point directly, or to enter protests against their resolutions, and by a decided separation from them provoke them to an opposition by which the Nabob might eventually lose even the little support which he derived from their ineffective opinions. Yet I omitted no argument that could apply to their judgments or make them individually feel for the consequences of suffering an injustice which reverted on them in the first instance for permitting it, and I particularly alluded to the claim which the Nabob had on Mr. Wheler as a gentleman and a man of honour, to relieve him from a state of distress brought on him by an act, in the formation of which Mr. Wheler was personally concerned, and with me exclusively. My sentiments were well known to Lord Macartney, however communicated, and were, I believe, as publicly known here, though I am myself very reserved on all points of a political nature. To the members of the Board in verbal conversations, both separately and collectively, I have from the beginning urged every argument and inducement to bring them to a determination, and have often declared that, though I should forbear it as long as I could with propriety, I would finally stand single in the avowal of my own opinion. To have done it earlier would have answered no real end, nor any purpose but that of grounding a separate credit, if any was to be gained, by a specious but ineffectual motion. When at last I did make it, I was careful to strengthen it by every argument which could justify it, without making it offensive to them; and I am told that they have privately expressed their approbation of it, and they have only suspended their decision upon it, not absolutely rejected it. In short, my own opinion is, and to you, Scott, I can confidentially mention it as a certain fact, that the members of the Board see less danger in doing nothing than in acting, and seeing a standing Committee of the House of Commons on the watch for matter of crimination against us all, and determined, right or wrong, to condemn whatever is done; a powerful party covetous of our places; a weak administration courting support from all quarters, and this government affording a wide field of profitable patronage; they do not choose to add to the number of their enemies the connexions of Lord Macartney, or give them fresh and strong ground of attack. This Mr. Wheler has confessed. As to the other two, they received an early hint from their friends not to attach themselves to a fallen interest, and they took the first occasion to prove that, if I was to be removed, their removal was not to follow as a necessary consequence of their connexion with me, by opposing me on every occasion on the most popular ground, on the plea of economy and obedience of orders, which they apply indiscriminately to every measure which I recommend;—and Mr. Stables with a spirit of rancour which nothing can equal but his ignorance. His friend, with the most imposing talents, and an elegant and unceasing flow of words, knows as little of business as he does, and Mr. Wheler is really a man of business. Yet I cannot convince him of it, nor persuade him to trust to his own superiority. He hates them, and is implicitly guided by them, and so he will always be by those who command him, and possess, at the same time, a majority of voices. But to return: if Lord Macartney's conduct at home is approved, let my opposition to it be known and condemned; if otherwise, let it be publicly known that I did all that I could do to check and punish it.

Attend particularly to the minute of the 20th March, the close of my long minute of the 11th July, my minute of the 31st of the same month, and the whole of that of the 13th of October. These contain the strongest vouchers of my intentions, and the last in express terms. Let not this pass unnoticed.

My minute upon the proposed visit to Lucknow was delivered yesterday, the 20th. I have written a note to Mr. Wheler, entreating him to give his opinion upon it to the secretary. As to Stables, his may wait, as usual. Mr. Macpherson is gone to Ganjam for his health. You shall know Mr. Wheler's answer in the close of this. I have used every argument and incentive to gain his assent. I have talked with him myself, and thought that I had fixed him; I have used the mediation of a common friend. I have also employed private means to prevail on Mr. Stables, though with little expectation of effect. In short, I have laboured with as much perseverance, and employed as many instruments, to carry this point as if I had it at heart; but in my heart I shall rejoice if I am defeated, for if I am committed in it, it will be the most desperate service I ever undertook, and may ruin my reputation by its failure of success; and here I leave it.

25th January.—I am now enabled to close my letter with the issue of the depending question. Mr. Stables has refused his assent to it, urging as his ground of it that the Governor cannot legally quit the Presidency, and that we are in expectation of new arrangements, that is, that I am soon to be dismissed from my office. The first objection is founded on no point of law, and contradicted by the practice of all my predecessors, and my own, known and approved by the Directors themselves; for though they have reprobated my measures, they have never intimated even the remotest doubt of the legality or propriety of my leaving either Calcutta or their own provinces. Mr. Wheler, indeed, has told me that his friends have blamed him for giving me full powers, and thereby abandoning his own; but if I could only have acted by separate powers given to me, on every occasion, and must have waited the tedious effect of repeated references to Calcutta when I was at such a distance, the design of my commission would have been defeated, and I might as well have staid where I was; besides that, such powers were ever given to my predecessors whenever they went on such deputations, and even the creature Bristow has effectually possessed them and exercised them with a vengeance, abetted and justified by the members of the present Board, and no doubt he will find advocates even among the Directors at home. His last plea (I mean Stables's), viz., the expectation of a new arrangement, is a wicked pretext, because it is calculated to destroy my influence by exciting distrust and presumption at a time and on an occasion requiring every support that could be given me. He may shelter himself under the specious covering of the constitutional secrecy of the department in which his minute was recorded; but that is no preservative against the notoriety to which all our measures are liable when the members of the Government are divided; for our actions and discussions, and the points on which we differ, are as well known and as early to the public as to ourselves, and sometimes before they are recorded; nor are my colleagues themselves very delicate in the publication of their sentiments concerning me, for I am assured that Mr. Stables offered to lay a wager at table (I believe his own), and in a large company, that I was actually dismissed. I have not time now, but I believe I shall address the Court of Directors by the next despatch for the purpose of stating this species of counteraction, and I may thank them for it.

Mr. Wheler's minute is sensible, and, what all his compositions are, sufficient to the purpose, and not too much. One passage only is a little exceptionable; but I had provided against it, and perhaps it was necessary for him. He kindly showed me the minute before he delivered it, and candidly offered it for my correction of whatever I might disapprove in it; but I was satisfied with it as it was. I am now making my preparations for the journey, and have fixed on the 15th of next month for beginning it. I hope to receive an answer in the mean time to my despatches by the Surprise. If my destined successor is likely to be cordial towards me, I will stay above and prosecute my plans till they are in a train for their accomplishment; if hostile, I will either return and take my departure for England, or stay, as the circumstances of affairs, combined with the advices from England, shall direct. I hazard much by this undertaking; but I am convinced that if the disorders in Oude are to be retrieved, I am most likely to retrieve them. Cashmeeramull, the banker, is come to Calcutta, and yesterday made me his first visit. He is a sensible and well-informed man. He painted the distracted condition of Oude in the same colours that they appear in from every representation of them, and urged the necessity of my proceeding thither in person. I told him that the Council had left the affairs of Oude wholly to my separate management, and that I should invest Major Palmer, whom the Nabob and his ministers considered the prime instrument of their deliverance, with all my authority; and I asked him whether that would not be sufficient. He said it would not. Major Palmer, he added, might effect much, and for the Nabob and his Court he would be competent to act; but that my own presence, and nothing else, could quiet the minds of the people, or give confidence to the acts done by my instructions; and he believed that I should find matters easy to be settled, though so large a collection could not be made this year as formerly, because of the late distractions and the effects of the late drought.

Your brother Jonathan shall be one of my few and chosen companions, and will be of great use to me. Adieu; remember that Sir E. Impey is to see all my despatches. Yours, most affectionately.

P.S. I had forgot to tell you that the detachment under Colonel Charles Morgan was at Handia, fifteen coss from Hoosingabad, on the 17th of December, and was expected to reach Elaya by an unnecessary length of route on the 1st of February. On the 19th we passed an order for the reduction of six regiments of sepoys, and the detachment itself to be reduced, and the parts of it posted with the brigades. I have a promise of bills for the arrears due to Colonel Pearse's detachment, and shall propose a fresh requisition for its return, the Europeans by sea, and the sepoys by land; the gross amount of the arrears to be paid at Mussulipatam and in Calcutta.

The following, to Sir Elijah Impey, whom the violence of party spirit had by this time recalled, seems too valuable to be omitted. If it contain several repetitions of matters in detail, it exhibits also in a new light the affectionate tone of the writer's mind.

To Sir Elijah Impey.

Fort William, 25th January, 1784.

My dear Friend,—I am obliged to write with a divided attention, but I shall not have much to say, having already written to Major Scott all that you may wish to know of my public situation, and he will show you of course my despatches. This letter therefore will be little more than a chapter of heads. On the 16th of last month I called on the Board to take decidedly the charge and responsibility of the affairs of Oude into their own hands, or leave both to me. This produced a series of committee meetings, which at length produced a joint offer, with a number of provisions and reservations of the whole charge, if I would be answerable for the discharge of the Company's debt, (I mean the Nabob's,) which was above fifty lacs, in three months, and the regular discharge of the current demands in the fixed monthly payments. I refused: They explained away their former requisition; agreed to let me have the exclusive charge, and to recal Mr. Bristow and his office on the delivery of the engagement to pay the balance and current demands without any specification of time, and the security of good bankers for the performance of it; and my responsibility was limited to the "propriety" of the measure. I agreed, and Wombwell set off post (a little too fat for an express) with letters to the Nabob Vizier and Bristow on the sixth of this month. This accommodation passed on the 31st.

As they had promised me their fullest support, and Mr. Macpherson dictated my expression of my reliance on that promise in my minute of acceptance, as the ground of the latter; and as I received many successive letters, stating the absolute necessity of my presence at Lucknow, to restore the quiet and order of that country, and to give confidence to the Nabob and his people, I tendered an offer of my services for that purpose. This was done on the 20th instant. Mr. Wheler has promised his consent to be given when the Nabob's requisition shall arrive, and Mr. Stables, in his usual coarse and surly style, has objected. He has wickedly insinuated that I shall be dismissed from my office, in the expression of the expectation of new arrangements from home. I shall however avail myself of this decision to depart, and have fixed on the 15th of next month, but not absolutely, for it. I shall go post to Patna, and take but a small attendance with me. I am not afraid of my colleagues when I am gone. They want courage and decision to counteract me with any effect; and my authority and influence, with the command of the army, and I shall not go without it, will be proof against all their teazings. I only fear the suspension of business at the presidency, and orders from home tending to the further reduction of my authority. I will at least do all I can to put my plan in train, and will assuredly leave affairs better than I found them.

We have no new alarms of the drought, and I have been inflexible to every argument and artifice used for making exceptions to the embargo. I verily believe it will have saved the lives of thousands.

We have ordered a reduction of six regiments of sepoys on Morgan's return, expected by the 1st of next month, and I hope to get back Colonel Pearse's very shortly, having made a provision for the arrears of pay.

Mrs. Hastings left the river in the Atlas on the morning of the 10th. In parting from her, I made a sacrifice of my own judgment, my ease, and possibly the comfort and happiness of my whole life, to the opinions of others. God grant that the event may prove it otherwise. I have a resource in the continual succession of occupations, which prevent my feeling so severe a sense of my loss as I should otherwise do; but it is never absent from my mind. She has no resource. I expect daily to receive accounts of the arrival of the Surprise, and some answers from Major Scott to my despatches by her. Whatever they are, my resolution is unalterable, though every voice in England were to cry out to break it.

I beg you will present my affectionate compliments to Lady Impey. I sincerely hope that you will have had a pleasant voyage, and landed your family in perfect health in England, and received unmixed pleasure in meeting with that part of it which you left there. You are a happy man! God keep you so! I am ever, my dear Sir Elijah, your affectionate and truly faithful friend.

To Major Scott.

Fort William, 8th February, 1784.

My dear Scott,—On the 31st of December it was agreed, after a length of debate, to recal Mr. Bristow and his office, and to leave to my separate charge our concerns in Oude, provided that the Nabob Vizier would give the security of creditable bankers for payment of the Company's arrears and current demands. In the mean time, on successive advices of the disorderly state of that government, and repeated assurances of the desire of the Nabob, and the general expectation of my presence, to assist in retrieving it, I represented this to the Board, and offered to go, but desired their early determination. It was agreed by Mr. Wheler conditionally that the Nabob should write that he desired it. The Nabob and his minister have furnished the securities, but Mr. Bristow demurs, on pretence that they may not be such as the Board may require. The Nabob was on a hunting party 110 coss distant, but expected to return on the 31st ult. This will cause some delay in his reply to my public letter, but I expect to receive it in two days more, and to leave Calcutta not later than the 20th. I dread the loss of time. The Company, exhausted of its wealth, and actually suffering the first effects of an impending famine; the government weakened by a twelvemonth's distraction; the revenue dissipated; the Siecs approaching with a numerous army, and threatening an invasion; our council divided, and the majority of its members hostile to me; rumours, and worse than rumours, of an impending change in this government; my own knowledge of the strong grounds which I have furnished for it by the Surprise—the possibility of its coming to pass before I have begun to act, and the certainty of new assaults in every general letter, with probably repeated orders to my colleagues to oppose me: these are the evils which I have to encounter, and they require despatch, lest I should be compelled to end before I have well begun. Add the approaching hot weather, and my constitution unable to cope with the sun. On the other hand, I know that I can do more good, if I have time allowed me, and it is my ambition to close my government with the redemption of a great government, family, and nation from ruin, and however I am defeated in the extent of my design, I am confident that I shall leave affairs at least not worse than I found them. I depend much on the dependence of the Nabob and his ministers, who have no resource if they forfeit my friendship, and on the public opinion. This will greatly facilitate my measures, though in the result it may hurt my credit, as I shall certainly disappoint it, do what I may. In a word, it is the boldest enterprise of my public life, but I confidently hazard the consequences. Colonel Morgan, with the Bombay detachment, is by this time returned to the Jumna, and the detachment will be instantly reduced, and six regiments disbanded, to make room for them. This will be a great saving, and we have made and shall make others. We will begin to pay off our interest bonds in December next.

The Mahrattas press the renewal of hostilities against Tippoo, which they have already begun, and the government of Madras is prepared for war, having heard nothing from the commissioners for seventeen days. Yet I scarce think that Tippoo, savage and wild of judgment as he is, will hazard it.

Our apprehensions of a famine daily abate, though the drought has prevailed universally, and without relief. The upper provinces have had rain, which will be of service to the harvests of wheat. Mr. Macpherson is sick at Ganjam. Yours, &c.

CHAPTER V.

Hastings's care of Science and Literature.

ARDUOUS as Mr. Hastings's public duties were, and indefatigable as he was in his attention to them, it is not to be supposed that he was indifferent all this while to the more ennobling demands upon his fostering care of general science and the literature of the country. If not the founder of the Asiatic Society, he was one of its earliest and most zealous promoters; and he made way for Sir William Jones in the President's chair, simply because he felt that there was not at his command leisure sufficient to do justice to the office. Of his eagerness to push, whenever an opportunity offered, geographical inquiries into unknown regions, a specimen was given in the account which I judged it expedient to introduce of Mr. James Bogle's journey to the court of Teshoo Lama. But this was not the only, nor perhaps the most important voyage of discovery which Mr. Hastings sent forth. He caused the harbours and rivers of Cochin China to be surveyed; directed Mr. Chapman to penetrate as far as he could into the interior; and received from that gentleman a report which was afterwards published, and added greatly to the stock of geographical knowledge previously possessed by Europeans. In like manner he examined the shores of the Red Sea, with the view, ultimately effected, of opening by that line more direct means of communication between England and India. Neither did the kingdom of Ava escape his notice, as well on its inland frontier, as along its coasts. He collected, in reference both to it and to the districts adjacent, almost all the useful information which was in our possession, not only during the administration of the most illustrious of his successors, but up to the commencement of the late war, in 1827.

I have noticed elsewhere the eagerness with which he promoted the compilation of Mr. Halhed's valuable Digest of Hindoo Laws. His zeal, however, in laying open to European inspection the stores of wisdom which were hidden in the languages of Asia, by no means exhausted itself in this. He encouraged bodies of learned pundits to settle in Calcutta, and supported them while they translated out of the Sanscrit into more accessible dialects, the poems and mythological and moral treatises of their native land. He founded colleges for the instruction of native youths in the laws and usages of their own country. He held out inducements to the study by the natives of English literature and English science. He laboured, in short, to promote not only the political, but the moral and rational improvement of the provinces. The following letters, which refer to these matters, seem to me to demand insertion, and I therefore transcribe them without further comment.

To the Honourable COURT of DIRECTORS.

On the River Ganges, 21st February, 1784.

Honourable Sirs,—Having had occasion to disburse from my own cash many sums for services which, though required to enable me to execute the duties of my station, I have hitherto omitted to enter in my public accounts; and my own fortune being unequal to so heavy a charge, I have resolved to reimburse myself in a mode the most suitable to the situation of your affairs, by charging the same in my Durbar accounts of the present year, and crediting them by a sum privately received and appropriated to your service, in the same manner with other sums received on account of the Honourable Company, and already carried to their account.

The particulars of these disbursements are contained in the enclosed accounts, Nos. 1, 2, 3, and 4, of which No. 5 is the abstract.

I shall subjoin a brief explanation of each.

The sum of the account No. 1 is the difference between the allowance of 300 rupees a month, which was the customary pay of the Governor's military secretary, and that which I allowed to Lieutenant-Colonel Ironside during the time that he acted in that capacity, on account of his superior rank. It was referred to your Honourable Court in one of the general letters of the year 1773 or 1774, but I presume that it was overlooked in the pressure of other more important matters which at that time occupied your attention.

Nos. 2 and 3 are explained in the accounts themselves.

No. 4 consists of three several kinds of charges, which I confess to have been unauthorized, but which I humbly conceive neither to be of a private nature, nor unworthy subjects of the bounty of a great and rising state. The first is inconsiderable, consisting chiefly in the subsistence of the Pundits who were assembled in Calcutta, and employed during two years in compiling the code of Hindoo laws for your use. The sum allotted to them was, as I recollect, one rupee to each per diem. A larger recompense was offered, but refused; nor would they receive this but for their daily support. They had, indeed, the promise of some public endowments for their colleges, which yet remain unperformed. The second is the amount of sundry monthly salaries paid to some of the most learned professors of the Mahomedan law, for translating from the Arabic into the Persian tongue, a compendium of their law, called the Hedaya, which is held in high estimation, and part of a more voluminous work, which I could not prosecute. Your Honourable Court is in possession of a part of the English version of the Hedaya, made by Mr. James Anderson, and the subsequent part of the same work has been lately translated by Mr. Hamilton. Thesé gentlemen are both engaged in the completion of it, and are both eminently qualified for it. It would exceed the due bounds of this letter to expatiate on the utility of this work; yet I may be allowed to vindicate the expense of it by one summary argument, which is, that while the Mahomedan law is allowed to be the standard of the criminal jurisprudence of your dominion, under the control and inspection of your English servants, it seems indispensably necessary that the judges of the courts should have a more familiar guide for their proceedings than the books of the Arabic tongue, of which few have opportunities of attaining a competent knowledge; and as necessary that your servants should possess the means of consulting the principles on which those judgments are founded, which in their ultimate resort, and in extraordinary cases, may fall within their immediate cognizance, and of the laws of which they are the protectors.

The third charge is that of an academy instituted for the study of the different branches of the sciences taught in the Mahomedan schools. After a trial of about two years, finding that it was likely to answer the end of its institution, I recommended to the Board, and obtained their consent, to pass the subsequent expense of the establishment to the account of the Company, and to erect a building for the purpose, at my own immediate cost, but for a Company's interest note granted me for the reimbursement of it. It is almost the only complete establishment of the kind now existing in India, although they were once in universal use, and the decayed remains of these schools are yet to be seen in every capital, town, and city of Hindostan and Deccan. It has contributed to extend the credit of the Company's name, and to soften the prejudices excited by the rapid growth of the British dominions; and it is a seminary of the most useful members of society.

I humbly submit the propriety of carrying these expenses to your account by the consideration that it was not possible for me to have been influenced in incurring them by any purpose of my own interest. Something perhaps may be attributed to the impulse of pride in the share which I might hope to derive of a public benefaction, but certainly not to vanity or ostentation, since I believe it to be generally conceived that the whole expense, of which the greatest part is yet my own, has been already defrayed from the treasury of the Company.

I will candidly confess that, when I first engaged both in this and the preceding expense, I had no intention of carrying it to the account of the Company. Improvident for myself, zealous for the honour of my country, and the credit and interest of my employers, I seldom permitted my prospects of futurity to enter into the view of my private concerns. In the undisturbed exercise of the faculties which appertained to the active season of my life, I confined all my regards to my public character, and reckoned on a fund of years to come for its duration. The infirmities of life have since succeeded, and I have lately received more than one severe warning to retire from a scene to which my bodily strength is no longer equal, and am threatened with a corresponding decay in whatever powers of mind I once possessed to discharge the laborious duties and hard vicissitudes of my station. With this change in my condition, I am compelled to depart from that liberal plan which I originally adopted, and to claim from your justice—for you have forbid me to appeal to your generosity—the discharge of a debt which I can with the most scrupulous integrity aver to be justly my due, and which I cannot sustain.

If it should be objected that the allowance of these demands would furnish a precedent for others of the like kind, I have to remark, that in their whole amount they are but the aggregate of a contingent account of twelve years; and if it were to become the practice of those who have passed their prime of life in your service, and filled, so long as I have filled it, the first office of your dominion, to glean from their past accounts all the little articles of expense which their inaccuracy or indifference hath overlooked, your interests would suffer infinitely less by the precedent than by a single example of a life spent in the accumulation of crores for your benefit, and doomed in its close to suffer the extremity of private want, and sink in obscurity.

I have thought it proper to complete the present subject by the addition of a charge which I intended to have submitted regularly to the Board, but which, if divided at this time from the others, might have admitted an unfair construction. It is in the account No. 6, and consists of charges incurred for boats and budgerows, provided by me for my own use, on such public occasions as required my departure from the presidency on extraordinary services.

My predecessors have always had an establishment of this kind provided for them, and my successor will have a provision devolve to him superior in convenience and in elegance to any that I have yet seen, and furnished with a cost which would not be credited by those who have seen the subjects of it. I have the honour to be, with the greatest respect, honourable Sirs, your most obedient and most faithful servant.

To Lord MANSFIELD.

The Province of Benares, 10th March, 1784.

My Lord,—I received so much satisfaction from the perusal of the enclosed papers, that it has tempted me to send them for your Lordship's perusal, in the assurance that they will afford you equal entertainment. They are a part of a report made by Lieutenant Turner, a young kinsman of mine (and I have a pleasure in acknowledging the relation, because his conduct has done credit to my choice of him for the service to which it relates), who was deputed, about the middle of last year, to visit the Lama of Tibet. I believe I may, without much licence, term it a physical curiosity, since it is perhaps the first example which was ever produced to the Western world of the effect of education on an infant mind, for such it surely is, as it is impossible to attribute the same effect to any other cause, without adopting the superstition which gave it birth. I will be your Lordship's pledge for the veracity of the narrator, whom I know to be incapable of uttering a falsehood, or enlarging the truth, for any consideration even of interest, and in this instance he had no inducement; besides that I should have the means of detection in my communication with other persons who were either present at the interview which Mr. Turner had with the Lama, or had other opportunities of seeing the same phenomenon.

I am very delicate in my intrusion on your Lordship's attention, but I consider this a tribute due to your eminent taste, and therefore not inconsistent when offered under such an impression, with a respect which I feel for your Lordship, exceeding that which I bear for all the rest of mankind. I have the honour to be, &c. &c.

Of the preceding letters, the two last were written while Mr. Hastings was prosecuting his journey to Lucknow. It was an expedition replete with interesting results both to himself and to the parties for whose sake it had been undertaken; yet I will not for the present enter upon that part of my subject, because the occurrences which kept pace with it elsewhere, in point of time, at least, make large demands upon our notice, and to these I feel that it will be proper, in the first instance, to direct the reader's attention.

CHAPTER VI.

Transactions in England.

NOTHING could be more bright, nothing more satisfactory or full of promise, than the aspect which Mr. Hastings's fortunes appeared to have assumed at home during the earlier portion of the year 1784. The King's councils were then directed by men who owed, and made no secret of owing, their elevation to office mainly to him. Of the members of that administration some were among his most ardent admirers, and all, Mr. Dundas himself not excepted, avowed themselves his friends. In the Court of Directors, likewise, a great change of opinion seemed to have taken place; while the proprietors were now, as they had ever been, his steady supporters. No doubt the faction in the House of Commons, which had sought his ruin with so much eagerness in other years, abated not a jot of their hostility; but though powerful in point of numbers, they were weak in influence as well as in character, and both to the King and to the mass of the people they had become peculiarly distasteful. No man's prospects, therefore, could appear more bright or more full of promise than those of Mr. Hastings at the opening of 1784; nor were his correspondents backward in assuring him that the day would answer to the dawn, and that an abundant recompense for all the mortifications which he had suffered would, without fail, attend him.

The first decided proof afforded of a change of sentiment among the Directors was their repeal of an order formerly issued to reinstate Cheyt Sing in the Rajahship of Benares. In performing this act of justice, they did not, indeed, pass all at once into a strain of encomium on the Governor-general. That would have made them ridiculous in their own eyes and in the eyes of the whole nation; but they cancelled instructions which in a moment of irritation had been drawn up, whether with a view even then of having them carried into effect may be doubted. Again, the feelings of the majority were all in favour of Mr. Hastings in reference to his quarrel with the Madras Government. So decidedly, indeed, was this the case, that the Surprise packet, after clearing at the Custom-house, was detained three whole days in order that she might carry out orders such as should enable him to settle in his own way the points in dispute between Lord Macartney and the Nabob of Arcot. By Mr. Hastings's correspondents I find all this attributed mainly to the influence of Lord Thurlow, Mr. Pitt's new Chancellor. Probably these gentlemen were right, for of the many distinguished men who befriended Mr. Hastings, through good report and through evil, Lord Thurlow was at once the most consistent and the most able. But however this may be, the effects of the arrangement were to hold out to him, for a brief space, the promises of power at the close of his administration, which, had they been afforded a few years earlier, would have saved him much personal annoyance, and the Company many severe losses. On the other hand, the friends of Lord Macartney, and they were both numerous and active, ceased not to inveigh against Mr. Hastings in all quarters. They charged him with having kept up a secret correspondence with General Stuart. They alleged that the latter had by him been encouraged in every act of contumacy towards his immediate superiors, of which he had been guilty, and they justified the General's supersession and arrest on the ground that he waited only for Mr. Hastings's direct command in order to supersede Lord Macartney and send him home a prisoner. Nor did their inventive malice end there. They circulated a report that Mr. Hastings had thrown off the English yoke, and was reigning in Calcutta as an independent prince; neither were there wanting those, even among his best friends, who declared, that, considering the amount of provocation which he had received, the proceeding, supposing it to be real, would be very little to be wondered at.

Such was the state of public feeling in England,

when the ship Nerbudda arrived from Calcutta, bringing intelligence of the Nabob Vizier's dissatisfaction with Mr. Bristow's administration, and of the applications which he had made to the Governor-general for redress of wrongs already received and protection for the future. The perusal of these despatches gave great joy to Mr. Hastings's friends, because they found in them ample confirmation of the opinions which they had uniformly expressed, namely, that the Governor's policy in reference to Oude was both just and humane throughout, and that the Nabob reposed in him unlimited confidence. When, therefore, Mr. Hastings's project for the withdrawal of a resident from Lucknow came to be discussed, they easily carried the question in the affirmative, and he was formally empowered to act in the matter according to the dictates of his own judgment. In like manner Lord Macartney's conduct, especially in the arrest of General Stuart, was severely censured, and the whole tenor of his policy, as opposed to that of the Governor-general, condemned. Yet the tide which appeared to flow so strongly in Mr. Hastings's favour had even then reached its height, and, for reasons not in every instance palpable, yet scarcely such as to be hidden from the careful inquirer, Mr. Hastings was destined once again to become the object of ungenerous suspicion and unlooked for hostility.

On the 6th of July, Mr. Pitt, who on the preceding January had sustained a defeat, and in the following March, after a stout contest, had dissolved the refractory Parliament, introduced into the House of Commons his great measure for the better management of the affairs of India. It was largely assisted in its progress through both Houses by the friends and admirers of Mr. Hastings, and early in the succeeding month received the royal assent. Nevertheless, the expectations which the supporters of the measure had cherished,—whether they looked to its probable effects upon the Company's affairs at home and abroad, or limited their views to the actual condition and future prospects of the Governor-general,—were not destined to be fulfilled. In the former case, the antagonist powers of the Board of Control and the Court of Directors were found not to work, at least at the outset, in harmony. In the latter, Mr. Hastings's claims on the gratitude of the Minister appeared to fade away so soon as Mr. Hastings himself ceased to be useful as an engine wherewith to effect a particular purpose; nor were there wanting those who accounted for Mr. Pitt's coldness on grounds scarcely less questionable, though far more contemptible. The King was well known to hold Mr. Hastings's talents in the highest esteem. The people asserted that it was Mr. Hastings's influence which kept Mr. Pitt in power; and the great attention which was shown at St. James's to Mrs. Hastings, who arrived about this time in London, was not calculated to destroy the illusion. Now if Mr. Pitt was, as his enemies represent him to have been, peculiarly open to the movements of political jealousy, it is by no means impossible that in the instance now before us, the feeling, quite unworthy of his position and talents, may have been brought into play; at all events, it is past dispute that the opinion obtained extensive credit not only among those who envied, and therefore hated the minister, but among his own personal adherents. Let me, however, adhere to the rule which has guided me throughout, as often as I have been called upon to criticise the motives or behaviour of those among the leading politicians of the day at whose hands Mr. Hastings suffered wrong. The following letters throw a strong light upon the state of feeling in the Cabinet at the time, and are in other respects of too much value to be overlooked :—

From Major SCOTT.

London, Queen-square, 15th August, 1784.

My dear Sir,—I despatched a packet to you overland on the 14th of last month, and another on the 3rd of this month; the last to convey to you the happy intelligence of Mrs. Hastings's arrival in England. This goes by Captain Rayne, who carries out the government despatches overland, and by the Fox and Cygnet.

Our India bill has now passed both houses, and received the royal assent on Friday. The Chancellor supported it, though he does not entirely approve of every part; and Sir Elijah Impey thinks there are parts which you will not like. He wished, so did we all, that the Governor-general should have a negative; but Mr. Pitt was afraid to propose so strong a measure, and therefore he determined to reduce the Supreme Council to four, by which means your casting vote would operate.

In debating this clause of the bill, I had an opportunity of stating that many of our misfortunes, indeed all, were owing to decided parties being formed against you in the Council; and I had two or three fair slaps at Francis upon this occasion; but the printed accounts will show you the whole. The Lord Chancellor spoke admirably in the House of Lords. There is a clause in the bill which directs that every person returning from India after the 1st of January, 1787, shall deliver in the amount of the fortune he acquired in India. Lord Carlisle insinuated that this distant period was fixed upon, in order to give some persons an opportunity of returning with larger fortunes in security, and glanced, as the Chancellor understood, at you.

His Lordship replied, with infinite force and spirit, "If the noble Lord means to insinuate that the great and respectable character who has presided so many years in India will have an objection to declare the amount of the fortune he has acquired in three-and-thirty years, I will venture to assert that that gentleman will be ready at any time to make such a declaration; and the only risk he will run, my Lords, from such a discovery, will be that of being thought in this instance a weak and foolish man; for I am sure it will be found that, in the course of his long and important services, he has not acquired a third of the fortune which many obscure men have accumulated in three or four years."

You will see in the printed debates how very unfairly Francis stated the business of presents, and that I had a good opportunity of clearing up that too. Sir Elijah thinks you will be chagrined at that clause; but the Chancellor declares that there is not the most distant idea of a reflection upon you meant by it, but that, on the contrary, his Majesty's ministers most warmly applaud every part of your conduct relative to presents, and that they highly approve of our making the application for the ten lacs, upon the plea of your having paid into the Company's treasury above three hundred thousand pounds which you might have appropriated to your own use.

In a bill of regulation it was thought better that the practice of receiving presents should be universally abolished; but this, without intending anything like a reflection upon you.

You will see also, my dear Sir, that I had a fair opportunity of clearing away all the slanders that had been thrown upon you, and of triumphing most completely over that reptile Mr. Burke. But we were most miserably disappointed indeed in one particular. The opposition Lords had assembled their whole force in order to debate the India Bill at the third reading on Monday last. I had been with the Chancellor every day previous to that time in order to give him full information, and I am convinced he would have pronounced the finest speech ever made in Parliament, in justification of everything you have done, and that he would also have given Mr. Francis a precious trimming; but when the hour arrived, the opposition Lords were afraid to meet us, and they suffered the bill to pass without saying a single syllable. This was a bitter disappointment indeed, and only made up, in a very small part, by a speech of the Chancellor, in passing our Dividend and Relief Bill; but he then challenged any man to come forward and debate what they might have debated on the third reading of the India Bill, and declared that the state of India was most prosperous; that you had concluded peace with all our enemies; had preserved all our possessions, and greatly improved our revenues. The speech goes inclosed, though not so well given as he pronounced it.

The Lord Chancellor has all along said that the ministry ought to give you a peerage and a red ribbon; I spoke to him two days ago upon the subject, and he took it up instantly with warmth. He said, "I do not know a man who cuts so great a figure upon the stage of the world as Hastings: to his other extraordinary actions must be added, that of giving a ministry to Great Britain, for whether we may choose generally to confess it or not, the fact is, that this is Hastings's administration, and that he put an end to the late ministry as completely as if he had taken a pistol and shot them through the head one after another. It would therefore be base and dishonourable in ministers not to advise his Majesty to confer some mark of his royal favour upon a man who, to his other great and important services, can boast of performing this meritorious action also."

His Lordship said he would speak that day to the two Secretaries of State, and sent me away instantly to Mr. Pitt. As he was not in town, I wrote to him, and went to the House of Lords, where I saw the Lord President, Lord Gower, who said it must be done immediately, and added:—"I always admired Mr. Hastings, but the late events in India and in England are of such a nature as to raise him in my opinion above all praise."

The Chancellor spoke to Lord Sydney and the Marquis of Carmarthen, the two Secretaries of State, and instantly obtained their concurrence, as also Lord

Weymouth's, so that it now only remains to get Mr. Pitt's consent, which, I trust, I shall communicate before I close this letter.

It is the desire of the Chancellor that you should be created an English peer, but if that cannot be accomplished, he says he will condescend to accept an Irish title just now, though so greatly inferior to your merits. You cannot, he says, be created Lord Hastings, because that barony is in Lord Huntingdon. I mentioned your taking the title from Daylesford, the place which was so many years the seat of your family, and he thinks it would be better than any other. I shall not be at ease, my dear Sir, till this business is accomplished. I assure you, I want words to convey to you an adequate idea of the Chancellor's warmth of friendship for you, and the admiration he expresses for your character. He is the first man in the kingdom, I think, for firmness and independence of spirit.

Burke has never made his appearance in the House since the day he moved for your instructions relative to Almas Alli Cawn, and the conclusion of that business has rendered him completely ridiculous, and indeed thrown great ridicule upon the whole party; for, from Burke's mode of opening the affair, they thought something might be made of it; but when I seconded his motion, and afterwards, in his absence, moved that the instructions should be printed, they saw what scrapes so wild a man would lead them into. Great expectations, too, were formed from Francis. He also is rendered as ridiculous as Burke, first, by his gloomy representations, and next by stating that there was no prospect of peace with Tippoo. Not the smallest attention will be paid to his predictions in future, even if he should attempt to speak, which, I believe, he hardly will. In short, my dear Sir, we have fully and effectually confounded all your enemies, not by the common mode of carrying points, by a dead majority in the House of Commons, but by reason and argument.

Mrs. Hastings returns from General Caillaud's today, and is to be presented on Thursday to their Majesties, by Lady Weymouth.

As the ships will not go till next week, I shall write again then, and remain, with every sentiment of respect, gratitude, and affection, my dear Sir, your much obliged and faithful humble servant.

From the same.

London, Queen-square, 4th September, 1781.

My dear Sir,—My packet overland with the pleasing intelligence of Mrs. Hastings's safe arrival, and covering a letter from her to you, has, I hope, reached Constantinople by this time.

I have given the strictest injunctions for its being forwarded, without the loss of a moment. I have since despatched another packet overland, with an account of the very honourable and gracious reception she received from their Majesties.

We were again at court on the 2d instant, according to the etiquette, and Mrs. Hastings was received with still greater marks of attention, if possible. The Chancellor had taken me aside to speak to me, while the Queen was talking to Mrs. Hastings, and when her Majesty spoke to me afterwards, she said, "I am very glad to observe that Mrs. Hastings is so much recovered; she looks infinitely better than when I saw her a fortnight ago, and I hope this country will soon restore her to perfect health."

These are precisely the Queen's words, I assure you, and they convey the most pleasing and pointed mark of attention that it was possible for her to show. Since my last letter the Directors have made several arrangements. The ministers wished exceedingly to remove Macartney, but when it came to the point, they were afraid of the Bute interest. The King highly disapproves of his conduct, and it is generally expected that the full and complete power given by the new Bill to you will effectually keep him in order in future, and orders will go from hence relative to the assignment.

In my last letter I informed you, my dear Sir, how the peerage stood. I cannot sufficiently express to you the kindness and friendship of the Chancellor on this occasion. He told me he would make a point of it, and peremptorily enjoined me to leave it to him. When I was with Mrs. Hastings at the drawing room on Thursday, Mr. Pitt came up to me and spoke exactly as follows: "I am really ashamed, Major Scott, that I have never yet entered upon the business you wrote to me about; but as I have always found you free and open, I will candidly and honestly give you my sentiments. I look upon Mr. Hastings to be a very great, and indeed a wonderful man. He has done very essential services to the state, and has a claim upon us for everything he can ask. My only difficulty, and I confess it appears to me to be a material one, is, the resolutions of the House of Commons, standing upon our journals: for though I admit that the charges against Mr. Hastings were ridiculous and absurd, and were, as I really think, fully refuted, yet until the sting of those resolutions is done away by a vote of thanks for Mr. Hastings's great services, I do not see how I can with propriety advise his Majesty to confer an honour upon Mr. Hastings. On the other hand, there are many powerful reasons to be assigned for our not waiting till we meet again."

I observed to Mr. Pitt that your situation was a cruel one indeed, if resolutions so totally unfounded, and carried in so shameful a manner, were to prevent you from receiving a mark of the sovereign's favour; and I desired Mr. Pitt to consider that the very same House of Commons which had voted resolutions against Mr. Hastings had also voted resolutions against Mr. Pitt, and that it was deservedly punished by a premature dissolution. Pitt told me then that he was undetermined, but I should hear further.

I saw the Chancellor the next day, and related this conversation to him. He told me he had laboured to carry the point now, and still had one hope left. "I mean (says his Lordship) to desire Mr. Pitt will permit me to take the responsibility of the measure upon myself, since he is afraid of the House of Commons, and I will ask the King to create Hastings a peer; I am sure he will not refuse me."

Thus the matter stands at present, my dear Sir, and I trust it will be done, because a vote of thanks may follow with the greatest propriety.

Mr. Pitt had manifestly taken his line. He praised Mr. Hastings both in public and in private; he spoke of him as the fittest of living men to control the destinies of British India; yet he positively refused to confer upon him any especial mark of royal favour. It seems idle to suppose that the motive assigned by him for this reluctance could be the true one. Mr. Pitt had influence enough in his own House of Commons to obtain the repeal of the vote of censure had he desired it, or if not, I cannot see how such a vote passed by a defunct Parliament ought to have operated as a bar to the advancement of him who was the object of it. For either Mr. Hastings deserved the censure, in which case he deserved much more, or the censure was unmerited, and therefore in itself a dead letter. Nevertheless, Mr. Pitt could not be moved. Moreover, the dissensions between the Board of Control and the Court of Directors, which almost immediately began, were not without their effect in obstructing Hastings's career of honour. I find for example, that the Directors, while they took part with Mr. Hastings against Lord Macartney, inserted in their despatch a clause, to the effect, that, within a year from its receipt, Mr. Hastings should resign his government. The Board of Control, on the other hand, though compelled by the Bute influence to cast their shield before the Governor of Madras, erased the paragraph relating to Mr. Hastings, and left him free to choose his own period of retirement. These may be regarded as trivial matters by an indifferent person. To Mr. Hastings they were big with important results, and the following letter will show that by more than Mr. Hastings they were regarded as important.

From the same.

London, 6th November, 1784.

My dear Sir,—I despatched a letter to you overland on Tuesday last, and a copy of it goes by this ship. There was a letter to you from Mrs. Hastings by the same despatch, so that I am doubly anxious for its safe and speedy arrival.

Two days ago I dined alone with the Lord Chancellor, and we had a very long conversation upon India affairs. He does not perfectly understand what his brother ministers mean, but matters he assures me cannot long remain upon their present footing.

The dissent of the Board of Control to the Directors' resolution for your quitting at the end of one year after the appointment of a successor, he approves, though he did not construe that resolution into an ungentlemanlike dismission from the service at the end of the year, which was the light in which many of your friends had viewed it. He thinks too that there is a more powerful leaning towards Macartney than he expected there would have been, at the same time that they substantially adopt your system, and blame and censure his lordship for those breaches of a solemn treaty which you have so justly condemned.

The Chancellor has promised he will make himself master of this subject completely, and I have put all the papers into his hands. Finding there was so great a backwardness in Mr. Pitt to do you justice, by elevating you to a British peerage, the Chancellor was determined to enter fully into the business, and I shall now copy for you, my dear Sir, as faithfully as my memory will permit, what passed between them.

I went, said his Lordship, to Mr. Pitt at Putney, and I told him that it was absolutely necessary we should do something decisive relative to Hastings, for though I had always declared, and was always ready to declare, that Hastings had made me a minister, and made Mr. Pitt one too, yet if there was anything in the character or conduct of Mr. Hastings which would not bear a scrutiny, or if he had been unprincipled, corrupt, or inefficient in his great office, I was just as ready to crush him as Mr. Pitt could be; for though he had made me a minister, and though I had declared so in the House of Peers, Mr. Pitt should never find me an advocate for, or a protector of, a delinquent. I saw Pitt was rather distressed to be so pushed; but he told me that although in many instances, and those important ones too, he allowed Mr. Hastings great merit, yet there were charges against him which, till explained, he conceived would render it dangerous for his Majesty's ministers to grant him a peerage, as it would excite the popular clamour to a very great degree.

I then desired Mr. Pitt would tell me what were the objections against Hastings, and he said there were four.

First, he had attempted to extend the British dominion in India, a system Pitt highly disapproved. Secondly, he had by his conduct forfeited the confidence of the native princes of India. Thirdly, he had, in various instances, disobeyed the orders of the Court of Directors; and fourthly, he had fixed enormous salaries to offices in Bengal, and wasted the public money to gratify the servants of the Company who were attached to him.

I told Mr. Pitt we were now nearly coming to a point, and all I wished further was to have him specify any instances under these general heads, to which I would engage to reply so as to satisfy his mind. Pitt seemed staggered a little, and I said to him, Come, Mr. Pitt, I see you know as little of the matter as I do, but let us talk this business over as friends, or if you please, as statesmen. Do not look upon me as the advocate of Hastings. You will see Mr. Dundas in half an hour, and perhaps he may point out some instances under each head of accusation. Perhaps he may not, for I suspect Dundas to know as little of India affairs as you and I do; but I'll tell you what I will do. You shall employ Dundas to employ any man or set of men he pleases, to point out the instances in which Hastings has profusely lavished the public money, disobeyed orders, forfeited the confidence of the native princes, or attempted to extend the British empire in India: and if I do not produce a full and satisfactory answer to each charge, why, then I not only will consent to sacrifice Hastings, but I will insist upon his being sacrificed to national justice. At present it appears to me that you are afraid to support Hastings, and yet afraid to recall him, but it is impossible that this miserable system can go on. His merits are great and splendid: you allow them to be so. His influence also is great, but it does not arise from corruption or wealth. It arises from the high opinion men entertain of his integrity and extraordinary abilities. If you can prove that he wants the first, or is deficient in the last, he will sink in the public opinion, and you may reduce him in a moment to the situation of a private man. Every friend of Hastings with whom I have conversed will gladly consent that he shall rise or fall by his merits.

This, my dear Sir, is the substance of what passed between Pitt and the Lord Chancellor. When Dundas returns from Scotland, his Lordship assures me there will be some decision, and he said, if it shall appear that Hastings has in some instances given larger salaries than they approve (for all the other charges are nonsense), why the devil don't they order them to be lessened? but I hope they will, at the same time, give Hastings credit for creating an immense revenue at his own responsibility and for the improvement of the land revenues of Bengal.

The Chancellor told Mr. Pitt that what information he had, he drew from me; that knowing my connexion with Mr. Hastings, and the enthusiasm of my temper, he did not entirely depend upon me. He observed, however, that Lord Walsingham was as strong an enthusiast as I was. What he therefore wanted was, that those who thought unfavourably of Mr. Hastings, that his avowed enemies should state every thing they could against him; that the Chancellor should be permitted to call upon me for an answer to each head of accusation, and then he would willingly leave it to Mr. Pitt to determine.

I hope, my dear Sir, something of this kind will be done, but you now see the little pitiful manner in which you are attacked.

Upon all the great points you have completely defeated your opponents, and they are now attempting to whisper away your reputation. In this, however, by the manly part our friend the Chancellor takes, we shall effectually disappoint them. This mode of attack proceeds from the private letters of two of your colleagues in Bengal, who have been perpetually asserting, that contracts, salaries, and agencies have been given away at an extravagant rate. When we can once bring them to specify the instances, we shall soon refute them.

10th of November.—I was two hours yesterday with our friend Lord Walsingham, and related to him, by the Chancellor's desire, what had passed between him and Mr. Pitt.

Lord Walsingham said that the three first charges were nonsense; that the Board gave you credit for holding high the British character in the East, and that the charge of disobedience of orders was contemptible, but that on the last head you would certainly be pushed when the subject came forward, in consequence of the minutes and private representations of Stables to John Robinson. It is impossible, my dear Sir, they can push you without condescending to specify the particular instances of larger salaries, &c.; and when once they will do that, I have not a doubt of explaining your conduct satisfactorily; but the Chancellor says, admitting the fact to be so, that their ideas of what are handsome salaries shall be more confined than yours, they have only to order them to be lessened in future.

What the Board and the Directors want, is to bring the civil expenses within thirty lacs a year, and whether they will order you to do this, or go into the detail is uncertain yet, but I believe the latter.

As the Fox is still to stay some days, I may be able to tell you further in another letter. I am ever, my dear Sir, most faithfully and gratefully yours.

CHAPTER VII.

Journey to Lucknow—Communication with the Prince of Delhi—Preparations to return Home—Letters to Mr. Hastings.

WHILE parties were thus confounding themselves, and losing sight in their bickerings, not unfrequently of what was due to justice, almost always of what they owed to sound policy and common sense, Mr. Hastings was putting forth his strength so that the affairs of the province might as speedily as possible be reduced to order, and himself left free to indulge his own wishes by departing for England. His journey to Lucknow went forward, as has elsewhere been explained, without the occurrence of any adventure of which it is necessary to give an account. In its results, however, it proved eminently advantageous, both to the Company and the Nabob, for the former received on the instant a considerable portion of the sums that were due; while the latter was placed in such a situation as to afford good hope of his being able thenceforth to support his own dignity. Yet greater things still would have questionless followed, had Mr. Hastings been, as his friends at home believed him to be, absolute in British India. Mr. Hastings found at Lucknow an illustrious exile, the eldest son of the fallen Mogul; who escaping from Delhi had come to implore the assistance of the English, in restoring to his father some portion of the power of which his enemies had deprived him. The project, bold as it was, seems to have been readily, I had almost said eagerly, embraced by Mr. Hastings. It agreed well with the expansive nature of his genius, which delighted to consider rather the ultimate results of things, than the inconvenience which might attend the effort to attain them; and he was the more disposed to assist the prince, that he believed the moral influence of the Company of sufficient weight to bear down all opposition. But his colleagues, to whom he referred the matter, shrank from it with dismay, and it fell of course to the ground. The following, which contains a summary of his proceedings in this and in other matters, will, I think be read with great interest.

To Major Scott.

Lucknow, 12th June, 1784.

My dear Scott,—On the 15th and 17th ultimo, I sent despatches to Mr. Bodham to be forwarded to England by the way of Bussora, containing duplicate letters to the Court of Directors, and two to you, with one in each for Mrs. Hastings. I can neither detail what I have done, nor send you materials. I have furnished the Council with bills for five lacs at a reduced exchange of three and a half per cent. instead of sixteen and twenty. I have paid up all the arrears of the different corps, the Surat included, of these provinces. I have just got bills for five lacs, also with a reduced exchange of four per cent. from Bombay, where they are in the last degree of want. I had realized above forty-six lacs when my accounts in those despatches were closed. The season of collection closed with them; but something, I do not exactly know what, has been received since. I have adjusted all the disputed accounts between the Nabob Vizier and the Company, and formed the mode of monthly adjustment with the joint signatures and interchange of the minister and our accomptant, which will preclude all future differences, the past being the accumulation of years. The minister has formed all his plans for the ensuing settlement, for the retrenchment of expenses, and the establishment of new and necessary offices; and promises that all will be in complete execution within a month from this time. He desires me to remain a little longer to give them effect in the first operation, and I have fixed the day of my departure. The settlement will be generally fixed for five years, and if the rains set in well, there will be a sufficiency to pay all the debt of the Company considerably within the next year, *i. e.* from 1st September to 1st September, and provide for a new military establishment to replace Sir John Cummings, which I shall withdraw. I have had few occasions to apply to the Board, but on these I have constantly received flat and ungracious refusals, after having been made to wait a length of time for answers on subjects stated to require instant decision; I wrote them a long letter representing the management of Benares, and offering to correct the abuses. They made me wait a month, and then asked for my plan. I have given them one, and they refuse to accept it; I shall have exposed the names of individuals to personal vengeance, and done no good to the country. If they accept it, I have pledged my credit for the prosperity and safety of the country and its revenue. If they do not, I will return by the river Gagra under pretext of a visit to the Begums at Fyzabad, that I may not pass Benares, for I underwent the persecution of mobs of complainants from Boxar to Joosee in my way hither, and there is now a little mob parading even at my gate.

I have desired powers to relieve the King, declaring that I believed I could do it without hostility or expense, provided I had the power of the former, and that I would undertake nothing without a moral certainty of avoiding both. They have "exhorted me to avoid most sedulously and cautiously in my correspondence with the different princes of India whatever may commit, or be strained into an interpretation of committing the Company, either as to their arms or treasure." These are their words, and they are fulsomely loud in their applause of the "*wisdom and sound policy*" of the Company's orders against our interference "in the objects of dispute between the country powers." Yet they "hope that I shall be enabled to effect the return of the Shazada to his father with safety and credit to the prince." As if I could negociate with my hands tied. I have, however, stated the necessity of my having powers so strongly, that I think they will be perplexed to justify their refusal. Yet I know they will refuse, and sincerely hope they will; for though I have urged this point with all the vehemence of a man whose heart is devoted to the point which he pursues, I have opposed my own interest, ease, and inclinations in it. Some good I will yet do, and may draw the means of it from the overshot caution with which the instructions of the Board are guarded. But I am led unawares into a subject which I meant to have left entirely to your brother: to whom I now leave what remains of it.

You will hear enough of the treaty concluded with

Tippoo Sultan. Our Board have ratified it, and sent a copy to me for a second ratification of it with my signature. I have assigned my reasons why I ought not to sign it. Indeed there is an absurdity in the very form of it, for it expresses that the Governor-general and Council have signed it on such a date in Fort William when I am at the distance of 800 miles from it. I have drawn out another, in which I rendered that part of the ratification more accurate, and accompanied it with a declaration on the part of the Governor-general and Council that we have acceded, to the treaty under the construction of the Nabob Walla Jah being understood and included in it wherever the Carnatic is mentioned; and I have signed both the copy which the Board sent to me, my amended copy, and the declaration, that they may make their choice of them without loss of time. They have approved the two latter, and intend to depute a person to see that they are delivered. Upon this occasion I have again condemned their forbearance, and urged their dismissing Lord Macartney and the committee for breach of orders. For they have studiously excluded the Nabob Walla Jah, though the principal in the treaty, and the Mahrattas, though it was concluded in virtue of the treaty made with them. I wish to send you copies of my protest and letters on this subject; but I want hands and time. I gave early information to Mahdajee Sindia, taking blame for the neglect of our treaty with him, and acknowledging that it was to his good offices and the Peishwa's interposition that we were indebted for the peace, such as it was. This has prevented him from taking offence at it, and he is gratified by the personal merit which I have assigned to him in the business. It might have created a breach between us. What a man is this Lord Macartney! The wit of man could not devise such effectual instruments of a nation's ruin, as this black eagle portends to every land and state over which he casts the shadow of his wings, not like the fabulous eagle of the Arabians, whose shadow confers crowns, victory, and prosperity to those over whom it passes. I yet believe that, in spite of peace, he will effect the loss of the Carnatic.

I must not forget that Mr. Wheler has behaved well. He is overruled, and has contended with the ungracious spirit of his colleagues as strenuously as could be expected from his disposition. I cannot expect more. I hear that Mr. Stables has taken Mr. Cowper into his family, and I will write to Calcutta that it may be ascertained, and you will know from thence the truth of it; his conduct is indecent beyond all bounds. My dear Scott, yours ever most affectionately.

To this I subjoin a letter to Mr. Wheler, in which the reasons that swayed Mr. Hastings to the adoption of his own peculiar views are set forth. Whatever we may think of this document as a piece of practical reasoning, it describes a mind deeply imbued with the principles of justice and magnanimity, and the loftiest order of ambition.

To Mr. Wheler.

Lucknow, 9th June, 1784.

My dear Sir,—You must not be offended at the distant and peremptory style of my secret letter. It bears your formal address, but is substantially less yours than theirs to whom I have desired you to impart it. By the unhandsome reception of my former letters I judge of the effect of this. I have simply done my duty, and am careless whether I am permitted to go further or not; because though I do most ardently wish to close my service with some act that will reflect a credit on my nation, with little cost or trouble, and feel an interest in the cause for which I am an advocate, proportioned to my actual proximity to it, and am not apt to enter coldly into any political measures,—yet I have numberless reasons to wish, could I oppose my private to my public feelings, that I may fail in my present application; and therefore I do not choose to solicit where I do not choose to be obliged.

I have used many arguments, and those, I think, of much weight, to induce the Board to afford such a degree and mode of assistance to the King as may prove effectual to his relief, and not implicate the Company in wars or expenses, so far as these, or either of these, consequences may be avoided. But I have omitted many other reasons applicable only to the present occasion, because I did not chose to overload the subject, having without them made my letter more than sufficiently long. I will endeavour to recollect them, and if you think them deserving your own notice in the consideration of the question which I have proposed for the Board's decision, it will be highly gratifying to me if you will make them in any way that you please your own. It is possible that they may not so obviously occur to you, as you are at too great a distance to receive that impression from the general subject, which a nearer view, and a daily intercourse with those who are interested in it, naturally force on me.

1. The daily indignities which have been imposed upon the King since he chose to abandon our protection have so much debased the credit and respect of his house, that unless some powerful effort is made to relieve it, it will very shortly be extinct; and there is no power but ours that can relieve it.

2. Its extinction will probably be followed by that

of the miserable influence which at this time oppresses it; for Affrasi ab Cawn himself possesses neither ability, spirit, nor birth to support the power which he has assumed, without the sanction of the royal name; and it is by no means improbable that, in the confusion which will ensue, some new adventurer may start up from the general mass who will constitute a new dominion, and join to it all the powers and prerogatives of the past. I would almost venture to foretel that such will, in the case which I have supposed, be the event of it; and whenever this happens, our dominion, which subsists but loosely on the weakness of our neighbours, and on the illusion of popular opinion. at least as much as on our military strength, will be exposed to greater dangers than any which it has yet had to encounter, though it has been many times near the brink of destruction.

3. There never yet was an instance of the flight of a prince of the house of Timur from the presence, that did not produce some great event; and such is expected from the late extraordinary effort of the Prince Mirza Iowan Bukht, for he is the eldest of the King's sons; supposed to be greatly superior to any of the family in ability; the declared heir of the throne; and regent, whenever the King himself is absent. It has already produced one event, by the imprisonment of the King's confidential servant, Mudged o'Dowla, which, if no exertion is made in favour of the King, may complete his debasement; but might prove the reverse by the universal dissatisfaction which it has occasioned, were an immediate advantage taken of it, while the minds of the ruling party are wavering, and their authority undetermined. If no other consequences follow such portentous movements, the veil which has hitherto concealed the nakedness of the royal authority will fall off, and it will lose even the little respect which it has hitherto retained.

4. The present reduced state of the royal authority may be principally ascribed to the indolence and passive spirit of the King. His son seems to be of a different character, and has given proofs both of his courage and attachment on some pressing exigencies. Indeed on such occasions his father has always had recourse to him as his principal dependance; but his services have been constantly forgotten as soon as the danger that called them forth was past. It is probable that, if the prince can be instrumental to his deliverance at this time, the magnitude of the service, and the unquestionable evidence which it will afford of his attachment, added to the confidence which the King will (or ought to) repose in the honour of our nation, which will be a security against the perfidy which is too often practised even by sons against their parents in the course of Asiatic intrigues, will attach the King to him, and induce him to invest him with that share of the executive administration which he has hitherto suffered to be usurped and exercised by the meanest and most unworthy men. I state this as a probability; but I own, I do not dwell with great reliance on it; for there is no answering for a spirit so weak as the King's, and so much under the dominion of whisperers and incendiaries.

5. Hitherto, when any calamity has befallen the King, it has passed at such a distance from the observation of our Government, that the occasion has seemed to have produced its own remedy before it was well known to us. It was known that we had work enough of our own upon our hands; and the distance between us (to recur to the first argument) has served for an excuse to our indifference. It at least prevented the appearance of a direct refusal. The case is now widely different. The proximity of the person who is supposed to possess the executive powers of our Government; his residence and intimate communication with the first servant of the Crown.; the superior

claim which the King has on me, derived from his deprivation of the tribute, which was my own personal act; the professions continually made by our Government through me from the time of that act, which includes a period of almost eleven years; the hopes excited by my arrival here, which were the declared and undoubted motive for the prince's flight; his flight attempted and effected with great personal hazard; that followed by the recent outrage which has been offered to the royal authority, of which I myself, though innocent of it, have furnished the original ground; the King's interests, cause, and inclinations, united by this event, if not always the same, with his son's; his application for our aid, and the pathetic expostulation with which he has since repeated it; the great advantages which the presence and influence of the prince would give to any plan undertaken for the King's benefit, and the weakness of those who might oppose it; and lastly (for I pass other points of less note, and many of equal may have escaped my recollection), our relaxation from every other external concern: these are all of such public notoriety (except one only, which will soon become as well known as the rest), that they may be said to constitute the crisis of the fortunes and destiny of the house of Timur; and it will most probably (I am almost impelled to say, assuredly) terminate in the utter subversion or the temporary relevation of its dignity. Of one or other of these events we shall be the instruments. I am not sure, but I believe, that we shall be applauded at home, if we take the generous side of the question; but I am quite sure that we shall be loudly reproached both by our own countrymen, and by all mankind, if we suffer so illustrious a family to perish, being able to prevent it, and having been the instruments of the causes which led to it.

6. I have said nothing of the King's absolute rights, having sufficiently discussed them in my secret letter. But I must add the right of gratitude, for he has asserted it. He pleads that when the French and Hyder earnestly solicited his grants of the Carnatic, and offered large sums to obtain them, he constantly and steadily refused them. We know by undoubted evidence that this is true; and though we have ever treated the King's sunnuds and firmauns as waste paper, and they were certainly no better, yet our enemies held them in high estimation, and his merit was proportionably great in disappointing their expectations.

7. If we meant to withhold all interference from the concerns of the King, we ought not to have appointed a public minister at his court. The Board appointed Major Browne for the express purpose of tendering our assistance. It was an act of the most complete authority; for it passed when the members of the Board were in entire confidence and good humour with each other, and all their judgments were concerned in it. It was a proclamation to the world that we acknowledged the King's right to our assistance, and a pledge equally public for the substantial performance of that acknowledgment. The member of the Board who was not present, nor his appointment known, at the time when this measure was adopted, may complain of it, as I have heard him; and may propose that it be reversed, if he considers no act of Government valid which he had no hand in. But it will be difficult for you, Mr. Macpherson, or myself, to find a reason to justify us in undoing it, or in making new declarations which are the reverse of those made and understood by so authentic a publication. Yet, if it shall be resolved to leave the King absolutely to his destiny, I shall not, of my own authority, send back

Major Browne, nor advise the Board to continue his commission.

After this long discussion (which I fear will tire you), I find it necessary to recur once more to the object of it. I do not want to send armies into the field, nor to disturb the repose which our Government enjoys and requires after the fatigues and bruises which it has sustained from a long and accumulated warfare. I want no more than the power to dictate, and I am persuaded that I shall have no need to enforce it: neither is it my wish or intention to stay beyond the term of my original commission, though all the wealth of Akbar should be offered to tempt me. I do not expect that the Board will approve of my recommendation, and I secretly wish, in spite of myself, that they may not; but I do sincerely hope that your sentiments will concur with mine, because I am convinced that you will gain credit by it, though we may be both overruled.

I think it proper to mention, though you will of course so understand it, that I mean this letter for your own perusal only, but with a latitude to apply it as you think proper. I am, my dear Sir, your faithful and affectionate friend.

The Board would not sanction the adoption of a policy so bold, perhaps so perilous, as is advocated in this letter, but they did not object to his taking the prince under his protection; and placed at his disposal resources enough, both in men and money, to secure for the young man a safe return to his father's capital. This was ultimately effected; but in the meanwhile Mr. Hastings had other business to conduct, and it pretty well engrossed both his time and attention. Through this, however, I cannot venture to follow him, because I am unwilling to embark upon a complication of details, every effort to unravel which would serve but to weary, without at all exciting my own interests or those of my reader. I, therefore, content myself with stating, that by his dealings with the Vizier, he delivered that prince entirely from the pressure of the resident's domination, and that having found for him ministers, both able and willing to manage his affairs, he left him in their hands, and never had cause to repent the arrangement. In the province of Benares, likewise, he affected great and important reforms. The city appears, indeed, to have flourished under the management of Mohammed Reza Cawn, a native of whose integrity and talents Mr. Hastings entertained the highest opinion, and whose portrait hangs, or did hang when I was last there, in what used to be Mr. Hastings's library at Daylesford. But into the rural districts Mr. Fowke had contrived to introduce the most exquisite confusion; and these it became the Governor's duty to remodel. He was not so immediately successful in this case as in the regeneration of Oude, partly because things were politically more confused, partly because over Benares the famine had spread with fearful violence. Nevertheless he constructed a machinery for the future working of the state, and in due time the state reaped ample benefit from it. After this he set out on his return to the Presidency, his progress towards which, as well as his final preparations for quitting India, I shall leave him to describe for himself.

The following letters, addressed to Mrs. Hastings, seem to me to be full of interest. They certainly do not describe the Begums as harbouring any vindictive remembrance of injuries sustained, though they make a good deal of mention of these ladies and of the feelings which they cherished towards both the writer himself and his interesting correspondent, though now far removed from them :—

Benares, 24th September, 1784.

My dearest Marian,—My last letter was closed the 27th of last month, the day on which I left Lucknow. I had a very unpleasant and tedious journey, though but of fifty miles, to Doondea-kéry where my boats lay ; for it began to rain as soon as I began my march, and continued almost without remission to the 2d of this month, The plains were overflowed, and every hollow way became an impassable river ; insomuch that many people, and some of my own, were drowned in attempting to pass the depths, which but a fortnight before were dry ground. I myself was obliged to cross one new born river on a raft which sunk below the surface with my single weight, and a few hours after wrecked my buggy, which is yet lying in the channel where it fell. The horse, with my two other favourites, were swum over, and safely landed in my own presence. The Nabob was with great difficulty persuaded to return to Lucknow, on the 2d, having resolved to accompany me, not from affection, to Benares. We parted in great good humour, and I do verily believe that his feelings and sentiments do justice to the kindness which I have shown him. Yet he is in vile hands, and it was to carry a paltry point for his unworthy favourites that he was so earnest to go with me, beyond the personal influence of his ministers. These men have urged him to some alarming acts since his return, but without consequence; nor have I much apprehension for his future behaviour. He well knows that if he loses my support he will be a ruined man, and I have left Major Palmer, on whom I can securely depend, to remind him occasionally both of his obligations and engagements; and I shall stay at this place one month, partly for the purpose of guarding against any mischief that may be practised; and, if necessary, which God forbid, to return to Lucknow for the last resource; I can be there in a journey of two days, but I do not suspect that it will be necessary. The Nabob solemnly promised that he would not break a single thread of my arrangements, and these, if undisturbed, will discharge all his debts to the Company in the course of a year, and leave him a free and independent man. His uncle, his mother, and grandmother, the most respected of his family, are all in my interest, and look upon me as the guardian of their house; nor do I believe that I have left an enemy in all the Nabob's dominions, except among the most worthless, whose influence I have been the means of repressing. But to return to my travels: in these the prince accompanied me, or to speak with more propriety, I attended him. On the 3d, we reached the Ganges, and on the 5th, in an evil hour, put off, or rather attempted it, against a strong wind, beating us on a lee shore. My beautiful budgerow became almost in an instant a complete ruin. I reluctantly detail the particulars. The rudder had been broken on the way, which the sarang concealed from my knowledge, and instead of repairing the damage, had loosely patched and covered it from view. The budgerow was of course unmanageable ; she was driving fast towards the bank, the Daudees being unable either to keep her off, or turn her, and a rapid stream hurrying her down at a most furious rate. I ran up to the poop to see what was the matter, and no sooner was my back turned, than the frosh opened every window which I had left fastened on the left side, which was presented to the shore, which the blockhead had no sooner accomplished than the stump of a tree, which my evil genius had planted for the purpose, shaved them all from their hinges in less than ten seconds, with a crash that I am sure you must have felt, and will remember, if you can remember where you were, and what were your thoughts, at the time, which answers to two o'clock in the afternoon of the 5th of September, in the longitude of Doondea-kéry. At the same instant I saw the rudder gone, and the old sarang in a state of stupefaction. It was a long time before he recovered his senses enough to tell me that it was impossible to move without a new rudder. I could not wait for so tedious an operation, nor bear to look at the destruction around me; and having given vent for a reasonable length of time, to a something too intemperate anger, I began coolly to reflect that I had been attended with a long train of fortunate events ; that it was the lot of humanity to receive a mixture of good and evil in the cup of life, and that it was well that my portion of the bitter had been administered to me in a substance which could only give a temporary affliction. The damage of a budgerow was not a subject of internal or lasting grief; and I said it was well if it were no worse. To avoid worse, I resolved to fly from the spot to which my ill fortune had attached itself, and leave it to complete the mischief which was yet in store for me. Accordingly, having given the necessary orders for the care of the budgerow, I took to the feelchehra, Mr. Sulivan and Major Toone, who with Sir Thomas Mills chanced to be with me, accompanying me. Sir Thomas was sick and stayed. I called upon the prince, made my excuses to him for leaving him, telling him my melancholy story, and took my leave. The next afternoon at three o'clock, we arrived at Mirsepoor, landed and found Mr. John Scott there, and at dinner. We stayed that night with him, and renewing our voyage the next morning by daylight, we reached Chunar before eight. We were accommodated by Colonel Achmuty in the new house built by Colonel Blair in the fort, and continued his guests till our companions joined us. In the mean time I was alarmed with the report of a fresh calamity. The pinnaw, which your sarang (for I have not yet turned him away) had stuck upon every sand between Calcutta and Allahabad, was not arrived when I left Doondea-kéry; and two gentlemen assured me that they had passed it near Manniepoor (see the chart) upon a shoal where, as the water had fallen considerably, she was likely to lie till the next rains. I had no remedy but patience, and never bore misfortune with so much philosophy. If you have ever seen me otherwise, it was because you had a share in my vexations, and because I feel more for yours than for my own. In the mean time I indulged in a long interval of repose and comfort, and had arrived in time to intercept a packet filled with all my letters from England by the Surprise. These would probably have passed me, had no accident obliged me to deviate from the quiet track of my voyage; and from these I learnt the complete overthrow of the men who had been aiming so much mischief through me at the Company, and the establishment as complete of my own reputation. On the 11th I had the pleasure to see my pinnaw arrive in safety, and the prince, who had met with some accidents with his own, in possession of it. I conducted him that evening in great parade to the fort, where a small mistake was committed in letting him see Mrs. Achmuty and Mrs. Showers. It was her fault, and I was not on my guard. I privately apologized for it, desiring him not to form his idea of English beauty from these models, assuring him that we had better. I carried him the next morning in the feelchehra to your gaut, and from thence conducted him in safety to Mahdewdass's garden, where I left him as happy as a prince ought to be proverbially. I am quartered partly at Markham's house on the plain of Schrowl, where I pass the day, and partly at a bungalow of Fowke's in which I sleep. Thus ends this chapter of my travels, which may be properly named the chapter of accidents. I should tell you that the budgerow is now at Chunar, and I have the promise of seeing her again very shortly in a state of complete repair.

It will be of consequence to you to know that, though I have been much exposed to both extremities of heat and wet, I have not suffered from either, having invariably preserved my health in every occasion of exertion, and never complaining but when I have been at rest. My complaints, such as they are, evidently proceed from the weather, and are languor, lassitude, and inactivity. I eat sparingly: I never sup, and am generally a-bed by ten. I breakfast at six. I bathe with cold water daily, and while I was at Lucknow twice a-day, using sooreys cooled with ice. Though my mind has laboured under a constant and severe load, yet the business which has occupied it has been light, with no variety to draw my attention different ways, and with little vexation. To these may be added, that unless every body was in a conspiracy to deceive me, all ranks of people were pleased, not because I did good, but that I did no ill. With such advantages I ought perhaps to be better. I am indeed infinitely better than I was at this season the last year, for then I was miserably bad: but the best health that I gain or can hope to gain in India, is but a palliative acquirea with continual sacrifices and unmanly attentions. I want a multitude of aids to cure me thoroughly, all which may be included in two comprehensive but comfortable terms, a hard frost and my own fireside.

I cannot ascertain the time that I may remain here; the business of this place need not detain me ten days. But I must wait a little longer to watch the course of the business which I have lately quitted; and I must allow a longer time to dispose of theinlustrious youth who has in so extraordinary a manner thrown his fortunes into my hands. I cannot abandon a person of such eminence who, on the credit of my will and ability to serve him, has voluntarily encountered so many difficulties to get to me; and I feel for the honour of my nation, which is concerned in it: but my hands are tied, and I can only work with poor expedients and borrowed aids. But my fortune is in its flood, and as the current of popular opinion floats with it, these together may bring about my decent acquittal of this charge more effectually than anything that I can do to accomplish it. Unfortunately his character gains, instead of losing, by acquaintance. His faults are trivial, and all grow out of his good qualities, and the best of these is his temper, which is incomparably cheerful and accommodating to every situation that he is placed in. Was he mean, or arrogant, or petulant, or unfeeling, or a fool, or vicious, I could easily let him shift for himself. As he is the reverse of all this, I must either contrive to restore him, "with credit and safety," (these are the terms of the Board's instructions,) to his father, or leave him here, or be loaded with him to Calcutta. The first is scarcely to be effected but by means which I may not use, and the last I cannot allow even in supposition; and I have many great objections to his remaining at Benares, which I regard as the place of my own peculiar patronage, and I am afraid that his presence and influence (for he has sad people about him) will hurt the police of the city, which has gained me great and extended reputation. God knows how it will terminate. The expectation is not a great encroachment on my time, for I am not very anxious to change the dry and open plain of Sukrowl for the deadly steams of Calcutta at this season of the year; nor, was I in Calcutta at this time, should I be of much service. Yet it is probable that I shall think of moving about the middle of October. I think to make another short visit to Chunar, partly to gratify the hospitable inclination of the good old colonel, and partly my own curiosity, as I was unable to go abroad while I was last there, on account of the excessive heat of the weather. We have had a late repetition of heavy rain, and hope we shall have no more disagreeable heat.

Sir Thomas Mills, whom I left sick at the time of the crash of my budgerow, has been since in great danger. He is now on the recovery, and mends fast; but it will be long before his constitution can have got the better of the shock which it has received.

The above has been written with a view to its being copied by another hand, as I mean to send the whole letter in duplicate, not for the value of what precedes this, for if you can interest yourself in the detail of the little events and casualties of my life, there is no one else to whom they would not be disgusting. I now proceed to the purport for which the letter was intended, and for which, as it is of consequence that you should be fully apprized of my intentions upon the subject of it, I shall make a duplicate of it.

On the 8th instant I received the packet of the Surprise, with letters dated down to the 24th of April. By these I received the first knowledge of the dissolution of Parliament, and the confirmation of the power of the administration which then existed. Some intimation was also imperfectly given me of an intention to begin the new sessions with a Bill for the regulation of the superior government of India, with assurances that my credit stood very high both with the Company, the Ministers, and the public, and that new and distinct powers were to be added to my office. Scott, in all his letters, mixes, with a natural apprehension for my health, and a feeling for what I must suffer in a protracted separation from you, both his own wishes, and those which he assures me are the wishes of the public, for my continuance another year in India. He will doubtless have told you what he has written, and you will also know the more recent expectations of others upon this point, and these may deceive you with wrong conclusions respecting my own resolution upon them. Hitherto nothing has passed which either has, or ought to have made any change in my original plan. On the contrary, I am more confirmed in my determination of leaving India in January next, by every argument which has been urged against it. Major Scott tells me that people are greatly alarmed at the expectation of my going away, and that some person of high authority said to him, "Good God, what shall we do if Hastings should throw up the government!" I am provoked at such exclamations, and almost displeased with Scott for being the dupe of them. If it is expected that I should remain, why am I not told so by authority, and trusted with the powers necessary to my station, and the expectations which they build upon me, that I may remain for some useful purpose? To me it is apparent, from every observation that I have made, that it is not the wish either of the present or any other administration that I should remain but as a cypher to keep the office open for the gift of their own patronage. I am not pleased to be made so pitiful an instrument, and had I no other reason, this alone should determine me to disappoint those who treat me so unworthily. That I may not appear too hasty in forming this conclusion, I will tell you why I do it. When Mr. Fox introduced his Bill, he began with declaring, for the satisfaction of my friends, that no injury was intended against me ; yet he immediately went on to a string of invective and abuse of my conduct as the only groundwork on which he could support his own question, or prove the necessity of wresting the authority from the Company, which he attempted to show was insufficient to control that which had been delegated to me. Mr. Pitt with great ability defended the rights of the Company, but weakened his own argument, by maintaining a profound silence with regard to every argument of his adversary which bore any relation to me. Had he replied to those, he must have said something in my vindication, and unless that vindication had been as strong as the charges which had been urged against me, his cause would have suffered in the debate. But if he had taken this line, he would have put it out of his own power at a future time to remove me, for with what grace could he attempt such an act against one to whose merits he had himself borne such ample testimony? His private declarations made to Major Scott in his closet are mere words, which cannot be quoted as binding on his future decisions, and may be forgotten, or explained to any arbitrary meaning, and were perhaps only intended as compliments of encouragement from Mr. Pitt, who wanted materials, to Major Scott, who could best furnish them, for the support of a great and critical question. He is now at liberty to act by me as he pleases, to reappoint me with proper powers to my office, or to extend his own interests by conferring it on another better able to repay the obligation. It was well known, when the Surprise was yet in England, that I had fixed the period for my departure, and that period must have been as well known. If it was expected that I should defer it, I ought to have been apprized of it by the only packet that could apprize me of it in time. I shall not probably receive any subsequent despatches of a much later date before the month of November, and by that time I shall have made all my preparations, at least all that require expense, for my return. I have already spent a little fortune in changing my first purpose of returning to England when you did, for one charge would have sufficed for both, both for the voyage, and for our future household. I cannot afford to lay out another sum and allow the purpose of it to be defeated. Perhaps it was intended to wait till something more decisive should have passed in Parliament. That cannot have happened, for it is not possible, before the month of July, or at the soonest very late in June, and at that season of the year, allowance being also made for the time requisite to prepare the consequent despatches, no advices could be sent to Bengal which could arrive there before next February. And who will say that I ought to wait their arrival, in the uncertain and surely unreasonable expectation of their containing the motives for my longer stay? Or on what pretext can I wait? I have declared my peremptory resolution to depart, and have called upon the Court of Directors to obtain the nomination of my successor. The execution of this declaration was indeed announced for the last year, but protracted on account of the distracted state of the province of Oude, and my sense of the obligation which it imposed upon me to continue for the means of retrieving it. I am now pledged, or committed, to use a more fashionable word, to give up my place; and if I do not, I must assign some reason for not doing it. I must either change my purpose, in obedience to authority, or assume an air of contemptible self-importance, and say on my own authority that my services cannot be spared.

If I was to be asked in what manner I could be authorized to remain, I would answer thus:—

The Court of Directors are authorized to send out what orders they please to the Governor-general and Council, which the Governor-general and Council are bound to obey. They may order the Council to yield me the lead, with the responsibility, in all points in which I shall think it of importance sufficient to assume both, and they shall differ from me. Let the Directors issue such an order, and require me, in virtue of it, to remain; let their superiors, if such be their wish, intimate it to the Directors; and let it be personally signified to each of my colleagues that such a conduct is expected from them, with a similar intimation to myself. I am far from presuming to expect such a deference to be paid to me. I only show the mode which might be adopted by those who think, or affect to think, more highly of me than I myself do. And with such a mode of application I should deem myself bound, against every consideration of domestic comfort, of life, and of fortune, though I were now to sacrifice them for ever, to remain. The mode is obvious. If it is practised, I must and will remain; if not, I will not, though all my friends should unite in soliciting it, unless you too joined them, which I hope and believe is impossible. Something like what I have written above, but not so full and explanatory, I have written in my former letters, if in more than one. You will now know by this with certainty whether you are, or are not to expect me, by the knowledge which you will possess of the orders which have been written to Bengal within the period necessary for my being in India to receive them.

For my determination, and the grounds of it, as I have stated both, I shall refer Major Scott to you, because I think it a subject in which you are most concerned; and because I wish to accustom you to a familiar acquaintance with such as have a near relation to my reputation, even though they were not, as this is, connected with our common happiness. I could assign other motives of equal weight in the scale of common sense for my adhering to my present purpose, such as my declining health, the loss of domestic happiness, the probability of rendering this everlasting by a longer residence in a climate become so noxious to me, my inability to conduct the necessary measures of this Government, with associates who are bound in an opposition to me, and will not act on their own authority; the certainty of incurring censure for the effects of such an opposition, both for what is, and what is not done, for who will distinguish? and the hazard of some fatal disaster, perhaps of utter ruin, in consequence of the same want of union, which is a want of government. Add, that my income is not equal to all my present expenses; that I shall have hardly a competency, let me arrive in England at whatever time; and that, as I must go at some time, or yield to the course of nature, I cannot go at a time of more quiet or public ease than the present; that it seems now necessary to compel my superiors to put an end to a state of suspension which has now lasted thirteen years, if anything will; and that it is yet possible for me to arrive in time to yield my assistance, if I may be thought of consequence enough to be consulted, in framing some plan for the government of our possessions in India, which may render them more profitable and lasting; or in preventing some plan that may accelerate their ruin. It is hard to see the good that I could do, and am not permitted to do it; and harder to be made accountable for the acts of others, and to be regarded as the only manager of affairs, when I have no more than a single vote with others who are determined to say no to all that I propose.

So much for my public concerns. Read as much of this to Major Scott as you think necessary for his knowledge, and store it all in remembrance for your own. What a letter have I written; and who that read it without the direction would suspect it to be written by a fond husband to his beloved wife? Perhaps my other letters, if intercepted, would appear to bear too much of the real character of their writer, and atone more than they ought for the contrary deficiency of this. But the subject and occasion required it. The first part was intended for a duplicate by another hand, and all that follows to this page for communication. I have now carried forward the history of my life from the 10th of January to this time, comprising the following parts or divisions: 1st, My residence in Calcutta to the 17th of February; 2d, My journey to Lucknow, ending the 27th of March; 3d, My residence at Lucknow, a long chapter, closed the 27th of August; 4th, Journey to Benares, 12th of September; Lastly remain to follow; 5th, My residence at Benares; 6th, My return to Calcutta; 7th, Preparations for my voyage; and 8th, The voyage. What variations, fortune, or the will of God may have yet in store, I dare not attempt to conjecture. I fear a multitude of unseen obstructions, for the great and interesting events of my life have hitherto been ever regulated by an influence overruling and defeating my determinations, making these the instruments of its own decrees. But, excepting my separation from you, I have no great cause to murmur; but the contrary. In one instance of disappointment, which I thought at the time a cruel one,

I now believe that I was most fortunate. You will probably recollect to what I allude. I will flatter myself that the worst is past, and the best yet to come at the period to which my hopes originally fixed it. I have yet no news of the Royal Charlotte, the ship expected from St. Helena.

1st of October.—I am indeed a fortunate man, and am tempted to adopt the term even to superstition; and no wonder, for the belief has seized others long since, and universally. The last sentence of the preceding paragraph was the beginning effort of a continuation of my letter, and would probably have been followed by some very foolish reflections, which were prevented by some abrupt, I know not what interruption. Last night, at about nine o'clock, Major Sands brought me the news of Phipps's arrival at Calcutta, and may God bless them both for it! a short but blessed letter from you, dated the 15th of May, the day of your departure from St. Helena, and written on board the Atlas. It tells me only that you were safe on board and well, but it tells enough, and it is written in the language of cheerfulness and of affection. I have also letters from Mr. Corneille, Markham, and Phipps himself, which all assure me that you had received benefit from the voyage, and looked better, Markham says, than he had ever seen you. I am satisfied; I have no fears for what was to follow. My dread proceeded from the reiterated affliction which you had suffered from the first ceremonious parting with your friends in Calcutta, and with Calcutta, to the departure of the pilot, and from the violence of the sea-sickness, with poor Cleveland's death in addition, acting on a frame too delicate for such accumulated agitations. All my past doubts, and the fixed gloom which has so long overspread my imagination, are dissipated, like the darkness before the equinoctial sun rising on the plains of Suckrowl—(do, my Marian, allow me to talk nonsense,) and have given place to the confident hope that every dreaded obstruction will follow them, and that I am once more destined to happiness. I am already happy; for as God is my witness that I prefer your happiness to my own, I feel the measure of my present joy full, with the information which I have recently received. Captain Phipps writes that he had your orders to deliver your packet to me with his own hand, and he is coming with it. I have written to accelerate his coming by relays of bearers from two or three stages beyond Patna; but as the roads have been unusually overflowed by the rains and the swelling of the river, he may not be here this week yet. But I have food enough for my heart to feast on for more than a week to come. Now gravely attend to what follows, and judge whether I have not reason to be superstitious. The despatches which Phipps is bringing were closed, and delivered on the 15th of May, and were the first which you have written. My first letters which were written for conveyance by land, and probably the first that you will have received written after my departure from Calcutta, were also despatched on the 15th of May. The same coincidence of dates has likewise appeared in that of your arrival at St. Helena, and the departure of the Surprise from England, both on the 28th of April. I shall compare your journal with my own for more similarities.

At what a time will you have arrived in England! If nothing has happened between the Surprise's departure and your landing, to change the public opinion of your husband, (and I think it not likely that it should have been changed,) you will find his name standing in high and universal credit, and what a welcome will it be to you! I have now but one wish remaining—(yes, one more,) viz., to be able to leave the stage of active life while my fortune is in the zenith of its prosperity, and while I have a constitution yet repairable.

I must repress myself, for if I write all that the fulness of my heart is ready to dictate, I shall never come to an end, and I have this to copy. How it is to go, I know not. I shall trust one to Mr. Boddam, and the other to Mr. Hay in Calcutta, to be despatched as each shall find means. Adieu, my beloved, my most deserving and lovely Marian. May the God whose goodness I have so wonderfully experienced, bless you with health, safety, and comfort, and me with the repossession of my sweet Marian! Amen! Amen! Amen! I never loved you so much as I do at this instant, and as I have loved you since the delightful news of last night.

P. S.—Remember me affectionately to Mrs. Motte.

8th of October.—Phipps arrived yesterday morning before seven, and delivered me your letter. I am the happiest man living; but it is not in a P. S. that I can answer it, or say—no, nor can a folio volume describe—what my feelings have been, and are from the perusal of it. Let me only assure you that I will comply most sacredly with your injunctions. I leave you to recollect them. One you cannot have forgotten. May the God of goodness guard and bless you. How wonderful has been his goodness to both, and I will trust in its continuance. I will not believe that I have been raised in my hopes above the heights of mortality, to be dashed to the earth with a severer fall. Your permission, my Marian, was unnecessary. All mankind knew it as soon as I did, and some before, and in truth I think all the world is mad with joy for it. But I forgot myself. I shall hasten to Calcutta, and, if possible, leave it again before the end of this year. Adieu, my most beloved! Adieu!

11th of October.—The shawl commission which you gave to Johnson is executed. I have not seen the shawls; but Cashmeereemall has brought me others of his own taste, which are beautiful beyond imagination; and I have countermanded the shawl handkerchiefs ordered in your letter. Why should I provide paltry things for you, when I carry with me inimitables?

To the same.

Calcutta, 14th November, 1784.

My dearest Marian,—I despatched my last number on the 20th October from Benares to Mr. Boddam to be forwarded by land with public advices of the death of Mr. Wheler. This event determined me to quicken my return to Calcutta. Having accordingly crowded into two days the business which I had before allotted to ten, I took my leave of the Prince on the 21st, and began my departure the next morning at four o'clock; and thus ended the "Chapter of Benares." The Prince had before fixed on the 29th for beginning his march to Furrukhabad, there to treat for his return on terms of honour and safety to his father's court. I have given him the attendance of my own body-guard, and provided for the additional retinue of five battalions of the Nabob Vizier's sepoys; besides employing what personal influence I possessed to promote his success. My feelcherra carried me that night to Buxar, where I slept, and proceeded (to the great regret of Mr. Eaton) the next morning, the 23d. At eight that evening I arrived at Patna, halted one day, and returned to my boat after supper. At half-past ten the following night I reached Baugulpoor, where I found Mr. and Mrs. Chapman, with a host of friends; your good friend, Mrs. Powney, among the foremost, standing on the ghaut, and almost in the water, to receive me. I must not omit Miss Touchet. Here I waited two days for Dr. Balfour, who had insisted on accompanying me to Calcutta, and had promised to join me at Patna, but missed me. On the 27th, after supper, I took my leave of my two excellent friends, and departed. (Mrs. Chapman is, in your sense of the word, very happy.) At twelve we passed the dreadful rocks of Cohlgong, and as the moon was full, and shone very bright, I ordered the manjee to steer between them and the shore, expecting to find some remains of the memorable vortex of 1782; but my virtue was not worth the trial: my curiosity only was gratified by a clear display of the cause of the eddy, which was a nulla tumbling down in the month of August with a flood from the hills, and meeting the stream of the river rendered more rapid by the obstruction of the rocks. The nulla was now dry, and only showed a hollow, like a notch, in the bank. But I must abridge my journey. I arrived at Rangametty on the 29th, at sunrise, stayed there a day and a half with Sir John and Lady D'Oyley, and by making a small journey from Dowdpoor to near Nuddea by land, got to Sooksaugur at noon on the 31st. The Begum sent me more than one message expressive of her disappointment at my passing the city, as she had prepared an elegant display of your couches and chairs for my entertainment. These are since arrived, with a letter for you, recommended most earnestly to my care. There are two couches, eight chairs, and two footstools, all of the former patterns, except two of the chairs, which are of buffalo horn, most delicately formed, and more to my taste than the others; not designed for fat folks, nor romps; nor proper for you, my elegant Marian, to use in the presence of your husband. I had originally determined to make Sooksaugur the termination of my journey, and Mr. Stables's absence, whom I had left at Rangametty,—not so rapid a traveller as Mr. and Mrs. Hastings, rendered my speedier return to Calcutta every way unnecessary. Here I received letters from Major Scott, dated the 15th May, followed by an overland packet, without a letter from him; it was not his fault; but with one from the Court of Directors, dated the 15th June, as unpleasing as any that I ever received from that body in the time of General Clavering. Scott will tell you its purport, and my conduct regarding it. I can learn nothing of my own destiny by this packet, and indeed I suspect that it was hurried away without notice, lest I should. The only circumstance which it contains to please me is that the news of your arrival at St. Helena had already reached England. I hope it will contribute to make them more decided before the next despatch. I am literally *sick* of suspense; yet I will wait for one more packet to take my final resolution. In the meantime I have engaged a passage in the Barrington, and as the Board (that is Mr. Macpherson) had before destined her despatch to take place on the 20th of this month, I have desired them to revoke the order, which they have agreed to, and she is to wait for me. Thus far I have proceeded with great deliberation. My most zealous friends are very desirous of my remaining till I am relieved by an appointed successor; but their reasons are such as I can never adopt, nor allow; nor will I on any consideration stay till my successor arrives, if I can get away, though it be but a day, before his arrival. I still abide by the resolution which I communicated to you in my letter of the 24th of September, that is to say, "If I am required by authority to stay, and have the powers given me which ought to belong to my office, and proper objects are assigned for my stay, I will stay, however repugnant it may be to my own feelings, or hazardous to my health: but I will not stay with my present colleagues to thwart me, and impede all my endeavours; nor will I stay, merely to fill up the gap of my office until it may suit the convenience, caprice, or worse motive, of my superiors to fill it." As yet I am at liberty to make my option; but I think that I cannot remain so longer than till the arrival of the next despatch from England, which I suppose must be here in another month. I am not sure that I ought to wait longer for it, but form my conclusions and my determination on the delay itself. My health I shall make no consideration, nor will I form my determination on any injuries done me by the Directors, *my new friends*. At the same time I must tell you that I fear that I have gained no more than a suspension from sickness, but have added nothing to the strength of my constitution by my late absence from Calcutta. I have been ailing ever since my return. Every night I have a regular return of feverish symptoms, for I cannot call them a fever; and the swelling in my ancles, which I thought had totally left me, has again returned. In short, I am little better, but surely something better, than I was this time last year. I am resolved, however, that I will not be sick; nor, if I shall be compelled to sacrifice another year of my life to the service, will I stay beyond June in Calcutta, while there are such climates as Baugulpoor and Benares to repair to. I intend to get the Barrington's saltpetre given to her immediately, and shall propose to load her, with the declaration of my resolution to depart. I do not apprehend that either of my colleagues will attempt to stop me. I wait with inconceivable anxiety for the news of your arrival, and with terror for the event which must have passed long before this. May God preserve you, whatever may be my lot; and yet, if possible, reunite us! Adieu, my beloved!

We have yet met but three in Council, but hitherto have sat in good humour. Macpherson is sick; and so am I; yet I am sure that it is wholly constitutional. I have laboured hard, and my mind harder: my spirits sink with the state of suspense and doubt which I remain in. O, that I could reveal to you all that it is filled with. Gloomy as my thoughts are, you would be pleased with the review of them. Again, may God bless you, my beloved! I dare not add more, though my heart swells with the addition.

To the same.

Calcutta, 26th December, 1784.

My beloved Marian,—I have received your letter of the 3d of August, informing me of your safe arrival in England. I received it on my return from the play. I could not go to bed, but sat reading it till past two, and afterwards lay long after counting three without being able to close my eyes. Whether I was happy, or unhappy in reading it, I cannot tell you. I fear, my disappointment on one subject equalled my joy for your safety, the close of your perils, and the promise that you would soon be as well as you ever had been at any period of your life. I have since thought only on the good; and I thank God for it. The attentions shown to you on your arrival, though what I expected, make no small part of my rejoicing. Something might at the first have been yielded to you on my account; more, surely, to your character which had preceded you, and your character is marked with virtues, all original, and such as would naturally excite curiosity and respect; but I am certain that they who were your first visitors would have wished to repeat their visits early and stimulate others with the same desire to see you.

I read much in your letter to admire, to be delighted with; but nothing that I can reply to. I am pleased that my sister received you at Portsmouth, and that you like her. I am pleased, too, that you are pleased with Mrs. Caillaud.

You say, "you fear they will keep me another year from you." No, my Marian; they shall not; nor do I apprehend it to be the wish of those who have it in their power to detain me. Upon this subject I have written fully to Scott, who will show you what I have written. The sum of it is, that as I have received the most incontestable proofs of the minister's indisposition to me, if I receive no other advices, or no letter from England by the 31st of January, I will wait no longer, but instantly embark. Still one chance may detain me, which will be the refusal of my present colleagues to give me the assurance, which I promised the Nabob Vizier that I would demand, of their punctual adherence to my engagements with him. I have no doubt that they will promise it in the manner that I shall prescribe; and it will not be safe for them to break it. As to the Fox, I do not expect to see her here, though I should wait for her till the end of February.

I have written so much by the Surprise, that I have nothing left but repetition. She sailed from Culpee the 14th, and carried four letters from me. One, No. 26, a duplicate; the original gone to Bussora. No. 27 contained a copy of my letter to the Court of Directors, dated 22d of November; a translation of your firmaun, and a list of shawls given in charge to Captain Price. No. 28 contained a letter from Munny Begum, a letter written to you by the Prince, and translations of both. Both letters, indeed all three, are intolerably long. The captain had also charge of two shawls in one package, and your firmaun. The first was a present from the Prince; but of no other value.

I shall enclose in this nothing but a correct copy of the Prince's narrative. If it is good for nothing else, it is at least a beautiful specimen of good penmanship.

But what have I to do with letters or enclosures? If I am in luck, I shall be with you as soon as this; for since I wrote the preceding, I have received and studied Mr. Pitt's bill, and receive it as so unequivocal a demonstration that my resignation of the service is expected and desired, that I shall lose no time in preparing for the voyage. It is now determined, not absolutely, because I must first exact from Mr. Macpherson his engagement to abide by my settlement with the Nabob Vizier, and I have no doubt of his acquiescence. This point settled, it is determined absolutely, absolutely. I will wait for no advices. They have given me my freedom, and opened the road to my happiness. Yet, my Marian, forgive me. I do not feel the joy which I ought. I am too much attached to my public character and its relations, and dread the ruin which I see impending over them. But I have acquitted myself of all my obligations, and am not accountable for the crimes or errors of others. I have given Sands and Francis their charge for preparing everything for the embarkation, and am going as soon as this is closed to whisper Mr. Barton to hasten the lading of the Barrington. May Heaven prosper my design, bless my Marian, and speedily reunite us with every necessary means of happiness in our possession! If I have enough for a decent subsistence, I want no pensions, and despise titles. At this instant I have but one wish, and a *little one* annexed to it; and, O God, grant them! Amen.

To the same.

Calcutta, 10th January, 1785.

My dearest Marian,—I believe I said in my last that I should sail early in this month. I did write so to Major Scott; but it was from a recent impression, which a slight consideration effaced, and left in its place the resolution which I had before formed of waiting till the 31st; and on the 31st I intend to take my leave, if no great event intervenes, and I can form no conjecture of any that can detain me longer. It is, indeed, very much my desire to be gone before any advices can arrive from England for a reason which I cannot trust to writing, but which you, my Marian, will applaud, and the public ought to applaud if they knew it.

I have declared my intention to Mr. Macpherson and to Mr. Stables. Both have assured me that they will not break my engagements with the Nabob of Oude; and Mr. Macpherson has promised me in the most pointed manner that he will in everything make my example the rule of his conduct.

We shall touch no where in the voyage, and Captain Johnson hopes to complete it in four months. It is therefore probable that I shall be with you before you receive this letter. Why, therefore, should I lengthen it?

I have not been well since my return to Calcutta; but I do not charge my complaints entirely to my constitution, nor entirely to the climate, nor to both; for my mind has been kept in continual fatigue, and will have little repose till I am out of pilot's water.

May God preserve you in health, and promote and prosper our meeting!

Till then, adieu, my beloved! Look at the date of this. How different are my present prospects from those which I had at this time the last year.

This day I shall keep sacred. I shall give much of it to business, but no part of it to society. Remember me affectionately to Mrs. Motte.

To the same.

Calcutta, 31st January, 1785.

My dearest Marian,—To-morrow morning I take my leave of Calcutta. The captain is gone, and will be ready to weigh as soon as he sees my flag. The Hussar, a Danish ship, is also on the point of sailing, with Mr. and Mrs. Halhed, passengers. As she has the reputation of greater speed even than the Barrington, and Captain Johnstone himself (our captain) thinks that she may get home before us, I therefore write this in prevention of such an event, lest you should be alarmed by it, to inform you of the probability that it may happen, that I am on the way, and that I am well, in defiance of all my cares, anxieties, and troubles. More I need not say, as I cannot easily support the thought of its being of use to say even so much as I have said.

May God prosper me in my voyage, and preserve you, my sweet Marian, in health and safety.

CHAPTER VIII.

Mr. Hastings's position at Home and Abroad—Departure from India—Return to England—Reception—Re-union with Mrs. Hastings—Correspondence with the Court of Directors.

BEFORE I turn my page in the history of the great man of whose long and chequered career I have undertaken to be the chronicler, it will be necessary to advert to certain circumstances, which, though vaguely hinted at in some of the letters introduced into the previous chapter, have not yet received, either there or elsewhere, the full measure of notice which they deserve. Enough has, indeed, been said to show, that of his high, and responsible, and thankless situation, Mr. Hastings had for some time become weary. Thwarted in all his favourite measures, or else compelled to carry them out by a species of moral violence; checked and reproved by his superiors at home in cases where he had a right to anticipate praise; made the subject of frequent and bitter and acrimonious debate in the House of Commons, and of censure in the King's Cabinet; no motive of inferior weight to that which swayed him, namely, an earnest desire to serve his country in spite of herself, could have detained him one moment, after the departure of Mrs. Hastings for Europe, upon the stage of public life. Yet such was the strength of his feeling on this head, and so clear and well arranged were his ideas regarding it, that to the last he seems to have deluded himself into a persuasion that all would come right in the end. From the change in the King's Councils, which brought Mr. Pitt and his friends into office, Mr. Hastings anticipated much. He was aware, no doubt, that they, not less than their predecessors, were, in some sort, pledged to effect great and important changes in the constitution of the Company's governments. But he believed that these changes would neither affect the existence of the Company's rights, considered as a chartered body, nor fail to strengthen the hands of the local authorities where they most required it. Moreover, Mr. Hastings, having repeatedly communicated with the different Cabinets, and stated his own views clearly and explicitly on the subject, was encouraged to expect not only that they would serve as a groundwork for the ministerial device, but that to him, as the real author of the improved system, the care of bringing it first into play would be entrusted. Accordingly he lingered on, after all the ties of his home were severed, and he had formally communicated to the Court of Directors his desire that a successor might be appointed, for the single purpose, as his correspondence shows, of ascertaining how far in the Bill which Mr. Pitt was understood to have proposed, justice would be done, not to his views alone, but to his public and private character as a statesman. It is not worth while to insert any of his letters, written at this time, which, whether official or otherwise, breathe the same spirit throughout, namely, a self-devotion, a zeal for the public service, and a total forgetfulness of personal interests and feelings to which I have nowhere found a parallel. For the only one among them all which might have thrown some new light on the history of the writer's character, namely, that addressed to Mr. Pitt, I have not been able to discover, though I have searched for it in every quarter where there appeared the smallest chance of success, and find constant allusions to it in other portions of the correspondence which he kept up all this while with his friends and supporters.

Mr. Hastings's opinion of the talents and disposition of Mr. Pitt appear to have been at one time very high. "I wish," he says in a communication to Major Scott, in which the fact of his having written to the new prime minister is noticed, "that he would take the trouble to read my other letters concerning the prince, which you will have in succession in the present despatches. Do you present my letter to him. I do not choose to give you a copy of it, out of respect to the person to whom I have addressed it. Indeed, I have not time, if I thought it right, as it was with difficulty, with the aid of two hands, that I could get it written fair in time. It contains much information little known, and though laboured to be concise, it fills six sheets. Would to God that I was in England. I could give to such a man my labour with pleasure, without office or reward, or desire of either." The letter from which this extract is taken bears date 11th December, 1784. It was written ere any information respecting either the India Bill or Mr. Pitt's method of introducing it into the House of Commons had reached him, and is therefore filled with proud and happy anticipations of the benefits about to be secured by it to the Company, to the people of India, and to himself. But the passage of a few days sufficed to dispel the illusion. The following tells its own tale in language which I could not improve, and I therefore insert it at length.

To Major SCOTT.

Calcutta, 26th December, 1784.

My dear Scott,—On the 20th I had the inexpressible happiness to receive your land packets of the 3rd of August, with one from Mrs. Hastings, containing the first intelligence of her safe arrival in England. Yours were dated the 11th June and 2nd and 3rd of August. I suspect that the original of the first, for this was a copy, was intended for the Directors' packet of the 19th June. All my feelings on the perusal of these despatches were engrossed by a private subject; I could, therefore, well bear my disappointment in the public advices. I regret that you could not send me a copy, or an abstract at least, of Mr. Pitt's bill. I received an abstract from

Mr. Boddam; but it was very imperfect, and in some parts erroneous. I have, however, studied and corrected it by the newspapers and printed debates, and have conceived a full idea of its tenor, scope, and substance. It has destroyed all my hopes, both here and at home; for, let its defects be what they may, I conclude that that is for some years at least irrevocable and irreparable. There is one which I suspect nobody foresaw in it: that it will throw all the wealth of the Company's servants into the hands of the foreign traders, and drive many, by the dread of a tribunal, which is already regarded with all the horrors of an inquisition, into other countries.

My situation is become worse than it was, and I fear I must form my final resolution upon this unofficial report of it, as I cannot expect the Fox to arrive before the month of March, to which period I cannot wait with the moral certainty that her despatches, come when they will, will contain the prescribed grounds of my recall.

Mr. Pitt's introductory speech is a very unpleasant indication of his disposition towards me, and is in effect more inimical to me, as, under the cover of moderation and candour, it admits all the slanders which Mr. Fox and Mr. Burke rendered ineffectual by the personal rancour which they manifested in their first promulgation of them. It contains the same indiscriminate abuse of the Company's servants, and this is expressed in the same trite epithets, on which he dwells with a most disgusting emphasis and reiteration. Nor will it avail me that my name is not mentioned, nor any allusion made to my conduct, since the criminations must have been heard and read in connexion with slanders, which were recent in every man's remembrance. Take the following examples from the printed debates which you have given me:—

Page 135.—"It must on all hands be admitted, that there doth exist a great and urgent necessity for the interference of the Legislature with regard to the East India Company and the future government of our possessions in India."

Page 140.—"The first and principal object will be to take care to prevent the Government (*i. e.* Bengal) from being ambitious and bent on conquest. Propensities of that nature have already involved India in great expenses, and cost much bloodshed. Ambition and trouble are companions but too often; and they have proved particularly hurtful to our interests in India, &c. &c."—What follows is worse in its principle than in its implication of my character.

Page 148.—"The retrenchment of our establishments in that country.—At present it is a well-known fact that all our establishments there are very considerably overcharged; at any rate, therefore, there must be no augmentation suffered, &c." "It will be necessary by proper provisos to compel the execution of these points, and the better to guard against the continuance of that rapacity, plunder, and extortion, which is shocking to the feelings of humanity and disgraceful to the national character, &c. &c."

Page 149.—With regard to disobedience:—"Such persons shall be considered as guilty of offences punishable in the degrees stated in the bill, which shall contain a special exception of those guilty of disobedience of orders, and other crimes, which, from the consequences being of a most fatal tendency, must be punished with great severity."

Page 150.—"Either a new process must be instituted, or offences equally shocking to humanity, opposite to justice, and contrary to every principle of religion and humanity, will prevail unchecked, uncontrolled, and unrestrained."

Page 152.—"And as a further means of rendering such a tribunal awful, and its plans of preventing the perpetration of crimes shocking to humanity from continuance effectual, it should be armed with the power of examining the parties charged as delinquents by interrogatories as to the value of their effects, &c. &c."

Why, Scott! what devil has Mr. Pitt dressed for his exemplar, and clothed with such damnable attributes of ambition, spirit of conquest, thirst of blood, propensity to expense and troubles, extravagance and improvidence in creating overcharged establishments, disobedience of orders, rapacity, plunder, extortion!!! It is a pity that the thirst of blood was out of its place. Had it closed the list, it would have made a complete climax, gradually heating the imagination to a degree of abhorrence due to the utmost perfection of human guilt. But lest this effect should be lost, Mr. Pitt winds up his description in a general display by which the great prototype of the mighty master's mind shines forth in the full blaze of complicated horror; armed with crimes shocking to the feelings of humanity, disgraceful to the national character, fatal in their tendency, opposite to justice, and contrary to every principle of religion and morality!!! And am I this character? Assuredly not: but most assuredly was it the declaimer's intention to fix it upon me; for much of this, and the whole in substance, but with less aggravation, had been before given to me by my avowed enemies, and no part of it to any individual but myself. I am therefore the sole proprietor of the whole aggregate allowance.

Perhaps, if I were to reproach him with the gross injury which he has done me, he would deny the intention. But why should he? He is above my reach; and a mind capable of using such insidious means to taint an innocent character with such a mass of infamy may easily affect to glory in the consciousness of its own virtue, and lay claim to the public applause for such a manifestation of it. But it may be said, that the crimes which Mr. Pitt has enumerated were designed only for argument, theoretically proving by a necessary deduction that such must be the consequences of a government not constituted on systematic principles, and subsisting without an efficient control. He has taken care to obviate this construction of his expressions; he does not state what might be, but affirms that it actually existed, and declares the object of his bill to be to prevent the "continuation" of it—a word six times implied by the construction, and thrice used in direct terms.

I will do nothing precipitately, nor determine on any act while I feel my mind warmed with a sense of personal injury; neither shall such impression be allowed to have any, even the faintest, share in forming my ultimate election; but I may be allowed to draw conclusions from the demonstration which the minister has afforded me of his dispositions towards me, in default of the arrival in time of those orders from home which I have declared shall determine me to resign the service or to retain it. It may not have been prudent or convenient for him to have proposed my removal from office directly; but it is impossible that, thinking me, or affecting to think me, such a man as he has described me, he should either desire me to remain, afford me his confidence, or add to my powers. And as the new system has thrown the whole authority of the Company into his hands, I may conclude with a moral certainty that the next regular official advices, come when they may, will be such as I have stated to be—if not an express, equivalent to an express, order for my recall.

If I hear no more from England by the 31st of

January, I will allow that period to elapse; but will most certainly form my determination then on the knowledge which I already possess, though not official, nor such as may be called authentic. This is in strict consistency with all my past declarations; but these seem not to be credited; and even you, my friend, write as if I had never made them.

By the Surprise I wrote to Mr. Pitt, and sent the letter to you sealed, deeming this a necessary respect, with a request that you would deliver it. I do now most heartily repent that I wrote it, though I most enthusiastically believed every syllable that either bestowed praise on him, or implied a trust in his candour for the effect of my opinions. These too I find, in all points, diametrically opposite to his; and the only reception that I now expect for it is such as Mr. Francis would give it—that it will be sneeringly called a fine poetical fiction. And let it be so. But enough of it.

I have begun a plan of retrenchment, which already comprises almost the whole civil establishment. On the 20th I read it privately to Macpherson and Stables in Council, the secretaries being ordered to withdraw; and I premised it by an offer to make it in terms the joint act of the Board, if they approved it. They seemed pleased with it; and Stables, in a very earnest manner, thanked me for it; but both desired to consider it (which I thought very proper), and Mr. Stables took it home with him. I have not talked with either upon it since; but I think it will pass; and I will follow it with a larger retrenchment of the military establishments. Both will be publicly ascribed to me, and will draw on me infinite odium; for a multitude of servants will be deprived of very lucrative emoluments, and some of them men who have strong claims upon me bv patronage from home. Perhaps, too, Mr. Pitt, instead of thanks, will reproach me with these attempts at reformation as demonstrations of the truth of his representation of the corruptions requiring it. Yet I will steadfastly pursue my purpose, and most fervently pray that this good act may close my service. I shall leave nothing else to be done.

One more good work has been effected; and that too is liable to the same unpopular consequences. I found Mr. Macpherson on my arrival engaged in a contest with Colonel Gordon about military authority. The Government of Madras had sent seven broken corps of the King's forces, with above eighty officers, to Bengal, to be subsisted or sent home; some without any official notice. Colonel Gordon, the King's senior officer, had received orders from General Campbell, his superior on the coast, restricting the recruiting service; and Colonel Gordon denied the right of the Board to act in this or any other point which respected the King's service but by his authority, and *that* he refused to grant, except in the terms of his orders from General Campbell. He on a late occasion went further, and protested against the appointment of a court martial held without his warrant.

On all these points the decisions have been complete. I will get copies of them made to go with this. The sum of all is this:—

1st. That as many of the King's officers as can be accommodated with passages to England on the Company's ships shall be allowed them, with an allotment of seven for every ship.

2nd. That such officers as choose it shall be allowed a liberal allowance as passage-money, and provide for themselves.—This has given general satisfaction.

3rd. That all the King's soldiers whose term of service is expired, according to the King's proclamation, and are willing to enlist with the Company, shall be recruited without regard to General Campbell's exceptions.

4th. That neither Colonel Gordon nor General Campbell, nor any King's officer, has a legal right to grant warrants for courts martial, that authority being exclusively in the Board.

The other regulations are mere provisions to render these effectual.

Colonel Gordon is a genteel and liberal officer; but he seems to be too much in dread of the reproach of deserting the cause of his corps. He and I are still on the best terms; and I yet hope to make him instrumental in procuring for us the recruits which we want. They are absolutely necessary, when we are on the eve of a large reduction of the native corps; for, if they should say we will not be reduced, I do not know how we could compel them but by a greater strength in our own countrymen.—I am, my dear Scott, your most affectionate.

P.S. I forgot to mention that Mr. Macpherson and Mr. Stables, who have both seen the debates, draw the worst conclusions to my interest, and no good ones to their own, from them, But their fears are over. They see themselves fixed, and me unsupported at home. I will put their moderation to the test in the course of the next week.

I thank you for your speech of three minutes in vindication of the service. Neither arithmetic nor geometrical reasoning can furnish a reply to such an argument; yet the flippancy of Mr. Francis's logic may prove, or affirm without designing to look for proof, that of the numbers who have not returned from Bengal with fortunes, one half spent them abroad with extravagance, and the rest are dead with debauchery.

December 27th.—I have seen, read, and abstracted Mr. Pitt's bill. It has determined me. I shall make an early trial of my colleagues on the affairs of Oude; and if they will engage to abide by my engagements there, I will depart as soon as the Barrington is ready. She is now loading.

The determination avowed in this letter Mr. Hastings lost no time in carrying into effect. He made his appeal to the Council; he received from them an assurance that the affairs of Oude would be carried on according to the system which he had devised; and he conveyed to the Court of Directors a formal resignation of his powers in the following terms:—

To the Honourable COURT of DIRECTORS of the Honourable United EAST INDIA COMPANY.

Fort William, January, 1785.

Honourable Sirs,—Some authentic advices which I have received by land from England since the despatch of the Surprise have determined me to leave this Government at the close of this month, and to take my passage for England in your ship the Barrington.

It would be to assume an unwarranted self consequence to assign the reasons for this departure from the letter, though with a strict adherence to the principle of the declarations which I made in my last address, dated 22d November, by the Surprise. Yet I may be allowed, in a very few words, to state that I conceive it to be now impossible for your commands to require my stay in the terms which I might have had the presumption to suppose within the line of possibility, were such to be your pleasure; that it is scarcely possible for your commands on any subject which could concern my stay to arrive before the season requisite for my departure; that I rather feel the wish to avoid the receipt of them than to await their coming; and that I consider myself in this act as the fortunate instrument of dissolving the frame of an inefficient Government, pernicious to your interests, and disgraceful to the national character, and of leaving one in its stead, such as my zeal for your service prompts me to wish perpetual in its construction, to every purpose efficient.

After a service of thirty-five years from its commencement, and almost thirteen of that time passed in the charge and exercise of the first nominal office of this Government, I do not part from it with indifference. I owe to my ever honoured employers the service of my life, and would with the devotion of a heart animated with the highest sense of gratitude offer it even with life, if the service could be accepted, or could, when accepted, contribute to the advancement of their interests, in return for the unexampled instances which I have received of their generous support and protection. Such professions are indeed easily made, and I know not how mine can ever be put to the test. But my conscience both avows them, and prompts me to declare that no man ever served them with a zeal superior to my own, nor perhaps equal to it. I have the honour to be, with the greatest respect and attachment, honourable Sirs, your most obedient and most faithful servant.

Having sealed and delivered over for despatch this official paper, Mr. Hastings turned his undivided attention to the adjustment of the petty matters, such as leave-taking, and the winding up of his private affairs, which alone stood between him and a satisfactory removal from the scene of all his labours. His property, inconsiderable in the extreme, when the length of his services is taken into account, and a comparison is instituted between his savings and those of men, I do not say of a rank analogous to his own, but in every respect his inferiors,—he had already converted into good bills, except only such ready money as sufficed for the purchase of two or three valuable diamonds. His houses and lands were either sold or ordered for sale, his old and faithful servants pensioned, and letters of farewell written to all the native princes and chiefs with whom, for thirteen years, he had been accustomed to correspond as an equal. Then followed,—to him the most trying ordeal of all,—the reception of addresses from his countrymen, who, whether in the civil or in the military services, lamented his departure as a private misfortune not less than as a public calamity. Finally, he made his will, entrusted it to the keeping of his friend and secretary, Mr. Thompson, and on the 1st of February rendered up, in the last Council which he attended, the keys of the public treasury and of Fort William. He accompanied the act by a minute strikingly characteristic of the man. I do not know how the document may be accounted of by others, but to me there is something very touching in the style, and I therefore insert it.

1st February, 1785.

Governor-general,—I have summoned this meeting of the Board to comply with the preliminary forms which the usage of the service has prescribed as necessary on my departure from the presidency. These do not require the formality of a written address, but I could not trust to the feelings, which would naturally be excited by the most awful and important act of my public life, for the verbal delivery of the sentiments which I may wish to express in the performance of it. The last duty which it will remain for me to discharge will be that of my resignation of the service, which I reserve to the time when the ship in which I am about to depart shall quit her pilot, and I shall send it in writing by the hands of Mr. Larkins, with whose attendance I request the Board to dispense, that he may accompany me so far on my way. I now deliver up to the Board my keys of the treasury, and to Mr. Macpherson the keys of Fort William, both under the necessary reservation of my right to resume them in the event (which God forbid) of any accident befalling the ship in her passage to the open sea, or any other contingency compelling my return.

I take my leave of the members of the Board with the warmest and most affectionate wishes for the prosperity and success of their public administration, and for their private ease, credit, and happiness. I regret that the custom of the service has not provided any regular channel by which my acknowledgments might be publicly made to the civil servants of the Company for the benefits which I have experienced from their labours. Yet it will be an alleviation of the pain of my approaching separation from them if the Board will permit my sense of their general merits, and the testimony of my particular estimation of them, to be recorded.

It is a pleasure to me to reflect that amidst the multiplied and the pressing occupations of my station, I have not been prevented from bestowing a large portion of my time in a participation of the current duties of the executive offices of every department; and these communications have afforded me the means both of knowing their several talents and of viewing those qualities which form the common character of the service, which I pronounce to be eminently marked with a liberality of sentiment, a susceptibility and firmness of attachment, a disdain of sordid emolument, with a spirit of assiduity, and the consequent expertness in business, exceeding, I dare venture to affirm, the habits of any community under the British empire. The time may come when my testimony, feeble as its present influence may prove, will help to disperse the clouds of prejudice with which the infection of party, and the malignity of particular vengeance, have obscured their real worth, and to display it in its full lustre. In the mean time it would not be presumption in me to attest it who know it, although my testimony were to be opposed by the clamours of a world of ignorance and infatuation.

From the council chamber Mr. Hastings returned to his own home, where a crowd of admiring and sorrowing friends waited to greet him. He accepted their parting adieus not without considerable agitation; and, as if anxious to shorten the trial, proceeded the same afternoon to the quay, where his budgerow, or barge, lay ready to receive him. He immediately went on board, Messrs. Larkins, Thompson, and Thornhill bearing him company, and began that night to move with the tide towards the Barrington's anchorage, at Kidgeree. On the 5th the ship was descried; on the 6th he was in occupation of his cabin; and on the 7th, which in his diary he has marked as Mrs. Hastings's birthday, the shores of India faded from his view. Next day the pilot left him, and his three faithful friends departing in the boat, Mr. Hastings was left to indulge undisturbed both in retrospects of the past and anticipations of the future.

I have nothing to record of Mr. Hastings's homeward voyage, except that in every point of view it appears to have been propitious. The letters in which he alludes to it, and of which it will presently be my business to insert a few specimens, all speak of the time spent on board of ship as spent agreeably; while the appearance by and bye of a narrative of the last three months of his administration, which he compiled during its progress, as well as of two or three imitations in verse of the odes of Horace, show that it was not left altogether unimproved. Moreover, a brief sojourn at St. Helena, where every mark of respect was shown to him, served to break in upon the monotony of a sea life, and supplied him with materials with which to fill up a few pages in his journal, with other records than those which owed their existence to changes in the weather. But the most agreeable feature in the whole matter lay in this, that the progress made from day to day was great, insomuch that within the space of little more than four months from the date of his embarkation, he found himself once more upon

English ground. Mr. Hastings landed at Plymouth on the 13th of June, 1785, and set off at six on the following morning, as rapidly as post-horses could convey him, to London.

I do not know that much good would arise were I to describe at length how great was his disappointment at not finding Mrs. Hastings in town, or how he sent off an express to Cheltenham, whither he learned that she had removed, urging her to return without delay, and proposing to meet her on the road. In like manner I suspect that the reader would scarcely thank me for dwelling on the facts that he waited, as in duty bound, upon the several members of the Cabinet, and on the chairman of the Court of Directors,—from the whole of whom, not less than from a wide circle of friends and admirers, his reception proved to be in the highest degree flattering. Let me, then, be content to state, in few words, that his proceedings were in every respect conformable to the temper and constitution of his nature; that he went with excellent tact through the routine which public duty required; and then flew off to embrace the object of his tenderest regard. They met at Maidenhead Bridge on the evening of the 17th, and on the following day came up again to London. But I must not pursue this subject any further, more especially as in the following letter Mr. Hastings has told his own tale in language more appropriate by far than any which I could select. It is addressed to the gentleman whom he had for some time employed as his private secretary, and for whom he was anxious permanently to provide in the civil service of the Company. It will be read, I think, with great interest.

To Mr. THOMPSON.

Cheltenham, 21st July, 1785.

My dear Thompson,—I have been unfortunate in missing the Surprise's packet, which I regret extremely, because I know that it will be a great disappointment to you and some other of my special friends, though you will know more particulars of my situation and prospects from others than you could from myself. The best that I can tell you is that I found Mrs. Hastings in better health than I have known her possess for some years, and that my reception has been as flattering as pride could wish it. I have experienced the distinction of *digito monstrari, et dicier, hic est;* but my humility preserved itself by the influence of a monitor within that whispered, All this will expire in less than three months. I think much of it is already gone. But as much of it as I wish to retain will, I am persuaded, remain yet for years,—the esteem of those whom all esteem.

I had a pleasant voyage, without bad weather; a clean and tight ship; officers of skill and attention, and even of science; a society that I loved; and a rapid course. The worst of the voyage was that my mind was stupid, and that I never passed a night without a slight fever. Thompson, never take the counsel of a physician that shall bid you go to sea for health. I believe that my first sufferings were from vexation; for you were scarce out of my sight when I recollected that my old bureau, which contained all my most secret papers, and some things of intrinsic value, had been left behind; Francis having, with admirable discretion, sent it out of my sight, and therefore out of my remembrance, as a piece of lumber, to the old house. What heightened my ill humour at this discovery was, the consideration that, though you were almost within hail, it would not be possible for me to apprise you of my distress in less than eighteen months; and that unless you or Larkins had the prudence to suppose that every article of my furniture that could contain anything valuable was worth looking into, these would not only be lost, but, what would be infinitely worse, fall into strange, and possibly scoundrel, hands. I wrote to you about this foolish business from St. Helena, but to little purpose. Your own good sense and recollection had long before provided my relief, or it is past for ever. I am yet vexed whenever I recur to the subject.

We landed at Plymouth on the 13th of last month, and passed through a Lucknow heat to London, where I passed two most uncomfortable days by Mrs. Hastings's being at Cheltenham. Having performed all the duties of loyalty, respect, and civility, I ran away to this place, where I have been since the 5th. We have been drinking the waters ever since, but without any benefit hitherto, and rather the reverse, which people say is a sign that they will do us good.

I had an early visit from young Mr. Anstey, who brought me a very polite letter from his father, whom I am anxious to see, as with his aid I may be more successful in a personal application than I have been by letters. The Directors are to a man friendly to me, and Mr. Smith both obtained the order for publishing the Gheeta with a very handsome preface, and himself attends to the impression. My friends tell me that I defeated my own recommendations in your favour and Turner's, by a subsequent remonstrance against overloading the service with writers and cadets. This checked their zeal, and served as a plea to others; and the next year appointments were made as usual, and mine were forgotten. I fear that in the article of patronage even the most virtuous men of this kingdom want virtue. Nevertheless be you sanguine. I cannot wholly lose my influence, and I will not desist from my purpose till I have obtained your appointment, with the arrears of time, though you may lose the intermediate advantages of emolument.

Tunbridge, 22nd September.—The preceding sheet, and if more it is lost, was written long ago under the impulse of recent disappointment, and the apprehension of losing the next packet, the despatch of which was uncertain, to me at least. I have since had the pleasure of seeing Mr. Anstey, and flatter myself that, short as our acquaintance yet has been, we shall not meet again as strangers, nor without a mutual welcome. I have received yours by the Cornwallis. It is dated the 4th of March, and is the first of yours that I have received. I wished for one by the Surprise, and expected one by the Lord Mansfield; and I must tell you that I shall feel a repeated and mortifying disappointment by every ship's arrival that does not bring a letter from you. But my greatest disappointment arises from your total silence in that which I have received concerning my bureau. It contained many letters and other papers which I would not for the world have seen by strangers, and some not even by you, implicit as my confidence is in you. There are also some miniature pictures which I should grieve to lose, and trash immeasurable. And why do I tell you this? The life of man will have run out much of its course ere you can avail yourself of this information, if you have waited for it; and how can you avail yourself of it? I have letters from Larkins, but these, too, give me no intimation of what I want.

I have led a most idle life, but not wholly unprofitable, having been allowed to contribute some little good to the service, which would not have taken place perhaps had I stayed in Bengal. I have not time to detail the particulars, nor am I sure that it would be proper. I am sanguine in the hope that I may be instrumental in undoing the mischiefs created by the last Indian Act. I will try at least, and shall think it the best deed of my life if I can effect it. Let my friends, but only special friends, know that I have such hopes and such intentions.

How much have I to write, could I indulge my inclination; but I must be short.

We are both well, but neither very well. Mrs. Hastings always remembers you, and speaks of you with an affection kindred to my own. We are at this time in a community, among which Lord Mansfield's partiality has made it fashionable to regard us with an uncommon degree of attention and respect. Indeed, my dear Thompson, I should wrong your sensibility, were I to conceal from you what would afford it the most pleasing gratification, that I find myself everywhere and universally treated with evidences, apparent even to my own observation, that I possess the good opinion of my country. Yet this blessing (for such it is, and I would not forfeit it for lacs), is not without its alloy, since it holds me up as an object of public calumny, which I could well support were I the sole object of it. Nor is it malice that assails me. Such is the profligacy of the ruling manners, that there are multitudes who get their bread by detraction; but so little of system is there in this vile science, that even the similitude of character is scarce ever preserved in the features which are held forth to the public in such compositions; and for the newspapers, even indifferent anecdotes of persons are often published without a spark of truth to justify them.

I am yet unsettled, but am in treaty for an old family estate of no value, which has employed me in a longer negociation than would have served for the acquisition of a province; and if I get it, I shall pay almost twice its worth, according to the common market price.

Your sentiments of the person who is the principal subject of your letter are literally mine, and, what is more, I hear them from the mouths of all men. Yet, bad as he is—but enough.

I did not tell you that I was early summoned to receive the thanks of the Directors for my services, and the chairman who read them dwelt with a strong emphasis on the word *unanimously*. From the King and Queen my reception was most gracious. The Board of Control has been more than polite to me, for they have quoted me as authority, and so have the Court of Directors—both a little more than I like, and in a way that I dislike. My friends expected more, but I can almost assure you that I have received the full recompense of all my services, and I am thankful for it; for the King cannot bestow any honour superior to a good name; and with a larger income I should lose what my present will compel me to—retirement. No, I have not said all. Lord Thurlow has been more substantially my friend than King, Ministers, and Directors.

Tell Wilkins that his Gheeta is printed, presented to the King, and published. Mr. Smith inspected the press, and zealously promoted my application for the patronage of the Court of Directors, by whose authority it was printed. I have yet but one copy, but I believe that some will be sent for his use. I don't know how the public will relish it. If it is abused, Wilkins has a good shelter by standing behind me.

In the voyage I amused myself in writing a history of the last three months of my government, in which I wound up all the preceding years. It has been of signal use, and is in the hands of the two rulers of the two great Indian Boards, *i. e.* Mr. Dundas and Mr. Devaynes, who both (and others with them) profess to have derived much instruction from it. I am myself not dissatisfied with it. It will be an antidote against the poison of false "*statements*." I wish you could see it.

Don't forget to send a good horse for Mr. Corneille. I promised him that you would write to him, and offered your services for other commissions. He is a worthy and most hospitable man.

My Arab arrived in excellent condition, and is wonderfully admired. I ride him in spite of his beauty and long tail, though both valid objections; for this is a land of ostentation, and therefore every body detests it in others. I give them little cause.

I must trouble you with a few commissions:—

1. All my shawl goats by Carr died in the voyage. Pray get me some, and send one, or at most two, but not more, by every ship that will take them, and bespeak an inclosed berth in each for them; otherwise they will die of ill usage.

2. Send me some seeds of the lichee. Tie them loosely in a coarse cloth or bag, and give them in charge to some one who will take care of them.

3. Seeds of the cinnamon in the like package. Both must be suspended so that a little air may get at them. Turner promised to send me some Bootan turnip seeds, and he must assist you with the goats; that is, he must get them.

4. Custard apple seeds, from my Allipoor trees, whoever is the proprietor of them. Adieu. Yours ever, my dear Thompson, most affectionately.

To the information conveyed in this letter I have very little to add. Mr. Hastings could not speak in terms too strong of the flattering reception which was meted out in all quarters both to himself and Mrs. Hastings, neither were the hopes which he ventured to build upon the circumstance by any means extravagant. For Mr. Hastings seems to have coveted retirement rather than the entrance on a new field of public life; and he was surely not sanguine if he presumed to anticipate that he would be permitted to indulge his own moderate wishes unmolested. Nevertheless he had not long breathed the air of his native country ere causes of discomfort began to present themselves; the first of which, strange to say, emanated from the very body which had loaded him on his arrival with praises and honours. He had resided but a short time in Cheltenham when he received from the secretary to the Court of Directors a letter, reiterating the Court's desire to be informed of the amount of the several sums which he had accepted as presents from the princes of India, and of the particular uses to which they had been severally applied. The following, while it gives of the subject all the explanation which the writer felt himself capable of communicating, refers to an occasion when the demand had been previously made, and specifies, neither peevishly nor in the tone of one whose self-respect has been wounded, the circumstances which caused him to treat the Court's request with neglect. I do not know how the letter may be regarded by others, but to me it appears in every respect satisfactory.

To Wm. Devaynes, Esq., Chairman of the Hon. East India Company.

Cheltenham, 15th July, 1785.

Sir,—The Honourable Court of Directors in their general letter to Bengal by the Surprise, dated the 16th March, 1784, were pleased to express their desire, that I would inform them of the periods when each sum of the presents mentioned in my address of the 22d May, 1782, was received; what were my motives for withholding the several receipts from the knowledge of the Council, or of the Court of Directors; and what were my reasons for taking bonds for part of these sums, and for paying other sums into the treasury as deposits on my own account.

I have been kindly apprised that the information required as above is yet expected from me.

I hope that the circumstances of my past situation when considered will plead my excuse for having thus long withheld it. The fact is, that I was not at the presidency when the Surprise arrived; and when I returned to it, my time and attention were so entirely engrossed, to the day of my final departure from it, by a variety of other more important occupations, of which, Sir, I believe I may safely appeal to your testimony, grounded on the large portion contributed by myself of the volumes which compose our consultations of that period, that the submission which my respect would have enjoined me to pay to the command imposed on me, was lost to my recollection, perhaps from the stronger impression which the first and distant perusal of it had left on my mind, that it was rather intended as a reprehension for something which had given offence in my report of the original transaction, than as expressive of any want of a further elucidation of it.

I will now endeavour to reply to the different questions which have been stated to me, in as explicit a manner as I am able; to such information as I can give the Honourable Court is fully entitled, and where that shall prove defective, I will point out the easy means by which it may be rendered more complete.

First, I believe I can affirm with certainty, that the several sums mentioned in the account transmitted with my letter above mentioned, were received at, or within a very few days of the dates which are prefixed to them in the account; but, as this contains only the gross sums, and each of them was received in different payments, though at no great distance of time; I cannot therefore assign a greater degree of accuracy to the account. Perhaps the Honourable Court will judge this sufficient for any purpose to which their inquiry was directed; but if it should not be so, I will beg leave to refer for a more minute information, and for the means of making any investigations which they may think it proper to direct, respecting the particulars of this transaction, to Mr. Larkins, your Accomptant-general, who was privy to every process of it, and possesses, as I believe, the original paper which contained the only account that I ever kept of it. In this, each receipt was, as I recollect, specifically inserted with the names of the persons by whom it was made; and I shall write to him to desire that he will furnish you with the paper itself if it is still in being, and in his hands, or with what he can distinctly recollect concerning it.

For my motives for withholding the several receipts from the knowledge of the Council, or of the Court of Directors, and for taking bonds for part of these sums, and paying others into the treasury as deposits on my own account, I have generally accounted in my letter to the Court of Directors of the 22d of May, 1782;—namely, that "I either chose to conceal the first receipts from public curiosity by receiving bonds for the amount, or possibly acted without any studied design which my memory at that distance of time could verify; and that I did not think it worth my care to observe the same means with the rest."

It will not be expected that I should be able to give a more correct explanation of my intentions after a lapse of three years, having declared at the time that many of the particulars had escaped my remembrance; neither shall I attempt to add more than the clearer affirmation of the facts implied in that report of them, and such inferences as necessarily, or with a strong probability, follow them.

I have said that the three first sums of the account were paid into the Company's Treasury, without passing through my hands. The second of these was forced into notice by its destination and application to the expense of a detachment which was formed and employed against Mahdajee Sindia, under the command of Lieut.-colonel Carnac, as I particularly apprized the Court of Directors, in my letter of the 29th December, 1780. The other two were certainly not intended, when I received them, to be made public, though intended for public service, and actually applied to it. The exigencies of the government were at that time my own, and every pressure of it rested with its full weight upon my mind. Wherever I could find allowable means of relieving those wants, I eagerly seized them; but neither did it occur to me as necessary to state on our proceedings every little aid which I could thus procure, nor do I know how I could have stated it, without appearing to court favour by an ostentation which I disdained; or without the chance of exciting the jealousy of my colleagues by the constructive assertion of a separate and unparticipated merit, derived from the influence of my station, to which they might have had an equal claim.

I should have deemed it particularly dishonourable to receive for my own use, money tendered by men of a certain class, from whom I had interdicted the receipt of presents to my inferiors, and bound them by oath not to receive them. I was, therefore, more than ordinarily cautious to avoid the suspicion of it, which would scarcely have failed to light upon me, had I suffered the money to be brought directly to my own house, or to that of any person known to be in trust for me.

I therefore caused it to be transported immediately to the Treasury. There, you well know, Sir, it could not be received without being passed to some credit, and this could only be done by entering it as a loan, or as a deposit.

The first was the least liable to reflection, and therefore I had obviously recourse to it. Why the second sum was entered as a deposit, I am utterly ignorant. Possibly it was done without any special direction from me. Possibly, because it was the simplest mode of entry, and therefore preferred, as that the transaction itself did not require concealment, having been already avowed.

Although I am firmly persuaded that these were my sentiments on the occasion, yet I will not affirm that they were. But of this I am certain, that it was my design originally to have concealed the receipts of all the sums, except the second, even from the knowledge of the Court of Directors. They had answered my purpose of public utility, and I had almost totally dismissed them from my memory.

But when fortune threw a large sum in my way, of a magnitude which could not be concealed, and the peculiar delicacy of my situation at the time in which I received it made me more circumspect of appearances; I chose to apprize my employers of it, which I did hastily and generally. Hastily, perhaps to prevent the vigilance and activity of secret calumny,—and generally, because I knew not the exact amount of the sum of which I was in the receipt, but not in full possession. I promised to acquaint them with the result as soon as I should be in possession of it, and in the performance of my promise I thought it consistent with it to add to the account all the former appropriations of the same kind; my good genius then suggesting to me a spirit of caution which might have saved me the trouble of this apology, had I universally attended to it; for if I had suppressed them, and they were afterwards known, I might have been asked, what were my motives for withholding part of the receipts from the knowledge of the Court of Directors, and informing them of the rest.

It being my wish to clear up every doubt upon this transaction, which either my own mind could suggest, or which may have been suggested by others, I beg leave to suppose another question, and to state the terms of it in my reply, by informing you that the endorsement on the bonds was made about the period of my leaving the presidency in the middle of the year 1781, in order to guard against their becoming a claim on the Company as part of my estate in the event of my death occurring in the course of the service on which I was then entering.

This, Sir, is the plain history of the transaction. I should be ashamed to request that you would communicate it to the Honourable Court of Directors, whose time is too valuable for the intrusion of a subject so uninteresting, but that it is become a point of indispensable duty; I must therefore request the favour of you to lay it, at a convenient time, before them. In addressing it to you personally, I yield to my own feelings of the respect which is due to them as a body, and to the assurance I derive from your experienced civilities, that you will kindly overlook the trouble imposed by it. I have the honour to be, &c.

It does not appear, from the tone of Mr. Hastings's correspondence, nor from any notices which I discover in his diary at this period, that the demand of the Court of Directors, alluded to in the preceding letter, gave him serious annoyance, or excited the smallest apprehension respecting the future. He wrote, indeed, to Mr. Larkins, and requested that from the records in that gentleman's possession, as much fresh light as possible might be thrown upon the subject; but he did nothing more. On the contrary, he resigned himself for some months to the pleasurable feelings which a reunion with a beloved wife, and a return to his native country, were eminently calculated to excite in a heart like his; and passed from place to place, happy in each as it received him, and adapting himself without scruple to the manners of those with whom each change of scene or circumstances required him to associate.

CHAPTER IX.

Personal Proceedings of Mr. Hastings—Purchases Beaumont Lodge—Correspondence with Mr. Dundas, Lord Thurlow, and Mr. Thompson—Mr. Burke's hostility—Charges brought into the House of Commons—Mr. Pitt's Defeat—Correspondence with Mr. Anderson.

FROM the date of the preceding letter up to the spring of 1786, the stream of Mr. Hastings's existence flowed on with so steady a current as to furnish few materials out of which his biographer might succeed in weaving a narrative worthy either of him who should be the subject of it, or of those to whom it might be offered. The ideas which had been generally entertained, previous to his arrival in England, of the enormous fortune which the Governor-general of India had amassed, the quiet and unostentatious tenor of his domestic life wholly dissipated. Mr. Hastings's only home was, for a while, a house in St. James's Place, which he hired ready furnished, and from which he passed by and bye into another, similarly fitted up, in Wimpole Street. His establishment went in nothing beyond what may be accounted necessary for the wants and conveniences of a private gentleman. His movements, no doubt, carried him from time to time to Cheltenham, and Tunbridge Wells, and Bath, and other places then in request; yet they were uniformly performed in the most inexpensive manner, and they invariably left him the very same man that they found him. It is true that his acquaintance was sought, by the noblest and most distinguished persons in the land; and that his own presence, and still more, the presence of Mrs. Hastings, at Court was always acceptable. But these were distinctions which his personal merits had thrust upon him; they were not the results either of sycophancy on his part, or of an unworthy deference to overgrown wealth on the parts of those who offered them. For there never lived a man of simpler habits, or more richly endowed with a becoming self-respect than Warren Hastings. He knew and felt that his legitimate place in society was among the most distinguished of his contemporaries, whether from rank or station; and he passed to and fro from the glitter of fashion into the absolute repose of his own happy home, without being in the most remote degree conscious that any remarkable transition had been effected.

I took occasion, at the opening of this narrative, to state, that one of the earliest dreams in which Warren Hastings indulged, turned upon the re-purchase of the Daylesford estate, where the evening of his days might be spent amid scenes which a thousand personal as well as traditional associations had endeared to him. More than once he had written from India, reminding his attorney that to this end his wishes pointed; and now the first movement which he made after having fairly established himself in London was to open directly a communication with Mr. Knight, who was then, as his family for two generations had been, in possession of the domain. Moreover, he went from Cheltenham to visit the spot; and wandered, in a state of excitement such as I cannot undertake to describe, over all the haunts of his childhood. For the mind of Hastings was of that rare texture which permits the enthusiasm, or, to express myself more correctly, the poetry of feeling to flourish side by side with the clearest judgment and the loftiest and best ordered ambition. It was, therefore, quite as natural to him that his heart should be touched, and his imagination warmed, at the prospect of recovering the patrimony of his ancestors, as that the laudable desire of winning an honoured name to himself, while he conferred lasting benefits on his country, should have carried him through a long career of labour, and difficulty, and annoyance.

It will be seen, from what he says in the concluding paragraphs of his letter to Mr. Thompson, that Mr. Hastings had early made up his mind not to allow the consideration of an exorbitant rate of purchase to stand between him and the accomplishment of his wishes. The offers which he made to Mr. Knight went in consequence far beyond the value of the estate, yet they were rejected. The London merchant did not choose to lay down the distinction which appertains to a landed proprietor; and Mr. Hastings, not without a bitter pang of regret, ceased to importune him. Yet as both the bent of his inclinations and the state of his finances rendered it desirable that he should establish himself somewhere in the country, Mr. Hastings did not abandon his efforts to discover a fitting residence. The results were that he became by and bye the purchaser of a small property on the skirts of Windsor Forest, called Beaumont Lodge, whither, so soon as the mansion-house was made ready for his reception, he removed, and where he spent two or three years in the enjoyment of as much of peace as was at all compatible with the extraordinary turn which party malice contrived, in the interval, to give to his fortunes.

It is not to be supposed that an active and vigorous mind like that of Mr. Hastings would abstain from all interference, even during its season of retirement, in public affairs. He had early conceived a dislike to some portions of Mr. Pitt's India Bill; and finding that it was about to undergo a revision, he freely proffered his assistance, in order to render it more equitable. Not that he wantonly or impudently forced his opinions on those in power. His opinions were held in too much value not to be eagerly sought; and he was too much of a patriot, in the best sense of the word, to withhold them from the members of the King's Government, be they, as individuals, whom they might. Accordingly, when Mr. Dundas applied to him for information concerning certain transactions in which the Nabob of Carnatic was mixed up, he supplied it with the same good will which actuated him in a correspondence into which soon afterwards he entered with Lord Thurlow. I subjoin one letter to the former of these statesmen, and two to the latter, all of them, but especially those addressed to Lord Thurlow, eminently characteristic of the writer. With Lord Thurlow, indeed, Mr. Hastings appears always to have stood upon the very best terms; and to his Lordship he at this time propounded his own device for the better government of the British provinces for the future. But the paper, however valuable, is too voluminous for insertion here. I must, therefore, for the present, lay it aside, not without an impression upon my own mind that it may yet find a place among the literary remains of one who, if he had not attained to greatness as a statesman, would have certainly become great as an author.

To the Right Hon. HENRY DUNDAS.

Cheltenham, 21st August, 1785.

Sir,—I had not the honour to receive your letter till late yesterday. I well remember the letters of which the enclosures in yours are copies, and the construction which the Nabob put upon them. I am certain that these are the same in substance, and of course they must be literally the same, as the copies I received from the Nabob, whether by the hands of the minister Assim Cawn, or by any other channel, I do not distinctly recollect. There was no assurance expressed in either letter, such as the Nabob seems to have inferred from them, not even the most remote sense of it in that from the King; but in the conclusion of that from the Company, I then thought, as I do now, that a mind, sanguine and eager as the Nabob's was in the pursuit of a favourite object, might have allowably drawn such a conclusion from it; since it acknowledges, in very strong and pointed terms, the justice done them by so signal a mark of his confidence, which was ill placed, if it was received without any intention to verify it; neither could the "deposit" be said in any other sense to be "so momentous to his august house."

In a translation from a book of Hindoo morality, I lately met with the following definition of truth: "To communicate to another person what we have heard, seen, or know, in such a manner as to impress and convey the same meaning as passes in our own minds, without using any ambiguity of expression which may be true in one sense, and false in another." It is not impossible that the Nabob, whose reading is very extensive, may have met with this maxim, and applied it to the most obvious sense which the words of the letter conveyed, and in which it most suited his own wishes to understand them; but I cannot think that he intentionally asserted a claim without the conviction of its being well founded.

You owe me no thanks, Sir, for the communication of the manuscript presented to you by Major Scott, because it is my duty, and you have made it equally my inclination to offer you whatever knowledge or materials of knowledge I possess, which may be of use to you in the department over which you preside; but I am much indebted to you for the candour and indulgence with which you have read this paper, and you will allow me to say that I feel my pride highly gratified by your approbation of the sentiments which it contains. I have the honour to be, &c.

To Lord THURLOW.

Bath, 13th January, 1786.

My Lord,—I took the liberty, very soon after my arrival in England, to represent to your Lordship my apprehensions of the consequences which some clauses in the late Act of Parliament respecting India were likely to produce on the minds of the Company's servants, and the peace of our establishments in India; and your Lordship is since in possession of my opinion at large upon the subject. From the advices newly received from Bengal by the Swallow packet, I conceive yet greater cause of alarm; because what was before but predicted is now verified, as far as it can be, in the first operation of a general discontent, and affords the stronger reason to apprehend worse in the sequel, if early means are not taken to prevent it. If your Lordship is of opinion that the Act, or the exceptionable parts of it, ought to be repealed, permit me to suggest that it ought to be done before the receipt of any public remonstrance against it, that the repeal may appear the result of the justice and wisdom of the parent state, not a concession extorted by popular clamour, and by the dread of a revolt following it. For your Lordship knows that there is one great example running in a parallel line with the present case which will both warrant such a suspicion at home, and its success operate as an incitement abroad.

If it shall be determined otherwise, that is, if the Act is to stand, and to be supported by force, either it will not produce that extremity, but the Company's servants will passively submit to it, and the service will in consequence lose its best and ablest hands, which will be supplied with inefficient men from home, and necessity will introduce among those that remain the worst habits of perjury and corruption; or it will provoke a resistance to it which no power from England will be able to overcome: nor is it in the reach of human foresight to say what emergencies will arise out of the effects of such a resistance, when the bonds of subjection are once broken, not only with impunity, but with an ascertained superiority.

For these reasons, my Lord, if I could have had immediate access to you, I would have earnestly solicited it to state the necessity of some immediate steps to be taken for the repeal or amendment of the Act in question, that what is to be done may be done with dignity; and I believe I should have run to town for the purpose, but for a domestic impediment, and for the kindness of my active friend Major Scott who has offered on this account to anticipate the necessary term of his departure for town by a few days: and he will request your Lordship's permission to wait on you in my stead. To him, therefore, I shall refer for all that I could wish to say myself upon this subject, and I do a violence to myself in thus closing it. Only, my Lord, do me the justice to believe that I have a conviction amounting almost to a moral certainty of the truth of my own predictions, so far as they relate to consequences abroad, and that I can have no possible interest of my own in the earnestness with which I make this representation, unless the self-applause may be termed such, which I may hope to derive from being even thus feebly and remotely instrumental in saving a valuable part of the national property from ruin. It is only to your Lordship that I can look for the effective agency of this deliverance; and, had I the influence of your Lordship's place, and possessed the ascendant of such a mind as yours, I would command the redress for which, in my present insignificant state, I can only be an humble solicitor.

I beg your Lordship's pardon for this liberty and intrusion on your time. I have the honour to be, &c.

From Lord THURLOW.

Tuesday, 31st January, 1786.

Dear Sir,—After I saw you yesterday I had an opportunity of reading the plan for transferring the debt from India to England. And it is to you I must again recur at some time or other, for effacing the melancholy impression it left upon my mind; which, I hope, is, in some degree at least, the effect of my ignorance.

If the bills now expected are four millions sterling; if to these are to be added the Arcot debts, and the probable amount of accumulation vested in other funds; the amount of fortunes already amassed in India seems truly formidable. If the immediate investiture of six millions more is expected, that appearance is terribly aggravated, and yet it does not much exceed the conjectures of Sir Elijah Impey on the fortunes of the servants, particularly those officers of the army, the brigadiers, who have enjoyed advanced stations. Whether plunder or parsimony produces this aggravated amount, it seems equally pernicious to the country, if the whole is to be drawn out, never to return.

But does the mischief end here? Will not the same causes continue to produce the same effect, and produce a perpetual course of sending home, by a forced channel of trade, all the produce of Bengal, which the existence of the country can spare, for the benefit of the servants only? And is that preferable to the allowing the competition of foreign stations to be fed by that support, as far as that will sustain it, against the advantages which the possession of the revenue and country will give to the Company?

But, above all, is it necessary that the servan should be allowed to accumulate and remit above a million annually, beyond their current expenses? and if it be, where is the wisdom of calculating upon ten years possession of these provinces?

Perhaps these thoughts are too wide of all mark to be intelligible. But, whatever they are, I propose them only as the subjects of some future conversation; and not to give you the trouble of writing upon them. I am sensible that I have not got far enough into the subject to make that a convenient way of consulting you. I am, dear Sir, sincerely yours.

Early in the following month Mr. Hastings waited upon Lord Thurlow, and laid before him certain remarks which he had compiled with great care. The following correspondence arose out of that interview.

To Lord Thurlow.

1st February, 1786.

My Lord,—The subject of your Lordship's letter is indeed of an alarming nature. I wish it may be in my power to lessen its impression. I would not attempt to efface it, for the truth would be against me.

That the government of a great kingdom, equal in extent and population, and in its natural resources superior to great Britain itself, exercised by a power held at the distance of half the globe by foreign agents, who are precluded by the difference of complexion, manners, religious and political habits, and language, from assimilating with the native inhabitants of it, should be productive of the evil of which your Lordship complains, is a consequence so necessary, that all the powers of legislation, control, and executive, however complete in each, never will, nor is it possible that they should remove it. It is an evil which has arisen out of the constitution, and grown into bulk from the means which have been applied to it from home; and this too, my Lord, is one of the effects of a discordant administration, and the curse of patronage depressing the regular authority. In Bengal, to which I wish to confine the immediate consideration of the question, there are three distinct classes of British subjects; the civil servants of the Company, the military officers, and the free merchants, to which a fourth has lately been added, the judges and dependants of the Supreme Court of Judicature. These make up a number of about 1500 men, who rank in the line of gentlemen, and lay claim both to the means of present subsistence as such, and to a competent provision against the season of repose. The far greater part of this number die without acquiring more than a sufficiency for their daily expenses. Some amass enormous fortunes, which will of course find their way by some channel of conveyance to England, whether for the use of the original proprietors or their heirs; and numberless besides are the calls for little sums in England for the support of near relations or the purchase of necessaries. I cannot pretend to estimate the sums which have been yearly remitted on these accounts, nor prescribe the bounds to which the annual remittances might with proper care and suitable means be reduced. If liberal allowances are expressly granted, with the necessary checks to prevent excesses, they will be deemed exorbitant at home from their comparison with the salaries of similar offices in England. If they are reduced below the necessary means of subsistence, and present subsistence is not enough, the difference will be made up from perquisites—and when men are once let loose from the obligations of strict integrity, and get the habit of carving for themselves, the transition is natural, and will be rapid—to the extremes of fraud and corruption; especially if they are bound by oaths, and impelled by the pressure, or terrors of want to break them.

But your Lordship is not to form an opinion of the profusion of these drains from the plan lately adopted by the Court of Directors for transferring the Company's debts in India to England, nor from the amount of those debts. These are the accumulation of many years, and are the effect of a war, which immediately involved two of the presidencies as parties in it, and was chiefly maintained by the wealth of Bengal. In this war we had our paymasters, contractors, agents, commissaries, (proverbial titles of corruption at home,) commanders-in-chief, and commandants of corps: who all had the means of making, and many, no doubt, did make, large profits: though, if I may trust to common report, in no degree equal to those of similar appointments near home. Besides, there are to be reckoned the fortunes of men who have long quitted the service, and estates of deceased servants, which have remained for years in India, and which at this time constitute a large part of the Company's bonded debt, both in Bengal and the other presidencies, the service for many years affording no means, or at most but scanty means, of transferring them to England, and the foreign channels being such as the former might not deem safe, nor the assignees of the latter deem legal.

Of the debt in Bengal, much, and I believe the greatest part, belongs to the native inhabitants of

Calcutta, who have made it their practice to buy up the Company's bonds, since they have fallen in their value. I repeat, my Lord, that whatever regulations are made for the service, however wise in their institution, or forcible in their application, large fortunes will be made by individuals, which must be remitted to England, and by indirect channels, if direct are withheld: and that every remittance that is made will occasion a loss of so much of the circulation of the country; whether it be exported in specie, or by any other medium which would otherwise produce a return of specie.

To this must be added the Company's investment, and the supplies sent to Bombay, Fort St. George, and China, which have been of late years excessive. I have been aware of the ruinous consequences of drawing so much of the circulating specie from the provinces of Bengal, and have laboured incessantly to prevent it. During the war, indeed, the supplies of money given to Bombay and Fort St. George were indispensable, and they were made with a liberal hand. In the same period, too, we continued to send treasure, or opium, which was equal to treasure, to China.

This I constantly either opposed, or yielded with reluctance to the peremptory commands of the Court of Directors, and the prompt spirit of acquiescence which prevailed with my colleagues. But in the year 1783, the same causes becoming less urgent, and the urgency of our domestic calls very great, the Board resolved to discontinue the supplies to Fort St. George and China, and to limit those of Bombay to sixteen lacs. I soon after left the presidency, and was absent during nine months. On my return, I found that the Council had permitted the government of Fort St. George to draw upon them to an amount which grew, before their drafts could be stopped, to near ninety lacs; and from Bombay they had answered drafts for more than thirty lacs. It was then proposed and agreed, that no more money should be sent in the course of the year, which ended with last April, either to Fort St. George or Bombay, nor any to China. These arrangements have also, as I fear, been broken: yet, at this time the bonded debt is but what it had been these three years, about 160 lacs, and the Treasury orders and arrears of pay much diminished.

Many have been the remonstrances upon these subjects to the Court of Directors, but with little effect, as they still continue to press the Government of Bengal to make the same supplies, and in a late publication, that to China is mentioned among the advantages which are to facilitate the increased provision of tea for consumption in England.

Upon the same principle that I used all my endeavours to prevent the provinces from being exhausted of their specie, I have also laboured to open new channels for recruiting it. The first adventure to Egypt was undertaken with my encouragement, and partly at my own cost.

Had it succeeded, it would have thrown the whole internal commerce of Africa into our hands. It failed because the Court of Directors were in the habit of reprobating every measure that they could ascribe to me.

At the same period I began the first attempt to open an intercourse with Tibbet; and in defiance of all the discouragements which I met with, and notwithstanding the most untimely death of the Lama, who had eagerly adopted the plan, and had even solicited and obtained the countenance of the Emperor of China in favour of it, I had so far succeeded as to have obtained the permission of the regency of that part of Tibbet, with which our intercourse had been established, for the passage of a caravan from Bengal to its capital. I do not know what has been the event of it; but I doubt whether the plan is generally known at the India House, or if it is, whether it is not regarded as a project of mere whim or curiosity.

Yet, unless such expedients are tried and brought to effect, and more moderation observed in the calls upon Bengal for foreign disbursements, the time will come when its inhabitants will want money for the interchange of the articles of internal commerce; and when that happens, the failure of the revenue and investment will be consequence of it.

Why this calamity has been so long protracted many causes may be assigned. The trade of Bengal, notwithstanding the large share of it which is monopolized by the Company, and may be termed gratuitous, is still considerable. Its productions and manufactures are of a high price, and are paid for almost entirely with money. Two great divisions of our army have been subsisted for more than ten years past on two subsidies paid from the province of Oude, some part of which has been expended in Bengal. Above 800,000*l.* in specie have been sent to Bengal, from Oude, in payment of the stipulations made by the treaty of Benares in 1773. Large fortunes were made by individuals of our nation, during more than fifteen years from the same source, and these were also thrown into the circulation of Bengal, or into the Company's cash, which was the same in its effect.

The capture of Bidjeygur, a fortress belonging to Cheyt Sing, in 1783, yielded a booty to the officers in silver and gold to the value of near 400,000*l.*, which was almost wholly and instantaneously conveyed to the provinces of Bengal. The province of Benares also has since that time contributed a fixed annual revenue of 400,000*l.*, instead of an uncertain one, which it before paid of 240,000*l.*, and is well able to spare a large portion of that sum from its own currency, on account of the continual resort of wealthy pilgrims from all parts of India to its capital; and this has been so much augmented by late regulations made for that effect, that the present magistrate of Benares informs me, in a letter which I received by the Swallow, that in the course of three years, 2,500 new houses have been built in that city. Yet, this is now the only remaining source of supply; the others were all accidental, except that of Oude, which is dry, and all that it can now afford is the payment of a single brigade, residing within it, and returning a part of its subsidy in exchange for the necessaries of daily consumption.

The recapitulation and inferences of the preceding detail may be reduced to the following propositions:—

1. Bengal has been annually drained of its currency since British possession of it, by the Company's investment, by supplies sent to China, Fort St. George, and Bombay, and by the remittance of the fortunes of British subjects to Europe.

2. These drains must be continued in a degree both for the Company's investment, and for the remittances of the fortunes of individuals.

3. They may and ought to be diminished by the forbearance of supplies to China, and the other presidencies, and by laying equitable restrictions on private emolument.

4. If Fort St. George and Bombay cannot maintain their own expenses in time of peace with their own resources, and furnish besides a profit to the Company, the nation ought to part with or abandon them.

5. The means of laying equitable restrictions on private emolument do not consist in multiplying penal laws, or increasing their rigour at home, but in establishing an efficient control in the government abroad

in affording liberal allowances, in constituting proper and competent offices for checks on contingent expenses, and above all, for the speedy and regular audit of accounts.

6. Every encouragement should be given, and every expedient adopted, for the enlargement of the existing trade, for opening new channels of trade with other countries, and for drawing new inhabitants into our own provinces, which their fertility and security, and the miserable desolation of the royal demesnes, would render at this time an attempt of easy accomplishment.

7. But neither can the improvement of actual resources, nor the creation of new, nor the reformation of abuses, be made, except by a single, strong, and despotic hand. The members of a collective government are unresponsible : they will all have their claims to wealth and to remittances, each will have his favoured dependants, for whom he will claim a share in the emoluments of office, and protect them in the abuse of it: and the Governor himself, let his integrity be what it will, will be forced to yield in a degree to the general torrent, or he will be assailed and overborne by his associates, and not have a friend or an instrument in the service to support or assist him.

I beg your Lordship's pardon for the loose and incorrect state of this address. I have scarce had time to write it, as it is, and have omitted many facts and arguments which would have rendered the subject more complete ; and some which, I fear, will be necessary to illustrate or explain some of the positions of it. I have the honour to be, with the greatest respect and attachment, my Lord, your Lordship's most obliged and most faithful servant.

The following, written about the same time with the preceding, gives a correct view of the writer's position at the moment, especially as regarded his hopes of rest, if not of honour. How misplaced these expectations were, the lapse of a few weeks sufficed to show.

To Mr. Thompson.

Bath, 19th December, 1785.

My dear Thompson,—I write at a distance from your letters, and can neither reply to them, nor inform you which of them I have received. In all I miss what has been uppermost in my mind whenever I have received them, the news of my old bureau and its contents. These, as I have already mentioned, consisted of secret letters and other papers which I have ever kept concealed from all eyes but my own, and some valuable portraits, valuable both for their execution, and their representation of old and dear friends. It used to stand in my own apartment, and was the first package that I thought of, but by Francis's admirable care it was sent to the old house, and so either escaped my recollection afterwards, or recurred to it (if at all) as being dismissed to the ship. It is not possible, after so long a lapse of time, to recover either the bureau or the things that it contained, if you have not already and long ago secured them. Yet I must continue to write my feelings about them till you tell me that they are safe, or that they are lost for ever.

I cannot write many, nor long letters. This must serve both for you and Larkins, for in three hours it must go to the post, or miss the packet, and in three hours I have three hundred things more to do; things which stand in the place of obligations, but belong to no class of duties which morality enjoins, prudence prescribes, or pleasure recommends. Yet, such as they are, they are indispensable, and have filled up the great void of my life during the last six months of it, and, vanishing like a mist from my remembrance, have left the void of greater apparent extent than if they had never occupied it.

You and Turner stand where you originally did in my recommendations, but precluded, first by the spite of my enemies, and the indolence or pique of my own friends concurring, and lastly, by an Act of Parliament which prohibits all appointments to the service till lists of the necessary servants are received from India, and fixed establishments formed upon them. Yet it is a point which I will never lose sight of, and am determined to accomplish it.

I have described my life as unprofitable. But it has not been absolutely misspent. I had an early occasion given me to enforce the design of opening the Bengal treasury for bills to an indefinite amount; and to recommend with success some useful principles in opposition to others that would have done mischief. I drew up a recital of the three last months of my government with a review of the whole period of it interwoven with the events of that short interval; and it has been read and studied as a rule of conduct by those whom I wish to think as I do. I have drawn up a series of arguments in examination of Mr. Pitt's Act, and heads for a new one: these I have presented to the Chancellor, the only man who can make any useful application of them; and he was, I know not if he is, disposed to it. These papers are voluminous, and I have nobody to copy them; but if I can, I will send copies of them to you, for you and my friends to read, and see that I have not grown torpid to the interests of the Company or the rights of its servants. Another deed I have done very lately, which has effected no good, and I wish it may not have done myself harm; I mean, an attempt to prevent the conclusion of a weak or wicked agreement with the new French India Company. The effect has served only to open my eyes on some discoveries which I do not venture to commit to writing. Two conclusions only I may write, viz. that the directors have totally lost their agency, and that the property of the Company is to be cut into slices, and dealt out for the purchase of advantages to the general state, and those perhaps ideal.

My health is but feeble. Yet I certainly gain gradual strength, though tardily. My reputation stands as well as I can wish it, and I see or think I see, the beloved partner of my life stand as high in the public estimation, which I prize far beyond my own credit. She is also improved in health beyond what I had dared to hope, and I trust will be restored in time to a confirmed strength of constitution. As to rewards and honours, I have almost given up the expectation of either, though the wishes of many, and of many to whom I am personally unknown, are sanguine yet in the belief that they are in store and ready for me. With respect to the former, I have been informed that they were withheld by Mr. Pitt, when proposed a little before my arrival, on the plea that Mr. Burke having threatened to bring some criminal charges against me in the approaching meeting of Parliament, it would have been indecent to forestall them. Whether this man really means what he has threatened, I know not, having heard nothing about him for many months, nor have I ever made him the subject of my inquiries.

We have heard of Lord Macartney's flight to Bengal; but I do not learn what impression it has made on those whom it first concerns.

Tell Larkins I have received his letters in (I think) quintuplicate, and if the next that I receive are in the same tenor, I am afraid I must offer my service to those who will accept it, and begin the world again. Give my love to him, and other friends to whom it is due. I must make an end to this. Mr. Anstey and I are as much friends as if we had rode round the Calcutta course together every day for the last fifteen years. Are you not glad of this? Mrs. Hastings desires me to assure you that you have a place in her kindest remembrance, and that she reproaches herself even for her inability to answer your letters, which however she will do in time for the next despatches. I cannot omit to mention that I had a very pleasing testimony shown me by Colonel Gordon and the other officers of the King's army returned from India, of their esteem, in an elegant entertainment provided for me; many of them remaining in town, though eager to revisit their families and friends, for that express purpose.

Adieu. I am ever, my dear Thompson, your most affectionate friend.

From the tone of the preceding letter, as well as from certain entries in his diary, which, though brief, and in themselves unimportant, may be regarded as evidences of the state of his feelings when they were made, I am led to the conclusion that there existed at this time a settled conviction on the mind of Mr. Hastings, that the hour of his final triumph over all his enemies could not be very distant. No steps had indeed been taken to erase from the journals of the House of Commons the votes of censure which stood there on record against him. Neither had Mr. Pitt exhibited any remarkable zeal in favour of a man to whom, more, perhaps, than to any other subject of the Crown, he owed his present place in the councils of his sovereign. But if there was apathy in one of the great political circles, at least the rancour of party violence appeared to have subsided in the other, insomuch, that from the date of the accession of the Tories to power, and the introduction of their famous India bill in 1784, all mention of Mr. Hastings and of his supposed delinquencies had, in either house of parliament, ceased to be made. On the other hand, his reception at the India House, in the King's palace, and by almost every member of the Cabinet, the prime minister excepted, had been such as to evince the best feelings in his favour. And finally, the very fact that the discomfited Whigs were known to hate him; that Mr. Burke still threatened in private, and Mr. Fox and Mr. Grey joined in his threats,—this circumstance alone was sufficient to induce a persuasion among Mr. Hastings and his personal friends, that, even on the ground of good policy, if by no higher motive swayed, the Cabinet would to a man support him. Accordingly, when, on the 20th of June, a few days after his arrival in London, Mr. Burke, just before the close of the session, gave notice that "if no other member would undertake the business, he would himself, at a future day, make a motion respecting the conduct of a gentleman just returned from India," the indication was received not so much with indifference, as with satisfaction; because both Mr. Hastings and his friends looked forward with confidence to the opportunity which the motion would afford, wringing from Parliament, if not from a higher source, the rewards which the Governor-General's faithful and distinguished services had merited, and which had been too long, and too perversely, withheld.

It is no business of mine to determine the true nature of the principle on which Mr. Burke's implacable hostility to Mr. Hastings was founded. The admirers of the great orator assure us, that he never acted except from a sense of duty, and that, whether right or wrong in his views of this particular matter, they were taken up conscientiously, and conscientiously adhered to. This may be true; for Mr. Burke's mind seems to have been so peculiar in its construction, that with him prejudice no sooner matured itself than it became a principle; and he obeyed its impulses with the ardour of one who neither loves nor hates either men or things, except in extremes. I am willing to admit, for example, that Mr. Burke may have credited the tales which were told him by the enemies of Mr. Hastings, and of the East India Company; and that his original object was, not so much to punish the crimes of an individual delinquent, as to put a stop to a system under which such crimes could be perpetrated. But when the measure of 1783 fell to the ground,—that measure, of which, though called by Mr. Fox's name, Mr. Burke and the late Sir Arthur Pigot were the real authors,—when the bill was thrown out, which was to have secured to the Whigs for ever the patronage of British India, with all the influence which such patronage was calculated to ensure; when Mr. Burke and his friends not only sustained the loss of place, but were held up to the ridicule and scorn, over and above, of the whole nation; and all these evils were known to have overtaken them chiefly through the instrumentality of Mr. Hastings, and the powerful party which supported him; then indeed, the zeal which had heretofore animated Mr. Burke in favour of justice, or mercy, or truth in the abstract, merged in a sense of unmitigable and deadly rancour towards the individual whom he regarded as the personification rather than the main support of their opposites. I believe that Mr. Burke was by far too great a man to be swayed in a case like this by the impulses of mere personal feeling. The stories which were told at the moment concerning Mr. Hastings's neglect of his nephew; and the thirst for vengeance which a sense of outraged vanity created, I therefore hold to be without foundation. But political loves and political hatreds are to personal feeling what the hurricane of a tropical climate is to a gale of wind at our season of the equinox. Whenever men become the slaves of these, and no human being ever was their slave if we may not predicate the truth of Mr. Burke, they appear to lose all power of discriminating between fact and fiction. Mr. Hastings had defeated the favourite scheme of Mr. Burke's whole public life. He had driven Mr. Burke and his party from political power; and Mr. Burke in particular, and his party party in general, devoted themselves to crush their enemy; under the persuasion that by convicting him of the crimes of oppression, and cruelty, and peculation, they would justify, in the eyes of the world, the terms of their own India bill, and place themselves in the light of martyrs to the cause of justice and humanity.

It is by no means impossible, had Mr. Hastings been content to drop quietly into the shade of private life, but that the party which desired his ruin, and so long laboured to bring it about, would have abstained altogether from attacking him. They knew that he had many and influential friends in every circle of society; and they might have shrunk from the prospect of engaging in a struggle, the issue of which was, to say the least of it, doubtful. But neither now, nor at any former period, was Mr. Hastings disposed to avail himself of the political cowardice of his enemies. He felt that he had deserved high rewards from his King and country; he was not willing to compromise these for the mere absence of censure. He therefore encouraged his friends to press the subject forward; and to win for him, at all hazards, the justice which the House of Commons appeared reluctant voluntarily to award. Accordingly, when parliament met again in 1786, on the very first day of the Session, and on the first opportunity that presented itself, Major Scott reminded Mr. Burke of the notice which he had given in the preceding June, and desired that he would name an early day for acting upon it. Mr. Burke's reply is well known; and deserves all the praise, on the score of wit, which his admirers have heaped upon it; yet it seemed to indicate, even in him, a reluctance to proceed. For Mr. Burke stood well nigh alone at this juncture, in the desire to prosecute, of which the inexpediency had been warmly pressed upon him a day or two previously at a great meeting of the Whigs at the house of the Duke of Portland. Nevertheless, Mr. Burke felt that his own character was at stake, and he set the advice of his associates at defiance. The consequence was, that on the 17th of February, he caused the vote of censure which had been passed on Mr. Hastings in 1782 to be read, and then moved, in a committee of the whole house, "for a copy of the correspondence which had passed between Warren Hastings, Esq., late Governor-general of Bengal, and the Court of Directors of the Honourable East India Company, between

January, 1785, and January, 1786," including, of course, the letters written on both sides, subsequently to the return to England of the Governor-general.

From this date, the trial of Warren Hastings may, in strict propriety of speech, be said to have begun. A warm debate undoubtedly followed, in which some members of the Government took part; and the motion was resisted, among others, by Mr. Dundas, whom Mr. Pitt, as in duty bound, supported. But Mr. Burke was opposed, not upon the high ground of Mr. Hastings's eminent services, and of the benefits which had accrued from them to the Company and the nation, but on a point of form; which, as far as the subject of the debate was concerned, might as well have been waved. Neither Mr. Hastings nor his personal adherents ever entertained the slightest objection to the production of any papers which might tend to throw light upon his character or sentiments. Still, though the public, or at least that portion of it which was already disposed to view with favour the conduct of the late Governor-general, experienced and expressed a great deal of disappointment at the tone which the minister had assumed, the Governor's personal friends persisted in believing, that when matters came to a crisis Mr. Pitt would not desert them. The following letter, written in part by Mr. Hastings's dictation, sets the matter in a sufficiently clear point of view; and I therefore insert it.

To Mr. Thompson.

London, 25th February, 1786.

My dear Thompson,—The governor being so hurried as not to be able to write you in the manner he wishes, desires me to do it for him. He says that since his arrival in England, he has purposely, for various considerations, kept himself aloof from the Court of Directors, and indeed he has not received that attention from them which he certainly merits, therefore has not had satisfactorily the acquaintance with their proceedings which he could desire. He further observes that the decease of his worthy friend Mr. Sulivan has widened the distance between him and the Court, and its occurrence at the present crisis is peculiarly unfortunate. However, he still enjoys opportunities of having gratuitous information though unsought by him. Mrs. Hastings is making up the papers which will convey to you information of Mr. Burke's progress in his attempt to substantiate the charges he has so long boasted to bring against our friend. You must not however regard the statement of Mr. Pitt's and Mr. Dundas's speeches as fairly given, for they by no means spoke of our friend with such cool and sparing approbation as the paper describes. On the contrary (I was one day in the House myself), they both expressed the warmest applause of his conduct, and boldly declared their opinion, that, instead of censure, he merited praise and honourable rewards from his country as the man, who, beyond all doubt, had by his exertions alone, preserved to her her possessions in the East. Even Mr. Burke seems to have receded from his usual violence, seeing, no doubt, the airy dagger of his gloomy imagination fly from his grasp at the instant when he means to clutch it. Instead of criminal, he now seems to dwell most on charges of political error, and it is the general opinion that numerous as the motions are for papers, no criminal charge will be found in the House on their examining the papers called for, but rather that the perusal will open the mind of every member, who is not determinately set against conviction; and I believe persons of that description are now very few. It is lucky for our friend's cause that such papers are called for, as he will now have an opportunity of his conduct being judged of from the best evidence, his own correspondence showing the real sentiments of his heart unprepared for defence, against the attacks of an enemy, and which he could not have brought to public notice himself without a charge of ostentation. I have no doubt but that numbers of the opposition, when they shall thus see Mr. Hastings as he really is, will be ashamed and sorry for having so long been blind to his merit, and be ready to repair the injury by joining in his exculpation. Mr. Burke has not yet made any specific charge, and it is thought that he will not be able to form any that will meet the approbation of the House. On Tuesday the business comes on, and Mr. B. will then be pushed to make his charge. Thus the business stands at present, but be of good heart, and let not thy noble courage be cast down, for the clouds of error are dispersing, and truth must appear. Your ever affectionate friend.

To the same.

My dear Thompson,—You must yourself forgive me, and excuse me to my other friends, for I cannot write. Read all the preceding as mine, except my own praises.

I sent you a long letter, and list of commissions by

a late packet, I hope not the Halswell's. I cannot now repeat them, but request your particular attention to the following, viz.:—

To procure two large tiger skins, and six pairs of sheets of the breadth of a bed, I forget whether of the Massulipatam, or Vizagapatam manufacture: not to be very fine, but a degree above ordinary. Let these commissions be expressed to be for the Comte de Haganeck, the imperial ambassador, lest I should forget it. I have promised the speedy execution of this commission, and owe it for his civilities.

Captain Ley has promised to take charge of a horse for me. Procure a good one for me, if you can; one equal to Sulliman. It is for Mrs. Hastings, who cannot get one fit for herself in England. (My Arabian is in amazing health, spirits, and beauty.) Be kind to Captain Ley and introduce him to all my friends. He is a worthy gentleman; so is Mr. Caruthers, his chief mate, and Mr. Lindsay, who is gone in a former ship. Seek him and be kind to him for my sake.

Mrs. Hastings grieves that she cannot write, but charges me to say everything kind for her. She is pretty well, but not so well as I wish.

Your friends in the Crescent were all in perfect health last month. Adieu, Yours, ever affectionately.

The debate of the 17th had turned entirely upon this one point, namely, whether Mr. Burke was justified in calling for papers, no specific charges having been brought against Mr. Hastings; or whether the forms of the House did not require that the accuser should first of all state his case; and then ask for the production of documents by which it might be supported. The House decided that the latter was the more becoming course, and Mr. Burke in consequence requested and obtained time to arrange his materials.

On the 3rd of March, however, and again on the 6th and 17th of April, the question was in some sort reopened by a demand for papers explanatory of the negociations which had ended in the late peace with the Mahrattas. But Mr. Pitt appears not yet to have made up his mind as to the tone which it would be becoming or convenient for him to assume, in the threatened discussion. He therefore resisted this motion as he had done the last, on the broad and general ground of inexpediency; and his party acting as it is the custom of parties to act in like cases, Mr. Burke's proposition was a second time negatived by a large majority.

Nothing daunted by these repulses, which, to say the truth, were as little calculated to restrain the enemies, as to encourage the friends of the accused, Mr. Burke applied himself to the task of moulding his case into form; and on the 4th of April brought forward eleven out of the two and twenty charges, on which he proposed, and ultimately succeeded, in grounding an impeachment. In the preparation of these charges it is now universally admitted, that he was largely assisted by Mr. Francis. "The charges brought forward by Mr. Burke against Mr. Hastings," says one who, whatever might be the perversion of his views on other points, was in this respect very accurately instructed,* "were on those subjects which had been matter of discussion between Mr. Francis and Mr. Hastings, while the former gentleman was in India; the impeachment of Mr. Hastings was therefore a continuation of Mr. Francis's opposition to Mr. Hastings's government. All the materials for twenty-two charges brought forward by Mr. Burke were furnished by Mr. Francis." I believe that this is true, neither am I at all disposed to doubt that Mr. Francis, "in whose character strong resentment was a leading feature," aimed at little more, while supplying these materials, than the gratification of a personal revenge. But, as I have already said, we are bound to take higher ground, while attributing motives to Mr. Burke. His hatred was that of a thwarted politician, who has reasoned himself into a belief that he is the champion of abstract truth, at the very moment when he is but the representative of a faction. Accordingly his whole bearing, both on the 4th of April and subsequently, was that of one who believes what he is asserting. He inveighed against Mr. Hastings as a very monster among his kind, and made no secret of the desire with which he burned, to crush him. The reader, who is by this time familiar with the whole tenour of

* See Nicholl's Recollections.

Mr. Hastings's administration, and from whom not so much as one thought in that great man's mind while presiding over the destinies of India has been kept secret, will judge of the reasonableness of this feeling by instituting for himself a comparison between facts, as they have elsewhere been stated, and the following epitome of the eleven first and gravest of the twenty-two charges which his enemies in Parliament brought against him. I copy what is subjoined from the introduction to the history of the trial, which was published in 1796. On the 4th of April then, Mr. Hastings was charged—

I. With gross injustice, cruelty, and treachery against the faith of nations, in hiring British soldiers for the purpose of extirpating the innocent and helpless people who inhabited the Rohillas.

II. With using the authority delegated to him through the East India Company for treating the King, Shaw Allum, Emperor of Hindostan, or otherwise the Great Mogul, with the greatest cruelty, in bereaving him of considerable territory, and withholding forcibly that tribute of twenty-six lacs of rupees which the Company engaged to pay as an annual tribute or compensation for their holding in his name the duannee of the rich and valuable provinces of Bengal, and Bahar, and Orissa.

III. With various instances of extortion, and other deeds of mal-administration against the

Rajah of Benares. This article consisted of three different parts, in each of which Mr. Hastings was charged with a series of the most wanton oppressions and cruelties. He gave in papers concerning the rights of the Rajah, his expulsion, and the sundry revolutions which had been effected by the British influence under the control of the late Governor-general, in the zemindarry.

IV. With the numerous and insupportable hardships to which the royal family of Oude had been reduced, in consequence of their connexion with the Supreme Council.

V. With having, by no less than six revolutions, brought the fertile and beautiful provinces of Farruckabad to a state of the most deplorable ruin.

VI. With impoverishing and depopulating the whole country of Oude, and rendering that country, which was once a garden, an uninhabited desert.

VII. With a wanton, and unjust and pernicious exercise of his powers, and the great situation of trust which he occupied in India, in overturning the ancient establishments of the country, and extending an undue influence, by conniving at extravagant contracts, and appointing inordinate salaries.

VIII. With receiving money against the orders of the Company, the Act of Parliament, and his own secret engagements; and applying that money to purposes totally improper and unauthorized.

IX. With having resigned by proxy for the obvious purpose of retaining his situation, and denying that deed in person, in direct opposition to all those powers under which he acted.

X. With treachery to Muzuffir Jung, who had been placed under his guardianship.

XI. With enormous extravagance and bribery in various contracts, with a view to enrich his dependants and favourites.

Of the events which immediately followed the production of these articles, as well as the discussion of others which Mr. Burke brought forward in the course of the week, neither the space at my command, nor my own inclinations, permit me to take any notice. Enough is done when I state that Mr. Burke was listened to generally with silence; till on the 26th Mr. Hastings petitioned, through Major Scott, to be supplied with a copy of the charges, and to be heard in his own defence at the bar of the House. This petition gave rise to a sharp debate, for though Mr. Burke affected the extreme of liberality, he was not willing either to furnish the paper required, or that, in the present stage of the business, Hastings should be permitted to speak for himself. But both points were carried against him. A majority of sixty, in which Mr. Pitt was again included, determined that Mr.

Hastings's desire should be acceded to, and the 1st of May was selected as the day on which the House would be prepared to hear him. Mr. Hastings felt that the interval was by far too brief, and has made an entry to this effect in his journal. "I had but five incomplete days," says he, "to reply to a volume that could not be read in less than two." Yet he applied himself to the task with all the powers of his vigorous mind, and he entirely accomplished it. The following, to his friend Mr. Thompson, will best explain how he felt, and what he did on the occasion.

London, 20th May, 1786.

My dear Thompson,—I had only time for a short letter to Larkins by the Swallow, which was general for the information of all my friends. Yesterday I received a short and hasty letter from you by the Rodney, dated the 11th January. I expect more by the same despatch; two more boxes not being arrived, nor have I any letter yet from Palmer, and only one short one from Larkins. I look in vain for some tidings of my private bureau, but neither of your letters have yet mentioned a syllable about it; yet, surely, you had long ago received my first letters concerning it.

This will be carried by Mr. Willis, who sets off tomorrow for India by the way of Bussora, and has promised to take charge of a book of Mr. Burke's articles of impeachment and another of my defence. Shore has a part of the last; but you will now have it complete. It has produced an effect exceeding my most sanguine hopes. The publication of the charges (nothing appearing in opposition to them) had begun to impress the minds of all men with an opinion against me, and Mr. Fox exultingly said so to the House. Such is popular judgment! The world knew the character of my accuser, and had seen nothing but his accusations. It knew that something could be said on the other side; yet decided on the accusation only before it. In a happy hour, and by a blessed inspiration, I resolved to try the effect of a petition to be heard in person. Against my expectation it was granted; and everybody came to ask me why I had done so imprudent a thing. Some called it rash, others mad, and all men condemned it—all but my *great* friend the Chancellor. I had but five days granted me to defend myself against sixteen historical libels, to which three more were added, and other two, before the second day of my appearance. On the 25th of last month Major Scott presented my petition, and it was granted, the next Monday (the 1st May) being appointed for my appearance at the bar of the House. On the 1st I attended, and was called in a quarter before four. I read the three first parts of my defence, Markham and the two clerks of the House the rest till half-past ten, when I was dismissed. The next evening I read the rest. I was heard with an attention unusual in that assembly, and with the most desirable effect; for it instantly turned all minds to my own way; and the ground which I then gained I still retain complete possession of. When I had finished the reading, I prayed for leave to lay my minutes (*i. e.* the defence) on the table. It was granted; and they became records of the House. A motion was made by Scott that they should be printed, and that too was agreed to; both unanimously. Sir Robert Barker, the same evening (for I was dismissed by seven), examined as a witness, and Colonel Champion and C. Marrack the next day. On the 5th Mr. Burke desired leave to bring on another charge, declared the last; it was admitted. This was the twenty-second. I forget when it was presented. I received a copy of it on the afternoon of the 8th, and the same day petitioned to be heard to this. I was ordered to attend on the 10th. With some difficulty I was ready in time; and am happy that, stinted as I was, and indeed most dreadfully, in time, I did not demand an extension of it for any part of the defence, though the most unreasonable allowance had been asked and taken for framing the charge, when all the documents had been prepared. I attended, presented my defence, but was excused reading it; for I was fearful of wearying my hearers. This has been the close of my labours. Since that Captain Jaques, Major Balfour, Messrs. Gardiner and Gilpin, and Mr. Middleton have been examined. Middleton's evidence is not yet concluded. If Mr. Burke calls no more, Captain Williams and Colonel Popham will be called by my friends, though they too are the prosecutor's evidences. None are summoned on my part. Part of the next week will be given to the examination; and the 30th is fixed for debating the first question upon the first charge, viz. that the Rohilla war was a high crime and misdemeanor. It has been agreed to take the opinion of the House in the same manner separately on each article; but Mr. Burke said, he should consider the judgment of the House on the first as decisive of all the rest. This may shorten the process. But it is impossible to say that it will; for nothing can be more irregular than all the past. I dread the fate of the next unhappy victim whom this precedent may doom to the same scene of iniquity; for the purest integrity alone can stand it. In all this long scene, now exceeding three months, I have undergone only twelve or fourteen days of personal labour; and I have no reason to complain of much suffering, as it has never affected either my health or spirits, nor (except a few days of the publication of the charges), my credit with the public; which, I believe, now stands higher by many degrees than it ever did. I have now, too, a well-grounded hope that a short period will bring the whole to a conclusion; I mean in the House of Commons. This is the summary of the business of the last three months. The detailed history would fill volumes, and much of these as portentous as instructive. They have destroyed the energy of their governments abroad, and are precipitating their own destruction.

I have not visited any of the ministers since the prosecution began. I have not been at the levee nor drawing-room. I have not desired the attendance of a single member. I have broken engagements which were officiously, but kindly, made to bring me acquainted with members of the House. I have disdained every species of management. I have acted against all that the word calls discretion. Every artifice of a man who has long thrown away the check of shame has been practised against me. Yet, my friend, I promise you that he will be most foully discomfited, and my name shall shine the brighter for the means which have been taken to extinguish it.

I thank God I am not wholly useless beyond my own little sphere, nor inattentive to the scene of my past service; but I cannot enumerate particulars. I have some reason to believe, and I hope it was so, that my known esteem for Shore contributed to the choice made of him for his present office. It is the best thing done for India for these many years. Lord Cornwallis goes with good dispositions, and a fair and honourable character and gentle deportment. I have not been able to serve Davies. I early applied to Mr. Sulivan; but unfortunately he had already obtained the promises of his friends for the gentleman of that name who is now at Madras. But the Board of Control has opposed his appointment, and Davies will of course retain his post till the arrival of the ships of the next season. In the mean time, if I can find a fair occasion to promote his appointment to it, I will. At present it is too delicate a point to meddle with, as the two bodies are at variance about the Directors' appointment.

Remember my commissions, viz. the two tiger skins, and six pair of Massulipatam sheets, for Comte Haganeck; and the horse, shawl goats, and Bootan turnip-seed for myself. Remember, too, to inquire for, and to send my ivory cot. I have received the cinnamon seed.

But, above all, recover and send me the contents of my bureau. I also request you to send me the remainder of my papers. I miss many of the most valuable, and almost all the consultations, except those which were bought from Sir J. Clavering.

I have corrected a part of the defence. You must correct for yourself the errors which remain. Let all my friends read it.

I am yet unsettled, not having been able to fix upon a temporary place of retirement in the country. Indeed I cannot yet go far from town. Mrs. Hastings, who always mentions you with affection, is well, though not of such firm health as I could wish. I gain health, though but slowly; but no wonder. I have not time even for the society of my dear Arab, who is in fine health and spirits; but I cannot get a horse for Mrs. Hastings. If you succeed in procuring one for the Barrington, it will probably arrive before we shall have met with one of English breed; and it will lengthen her life, and with it mine. There is a spur for your exertions. When Shore arrives, remind him of my application to the Board for Mrs. Hastings's banyan, Etwarree, and Kulleem o'Deen.

Deliver the enclosed yourself to Lord Cornwallis. I intended to have written it by the Swallow; but his Lordship went away the 29th, and I was then in the midst of my defence, which prevented me. I have cut off the first charges, and sent you only the six last, to save package. The former you will have in abundance by the Swallow and other ships.

Tell Colonel Pearce I cannot write to him; but that I will labour for him as effectually as for myself when I have got through my present impeachment. I have spoken and written of him to Lord Cornwallis. Adieu, my dear Thompson, yours ever affectionately.

Mrs. Hastings desires me to acknowledge the receipt of your letter, and to inform you that the Begum's ivory chairs are of *very great value*, not of little, as you seem to estimate them. She requests that you will present her respects to the Begum (and mine, pray), and desire that she will not order any velvet or other worked seat to the chairs, as they will make the whole seizable by the custom-house officers. She also begs that they may be sent by a ship that will swim.

Tell Palmer that I have received his letter; but that I have not received a line from the Nabob Vizier, Hyder Beg, nor the Prince, not since I arrived in England.

Neither have I received the recovered letter, or any other from Nizam Ally Cawn; nor any from Moodajee.

I have not written to Palmer, because I expected him in England. I am at this instant pressed to the last moment, as Willis lives in the city, and goes away this evening. Be kind to him.

The peculiar phraseology of the preceding letter

seems to indicate, that Mr. Hastings was not at this time so sanguine as many of his friends touching the final issue of the inquiry which had just been opened. They, drawing their conclusions from the tone assumed by Mr. Pitt in the first debate, anticipated his steady co-operation, and that of the other members of the Government, in all their future proceedings. And when Mr. Pitt again joined them in their attack on the first charge, by voting that the Governor-general, for his conduct in the Rohilla war, was not deserving of censure; they no longer hesitated to declare in all quarters that the ball was at their foot. But Mr. Hastings was a great deal more sober in the view which he took of affairs; and, as the event proved, a great deal nearer the truth. Neither the vote of the minister on the Rohilla charge, nor his request that Mr. Hastings would furnish him with a correct view of the nature of a zemindarry tenure, sufficed for a moment to mislead that able politician. He drew up with great care such a paper as Mr. Pitt required; and sent it to him on the 8th of June. Yet he did so with a strong impression on his mind that Mr. Pitt would sooner or later desert him; and the event proved, and very shortly too, that Mr. Hastings's view of the case was the right one.

On the 13th of June the Benares charge was opened by Mr. Fox in a speech full of maligaity towards Mr. Hastings; whom he accused of violating every law both of national and individual faith. The friends of Mr. Hastings expected that Mr. Pitt, to whom the merits of the case were known, would defend the accused on the obvious ground that he was justified in every step that he had taken. And so far the minister fulfilled these expectations, that he scouted the notion of Cheyt Sing's independence, while he vindicated the right of the Bengal Government to demand from its vassal additional supplies during a season of great difficulty. Yet, strange to say, Mr. Pitt summed up by avowing his intention of voting for the impeachment, because the fine which Mr. Hastings had proposed to exact from the refractory vassal, was out of all proportion to the weight of the offence. "When the Benares charge," says an eye-witness, "was argued in the House of Commons, Mr. Fox rested his argument solely on this principle, that Cheyt Sing was an independent prince, no way liable to be called on for succour by the Bengal Government. Mr. Pitt resisted this opinion of Mr. Fox. On the contrary, he said, Cheyt Sing was a vassal of the Bengal empire, and as he received protection from that empire, he owed to it allegiance; and in consequence of that duty of allegiance, was liable to be called on for extraordinary aids on extraordinary emergencies. He also assented to an assertion which had been advanced in the course of the debate, viz. that Mr. Hastings having only put Cheyt Sing under arrest for the purpose of subjecting his conduct to examination, could not be criminated for having inflicted too harsh a punishment on him. But he said "that the whole of Mr. Hastings's conduct showed that he intended to punish Cheyt Sing with too much severity; this intention was criminal, and for this criminal intention he should, though with extreme reluctance, vote for the impeachment of Mr. Hastings."

I have no language in which to describe the surprise and disappointment, and in many instances the indignation, with which the announcement of this proceeding on the part of Mr. Pitt was greeted. The personal friends of Mr. Hastings were of course furious in the extreme. They asserted that they were betrayed; inveighed against the minister for deceiving them, and appealed to the country, through the medium of the press, against so foul a conspiracy. Neither were the members of the Cabinet itself unanimous in supporting its chief, either in the act which he had perpetrated, or the grounds on which he rested it. Lord Thurlow, in particular, openly denounced them both, making use, among other expressions, of this, that "if a girl had talked law in such terms, she would have been without excuse." Mr. Hastings alone received the announcement of the minister's defection without dismay. The following, to Mr. Thompson, gives so faithful a picture of his mind under the circumstances, that I cannot think of withholding it.

Baselden Park, 18th July, 1786.

My dear Thompson,—I just learn that I am almost too late to write to India by the Intelligence, which is to be despatched the day after to-morrow, and I am at too great a distance from my letters to write from them. Yours, indeed, are not on subjects which require reply. By the King George, the last ship, I have only one short letter from you. This seemed to promise a speedy termination of Ganga Govin Sing's vexations, and I trust that Lord Cornwallis's arrival will finally close them, and that justice will be done to his merits and abilities. You will hear from others what justice I have received. With ministry and opposition both united against me, I have been declared guilty of a high crime and misdemeanor in having *intended* to exact a fine too large for the offence, the offence being admitted to merit a fine, from Cheyt Sing. This has given consequence to my accuser, who was sinking into infamy, and had every reason to expect punishment for the baseness and falsehoods of his charges against me. It is new to me to see a criminal prosecution hang over a man's head the length of a Chancery suit in a land where the laws will not permit the jury to sleep over a trial for murder. What, or in what manner, the next proceedings are to be carried on against me I know not; nor can I take any measures whatever to direct them to a favourable issue. They will take their own course. Hitherto neither my credit nor character has suffered by the last vote,—no not, I believe, in the opinion of an individual. I have not solicited, nor will I, the interest of a single member of the House, and after what has passed am indifferent about the issue, provided only that it be speedy. It hurts me, I own, to be tried by judges who vote with their party in a judicial, as they do in a political question, and people talk of it as a thing of course. In the meantime, my prosecutors (for they are many, and they are also my judges) fill the papers with the most wicked lies to inflame the public against me, and my friends tell me that I must not give myself any concern about them; yet everybody believes every calumny so uttered, if they do not affect themselves, their friends, or party connexions.

The worst effect of this business is, that it keeps me at a distance from all men in business, and prevents me from attempting to do the good which I think I could do. I see nobody, but in the character of a mere idler; yet I have not been absolutely idle, nor unusefully busy. However this affair may end, I see in this, and in two others not very unlike it, strong symptoms of decline in the power of this empire.

I have bought a very pleasant little estate of ninety-one acres in Old Windsor, called Beaumont Lodge, a *modus agri non ita magnus, hortus ubi, &c.*, exactly answering Horace's wish; and if I live in England, I may probably end my days upon it; for I see nothing in England that I like so much. Mrs. Hastings is in health much as she has been; if anything, better since we came to Beaumont Lodge. We are much interested in the success of our haymaking, which has been prodigious, and never feel a tendency to be out of humour or spirits, but when we look towards London. Tell my friends that I am well, and remember them affectionately.

Whether life be long or short, it is wise to provide for its most distant wants. I therefore remind you of my commissions. Tell Turner that I thank him heartily for sending me the shawl goats; but I have not yet received them; and am told they are all dead. Two of Lord North's are arrived; yet let him continue to send others, and not forget the turnip seeds. Any other from Bootan would grow in England. I beg of you to send me seeds of the lichen, of both sorts; the custard apple; and, if possible, the mango, with such others as may have a chance of succeeding. I will make up a little collection for you.

It pains me to recur to the subject of my bureau. I have not yet received any intelligence from you or Larkins about it. You cannot conceive my anxiety about it. Adieu. Your ever affectionate friend.

I shall have an opportunity of showing, by and bye, that Mr. Hastings, when he spoke of himself as thrown aside like a worn-out habit, wholly mistook his position. The world is apt enough to turn its back upon a great man in adversity. Neither did the world ever behave too well to him. Nevertheless, his talents and acquirements were throughout appreciated as they deserved to be in the highest quarters; and more than one appeal was made to both in a way which could not fail to gratify, even though it brought no more solid benefit on their owner. As yet, however, his attention was occupied mainly in the conduct of his own defence. For he felt that the defection of the minister from the ranks of his supporters had so far changed the aspect of his affairs that he must thenceforth look only to the abstract justice of his cause, not to the good offices of either of the great parties into which the political world was divided. He therefore applied himself more than ever to the task of dealing with the subject so that it might be rendered intelligible to the thinking classes of his countrymen as well without as within the walls of Parliament. The following, addressed to his old friend Mr. David Anderson, seems to me well worthy of insertion. Though referring chiefly to a pamphlet which one of the many volunteers in his defence proposed to compile, and concerning which Mr. Anderson had been consulted, it gives, at the same time, such a clear summary of the chief events of his government and of the principle on which it was carried out, that crude and undigested as the style may be, I cannot bring myself to suppress it. Even the self-praise, of which the writer is evidently ashamed, and which he certainly never meant for other eyes than those of his correspondent, could not have proceeded except from one whose conscience assured him that it was merited. I will not, therefore, presume to draw my pen through it, confident that it cannot tell, in the judgment of any right-minded person, against either the good sense or the modesty of the writer.

To Mr. Anderson.

Beaumont Lodge, 13th September, 1786.

My dear Anderson,—I wrote and despatched a short letter to you yesterday, merely to acknowledge the receipt of yours of the 1st, as you would be anxious to hear of its safe arrival. I am much pleased with

Mr. ——'s reflections on the past mode of proceedings. He might have added to them, that by joining in one charge such a variety of distinct and heterogeneous matter, some of which was criminal, some doubtful, much of it perfectly innocent, and all involved in obscurity, and devoid of applied or express evidence, and putting the whole to one vote, it was impossible that the members, even if they were disposed to it, should give just sentence; because one thinking one point impeachable, another another, and all inclining to the belief that of course some part of the dirt, where so much was thrown, must adhere,—the majority could not avoid giving judgment for the impeachment, though on each point the same majority would acquit me. But when to this is added that one body is *conjuratum* against me, and another equally ready to join the caprice of the minister, the purest integrity has no security. When I appeared before the House in my defence, I declared my readiness to stand or fall by each charge, and protested against an acquittal produced by a general comparison of my good with my blameworthy actions. But I did then expect that the question upon each charge would be simple, that is, that it would involve but one position, and that either the leading one, or one following and dependent on another already decided. For instance:—"Was Mr. Hastings warranted in exacting from Cheyt Sing an additional subsidy for the extraordinary exigencies of the war?" To this every man who knew but little of the subject could reply Yea or No. The question following it would be:—"Was Mr. Hastings warranted in exacting a fine from Cheyt Sing for his refusal?" This also admits of an easy answer. If given in the affirmative, Mr. Pitt might ask, "Was not fifty lacs too much?" And this would be rejected by its absurdity, for the same question must have been repeated with a progressive diminution of the sum, till it should exactly hit the sense of the majority; and all the lawyers would condemn the question in the terms of it, as being contrary to all law, and incapable of being reducible to any determined rate by law. But to ask a mob of giddy and uninformed men, is Mr. Hastings impeachable for having "paired his nails, shaved his beard, put on two stockings not fellows, got drunk on the King's birthday, eat bad rice instead of wholesome flour, and entertained a treasonable design against Cheyt Sing, &c.," including five hundred affirmations, some of which were true, but innocent; some blameworthy on a good principle; some wrong, but of no consequence; some right, but applied to wrong construction; and many strictly right and most meritorious, but contrary to a false, wicked, or dangerous principle which Mr. Burke would establish in the stead of mine;—what is this but to punish me because the House of Commons cannot solve his enigmas?

In such a confusion prepared against me, I am willing to get rid of such a tribunal at any rate; though I think that the House will get as little credit by the mode proposed for dismissing the inquiry, as they have in their past conduct of it, or in entering upon it at all. But in this I have no concern. It is their concern, not mine. For I shall never admit the effect of any vote that they can give, as either conveying real credit or dishonour on my character.

I am upon the whole much pleased with what I understand of the proposed plan, and greatly obliged to you for your assent to the request made to you respecting it. But in this also you will meet with the same difficulties that have discouraged *your friend,* from the incapacity of the House of Commons to act in a judicial character even in the arrangement o materials provided for their information. Every document that he or you can want is before the House, and comprised in the numerous folio volumes which have been printed on India affairs, but so mixed and dispersed that it would take an age to find them out and give them connexion. I will try what I can do when I go to town, with the aid of Mr. Scott, who alone can give me aid of this kind. In the mean time the following are the points which will best deserve to be put forward in such a display.

Mr. Hastings found the government of Bengal, to which he succeeded in April, 1772, inefficient, in debt one and a half crores, and without resources. He constituted offices, all now extant being of his formation. He divided the departments of the Council. He brought the revenues from the charge of two provincial Councils, which kept the knowledge of them from the superior Board, to Calcutta; instituted new courts of civil and criminal justice, distributed at due distances over the province, with superior courts placed over them, the Board presiding over one of the last, and himself singly over the other. He and his Council, with great labour, reduced the expenses of every department, and formed a complete system of economical establishments. He rigidly obeyed the orders of the Court of Directors in revoking the authority and annihilating the influence of Mahmud Reza Cawn, for which he received their thanks, and the persecution of the same men united to support Mahmud Reza Cawn against him. He reformed and arranged the Nabob's household and expenditure. He first converted the funds of salt and opium from private emolument to the profit of the Company. The first of these was afterwards taken out of the hands of the Board by the Court, and given to the Board of Trade, where it declined to such a degree as to become a charge to the Company. He proposed its resumption; and lastly, having freed the management of it from the intricacies of its former varied tenures, he, on his own responsibility, and against the judgment of his colleagues, reduced it to a simple and easy system, yielding a yearly and unfailing net produce of fifty lacs (half a million sterling) for ever, not only without oppression, but by means which facilitated and equalized the circulation of the necessaries of life, and gave bread besides to thousands in its commercial progress.

He freed the provinces from the yearly incursions of the Seniassies, who never failed to visit them before his time, and from the second year of his accession have abandoned them entirely.

He received the thanks of the whole body of the Directors for the first acts of his government; and received the reproaches of the same body, under exactly the same signatures, as soon as the new Council proclaimed themselves his enemies.

In June, 1773, he left Calcutta with less than 50,000 rupees in the treasury, and after means unsuccessfully tried to borrow money. In September he returned with twenty lacs in specie, and with thirty more in actual receipt, with an annual fund established of twenty-five lacs more in the establishment of the army subsidy. This sum he settled for the army, whenever it should be wanted, for the support of our ally, the Nabob of Oude; and by making the terms fixed, and the employment and dismission of the troops optional to the Nabob, he most effectually rendered their appropriation, and the subsidy with it, perpetual. He established the alliance between the two states on conditions of such equal advantage, that the representatives of both parted equally satisfied; and had the succeeding governments pursued the same line, and the Nabob ul Dowlah lived, Oude would have been a shield of defence, and a source of wealth, to Bengal, while it derived reciprocal support and the means of wealth from Bengal. In the originating connexion and subsequent war with the Rohillas he did what all states ought to do. The invasion of the country threatened ruin to those of our ally, whom he joined in repelling it, the Rohillas giving a solemn pledge in writing for the payment of twenty lacs, in consideration of the expense and risk incurred in their protection. They obtained their safety, and refused to pay the price of it. We made war with them, on just grounds surely, unless any other process than that of the sword can be devised for recovering the rights of nations; defeated them, with the death of their ungrateful and perfidious leader; and annexed their dominion to that of Oude, which from that period became defensible throughout. The Directors, as usual, allowed the justice of our proceedings, and approved them, but condemned both when Clavering and his associates condemned them.

From this period Bengal has been growing in power, wealth, population, and greatness.

On the 20th of October, 1774, arrived the three members of the new Council, and for two years superseded that of which I had before the principal lead. I was a man unknown, unprotected, and unconnected at home, and possessed no other influence abroad than that which I had acquired by my own knowledge and practice, in the credit which the success of my measures impressed on the people of Indostan, and in the attachment of my fellow servants and citizens. Without time allowed for the pretext of provocation, the impatience of my adversaries hurried them to a declaration and to acts of hostility on the 3rd day after their arrival. They persevered in their persecutions, which were gross to personal outrage, till the death of Colonel Monson; and their opposition, which the death of General Clavering did but suspend for an instant, till their final annihilation by the departure of Mr. Francis in December, 1780. In so long an interval, what had I wherewith to sustain the weight of their oppressions but the superior weight of my own character, and the consciousness of superior desert, set against the claim of high names, which supported the respect of my adversaries; King, Lords, Commons, and Directors, and half the people of England against me; the power of patronage employed in the seduction of my fellow servants; and for a while the rule taken out of my hands, to be employed in a warfare against me, and in that only. Yet even in that time the confidence of my opponents allowed me to conduct the current business, in which they never interrupted me but for occasions of personal attack. I suffered in patience; I did my duty where I could; I waited for better and more lasting means; no act or word of intemperance escaped me; no meanness of submission ever afforded my assailants the triumph, even of a moment, over me; and I have been told that they themselves have been heard to confess themselves foiled, even when they had brought their long prepared plans of attack to the Board, and I was unprepared to resist them.

When intervals of accidental authority enabled me to act, and I never had more than intervals, I employed them in forming and setting in motion the greatest and most successful measures of my Government. When these were impeded by frequent changes of influence, I still contrived to keep them in existence, and again gave them energy when my power returned. My antagonists sickened, died, and fled. I maintained my ground unchanged, neither the health of my body nor the vigour of my mind for a moment deserted me, nor did my difficulties end here. New coadjutors became new enemies, with the same encouragement from one body, (the Directors,) but without the same personal consequence. Mr. Wheler, Mr. Macpherson, and Mr. Stables were, as soon as they could stand without me, my successive, and lastly my united opponents. Mr. Wheler has declared to me, that he was enjoined to oppose me, and complained that he was deserted. Mr. Stables pleaded the advice of one friend, and Mr. Macpherson showed me that of another, not to link themselves to a falling man, but save themselves by showing that the same policy that sought my removal did not require theirs. Yet even when they were all three in force against me, I awed them into a surrender of a wretch whom they had scandalously protected in the most infamous of all oppressions, and compelled them to yield me the charge of a province which he had reduced to the brink of ruin, with the national honour linked with it; and in spite of their wishes, for they durst not act against me, I succeeded. I need not expatiate on this subject. You know it all as well as I do.

From the month of February, 1772, to the 23rd of August, 1782, I had enjoyed so uninterrupted a state of equal health, though with a constitution by no means robust, that I had never had cause to postpone the meeting of Council, or other appointed applications o business, and scarce allowed myself an hour of indulgence from it. Even in the severe sickness which then seized me, many hours were still devoted to my duty, and I dictated from my bed what I could not write at my desk. Of my manner of living at Lucknow, and its effects on the Nabob's authority, and the peace of his country, you know as much, or more, than I can write.

I now proceed to the last subject, in which I must combine the wars with France, Hyder, and the Mahrattas (as to the insurrection of Benares, I leave it to shift for itself).

The first hostilities against the Mahrattas commenced unknown and unsuspected by our Government. They were built on the standing orders of the Court of Directors, and had not even the shadow of a plea to justify them, if that authority should not be allowed, as it certainly was not, a sufficient one. They took place about December, 1774. We heard of them some time in the beginning of the ensuing year. I urged the Board (then substantially consisting of Clavering, Monson, and Francis) to condemn the measure, and command the government of Bombay to retract it; but as the means of doing this, to proceed with their operations in the field till they could make peace without soliciting it. The majority resolved on peace at all events, and ordered back the army abruptly to its quarters. A peace was made, but on terms so loose, and with concessions on our part so degrading, that the conditions were never fulfilled on either side. I opposed the negociation; but when the treaty was concluded, I was its most strenuous assertor, for there are two letters to Bombay on record, both written by me after Monson's death, in one of which we indirectly threatened them with dismission if they were aggressors in the breach of it; and in the other we gave them long instructions for the accommodation of every point of their differences. In the mean time they were invited by a conspiracy of one part of the Mahratta administration to unite in a plan for the restoration of their former adherent Ragoba, on which the accession of Suckeram Babboo, the minister, and principal of the two only persons who were subscribers to the treaty of peace, served for a pretence for their concurrence. They agreed to become parties in it, prepared to take the field, and advised our Government of it, excusing their engaging so far without our licence by the nature and necessity of the project, which required both secrecy and instant decision and action. What could we do? I had then the rule with Mr. Barwell's aid. The design was more desperate than those who had adopted it were themselves aware of. I did not believe that it would take place; but that the government of Bombay, sanguine as it was, would shrink on the moment of execution. But I judged that they were yet involved too far to recede without some consequences of danger; that if they did act and succeeded they had not strength to maintain their ground; if they failed, they had not strength to defend themselves. Whichever way the subject presented itself, it displayed dangers which without our support appeared insurmountable, and the die was cast before we were apprized of the throw. It was not a time to blame, nor to distinguish between the measures of right and wrong. The wrong (for wrong it was) was theirs who did it. Our part was to hinder it from affecting the interests of our common masters, and, if possible, convert it to their advancement. At my instance the Board ratified what they had done, sent them money, provided a powerful detachment which was ordered to march by a route and through an untraced geography to their relief. I had previously sounded, and ensured an ally in the Rajah of Berar. Leslie, who commanded the detachment (and I had no choice of a better leader), disobeyed his instructions. We recalled him, but he died, and Goddard was appointed in his place. He marched rapidly by the prescribed line, was received by the government of Berar with every due of hospitality: but here the design received a check, and required a total alteration.

On the formation of the detachment I deputed Elliott to the Rajah of Berar, and entrusted him with a plan for engaging the junction of that chief with views to his own elevation. With these the Rajah was well acquainted, and had manifested an eagerness for Mr. Elliott's arrival, with many other symptoms which could assure me of his readiness to take the part which I wished. In the first draft of the orders which were sent to Bombay at the time of Elliott's mission I had, in peremptory terms, required their forbearance of every plan of their own till they should receive our instructions for their future proceeding in the event of his success. Unfortunately the Court of Directors had given their orders, of which we had recently received the copy, to Bombay, to resume the cause of Ragoba *in case of a breach* of the treaty, which in a manner directed the breach of it, and the expression strongly indicated that meaning. With such an authority strengthening and sanctifying the predilection of the government of Bombay, I was dissuaded from tying up their hands to give a preference to my own plan; and I altered the clause first drawn to a general and loose caution. This, indeed, might in common sense have appeared sufficient, since they had already abandoned their original design, and so weak was the party of Ragoba in his own state, that it was manifest he must have depended upon the English alone for his success; and we had not on that side of India any strength adequate to such an enterprise. The consequence was, that no sooner did they hear of Goddard's approach, than they precipitately rushed to the field, without plan, alliance, or weighed strength, with troops that had scarce ever seen service, under the command of an officer who was then actually bedridden. They were defeated, yielded themselves prisoners of war, and were ignominiously reconducted to Bombay. Poor Elliott died before he had completed his journey. Moodajee, anxious for the accomplishment of the negociation, pressed me to transfer his credentials to his secretary, Mr. Farquhar; but learning almost instantly the new engagements concluded with Ragoba, and the hurried preparations which marked equally a want of judgment portending what actually happened, and a want of union and consistency in the councils of the ruling and dependant state, he wrote a second letter revoking all that he had written in the first, complaining of our want of power to enforce our own plans and orders, and earnestly pressing the return of General Goddard.

Goddard, however, had orders to proceed, arrived without opposition on the confines of Surat, acquired possession of a large territory, which, though of little use to us, was a loss of revenue to the Mahrattas which they could ill afford; and a campaign ensued in which our arms recovered their lustre, and the British name more than the credit which it had lost. But no substantial advantage was gained.

Now, my dear Anderson, I need not go on any further. You well know the rest. Carnac's detachment drew off Mahdajee Sindia, and induced him to conclude a separate peace.

The history of the confederacy should follow. The wrongs and revenge of Nizam Ally Cawn; the combination of Nizam Ally Cawn, the Peishwa, Mahdajee Sindia, Moodajee Boosla, and Hyder Ally, with the parts severally allotted to each; Sindia withdrawn from it by Carnac's diversion, his own policy coinciding; Nizam Ally Cawn won from the party by the interposition of Bengal seasonably affording him an ample and unexpected redress of all his grievances; Moodajee kept faithful to us by secret intercourse, and his army removed and induced to return by negociation (nor let its withdrawing to give Pearse's detachment a free passage, the assistance given to him in his march, nor the horse sent, though but ostensibly, to his support, be forgot). The next subjects are the war with Hyder, and the war with France, and finally the peace concluded with the Mahrattas, which eventually produced one with Hyder, in the terms of which I had no concern.

What a world of various and interesting matter does this abridgment include, were it spread out into all its detail! But your great task will be to select and reject, not to amplify. I would not have it forgot, that every design of the Surat expedition (which was undertaken against the judgment even of the most experienced officers in Bengal) was explained in a series of letters to the ministry of Great Britain, its causes, its motives and objects, and its dependencies discussed, and its expected consequences foretold; every successive letter verifying the expectations of the preceding, and proving that the plan was well digested, as its various checks and counteractions, all notwithstanding terminating with success, demonstrated the solidity of its composition.

Let it be also remembered that to conduct so complicated and vast a plan as it became in its progress, I sometimes had power, sometimes wholly, sometimes in part, often overruled; yet I persevered and carried it in triumph to its destined end. Nor that my exertions were the most vigorous under the pressure of the greatest difficulties; and that my confidence and pretensions rose in proportion to the despondency of my rulers at home and my colleagues of the other presidencies.

Let not my allusion to the plagues of Egypt and the land of Goshen be unnoticed; nor that, like Augustus, *urbem lateritiam recepi, marmoream reliqui.*

If I might be allowed to point out the best features of my own character in office, I should place these in the catalogue:—Integrity and zeal; affection for my fellow servants, and regard for the country which I governed; official regularity; accuracy and collateral provision (you must find out the meaning of these words) in the creation of new offices or systems of policy, in instructions for political negociations, and in the construction of treaties; sincerity and unreserve in my dealings with the chiefs in connexion with our Government; a study to choose agents most fitted for their trusts, confidence liberally given to them, and their conduct guarded from the hazard of every responsibility which belonged in right to myself; and lastly, patience, long suffering, confidence, and decision.

My dear David, let no man see this. I am ashamed of my own praises bestowed so lavishly by my own pen. But I mean this only as a farrago of hints to help your sounder judgment and clearer recollection. I fear that it may tend only to confuse and embarrass you; for it is most unmethodically arranged, and almost illegibly written. In truth, I am not qualified at any time for such a work, and now less than ever, as all that I have written was written by fits, and with a mind disturbed by pain. I intended as I went on to mark the official records required as vouchers for the facts as they occurred, but I wanted time and patience If you, as you proceed in your own work, will make out such a list, and send it to me, I will furnish you with the papers.—Adieu, my dear friend, yours ever most affectionately.

P.S. I have read over the above, and think that it may be of use to myself hereafter, if it should not be so to you; so keep it.

I subjoin to this another letter addressed to the same true and well-tried friend, not because it throws any fresh light on the state of the writer's affairs at the moment, but because it illustrates—what far more deserves the attention of the world

—the temper of his mind and feelings under every variety of circumstances. Mr. Anderson had misunderstood some expressions in Mr. Hastings's communication of the 13th, and replied to it with a slight tone of vexation. How kind, and gentle, and beautiful is the rejoinder.

To the same.

Beaumont Lodge, 28th September, 1786.

My dear Anderson,—I have received yours, and am glad that mine reached you in safety. David Anderson is the last man living whom I should have suspected of *cavilling*, and Warren Hastings is the last man living at whom he should *cavil;* for you have not misapplied the expression. I meant no more by the words *your friend* than to avoid the mention of the name to which I alluded, in conformity to your recommendation of secrecy and my own sense of the necessity of it; and for the same reason I left a blank for the name (as I well recollect) in the beginning, where the context sufficiently indicated the person intended by it. I am hurt to think that you could for an instant judge me (I am sure against experience) capable of little jealousy, and of yourself too; and on this occasion I have the additional mortification to know that the misconception will last for a fortnight before my explanation can remove it.

I am satisfied with the fulness of your brief conclusion on the Rohilla and Benares subjects. I had intended to have given you a few more hints about the interposition with Madras, but I have been lazy through the effects of my rheumatic complaint, which grows worse and yet hangs upon me.

I will write to the Chancellor about Shore's brother. Had it not been for his late desperate sickness, I should have performed my promise many months ago. —I am, my dear friend, your affectionate.

I need scarcely add that there needed no further explanation to restore these two men to the footing on which they had so long stood towards one another. Among all his friends, and he had many, none were more devoted to Mr. Hastings than David Anderson; among all whom he loved, and his benevolence was as extensive as it was sincere, Mr. Hastings, I am inclined to say, loved David Anderson the most.

CHAPTER X.

Proceedings in the Commons—Hastings arraigned at the Bar of the House of Lords—The Impeachment opened.

It will not be expected that I should follow, step by step, the order of events which terminated in the trial of Mr. Hastings; much less can I pretend, within the compass of a memoir like this, to give an analysis, however brief, of the proceedings which characterized the trial itself. It is matter of history that, after separating on the 19th of July, Parliament met again on the 23d of January; and that on the 1st of February, 1787, the House of Commons returned to the examination of witnesses which the summer recess had interrupted. Then followed debates on the different charges, as one by one they were brought forward; almost all of which terminated unfavourably for Mr. Hastings: till finally, on the 3d of April, the House came to the determination of exhibiting articles of impeachment against the late Governor-general of Bengal at the bar of the House of Lords, and of nominating a committee to whom the management of the business should be entrusted. The names of the gentlemen thus honoured are, I doubt not, familiar to many of my readers; yet for the benefit of such as may not be at home in this department of history, I subjoin a list of them :—

Edmund Burke, Esq.
Right Hon. C. J. Fox.
R. B. Sheridan, Esq.
Sir James Erskine.
Right Hon. Thomas Pelham.
Right Hon. W. Wyndham.
Hon. Sir Andrew St. John.
John Anstruther, Esq.
William Adam, Esq.
M. A. Taylor, Esq.
Charles Grey, Esq.
General Burgoyne.
Welbore Ellis, Esq.
Right Hon. Frederick Montagu.
Sir Grey Cooper.
Sir Gilbert Elliot.
Dudley Long, Esq.
Lord Maitland.
Hon. G. A. North.

An attempt was made to add to this list the name of Philip Francis, but the Commons would not consent. They positively refused, in defiance of Mr. Burke's adjurations, to employ as their agent in the prosecution of Mr. Hastings, one whose personal hostility to the accused wa notorious; whereupon the managers, as if to evince their contempt for the decision of such a body, appointed Mr. Francis their assessor, in order, as they said, that the benefit of his talents and experience might not be lost to a cause in which the very first principles of moral right were involved.

Meanwhile Mr. Hastings, whom the events of 1786 had prepared for much that was to follow, was not inattentive to his own honour, nor negligent in preparing the means of its vindication. He bestirred himself during the recess to set his character right before the world; as well as to draw up such a statement of facts as might, when the proper time comes, be read as his personal defence. The following letters, which relate to these proceedings, I judge it expedient to insert, for this among other reasons, that they do justice to the many friends who volunteered to aid him in his difficulties. To Lord Thurlow he had been indebted all along for countenance and support, while struggling to maintain himself in power. They were not, it will be seen, withdrawn, now when the question to be determined was, whether he should spend his latter days in peace, or go a dishonoured and ruined man to his grave.

To David Anderson, Esq.

Ewell, 27th October, 1786.

My dear Anderson,—On my return to town the evening before last I received your favour of the 15th, and yesterday morning I again left Beaumont Lodge for this place, which is in Surrey; where I write with interruptions, impending engagements, and restricted time; so I must come quickly to the material point. I have many reasons to wish for your early return to town. You cannot possibly work without materials, and you have none where you are. Major Scott has promised to assist, and will be much advanced by the time that you can come. As to myself, I literally do nothing, nor can bring myself to do anything till I know what is to be done against me; and indeed I feel a mighty repugnance against it from my contempt of my accusers, and something like it for those who, not having the plea of malice and revenge, permit both to operate in so unworthy a manner against me; and I know, besides, that if the former could carry the question for impeachment, they would not dare to do it.

But my wish to see you early arises principally from another cause. I know not to what I may be early destined; early, for my destiny must be now soon fixed. If to a public life, which is possible, I wish to have the benefit of your counsel in the crisis which may precede it, and I should have a pleasure in its being early seen that I have a proper estimation of your talents as well as attachment. But I may not pursue the subject; it would look too like profession, which I hate.

My memoir was surreptitiously obtained by a mercenary stationer, who printed, and had actually published it. I could only punish him by giving the property to another, Murray, the editor of the English Review; and by him it has, I believe, been, or is near being, published. I am sorry for it; for it will draw cavils upon me, which will pass because I shall not answer them; but it could not have been longer suppressed, and the impression now made is a correct one.

Mrs. Hastings desires me to make her compliments, and hopes you will pass your Christmas at Beaumont Lodge. We are both well. I rode yesterday to this place, a journey of at least twenty-two miles, without baiting. Adieu, yours affectionately.

I am pleased exceedingly with what you write of Dr. Adam Smith's approbation.

To the same.

Ewell, 29th October, 1786.

My dear Anderson,—I wrote you a short letter three days ago from this place. For fear of a miscarriage, I repeat my wish to see you in this end of the earth before the meeting of Parliament, which is now fixed for the 20th of January. I am afraid that I must myself undertake the drudgery which in your hands would have been a more pleasing and more easy labour; for my great *Gooroo* has enjoined it. Still you must take a large part in it. We shall not leave Beaumont Lodge till the meeting, and shall be very happy to have you for our guest to that time. forgot to tell you that I wrote immediately after receiving your letter, with Mr. Shore's enclosed in it, to the Chancellor, but he received it while he was leaving Buxton, and has been so good as to commission Scott, whom he has seen, to mention that as his reason for not answering it, adding his wish that the object of it was already within compass. I write this only to you. I should be glad, however, that when you write to Mr. Shore, you would let him know that I have not neglected him. Your affectionate.

Mrs. Hastings desires me to join her request that you will make Beaumont Lodge your immediate residence, and save yourself the fatigue of twenty miles out of your destined 400.

To the same.

Beaumont Lodge, 9th October, 1786.

My dear Anderson,—I hope you have received my last, as I should be sorry indeed that you should retain, a moment longer than was necessary for its removal, the impression of such a mistake as you committed in yours. I see advertised for publication a pamphlet written by a new volunteer in my cause, whom though I have not seen, nor know, I have seen his book, and will order it to be sent to you, because it sets the matter in a new light, and by assuming only one general principle, equally applicable to all the charges, and avoiding the discussion of each, which nobody could understand, is likely to do more service than publications of more knowledge and better composition. I was assured, when I was last in town, that Parliament will certainly meet in November, and that this abominable business would be first and speedily despatched. They seem to have enough prepared for the next sessions, without such unprofitable matter.

I understand by the Winterton's despatches that your brother and Sindia have had a serious quarrel, which was occasioned by Sindia's giving protection, and bestowing public honours, on Mowlary Hyroodeen and his brother Sala o'Deen, whom James had dismissed for treachery. Your brother insisted on their being turned out of the camp, and this being evaded, himself left it in resentment, and retired to Agra, where he was waiting the Board's commands, Sindia having in the mean time made a proper atonement for his behaviour. The Board had expressed a wish that he might return, but properly referred it to his discretion. Perhaps you have not heard this; the latter part you very probably have not. I hear little besides; but that little I dislike: nor do I know a syllable of what passes in the India House. Turner has sent me an abundant supply of turnip seeds, ingeniously packed, and in excellent preservation. They will do admirably for Scotland, and you shall have some for trial. At what time of the year are your turnips sown? Where has Sands fixed himself? I have also got a Bootan bull, of the

Chowry species, one female shawl goat, and I am told that there is a male for me in the Dublin, some time arrived. The bull is in fine health, and I am in quest of a mate of his own size, to secure what I can of the breed; for I doubt if we shall ever get another from India.

Did I tell you that the Chinese only use the seeds of the red palma christi, accounting the green unwholesome? I don't know which is the sort used in England; but it is worth inquiring. I am yet unable to ride; in other respects well. Mrs. Hastings is, I thank God, in better health than she has known since I arrived in England. Whether Beaumont Lodge has contributed to this, God knows. I think that we should be both better for a month's residence in a drier atmosphere than this island, I fear, can afford in any part of it. Adieu, your affectionate.

Thus far Mr. Hastings proceeded with his arrangements, ere the session of 1787 opened. He soon found, after the investigation of his case was resumed, that more would be necessary. He therefore determined to meet his enemies on the ground where they imagined that they were most secure, by obtaining from the people of India—the Hindoo and Mussulman inhabitants of the country which he had so long governed—testimonials of the estimation in which, both as a ruler and a man he had been and still continued to be held. The following letters to Sir John Shore, afterwards Lord Teignmouth, and to Mr. Thompson, his friend and ancient secretary, explain themselves.

To Sir JOHN SHORE.

St. James's Place, 19th February, 1787.

Dear Shore,—As I have now every reason to believe that an impeachment will be carried against me to the House of Lords, and have had a severe warning given me not to trust to my own integrity, or services, as I may conceive them, for the event,—and as I fear no issue of the trial so much as its influence on my future and lasting reputation,—I apply to you, my friend, to afford me such assistance as, I hope, may be in your power to obviate such a conclusion, by collecting the testimonials of the most respectable inhabitants of the provinces of Bengal, and such other creditable vouchers, of whatever kind, beyond the provinces, as may refute the calumnies with which I have been loaded, and ascertain whatever pretensions I may have to more positive merit.

I am charged with cruelty, oppression, violation of treaties, and with the general guilt of having sacrificed every duty to the views of interest, ambition, or private vengeance. I am not sure that rapacity makes a part of the catalogue of my imputed crimes, because the instances which have been adduced in evidence to prove it apply only to acts done for the relief of the public necessities, and it is scarcely (I believe not at all) insinuated, that I have practised it for any profit of my own.

I wish to make my appeal to the justice and generosity of those to whom it best appertains, to pronounce upon my real character, according to their several relations or concerns with the government of Bengal during the periods in which I held an efficient share in its powers; that they may declare whether I deserve these imputations, or whether I am entitled to their testimony of the reverse.

Whether I have extorted money from individuals to

gratify my own avarice; or whether I have not notoriously abstained from every means which might have promoted my own interest, with the injury of individuals or the public:

Whether I have countenanced, or permitted; or whether I have not, on the contrary, to the utmost of my power prevented men in office or favour from oppressing or plundering those who were subjected to their authority or influence:

Whether the provinces have been infested with robbers, or plundering Seneassies, as much during my administration as in the times preceding it:

Whether the provinces have suffered the calamities either of war or famine during my administration; or whether they have not enjoyed both uninterrupted peace and abundance, though our Government and nation were for years engaged in wars with powerful states and neighbours, and were at one time threatened with a dearth from the same causes which produced one in 1768:

Whether I have oppressed the reiats by intolerable or unequal taxes, for the public service; or whether I have not rather multiplied the sources of public wealth, and equalized the burthens imposed on the people:

Whether I have neglected the administration of justice; or whether I have not established Courts of Civil and Criminal Justice, and supported both in the exercise of their functions beyond the experience of any former times:

Whether I have offended, or discountenanced the laws, customs, and religious worship of the country; or whether I have not respected, protected, and conformed to them:

Whether I have shown a disregard to science; or whether I have not, on the contrary, by public endowments, by personal attentions, and by the selection of men for appointments suited to their talents, given effectual encouragement to it:

Whether in my public negociations, and in my general intercourse, I have made use of artifice and trick, or of truth and plain-dealing:

Whether I have affected a display of state; whether I have ever shown an inordinate solicitude for my personal safety; or whether I have not been thought to err in the opposite extremes:

Whether I left the country in a worse or in a better state of population and cultivation than I found it:

And lastly, whether the English name, power, and influence were ever greater, more respected, or more extensively known in India before than during my administration, and particularly at the close of it.

The persons who can be most instrumental in collecting the suffrages which I require, are Gunga Govin Sing; Allee Ibraheem Cawn; Beneram, or Bissumbes Pundit; Rajah Govindram; Tofuzzel Hossein Cawn; Mowlary Majud O'Deen, or his brother Muftee Ahmed; and I believe I may venture to join Mahdajee Sindia. I would wish at least to have his testimony, and those of every other chief with whom our Government was in connexion; Moodajee, the ministers of Poona, Nizam al Moolk, Assof o' Dowlah, and the Nabob Wallah Jah.

I cannot prescribe the means. Perhaps I have been too particular in detailing the ends. But you must make allowances for my anxiety, and the cause which I have to make me more than ordinarily anxious.

If you think that you can undertake this commission with an assurance of its complete execution, you will of course (as I should on every account wish) first propose it to Lord Cornwallis for his approbation. If he objects to it, there must of course be an end to it. Even from the little which I know of his Lordship, and from his general character, I give him credit for qualities incompatible with such a supposition, and assure myself besides that he will not in Bengal have changed the opinion which he entertained of me in England for a worse.

I will not ask your forgiveness for wishing to impose on you so much trouble; but I ought if I thought that it might eventually draw on you the same enmities which are now directed at me. I confess, I think such may be the consequence, though I rather hope that the crisis of this phrenzy may terminate with me. If it does not, I am not sure that any conduct will be a safeguard against it.

You will readily comprehend that I do not mean to use the justification which I solicit from your means for any purpose of meeting the impending trial; for though I am certain that every artifice will be put in practice to protract it, it will be impossible to extend the delay beyond another sessions; I mean another after the present. The result, therefore, of this plan can be of no other benefit to me than that of retrieving my character from the injury which it may have received from the present prosecution, and its legal consequences. These must all have ceased long before the result of my commission can arrive in England. I am not sure that the House of Commons will vote an impeachment. I cannot be certain that the same prejudices, the same intrigues, and the same influence may not follow me into the House of Lords, though in judicial matters the character of that assembly stands hitherto unimpeached. But I have been told by judgments much better informed than those of common men, that much is to be apprehended, even in that assembly, from the respect paid to a decided judgment of the House of Commons, and yet more to the ascribed inclination of the minister; and I myself have my doubts of another kind. The charges may prove so numerous and complicated, that every mind will not be able to comprehend them, or to retain even what they do comprehend; and the tedious and artificial examination of the witnesses to every charge will, with the other process, take up such a length of time, that the aged, infirm, and indifferent will not sit out the trial. I may therefore lose many verdicts in my favour. None will be lost of those which are predetermined against me. I am almost ashamed of these suspicions; yet, after what has passed, how can I avoid them? I have been condemned by one assembly for having intended by a resolution, which was confined to my own breast, to exact a fine from Cheyt Sing exceeding his offences, admitted to be great, and a fine, if moderate, admitted to be a legal and proper punishment. I have been condemned for permitting the jagheers and treasures to be taken from the mother of the Nabob Assof o' Dowlah, because in the evidence adduced by my prosecutor to prove my guilt, I had not brought proofs sufficient of the Begum's rebellion against her sovereign, and hostility to our nation; though the charge, black and rancorous as it is, and the admired harangue of the mover of the charge, fabricated with the labour of months, and the combination of all the powers of a great party, both stated in terms that the money produced by these exactions was applied to the relief of the public necessities, and they have not dared to suggest that I took or attempted to take any part of it to my own use. Let, however, this business end as it will, a great portion of mankind will think they judge with candour, if, unable to comprehend any part of the accusations, they acquit me, at a guess, of some, and conclude that where so much is alleged against me, much of it must be necessarily true. The plan which I have recommended may be productive of that species of evidence which the meanest capacity will understand, and which will most effectually and totally efface every prejudice against me. Let it arrive when it will, whether I shall have received an absolute and unqualified acquittal, or a condemnation; whether I am alive or dead, it will answer the end for which I want it. I am ever, my dear Shore, your most affectionate friend.

To Mr. THOMPSON.

St. James's Place, 19th February, 1787.

My dear Thompson,—If the letter which I have written with this to Mr. Shore should be delivered to you according to its direction, and God forbid that it should be in one of the events supposed in it, I request that you will open and read it as addressed originally to yourself, and then you will conform to the contents of it. Yours affectionately.

To the same.

St. James's Place, 29th March, 1787.

My dear Thompson,—I have not time to write answers to your letters. I have not yet paid your draft, because I could not raise the money without loss. It will be paid in the course of next month. I have written a letter to Shore, which I have directed, in case of his absenc or death, to you, and in either case I have desired you to execute the commission which is contained in it. I sometimes flatter myself that, as the thought is obvious, my friends in Bengal will have anticipated it. I suppose that of course Shore will show you the letter. Mr. Pitt has shown himself so unequivocally on the same side with Mr. Burke in the business of my impeachment, and they have so many followers, that there is no doubt of its going to the House of Lords. I am only fearful of delays. I shall be perfectly contented if I am completely out of the hands of the Commons this sessions. But that the impeachment will be voted you may be assured, though it will be strongly contested, (and on grounds with which I have but a remote and accidental concern,) and the two sides of the house disagree upon the articles, each condemning and approving what the other approves and condemns. My friends in India will hear with indignation, and my enemies with ridicule, that in one charge I have been condemned for removing Mr. Shea from Furrukhabad, and leaving Mozuffer Jung unprotected, and of course oppressed. I send you a paper which contains a brief state of the charge which is to be debated to-morrow. I have caused sixty to be printed, with the intent of distributing them among my friends: but am advised that it will not be prudent, as my friends will give them to my enemies, and these will turn them to ridicule, extract centos from them to turn my own words against me; and as no one will read them but those who mean to pervert what they read, the rest will believe whatever is asserted to be quoted from them. This was done with the charge of the Begums.

I cannot yet give up my bureau. I am sorry that you did not make public search for it. I now beg you to do so, and obtain the support of Lord Cornwallis for making it. It is strange. Every January did Larkins's writers, and my banyans, take an accurate account of my dead stock, and of the Company's dead stock, as they lay in my two houses. Yet you tell me that the Company's sircars claimed for the Company what they pleased, and were allowed what they claimed! but I know not why I complain. I beg that you will send home every paper of mine that was left, and that has existence. Many were left that I have eagerly sought for among those which I have, in vain. Not one of my pictures has been sent after me, none of my Tibbet pictures, not one, but Mrs. Hastings's of Zoffani's, and that packed so negligently that it arrived almost spoiled. I thank you for your intention of sending Sulliman. If he is not too old, he may yet do two or three years of service; at least his breed is invaluable. I have in vain sought for a horse that Mrs. Hastings can ride, and this is now my only chance. You will be pleased to hear that Mrs. Hastings gains health and strength visibly, though of a constitution still too susceptible. I am certainly better than I was the last year: yet I shall not be completely well till I can make trial of the drier atmosphere of the continent. I am, my dear Thompson, yours most affectionately.

The doubt which rested on the mind of Mr. Hastings, when the preceding letter was written, (if indeed he can be said to have doubted, even then, concerning an issue so obvious,) was not slow in receiving its solution. On the 21st of May, Mr. Burke moved that he should be taken into the custody of the serjeant-at-arms, and he was taken into custody accordingly. In this state he accompanied the managers to the bar of the House of Lords, where articles of impeachment were exhibited against him; and he departed from it on bail, being bound over to appear again when required, himself in the sum of £2000, and two sureties to the amount of £1000 each. Thus, after a long life spent in the public service, during no inconsiderable portion of which he had been at the head of a mighty empire; after having been repeatedly thanked in that position by the East India Company, and thrice continued in office by a solemn vote of the legislature; Mr. Hastings found himself called upon to defend his character, perhaps his life, against the violence of a faction, which accused him of crimes the most repugnant to his nature, and of which it seems hardly credible that the most rancorous of his personal enemies could have believed him to be guilty. For the only boons which he could now solicit, and which were not of course refused, were, that he might be furnished with a copy of the indictment, and be allowed counsel, and time for the preparation of his defence. He went forth, therefore, to the world, a branded man, whom nothing short of a formal acquittal, by the highest tribunal in the nation, could restore to his legitimate place in society.

From this time forth, throughout an interval of not less than seven years, Mr. Hastings continued on his trial. There was arrayed against him all the eloquence, and talent, and influence of a scarcely divided House of Commons; while he depended for support upon his own lofty sense of right alone, and the indefatigable exertions of the three distinguished lawyers to whom the care of his defence had been committed. But the questions at issue between him and the managers soon spread beyond the limits of Westminster-hall. Not England only, but all Europe, watched with intense interest the progress of events; while India sent home its countless testimonies to the public and private virtues of the man whom his own government rewarded for the benefits he had conferred upon them by a prosecution, which in every point of view has no parallel in history. As might have been expected, moreover, the passions of men began immediately to be roused, and the press teemed with pamphlets criminatory or otherwise of the accused. These had their day, and were certainly not without their uses; but as I cannot afford space to describe in detail the events of the impeachment itself, far less will it be expected of me that I should make further allusion to the countless pamphlets which discussed it, than by placing upon record the fact, that they once existed and are now forgotten.

A reference to the journals of Parliament will inform the curious in these matters, of the extraordinary solemnity with which the Peers met for the first time in their judicial capacity. "The House," says the historian of the trial, "met at ten, and by eleven a message was sent to the Commons, that the House was immediately going to adjourn to Westminster Hall, to proceed upon the trial of Warren Hastings, Esq. A message was immediately returned that the Commons were ready to substantiate their charges. The Lords were then called over by the clerk, and arranged by Sir Isaac Heard, principal king at arms, when upwards of two hundred proceeded to Westminster

Hall." From the same authority we learn, that "previous to their Lordships' approach to the hall, about eleven o'clock, her Majesty, with the Princesses Elizabeth, Augusta, and Mary; made their appearance in the Duke of Newcastle's gallery. Her Majesty was dressed in a fawn coloured satin, her head-dress plain, with a very slender sprinkling of diamonds. The royal box was graced with the Duchess of Gloucester and the young prince. The ladies were all in mourning dresses; a few with feathers and variegated flowers in their head-dress, but nothing so remarkable as to attract public attention. Mrs. Fitzherbert was in the royal box. The Dukes of Cumberland, Gloucester, and York, and the Prince of Wales, with their trains, followed the Chancellor, and closed the procession. Upwards of two hundred of the Commons, with the speaker, were in the gallery. The managers, Charles Fox and all, were in full dress; but a very few of the Commons were full dressed, some of them were in boots. Their seats were covered with green cloth—the rest of the building was 'one red.'

"Mr. Hastings stood for some time. On a motion from a peer, the Chancellor allowed as a favour that the prisoner should have a chair; and he sat throughout the day, except occasionally when he spoke to his counsel. His counsel were Mr. Law, Mr. Plumer, Mr. Dallas. For the Commons, Dr. Scott and Dr. Lawrence; Messrs, Mansfield, Piggot, Burke, and Douglas.

"A party of horse guards, under the command of a field-officer, with a captain's party from the Horse Grenadiers, attended daily during the trial. A body of three hundred foot-guards also kept the avenues clear; and a considerable number of constables attended for the purpose of taking offenders into custody."

I pass over the description of the fitting up of the hall itself, as well as of the order in which the Peers entered and arranged themselves, that I may extract the following account of the manner in which the business of the court began. "At twelve," says my authority, "the court was opened, and the serjeant-at-arms, with a very audible voice, made the usual proclamation; after which, in old blunt English, he summoned 'Warren Hastings, Esq. to come forth in court, and save thee and thy bail, otherwise the recognizance of thee and thy bail will be forfeited.' Hereupon Mr. Hastings appeared at the bar with his two sureties, Mr. Sulivan and Mr. Sumner, and immediately dropped upon his knees; but the Lord Chancellor signified that he might rise. He seemed very infirm and much indisposed. He was dressed in a plain poppy coloured suit of clothes.

"After Mr. Hastings appeared at the bar, a proclamation as follows was made:—

"'Whereas charges of high crimes and misdemeanours have been exhibited by the knights, citizens, and burgesses in Parliament assembled, in the name of themselves and of all the Commons of Great Britain, against Warren Hastings, Esq., all persons concerned are to take notice that he now stands on his trial, and they may come forth in order to make good the said charges.'

"Proclamation being made, the Lord Chancellor rose, and addressed the prisoner as follows:—

"'Warren Hastings, You are called upon, after every expedient allowance, for your defence. You have had bail: you have counsel. Much time also has been granted you, becoming well the circumstances of your case. For the matter in the charges is most momentous, and the dates are remote since the occurrences in those charges alleged against you are said to have been committed. These advantages you must understand, while you feel; you are to deem them, not an indulgence of this House, but the fair claim of right, a concession of nothing, but what you have in common with all around you—what every British subject may ask, and every British tribunal must allow. Conduct your defence, therefore, in a manner that may befit your station, and the magnitude of the charges against you, and estimate rightly the high character of those you have to answer—the Commons of Great Britain; who at once, perhaps, attach likelihood to doubt, and enforce authority, certainly on declaration.'

"To which Mr. Hastings made almost verbatim the following answer :—

"'My Lords, I am come to this high tribunal, equally impressed with a confidence in my own integrity, and in the justice of the court before which I stand.'"

Thus was the tribunal opened, which was to decide concerning Warren Hastings, not whether he had earned and should receive high rewards from his King and country, but whether or not he were covered with such a load of obloquy and crime, as never before attached to any high functionary under the British crown. The ceremony was grave and solemn as became the occasion, neither can any blame attach throughout either to the illustrious court or its distinguished president. But the feelings of him are, I conceive, very little to be envied, who can think of the conduct of the parties by whom that most iniquitous prosecution was carried forward, without indignation.

The following letters give so vivid a description of the state of the writer's feelings at this period, that I cannot resist the inclination to insert them. They are very beautiful, both in their tone and composition, and do infinite honour even to Mr. Hastings.

To Mr. Thompson.

Beaumont Lodge, 2nd August, 1787.

My dear Thompson,—I have not heard from you by any of the late arrivals, nor indeed for some time past; and the Barrington is yet expected, not without some fears for her safety. I am unreasonable; but I feel the disappointment of every packet that does not bring me a letter from you.

You will suffer by all the past advices from England in your concern for me. As for myself, I have made up my mind for the worst that can befall me; and can with truth affirm that I have borne with perfect indifference all the base treatment which I have had dealt to me, except the ignominious ceremonial of kneeling before the House of Lords, though I think it a usage that reflects more dishonour on that assembly for permitting the continuance of so iniquitous a form, than on those who are compelled to submit to it, and on whom it is inflicted as a punishment not only before conviction, but even before the accusations against them are read. I am prepared for my trial, and hope (whatever may be the result of it, for I should not be too sanguine, if the only crime laid to my charge was that I was concerned in the revolt of America) that it will be ended before the end of the next sessions of Parliament.

I have written to Shore in duplicate, and addressed both letters provisionally to you upon a subject which has a near relation to my impeachment, or rather to the event of it. Let me know only if you have heard anything about them.

I have the pleasure to tell you that I pass the best months of the year in the place from which this is dated, with great comfort, and almost delight, and have the satisfaction of seeing Mrs. Hastings's health proceed in improvement, though it is yet delicate, and subject to frequent and sudden ailments. She has suffered more than I have done from my prosecution, and I only from her sufferings (except the instances mentioned above).

I had the pleasure to see Mr. Anstey a few months ago in town, well, and cheerful, as I suppose he is always.

I can give you no news; I am not in the way of hearing any. I never see any official men who are concerned in affairs of India, nor know what they are doing. You will hear that we are likely to be engaged in the present contests of the Dutch, and in another war, the consequence of it, which, I believe, we are striving to avoid by, not the best of all expedients, negociation. If we fail, you will feel the first effects of it.

Mrs. Hastings always remembers you with affection, and desires me to tell you so. Adieu, my dear friend. Your affectionate.

Remember me kindly to Turner. I am too lately informed of this despatch to write to him. Make the same excuse for me, with the kindest remembrance of me to Colonel Kyd.

To the same.

London, 8th February, 1788.

My dear Thompson,—I hope to have sufficient leisure, before the last despatches of the season, to write to you with your unanswered letters before me. It would now take up more of my time than I could afford to select them; and you must be content to receive my annual report on the subject in which you will be most interested. Mrs. Hastings, in spite of some occasions on which she suffers her spirits to be affected more than they ought with the impending transactions, gains daily, though but gently, both in health and in the appearance of it; and I am well.

On Wednesday next, the 13th, I am to appear as a criminal before the first tribunal of the kingdom. How long the trial will last God knows; but I believe it is not yet in the power of man to conjecture. Sir E. Impey appeared on the 4th, and last night, at the bar of the House, and was allowed to defend himself on the charge of having deliberately murdered Nundcomar, which he did most ably, and with an effect that brought over every member of the House but his prosecutors, and confessedly some of them, though they will persevere. It is agreed to decide on this article immediately, and there is little doubt that it will be thrown out by a large majority, and without much delay, though it is probable that much art will be used to spin it out, and to afford time for the present impression to wear off, which it soon would do from minds so superficial and so finely polished as those of that House.

I wait with much impatience for the Ravensworth. Surely she will bring some materials that may afford me more service than the mere negative argument drawn from her producing no complaints against me, which, if the activity of my prosecutors could obtain them, I should not yet be surprised to see. I have but an imperfect recollection of my having mentioned in one of my letters to you, that I had written a letter to Shore in February, 1787 (I have not the copy, or any memorandum of the date by me), desiring him to collect authentic testimonies of the native inhabitants of our own provinces, and others in political connexion with our Government, respecting my conduct towards them. I did not then suppose it possible for him to execute this commission for the purpose of the present trial; neither do I now expect it, but that it may afford complete satisfaction to the world. Yet I sometimes persuade myself, that as I was never the personal enemy of any man but Nundcomar, whom from my soul I detested even when I was compelled to countenance him; and as no man in a station similar to mine, and with powers cramped and variable as mine were, ever laboured with so passionate a zeal for the welfare of a nation as I did to promote the happiness and prosperity of the people under our jurisdiction, the gratitude of some of them will have of itself suggested and produced the attestations which I wish. My own countrymen abroad, civil and military, have shown them, by two noble examples, what they might, I will not say what they ought, to do. I would rather have such testimonies, although the law should reject them, than any that could be offered here with its sanction for my acquittal. In the hours of solitude and secret reflection I have indulged myself with a number of fancies of what might have been done, and which I have almost wrought myself into the expectation of hearing that such had been done. It was not presumption to expect that that measure would be dealt to me which I have so often dealt to others; for what public merit has not had its due praise in various, and even some in lasting, means of publication?

I have desired Major Hussey to take charge of a small parcel, containing a few recent publications which may amuse you. One by Mr. Wilkes, published about eight months ago, is, I think, a most elegant as well as sensible composition. The others are all come out within these few days. Adieu. I am, my dear Thompson, yours ever most affectionately.

CHAPTER XI.

Results of the Impeachment—Specimens of Mr. Burke's Eloquence—Sir Gilbert Elliott a Manager—Proceedings at the India House.

THUS far the reader and I have journeyed onwards together, tracing the career of the subject of this memoir with strict attention to the chronological order of the events which, one after another, gave a colouring to his fortunes. It will be necessary that we deviate for a while from this course, because, however important to the individual the transactions of a strictly domestic life may be, they afford no materials out of which to construct a narrative calculated to arrest the attention of strangers. I must content myself, therefore, in reference to the impeachment, by stating, that for the space of seven entire years its issues hung in suspense; that every effort of Mr. Hastings and his counsel to obtain a speedy judgment was frustrated; that the three estates of the realm were repeatedly petitioned, sometimes conjointly, sometimes separately, but that no results followed favourable to the cause of justice and humanity. Long after it must have been apparent to themselves that they had failed in establishing their case, the managers persevered in attacks the very tone of which sufficiently indicated the spirit in which they originated, for it was that of personal vituperation and malignity throughout. But the Lords did their duty, as they have always done when appealed to for the administration of strict and impartial justice. On the 23rd of April, 1795, Mr. Hastings was commanded to present himself in Westminster Hall, when the Chancellor (Lord Loughborough), no friend of his from the outset, informed him that by a large majority he had been acquitted, and that he was in consequence discharged.

It is a gratifying thing, doubtless, to be dismissed from a lengthened inquisition into character, with a reputation freed from reproach by the verdict of our judges; and this gratification Mr. Hastings experienced in no ordinary degree. For though the determinately prejudiced might still cling to their own views of his case, by the universal voice of the nation, his acquittal was greeted as a triumph. Moreover, the congratulatory addresses which poured in upon him, not from his friends and countrymen alone, but from strangers and foreigners, and above all from the inhabitants of British India, told of the general interest which his wrongs had excited, in language that was not to be misunderstood. Yet Mr. Hastings came not forth from the ordeal unscathed. His good name might be saved, but his worldly prospects were blighted, inasmuch as the cost of the trial had swallowed up almost all the savings of a lifetime. Not less than seventy-six thousand five hundred and twenty-eight pounds were wasted in law charges alone; while the other expenses incident to such a protracted prosecution, during which it was necessary to communicate with all parts of the world, and bring witnesses from very distant quarters, reduced the party in whose favour sentence was given to a state of bankruptcy. Mr. Hastings, when for the last time he turned his back on Westminster Hall, could not tell whence the funds were to come by which the weekly bills of his household might be discharged; he was, as far as pecuniary matters were affected, a ruined man.

It was not, however, by these means alone that the impeachment operated with fatal effect upon the immediate condition and future prospects of Mr. Hastings. The doors of public life were, in a great measure, shut against him by it for ever. Acquitted he doubtless was, and society, in all its departments, from the palace to the cottage, hailed the event with joy; but as both the great parties in the state had united in carrying the prosecution forward, so they equally withdrew from the contest, as men are apt to do, when, in their efforts to accomplish some great purpose, they have been defeated. Mr. Burke and his friends continued to hate the man whom, in the spirit of undisguised hatred, they had dragged before the highest tribunal in the land. Mr. Pitt, and the supporters of his administration generally, could not forgive the same individual, because, in spite of their influence exerted against him, he had established his own innocence. The very extent of Mr. Hastings's deservings became in their eyes a ground of hostility; and having failed to destroy, they determined, and adhered to their determination, to neglect him.

Of the existence of this feeling towards himself, on the part of the King's Government, Mr. Hastings was not destined to remain long in ignorance. After a day or two devoted to the exchange of visits of congratulation, and paying his court, as became him, both at the levee and in the drawing room, Mr. Hastings drew up a petition to the House of Commons, in which he set forth the heavy expenses to which, by the impeachment, he had been subjected, and prayed for remuneration. He took this step in despite of the remonstrances of his most intimate friends, who prognosticated that no good would arise from it; yet it was not taken unadvisedly. On the contrary, as he had more than once, in the course of the trial, been given to understand, that in the event of an acquittal, his expenses would be defrayed by the country, Mr. Hastings conceived that he was entitled, both in law and equity, to the remuneration for which he applied. And he ventured to hope, in defiance of all apparent probabilities to the contrary, that the Chancellor of the Exchequer would himself see the matter in a similar light. He therefore commissioned his friend, Colonel Hastings, to carry the petition to Mr. Pitt, with a request that the right honourable gentleman would lay the case before the King, so that the application, when formally made, might carry with it the weight of a message from the Crown. Mr. Pitt seems to have taken a few days, and only a few, to deliberate on the proposition of Colonel Hastings. He returned the paper at their termination, with a short note to the effect, that, "under all the circumstances, he did not conceive that he should be justified in submitting the petition of the late Governor-general of India to the consideration of the sovereign."

To say that Mr. Hastings was either surprised or disappointed by the refusal of Mr. Pitt to interest himself in his petition, would be to advance an opinion for which I have no authority in fact. I am inclined, on the contrary, to believe, that the result of the application was scarcely different from that which he anticipated, because he seems, from very early times, to have counted little, if at all, upon the friendly disposition of the prime minister. How, indeed, could the case be otherwise? Mr.

Hastings was not ignorant that it was Mr. Pitt who stood between him and a peerage ten years previously; while the whole bearing of that right honourable gentleman, from the beginning to the end of the trial, had evinced towards him a feeling decidedly hostile. Still Mr. Hastings believed that there was a moral obligation upon himself to make the move, and he made it without much caring whether it might prove successful or the reverse. It was not successful, and the applicant felt chagrined for the moment. Nevertheless he found no reason in the end to regret having exposed himself to the repulse, because the fact of his having sustained one placed him in a better light towards the East India Company, and strengthened the hands of his adherents while appealing to that body for the justice (I cannot call it the bounty) which the Legislature refused to award.

Besides these more serious evils,—the loss of fortune, and the negation of merited honours,—Mr. Hastings was exposed, as well during the progress of the trial as after its termination, to annoyances which, by a finely tempered mind like his, are scarcely more endurable than the worst that can befall. He was prepared, as every man gifted with common sense must be against whom a criminal prosecution lies, to find his good name treated with little respect by those who might undertake the conduct of such prosecution. But on the extreme lengths to which the leading manager carried the system of vituperation he had never counted.

"We know," said Mr. Burke on one occasion, "that as we are to be served by men, that the persons who serve us must be tried as men, and that there is a very large allowance indeed due to human infirmity and human error. This we know, and have weighed before we came to your Lordships' bar. But the crimes we charge are not the causes and effects of common human frailty, such as we know, and feel, and can allow for, but they are crimes which have their rise in the wicked dispositions of men; they are crimes which have their rise in avarice, rapacity, pride, cruelty, ferocity, malignity of temper, haughtiness, insolence,—in short, everything that manifests a heart blackened to the very blackest—a heart dyed deep in blackness—a heart gangrened to the core." . . . "We have not chosen to bring before you a poor trembling delinquent." . . . "We have brought before you the head, the chief, a captain-general of iniquity—one in whom all the fraud, all the tyranny of India are embodied, disciplined, and arrayed." . . . "I charge him," continued the orator, "with having taken away the lands of orphans, with having alienated the fortunes of widows, with having wasted the country and destroyed the inhabitants, after cruelly harassing and distressing them. I charge him with having tortured their persons and dishonoured their religion through his wicked agents, who were at the bottom and root of his villainy. I charge him in the name of the Commons of England." . . . "Now, my Lords, what is it we want? We want to have the cause of oppressed princes, of undone women of the first rank, redressed—of desolated provinces and wasted kingdoms redressed. Do YOU want a criminal, my Lords? When was so much iniquity charged against any one? No, my Lords, you must not look to India to furnish one, for Mr. Hastings has not left in India substance enough to furnish such another delinquent." . . . "I impeach Warren Hastings in the name of the people of all India, whose laws, rights, and liberties he has subverted. I impeach him in the name of the people of India, whose country he has destroyed. I impeach him in the name of human nature, which he has cruelly injured and oppressed in both sexes."

Such is a specimen of the style in which the leading manager judged it not inexpedient to clothe the harangue with which the proceedings against Mr. Hastings were opened. The charges, though general, are all of the most atrocious kind; the prisoner at the bar, ere the case against him has been so much as stated, is overwhelmed with invectives, which would have been misapplied had he stood there to receive sentence as a convicted criminal. Does the reader desire to know how the same orator expressed himself when the progress of events carried him forward to the discussion of particular acts? The following samples are taken at random from Mr. Burke's speeches in 1789:—

The prisoner is "eminent for the pillage and destruction of provinces." . . . His are "crimes of great enormity, the ruin and expulsion of illustrious families, the total ruin of villages, the total expulsion of the first houses in Asia." . . . He is a man "who in his own person has done more mischief than all those persons whose evil practices had produced all those laws, those regulations, and even his own appointments." ... "A corrupt, shocking arrangement was made, and Bengal saw a dancing girl administer its laws." ... "He murdered that man (Nundcomar) by the hands of Sir Elijah Impey." ... "He gorged his ravenous maw with an allowance of two hundred pounds a-day. He is not satisfied without sucking the blood of fourteen hundred nobles. He is never corrupt without he is cruel. He never dines without creating a famine. He feeds on the indigent, the decaying, and the ruined, and them he depresses together, not like the generous eagle who preys on a living, reluctant, equal prey; no, he is like the ravenous vulture, who feeds on the dead and the enfeebled; who destroys and incapacitates nature in the destruction of its objects while devouring the carcases of the dead, and then prides himself on his ignominious security; and his cruelty is beyond his corruption. At the same time there is in his hypocrisy something more terrible than his cruelty. For at the same time that he exercises a proscription that sweeps off the bread of thousands of the nobility, he turns the precious balm that flows from wounded humanity into deadly, rancorous, and mortal poison to the human race." ... "His crimes are so multiplied, that all the contrivances of ingenuity to cover them are abortive."

Will these specimens of Mr. Burke's eloquence suffice, or shall we add to them one or two more? Let the following sum up our catalogue. They will at least show that it was not always in a spirit of generous indignation, because of wrongs done, or supposed to be done, to suffering millions, that the manager indulged his taste and talent for invective of the grossest kind. It is thus that he speaks of Mr. Hastings, not as the governor of a province, but as a man :—

"This swindling Mecænas—swindling of glory, and obtaining honour under false pretences—a bad scribbler of absurd papers, who could never put two sentences of sense together." . . . "A man whose origin was low, obscure, and vulgar, and bred in vulgar and ignoble habits; more proud than persons born under canopies of state, and swaddled in purple." . . . The proceedings of this man were, he says, "a traitorous and rebellious assumption of the power which belongs only to the King, as sovereign, with both Houses of Parliament." . . . Again: "Such are the damned and damnable proceedings of a judge in hell, and such a judge was Warren Hastings." . . . "Sir Walter Raleigh was called a spider of hell. This was foolish, indecent in Lord Coke. Had he been a manager on this trial he would have been guilty of a neglect of duty had he not called the prisoner a spider of hell." . . . Finally, he is "a captain-general of iniquity, thief, tyrant, robber, cheat, swindler, sharper. We call him all these names, and are sorry that the English language does not afford terms adequate to the enormity of his offences."

The freedom of speech claimed by every counsel, whether in the prosecution or defence of a prisoner, is doubtless very great; neither is he a friend to substantial justice who would desire to see it materially abridged; but I do not think that the wildest advocate of forensic licence will venture to justify expressions like these, even if the case be one where, to save life, it is necessary to appeal, not to the reason, but to the passions of an ordinary jury. Mr. Burke, however, had not even this poor excuse to offer for his outrage on common decency. His own passions were not, or rather ought not to have been, enlisted either for or against the accused. His appeal was made to a court in which reason, and reason alone, might be expected to preside. What right had he to load with opprobrious epithets, and cover with unmitigated abuse, a great public servant, against whom he had been commissioned to conduct a great public prosecution ? But this is not all. Far from desiring that his words should be received as the index of his own private opinion, no matter on what evidence formed, Mr. Burke had the audacity to drag the whole Commons of England at his chariot wheel; and to tell the Lords that as the libels which he had uttered were fully credited by the body which had commissioned him to speak in their name, so they must choose between the prisoner and the House of Commons, one or other of whom their sentence would overwhelm with disgrace. "Nothing," said he, "but the malice of the House of Commons could have instigated them to institute this prosecution if they had not been sure of his guilt. Nothing but a great party formed by his wealth could support him." . . . "I tremble for the event, because, if the prisoner is innocent, the Commons are guilty."

Such was the temper and spirit in which, from first to last, Mr. Burke carried on the prosecution of Warren Hastings; and such the insults to which Mr. Hastings, throughout nine long years, found himself under the necessity of submitting. Moreover, the utmost pains were taken to induce a belief, both at home and abroad, that the object of all this obloquy was rolling in wealth; in wealth, wrung from the blood of oppressed millions, and now dispensed with a free hand, in order to corrupt the springs of justice, even at the fountain head. Among other ridiculous stories, which had their day, though a brief one, I may be permitted to specify two—both of which made some noise at the time, though they are long ago forgotten. It happened on the 2d of January, 1786,—the very day on which the Commons came to the resolution of impeaching Mr. Hastings on the Benares charge,—that Mr. Hastings received, through Mr. Richard Johnson, the Company's resident at the Court of Hyderabad, a letter from the Nabob Nizam Ally Cawn; which, together with a small bulze, containing a diamond, the Nabob requested Mr. Hastings to present to the King. The diamond and letter were delivered to Lord Sydney, who conveyed them, as in duty bound, to His Majesty; and they were both graciously received. But the matter did not end there. In the House of Commons first, and afterwards in the newspapers, it was asserted, that the letter from the Nabob was an impudent forgery; and that the diamond, a jewel of incalculable value, had been given by Mr. Hastings himself as a bribe, wherewith to secure the royal countenance and support in his difficulties. It is scarcely necessary to add, that the caricaturists soon turned the story to account. The shop windows were almost immediately filled with representations of George the Third in a wheel-barrow, which Mr. Hastings trundled before him; while the legend ran thus:—"What a man buys he may sell." The good old King, it appears, was highly amused with the device. He laughed heartily when it was shown to him, and said, "Well, I have seen myself in many odd situations, but never in a wheel-barrow till now."

The story of the diamond was absurd and malicious enough; yet, in point of magnitude, it fell greatly short of another, which, a year later, obtained very general circulation. It was said that Mr. Hastings, finding it impossible to remit his enormous fortune by any ordinary means to Europe, had freighted several ships with the most valuable merchandise; and sent them to Amsterdam for the purpose of discharging their cargoes. So completely had this tale gained at one time the ear of the world, that the French Government appointed agents to treat with Mr. Hastings for the purchase of his goods; nor was it without some difficulty that Mr. Hastings could induce the French minister at the Court of St. James to mistrust the truth of a statement to which he had himself contributed to give circulation. At length, however, the French agents went to Amsterdam, where, sure enough, vessels lay to be unloaded; and it was ascertained, that not only was Warren Hastings not the sole owner of their cargoes, but that he had in their cargoes no interest whatever.

I say nothing of the thousand and one stories that got afloat relative to the enormous sums disbursed by Mr. Hastings in hiring writers to plead his cause, and the editors of newspapers to give circulation to their essays. Neither is it worth while to dwell upon Mr. Burke's attempt, so early as the month of January, 1787, to have Mr. Hastings committed to close custody; on the plea that three hundred thousand pounds had been sold out of the public funds, and that the owner of that enormous treasure was about to defeat the course of justice by fleeing from the country. The full disclosures which in due time came out, of the state of Mr. Hastings's pecuniary affairs, both at the commencement and at the close of his impeachment, set to rest these idle rumours for ever.

Yet they were sources of indescribable pain to him who was the object of them at the moment, because Mr. Hastings was sensitive of his honour to a degree which seldom consists with a long life spent in political warfare—more especially in political office; and being a poor man, he felt that his honour was compromised as often as his enemies spoke of him as the reverse. Moreover, they came not alone. Mr. Hastings was indignant with Mr. Burke, and scarcely less so with Mr. Pitt, who added this to his other acts of unkindness—that it was he, who, after sentence of acquittal had gone forth from the House of Lords, moved for a vote of thanks by the Commons to their managers in the impeachment. But a deeper and a more painful feeling possessed the subject of this memoir, when he beheld arrayed among the number of his most inveterate persecutors the brother of Alexander Elliott, on whom he had lavished so much kindness, and whose memory he continued to cherish with the fondest affection. Far be it from me to insinuate that Sir Gilbert Elliott would have been justified, had he, believing Mr. Hastings to be such as the articles of impeachment described him, stood forward from motives of personal gratitude or regard as his defender. But I cannot help thinking, and the world, I conceive, will go along with me, that at least it would have been more becoming, had he declined to appear as one of the managers on the trial. For Sir Gilbert Elliott had been a frequent applicant to Mr. Hastings, while in power, as often as some relative or protégé of his own stood in need of an appointment; and not in a single instance do I find that his applications were rejected. Yet he, after largely benefiting by the patronage of his father's friend, and his brother's protector, did not hesitate to join eagerly in a cabal, which, had it succeeded, must have covered the name of Warren Hastings with disgrace, if indeed it left the bearer of that name any further place in the land of the living. Sir Gilbert Elliott may have been, for aught I know to the contrary, as amiable in private life as he was consistent in politics; but I deceive myself if his name will not go down to posterity with at least one deep stain upon its brightness from which it might have been saved.

The issue of Mr. Hastings's negociation with the minister no sooner became known, than his friends importuned him to lay his case before the Court of Directors; and to demand of them as a matter, not of favour but of right, that his expenses in the recent prosecution should be defrayed by the Company. Mr. Hastings positively refused to act upon this suggestion. "I feel," said he, "equally with you, that I shall suffer great injustice, if, after having been acquitted on every charge, I be left to pay my own costs during the trial; but my claim lies, not against the Company but against the British nation. I have been subjected to a long, and, as the issue has proved, an unmerited prosecution, at the instance of the people of England, or at least of their representatives. It is for the country at large, not for any corporate body of its inhabitants, to replace me on the ground which I occupied ere the prosecution began; and if Parliament refuse this act of justice, I must submit. I can have no claim whatever upon the Court of Directors." His friends, however, thought differently. They argued that in his person the rights of the Company had been tried; and taking into consideration the eminent services which he had rendered, they came to the conclusion that the Proprietors would feel themselves bound to make good his losses during the trial, if, indeed, they went not further, by voting him a separate gratuity.

Foremost in the efforts to which a host of devoted admirers immediately gave themselves up, was Mr. Alderman Lushington; between whom and Mr. Hastings some interesting correspondence passed. It is highly honourable to both parties; for while, on the side of the Alderman, it abounds with reasons why Mr. Hastings should take the ground of one who has earned, and comes to claim his reward; on Mr. Hastings's part the tone is dignified and sober throughout. He is not too proud to accept a favour; on the contrary, he acknowledges his great need, and is willing to be relieved by the bounty of his employers But he abjures the idea of right, while at the same time he pays a becoming regard to his own position, by declaring, that unless he be placed on a footing of equality with Lord Cornwallis, to whom the Company were about to make a grant in testimony of their sense of his eminent services, no consideration of personal inconvenience should induce him to become their debtor for one farthing. Owing to some mistake, Mr. Hastings was a few days subsequently represented by his friend Mr. Vansittart as having, on this latter head, changed his opinion; and Mr. Lushington paved the way, in consequence, both with the Directors, and at the Board of Control, to obtain for him an annuity for life. But the question did not long remain in doubt. Mr. Hastings, informed of what had been done, wrote instantly to set himself right with Mr. Lushington; and it was finally settled that no more should be asked of the Proprietors, than a bare reimbursement of the expenses occasioned by the trial.

The first meeting of Proprietors especially called to take into consideration the case of the late Governor-general of India, occurred on the 29th of May, 1795. It was very numerously attended, and in all its proceedings evinced a spirit decidedly friendly to Mr. Hastings; for a vote in acknowledgment of his distinguished merits passed without opposition, and stands, with many more of a like tendency, on the records of the Court. Others, which had for their object, first, a grant, in compensation for sums expended in the conduct of his defence; and next, the insuring to him out of the Company's land revenue an annuity of five thousand pounds, were not indeed so immediately adopted. Yet, though referred to the ballot, the reference was carried out in the best possible temper, and a large majority in both instances appeared favourable to the proposition. Unfortunately for Mr. Hastings, however, recent enactments had greatly modified the power of the Company to deal generously by their dependants. It was no longer competent for either the Proprietors, or the Directors, or both combined, to vote away sums of money, under the head of remuneration for services performed; they must first of all obtain the sanction of the Board of Control; and the Board when appealed to, in the case now before us, showed no disposition to go along with them. I must again refer my reader to the history of the trial, for the particulars of a transaction which reflects, I write it not without reluctance, little honour on Mr. Pitt's administration. Enough is done when I state, that, taking advantage of certain clauses in the Act of Parliament, under which the Company's charter had been renewed, it was delivered as the opinion of the Attorney and Solicitor-general, that the obstacles in the way of the arrangement proposed were insurmountable. Thus the most pressing point of all—the act which was to relieve Mr. Hastings from a load of debt, under which he could with difficulty bear up —fell to the ground; while of the proposed annuity it was shortly said, that the Board of Control entirely and unhesitatingly condemned it.

The mortification occasioned by this issue to their movements among the friends and admirers of Mr. Hastings (and in the Court of Proprietors they constituted a large majority) appears to have been at least as acute as that with which Mr. Hastings was himself affected; neither were the Directors actuated by a temper different from that which swayed their constituents. They took the subject of his losses into consideration as often as they could find a pretext for doing so, and evinced throughout a laudable desire to discharge themselves of what they felt to be a moral obligation of the most pressing nature. Nor, indeed, was Mr. Hastings's a case which admitted of a moment's unnecessary delay. He was not only penniless, but reduced so completely to the condition of a bankrupt, that the sale of all his property, supposing it to have fetched its full value in the market, would have scarcely enabled him to compound with his creditors at the rate of ten shillings in the pound. Yet this was the man of whom his enemies declared that he had sucked the blood of fourteen thousand nobles, and never sat down to dine without causing a famine!

I am not sure that any good purpose would be served, were I to continue these details much farther. It is well known that, after much hesitation and delay—after frequent remonstrances from the two Courts, and a wavering resistance on the part of the King's Government—the question at issue between Mr. Hastings and the Board of Control ended in a sort of compromise. Instead of the immediate liquidation of his debts, and a pension of 5000*l.* for life, the Company was permitted to settle upon him, for the term of twenty-eight years and a half, an annuity of four thousand pounds; forty-two thousand pounds of which were paid in advance, while a further loan of fifty thousand, free from interest, was offered and accepted. Thus, after the most unreserved exposure of the state of his pecuniary affairs, which hopes, that were never realized, could have alone induced him to make, Mr. Hastings found himself benefited to a slender extent by the good will of his employers; inasmuch as the stream of their bounty was not only reduced to a very narrow volume, but the mode in which it was dispensed took away from its fertilizing influence to a degree which I shall take occasion by and bye to point out. Mr. Hastings never complained of having received harsh usage at the hands of the East India Company; but Mr. Hastings's contemporaries did—what posterity, I suspect, will continue to do. They considered that his eminent services scarcely met with the full measure of their reward, even from the body which had reaped from these services such unparalleled benefits. But I must turn to another page in my history.

CHAPTER XII.

Proceedings in Private Life—Familiar Letters.

So soon as it became apparent that the Government was determined to take part in the impeachment with which he was threatened, Mr. Hastings withdrew almost entirely from public life. He was too proud a man to solicit the favour even of the Crown, while the ministers of the Crown swelled the list of his enemies ; he was too good a man not to find in the quiet pursuits of his own home a compensation for the loss of honours and high station abroad. Of his purchase of Beaumont Lodge, and of the zeal with which he applied himself to its adornment, notice has elsewhere been taken. There in dignified retirement he spent a considerable portion of his time, not unfrequently surrounded by the friends of his early days ; and when he chose to vary the scene, he did so either by visiting London, in the season, or by passing to one or other of the watering places, which were then in fashion. Such migrations, however, like the habits of his domestic life, were all controlled and regulated by a principle of unpretending simplicity. There was nothing mean or sordid about him; quite the reverse; but he was too poor a man to indulge in unnecessary luxuries; and he was by far too wise to find the smallest pleasure in ostentation.

Neither the possession of Beaumont Lodge, however, nor the pains which he took to improve it, withdrew Mr. Hastings's thoughts for one moment from the favourite dream of his youth. He still desired to be the proprietor of the Daylesford estate; and he ultimately succeeded. From an entry in his diary, dated the 26th of August, 1788, I find that he that day completed the purchase, and that the first costs, including an annuity of 100*l.* a-year to Mr. Knight and his wife, amounted barely to eleven thousand four hundred and twenty-four pounds. This may appear a trifling sum for a retired Governor-general of India to have expended in the attainment of an object on which he had long set his heart; yet the reader must not suppose that it received no increase. Daylesford, on the contrary, soon became to its new lord a fruitful source of expenditure. The mansion-house was old and in ruins; he caused it forthwith to be pulled down, and erected a new one in its place. The grounds, greatly indebted to nature, had received no improving touches from the hand of art. He set himself forthwith to the agreeable occupation of planting, levelling, turning various water-courses into one channel, and otherwise embellishing with consummate taste the spot where he meant thenceforth to set up his rest. By referring to the statement of his accounts, which he in 1795 laid before the Chairman of the Court of Directors, it would appear that the total amount of outlay upon the improvements of Daylesford exceeded forty thousand pounds; and that before he had fairly established himself in his new home, Mr. Hastings was out of pocket little short of sixty thousand pounds by the purchase.

From the date of his final settlement at Daylesford, Mr. Hastings sank (if the expression be allowable when speaking of so great a man) into the condition of a country gentleman. In all the pursuits of an agriculturist he took the deepest interest. He bred horses, reared sheep, fatted bullocks, sowed and reaped corn, and exhibited in each of these occupations, as one after another they engrossed him, not less of knowledge than of enthusiasm. As a horticulturist, likewise, his name can never be mentioned without respect. His gardens were perfect models of that graceful style which, owing all its beauties to the skill of the artist, yet appears to be the production of untutored nature. He took infinite pains, moreover, to possess himself of the seeds of plants and herbs which he had admired in their native soil of India, and which he believed were not too delicate to be reared and brought to perfection in England. In a word, Mr. Hastings, in the seclusion of Daylesford, was precisely what he used to be when the fate of a great empire depended upon his will; he was constantly employed, and always had for the end of his exertions the attainment of some good and wise purpose, involving moral or physical benefits to his fellow creatures. It is not, however, to be supposed that he left himself without leisure either to watch as they befel the mighty events by which Europe was shaken, or to keep the fine edge of his genius from growing dull for lack of use. He never ceased to take an interest in public affairs; he never lost his taste for intellectual pursuits, and he contrived so to interweave them with the ordinary occupations of life, that the one seemed, in point of fact, to be a portion of the other. The following brief account of the manner in which one day at Daylesford was spent may be taken as a tolerably correct specimen of all the rest.

Mr. Hastings had always been an early riser: he was generally up and dressed before any other member of the family began to stir, and, shutting himself in his own little room, he devoted the first hour of the day to private study. Mr. Hastings breakfasted invariably alone, and his meal never consisted of any other viands than tea and bread and butter; in the former of which articles, by the way, he was a decided epicure, for he made it after a fashion of his own. It was with him a maxim, that the tea having been once infused, and the tea-pot filled, no second supply of water ought to be added. All the aroma, he would say, is carried off in the first decoction; you extract nothing from the wasted leaves by saturating them again, except a bitter and unwholesome beverage. In like manner, animal food of every description, down, I believe, to the fresh laid egg, was, on principle, excluded from his early meal. But though he never breakfasted with the family party, not even when Daylesford house chanced to be full of guests, Mr. Hastings would come forth from his own room, which communicated with theirs, and sit beside his friends and do his best to amuse them while they were demolishing their tongue and venison pasties. On these occasions he not unfrequently made his appearance with a copy of verses in his hand, the composition of which had employed either his sleepless hours by night or his first waking moments in the morning; and they were uniformly so graceful—so perfectly adapted to the situation of the party, because touching either on the occurrences of the past day, or illustrating some subject of conversation which might have called forth his own wit or the wit of somebody else—that every interruption of the pleasant practice was felt as a grievous disappointment.

There is no poet, however, whose Pegasus will always soar on the mere volition of its rider; and Mr. Hastings did from time to time join the family circle without bringing a poetic offering along with him. When thus reduced to matters of fact, he would either read aloud some passage from a favourite author, or, if public events happened to be peculiarly interesting, he took refuge in a newspaper. Whatever his text might be, however, he seldom failed to make it clear by an oral commentary; and I have been assured by those who enjoyed the best opportunities of judging that he was never more agreeable, never more animated, than at these early conversaziones. There was a playfulness in his humour which won the best affections of such as listened to it; there was a strength and power in his philosophy which commanded the respect of all to whom its maxims were propounded.

Mr. Hastings was a great advocate for bathing, which he regarded as conducive not only to cleanliness, but to health. He himself took the cold bath daily, the warm bath twice or thrice a-week, and, as often as an opportunity came in his way, he indulged freely his predilection for swimming. In like manner his fondness for horse-exercise, and indeed for the horse itself, was quite oriental. He rode remarkably well, and he piqued himself on the accomplishment to an extent which in almost any other man might have been accounted ridiculous: for nothing pleased him more than to undertake some animal which nobody else could control and to reduce it (as he invariably did) to a state of perfect docility. The following anecdote, which I have from my friend Mr. Impey, himself an actor in the little drama, may suffice to show the extent to which this passion was carried :—

It happened once upon a time, when Mr. Impey was, with some other boys, on a visit at Daylesford, that Mr. Hastings, returning from a ride, saw his young friends striving in vain to manage an ass which they had found grazing in the paddock, and which one after another they chose to mount. The ass, it appears, had no objection to receive the candidates for equestrian renown successively on his back, but budge a foot he would not; and there being neither saddle nor bridle, wherewith to restrain his natural movements, he never failed, so soon as a difference of opinion arose, to get the better of his rider. Each in his turn, the boys were repeatedly thrown, till at last Mr. Hastings, who watched the proceeding with great interest, approached.

"Why, boys," said he, "how is it that none of you can ride?"

"Not ride!" cried the little aspirants; "we could ride well enough, if we had a saddle and a bridle; but he's such an obstinate brute, that we don't think even you, Sir, could sit him bare-backed."

"Let's try," exclaimed the Governor-general. Whereupon he dismounted, and gave his horse to one of the children to hold, and mounted the donkey. The beast began to kick up his heels, and lower his head as heretofore; but this time the trick would not answer. The Governor-general sat firm, and finally prevailed, whether by fair means or foul I am not instructed, in getting the quadruped to move wheresoever he chose. He himself laughed heartily as he resigned the conquered thistle-eater to his first friends; and the story when told, as told it was, with consummate humour, at the dinner table, afforded great amusement to a large circle of guests.

Besides preparing the poetical effusions of which I have spoken as giving a zest to the conversation over the general breakfast table at Daylesford, Mr. Hastings was in the constant habit of amusing himself in literary composition. I find among his papers, essays, dissertations, criticisms, poems, on almost every conceivable subject; of which many appear to me to possess extraordinary merit, while all exhibit marks of talent, if not of genius. It is not, however, my intention to introduce into the present work any specimens of these literary productions. There are more than enough of them within my reach to form a moderate sized volume, and I shall greatly distrust my own judgment in such matters for the future, if the readers of this memoir fail to thank me, should I by and bye arrange them into something like order, and offer them for general perusal.

Having premised all this, there remains for me only the pleasant task of filling up the present chapter with some of Mr. Hastings's familiar letters, taken at random, from the multitudes that cover my table. It will be seen that I choose those which are addressed to his earliest and most trusty friends, in preference to others which bear more imposing superscriptions. My reasons for doing so require no explanation. It is only in such correspondence as the following, that we may ever hope to discover a faithful picture of the writer's mind and feelings.

To G. R. THOMPSON, Esq., referring in part to his Negociation with the Court of Directors about the Annuity, in part to the Congratulatory Addresses which had reached him from India.

Park Lane, 26th March, 1796.

My dear Thompson,—When you come to town I know that it is with such reluctance, and you have such powerful calls for your speedy return, that I never expect to have more than fleeting glimpses of you. My disappointment, therefore, is not so great as yours, if you are so near, and yet can afford me but little of your society, though no one of your friends sets a greater, if an equal, value upon it. Next time, however, do as you promise. Put up your portmanteau in Vere-street Hotel, or there is one in Oxford-street, or be anywhere near us.

Mrs. Hastings returned to town on the 14th, almost well, caught a new cough, added other and worse complaints to it, and is but within these three days well enough to go abroad.

The Directors have not yet closed my arrangements. I have desired them to purchase my annuity, to prevent my depreciating their bounty by selling it to a Jew, and to enable me to pay the remainder of my debts. A foolish motion of Lord Lauderdale in the House of Peers, giving occasion for a short delay, the chairman in that interval fell sick, and my letter remains unnoticed; but a Court is called for next Tuesday, for the express purpose, as I understand, of taking their sentiments upon it.

In the mean time, the copy of a letter from the British inhabitants of Calcutta, congratulating me upon my acquittal, with the annunciation of two similar addresses from the officers and native inhabitants of Calcutta, is seasonably arrived, and these are aids to the business on the principle of popularity. The paper which is come is admirably drawn up. As it is in the newspapers, I conclude you have seen it. It is, as our great Lord observed, "simple and dignified, evidently proceeding from a sentiment of more than it was thought useful or becoming to express." It consoles me for the want of money to throw away on the luxuries of a farm and a greenhouse, and on the tax of town residence.

Mrs. Hastings gives her love to you and Mrs. Thompson, and under her protection I beg leave to offer mine.

I had almost forgotten a material object of my letter. I forgot what you told me concerning the person for whom you wanted the cadetship which Mr. Inglis promised me. I think you said that he was otherwise provided for. Let me know by the returning post whether you still wish for it, as Mr. Inglis reserves the appointment for me, and must give in his nomination by the end of this month. If you adhere to the original recommendation, give me the person's name. At all events write an answer by to-morrow's post. Your affectionate.

The following to Sir John D'Oyley exhibits the writer in the light of an ardent agriculturist:—

Daylesford House, 10th June, 1799.

My dear Sir John,—I return you as many thanks as can amount to my sense of the strong testimony which you have given me of your affection, in the letter recommending Mr. Turton to General Ellerker, and the additional recommendation which you intend to give him to Captain Davies. This will be of more service to him than all my letters united.

I rejoice at the birth of your Indian calf, and hope that I and my cow shall both live to profit by his services, when he is arrived at full estate. I am yet not without hopes of a similar accession to my own Indian family.

Mr. Cooke has sent me the implements which you were so good as to bespeak for me; and I shall set the chaffcutter to work before I close this letter. I have already tried it—yesterday, God forgive me! I do not think that the simple examination of a thing which may be converted to the general benefit of all the society around me can be termed doing any manner of work in the sense of the commandment. But I am just come from working it with lucerne, and oatstraw as a substratum, and have distributed the produce among my best horses. Sir Charles and my new broke colt eat it greedily. Mrs. Hastings's horse only rejects it, and my grey mare seems only not to dislike it. I suppose the crudeness of the expressed juice of the plant is unpleasant to them from want of use. The instrument does not draw the lucerne alone, but works well with straw neatly laid at the bottom. If I am right in my recollection, P. L. Close gave his horses and cattle green and dry chaff mixed; and if his riding horse obtained his sleek coat by such provender, with (I conclude) a little addition of oats, there cannot be a better diet.

I have written to Mr. Cooke for a plough, and it will be in time.

I have fitted up a stand for two oxen, which I am now fattening on my idea of the principles (or rather of their application, for I cannot err in the principles) of Mr. Close's stables.

I find my bailiff heartily desirous to give my innovations a fair trial; but he, my groom, carter, and all are delighted with the chaff-cutter. I grieve that I want the bodily powers, which, if I possessed them, I am sure I could employ to the completion of my character as a farmer. I am resolved, however, to get back the cost of my machines by the use of them.

Having paper to spare, and a frank to cover it, I will fill it with some observations on the practice of giving cattle cut food.

From the frequent instances of oats growing out of horses dung, and the disorders to which elephants are liable from eating the leaves and succulent stems of plantain trees uncut, it is evident that it is only the soluble parts of vegetable substances on which the powers of digestion can act, the hard husk of the entire oat preserving the seed from undergoing any change in the passage, and the fibres of all grasses undergoing but little, especially the stems of lucerne and green tares near the roots, the greater portion of straw, and much even of hay. These of course often retain their original substance, and are connected together like ropes, through all the intestines. How far this may disturb what is called the peristaltic motion, or in what other way they may be affected by the prolongation of the same undissolved matter through vessels formed for different processes of digestion, I am not anatomist enough to conjecture: but I am confident of the cause, however it may produce its effect. In the instance of elephants the effect is visible.

Hence it appears that in all cases, where cattle have fibrous food provided for them, of whatever kind, it ought to be prepared for the stomach by being first cut into small portions. I have read that hogs will thrive in a field of clover, but die, if it is given to them as it is cut from the field. This (if true) must be owing to the cause above assigned. I wish you would suggest this to Mr. Close. You need not show him what I have written.

I add to this a letter addressed to one of Sir John D'Oyley's sons, who had recently gone out to India as a writer. It does full justice to the kind and gentle disposition which induced Mr. Hastings to take so much interest in the well being of young people, and endeared him in an extraordinary degree to all the young persons with whom he ever came closely into contact.

Daylesford House, 24th April, 1799.

My dear Charles,—I thank you for your kind letter, and for affording me this proof of your retaining me in your remembrance, which pleased me, though I was far from suspecting that you would forget me. If you follow one of the dictates of natural morality, to love all who love you, and with the same measure of affection, you will feel that sentiment in the fullest degree for Mrs. Hastings and myself as long as you live; and we wish for no better effect of it, than to be informed by your letters that you prosper and are happy. You have commenced your course so well, and seem to have laid down for yourself so judicious a plan of conduct, that I have no doubt of your attaining both these objects. Your excellent father, who unceasingly talks of you, and with what anxiety you need not be told, has gratified us exceedingly by permitting us to read your letters, knowing how interested we were in their contents, and how many sources of satisfaction they would, as they did, yield us.

You cannot too highly appreciate the benefits which you have received by your reception into Mr. Brooke's family; nor can you know so well as I do, be the present manners and fashions of the young men of Calcutta what they may, what perils you have escaped by having been thus withdrawn from their society. Against these your good sense would have been an insecure guard, and the goodness of your heart would but have more exposed you to them. Upon this subject I could give you a world of good advice; but you will not want it. Yet let me say thus much: cherish your present protection; and when you lose it, as you must in the course of a few years, resolve to be in every sense your own master, nor suffer any influence but the rectitude of your own understanding to prescribe your conduct in the pursuit either of pleasure, interest, or reputation.

Sir John and Lady D'Oyley made us very happy by deviating a little from the direct line of their route to Dublin, and passing a few, though very few, days with us in the last month. We expect them again in their way back in the beginning of the next, and propose to accompany them to Newlands. Your father appeared to be in better health than I have seen him in for many years, and your dear mother holds her head almost as erect as if her neck had never received any injury. Indeed I never perceived the effects of it after the day of her arrival. Your little brother was so far of the party. He is very much like what you were at the same age, in temper and person, and less delicate in his health than I had expected to see him.

I beg you will present my kindest regards to your good friend, Mr. Brooke. I ever remembered him with the respect which was due to a truly amiable character, and I love him for his goodness to you.

Mrs. Hastings desires me to assure you of her kindest affection and good wishes. I am ever, my dear Charles, your affectionate friend.

To Mr. THOMPSON, relative to electioneering matters, in which he had been solicited by more than one friend to interfere.

Daylesford House, 14th March, 1800.

My dear Thompson,—Much occupation embarrassing me at the time when I received your letter of a date so distant that I will not mention it, may account for my long apparent inattention to it; but will not excuse me. Reading it over now, and feeling the same sensations excited by it, as the recent perusal of it must have produced, I can better comprehend the reluctance which an indolent mind, like mine, had to encounter, and to conquer in entering on the discussion which any reply that I could make to it would require. To have governed the first and only valuable portion of the British Empire in India thirteen years, to have received at my departure and since the fullest assurance of my carrying with me the regrets and affections of my fellow servants and countrymen there, and to find myself without interest with those whom I had successfully served, and without influence with my associates at home, might have been a subject of mortifying reflection to a mind even less susceptible than my own: it has had less influence on mine by my incessant care to preclude or run away from it; and I am afraid this has grown so much into a habit, that I give way to it in cases where I ought not, as in the present. But one-fourth of a letter is too much for a preface. Let me proceed to the substance.

I have already done all that I could do for the late Mr. Dent, and was told that any further exertion of mine would be ineffectual. Something, too, I attempted, but I forget what, for his widow. If it be not too late, and I can repeat it by verbal application, I will, and will carry your letter with me to town for that purpose. Mr. Powney's kind interpretation of my silence to his application in favour of Mr. Porcher hurt me more than a reproach. I was sore, too, from other hurts from the same occasion. In the support (of whatever avail it may, or may not have been) which my old friendship for Colonel Toone exacted from me, willingly and zealously as I gave it, I yet felt grieved that I hurt two worthy people for whom I had a regard, at the same time that I broke through a fixed determination which I had long made and maintained. In the last contest I had two friends pitted against one another, and a friend of my friend's against them. If I could have departed from the line of forbearance which my reason had imposed upon me as an obligation, I should have given my interest (such as it is) to Mr. Auriol, to whom I was under pecuniary obligations. I excused myself to him, and stated my situation to Mr. Plowden, and expressed to both my disapprobation of the competitions of Indians with Indians, involving their common friends in mutual hostility, and too often in consequent hatreds, for the sole benefit of other candidates to whom the division of their strength was the means of success. Your letter arrived after these explanations, and when I had received private assurances that neither Plowden nor Porcher had a chance of success against the powers of Government and Directors united in favour of Mr. Thornton; so that, if I had been at liberty, I could not have exercised it with any hope of success.

I seldom keep copies of my letters, for I can hardly command time to write them. But I did make a copy of my letter to Auriol, and I give you the following extract of it, because I think it possible that you may have it in your power to apply the substance of it, and your energetic manner give it greater effect, in the trial of it on Powney and his friend, than I had on mine; for I used the same arguments, and recommended the same accommodation to Mr. Plowden, but in other words. . . . . . "In the present instance I should consider every vote that I could procure for you as remotely, but most surely, contributing to the success of the most powerfully supported of your rivals. In effect you, and Mr. Plowden, and Mr. Porcher, are labouring for the success of Mr. Thornton, by dividing that interest which, if united, might be a match for any that could be opposed to it; and it ought to be united. I might say in the words of Moses:—'Why smite ye your fellows? Why join the herd of your revilers and oppressors against each other, and against yourselves?'

"I own, it has long been a matter of painful regret to me to see the gentlemen from India so little regardful of the reproaches and contumelies which are cast upon them by their countrymen at home, and the universal combination which has existed against their name, reputation, and interests. I believe that my long trial, and the voluminous matter which it produced in evidence, may have served to remove a part, though but a part, of the odium which has so ungratefully, as well as unjustly, prevailed against the whole body of the Indian service; the members of which might both efface the rest, and render themselves respectable, if they would but assert their own rights, and yield to the dictates of that natural principle which all mankind obey, but themselves—self-defence.

"If you ask me how this is to be done, I will tell you, and apply my answer to the case in point.

"Let the present candidates (I mean the Indian) meet together, with their respective friends. Let each produce a fair state of his own force and expectations. Let the weakest consent to resign their present pretensions to the strongest, and join their interest to his for his support, reserving and assuring to the next their combined aid against all other competitors, when the next vacancy shall enable him to enter the lists.

"One of you by this accommodation might have a fair chance of succeeding; but if three members in their aggregate amount are not sufficient to produce that effect, I am sure that no one portion of it, if divided, will.

"I have long ago wished to propose to my brethren from India such a defensive plan of confederacy against their common enemies; but I have never been in a situation which suited with such a purpose. For many years I was so circumstanced, that a proposition of this tendency coming from me would have been liable to the imputation of attempting to form a party to elude the course of justice. Other considerations have since dissuaded—I should rather say, disabled—me. You have it in your power, let the state of your canvass be what it will. Let me conjure you to weigh well what I have written, before you reject my advice. If you follow it, the event may not indeed prove it to be right, but if you do not, I am sure that you will find it so."

I am sorry, my dear friend, to put you to the charge of double postage; but I have exhausted so much of my time and paper, as I shall your patience, on alien and unpleasant subjects, that I must add something, *quod magis ad nos pertinet,* and more pleasing, to relieve the foregoing.

Notwithstanding the querulous tone of some passages in the other sheet, I do not complain, nor have cause for it. Of the ingredients of happiness which I once enumerated in rhyme, I possess all (and the catalogue is pretty large) but one; and that occasionally comes and goes. Daylesford is very much improved since you saw it, both in its ornamental acquisitions, its comforts, and its husbandry. My beloved wife is what she was in her moral and spiritual substance, and I should and ought to be perfectly contented, if her health (which is not worse, but rather better) was more stable. The worst is, we live too much secluded from society, excepting that of our neighbours, and too remote from our friends; but our hearts turn to them with as much warmth as ever, and with as hearty an interest in their concerns, and in none more, hardly any so much, than in those of our dear friends at Penton. May their number go on increasing, and Heaven bless you with the means of providing for their future comforts, and with the fortitude of self-privation, if that should be necessary to that end! Present to Mrs. Thompson, and accept the assurances of our truest love, and believe me ever, my dear Thompson, your affectionate.

To Mr. THOMPSON, on agricultural affairs.

Daylesford House, 13th April, 1801.

My dear Thompson,—I have ventured to depart from your instructions, and instead of the coach, I have directed the sack containing your barley wheat to be sent from London by the Salisbury waggon; having, besides the direction on the sack, desired my waggoner to give special injunctions to the Salisbury people to drop it at Andover, where it will be left till called for. To have sent it by the coach would have imposed upon you a charge of at least fifteen shillings; I suppose five shillings will be the cost of it by the waggon. You will take care to intercept the sack at Andover, lest, by a not unusual negligence, the people should carry it on to their last destination.

The sack contains no more than two bushels, and the quantity of a peck taken from some that I had caused to be dressed for baking; and this I have packed in a small bag by itself, that you may make trial of it, if you choose it. My bailiff, with more expedition than I expected, had carried all the rest, with the reserve of one bushel, into the field; and I was only apprized of it in time to recover one bushel from it. This added to the first makes up the contents of the sack.

The quantity required for an acre will depend upon the process; three bushels would be required for broadcast; two for the drill, if the lines are eight or nine inches distant. I should recommend the distance of a foot at least, or rather eighteen inches. This last will afford more room for horse- (or any) -hoeing, and the roots will draw more nourishment by having space to spread in. With so small a quantity you can afford to hoe by the hand, and to earth up the loose soil to the stems of the growing plants.

If you make trial of the small parcel for bread, you should keep the flour, after it is ground, a fortnight at least before you use it, turning it often, that it may not ferment, and become clotted. I have tried it. It makes bad bread; that is, black and heavy; but it is well tasted, especially if sliced and toasted. I have sent four quarters to be made into malt; and the maltster says, it swells more, and promises to turn out altogether better than any barley that he ever malted. So much for barley wheat.

I wish my ability was equal to my inclination. I can only assist you by my inquiries. General Harris is in quest (I hear so). Chapman will be in England in August or September; but I may be able to afford you more information when I am in town. I do not go yet; but keep myself ready to start. Something will be done to day, or by and bye, in Parliament; the issue of which, as I have made it up in my own mind, will be the nomination of the Queen to be Regent, with a Council of Regency, in which Mr. Pitt will preside. The first possesses my most devout wishes; the last has not one good one for me.

Do not make excuses for not answering my letters. My last (which I had almost forgot) did not require one; and I should be glad that every friend I have would neglect me in that way now and then, to set my conscience at rest, which has always a dozen sins of this kind oppressing it; and suggesting the same reflections, word for word, as you have made upon your own omissions, with less cause than any man living.

Mrs. Hastings interrupted me while I was writing, to desire me to mention her in the most affectionate terms to you, and through you to Mrs. Thompson. To her I beg to be most kindly remembered. Your dear children have our best wishes ever. I proceed to attest a sentiment expressed in the close of your letter. To Mrs. Hastings we are both indebted for our mutual friendship; or rather to Providence, which made her personal danger the means of calling forth your humanity, and my gratitude for its exertion, when we were unknown to each other. You may have forgot this. It is fresh in my remembrance. Adieu, your affectionate.

To Mr. CHARLES D'OYLEY, giving him two commissions to be executed.

Daylesford House, 30th March, 1802.

My dear Charles,—I am greatly obliged to you for your kind letter, which, though dated the 7th of May last, has been but a few days in my possession. I am not afraid of your forgetting me: yet I am pleased with this proof of your remembrance. I read with a particular intesest your description of the characters of my young friends Waring and Impey, and even of Mr. Metcalfe, though I am not personally acquainted with him. They may be gratified with your praises: for yours have been imparted to me in terms equally honourable to you; and the distinction shown you by Lord Wellesley proves that you are deserving of them. I am grieved to understand that the Court of Directors are not disposed to confirm his collegiate establishment; because I think it well conceived, and likely, if it were prosecuted, to be of infinite service both to their servants and to their interests; and I regret that by placing it on so large a scale, his Lordship should have indisposed them to it altogether.

It is a long time since I heard from your excellent parents; but I often hear of them, and by the last accounts that they and all around them were well.

I wish to load you with two commissions; one relating to a matter of mere curiosity, in investigating which your own may be gratified equally with mine. In the other I have a substantial interest. Mirza Aboo Tauleb Khan, a native of Lucknow, now in England, has informed me, that in a small district, called Mohaun, about fourteen miles from Lucknow, if the ground be dug to the depth of fifteen yards, a stratum will be invariably found of a substance resembling wood in all its properties, and covering a bed of the purest water. As the Mirza is a man of good understanding, and something analogous to this matter, but ascertained to be an imperfect coal, is to be met with in Devonshire, I think it well worthy of inquiry, and that its existence, with all the circumstances appertaining to it, should be authentically and accurately ascertained. I shall be much obliged if you will obtain this knowledge and transmit it to me. The second commission is, that you will procure and send me some seeds of a grass which grows in the province of Gooracpoor, constituting its principal pasture, and remarkable for its nutritive effects on all animals that feed on it. This circumstance also I learn from the same person, who assures me that it is sufficiently known by the qualities which I have ascribed to it, though he does not know that it has any specific name. If you can obtain any of the seeds, be so good as to tie up the quantity of an ounce or two in a bag like a pounce bag, and give it in charge to any mate, or rather passenger, coming to England, with instructions to keep it where the air may have access to it in the passage. If too much confined it will not keep.

Mrs. Hastings desires me to assure you of her affectionate regard, and sincere wishes for your prosperity. She is, I thank God, at this time in good health, though she has been a severe sufferer this last year by the want of it. Adieu, my dear Charles. Believe me ever your most sincerely affectionate friend.

I enclose a more minute account of the substance mentioned in my first commission, written by Mirza Aboo Tauleb Khan and a P.S. on the outside of it.

To the same, on his marriage.

Daylesford House, 16th March, 1803.

My dear Charles,—I thank you for your affectionate letter of the 6th of September, and for your attention to my commissions.

The intelligence which we received of your intended marriage with Miss Greer was received by Mrs. Hastings and myself with a joy, that, as very prudent persons, we ought not to have avowed. We were pleased with the choice which you had made of an amiable, accomplished, and sensible companion; and for her sake we rejoiced that she was about to be united to a man whom we knew to possess a heart capable of the most generous affections, and to whom we gave credit for a principle that would preserve his affections from decay. May the Almighty bless you both with many years of mutual love and happiness!

My dear young friend, you are now on the eve of a great change which is to give the colour to all your future life; and that will depend entirely on the manner in which you enter upon it. For God's sake avoid one rock on which many young families have struck, and have been wrecked. Avoid entertainments: keep no table; and that you may avoid the obligation of returning invitations, accept of none, but from persons so much your superiors in age and standing as not to expect it: and firmly and intrepidly persevere in this cautionary rule, till your station, or situation in the service, shall exempt you from the observance of it. Upon this point, and upon every occasion in which you shall be called upon to determine upon your own line of conduct, first deliberately and dispassionately ask yourself what you ought to do; and when you have received the answer which your reason has dictated, make that answer your law, and never depart from it, whatever censures, sneers, or temptations may provoke or attempt to seduce you to depart from it. Be the slave of fashion in indifferent matters; but be your own master and independent in all such as may affect your moral character, or influence either your own happiness, or (which indeed is yours) the happiness of your family.

I intended, when I began the foregoing paragraph,

to confine my advice to one single and practical point. In attempting to enforce it by a general principle, I have imperceptibly extended it to an universal maxim. It is, however, the only one on which a true manly character can be built: but I revert to that with which I commenced, conjuring you to practise it, by all your hopes of returning to your country in time to bless the latter lives of your beloved and most affectionate parents; and to perform those other duties which will be required with a growing family, and which no parent ought to abandon to another, who can perform them himself.

Advice is hateful. I ventured upon this with that general prepossession against it: but, my Charles, I know that it is both useful and necessary, and of easy practice, and that it is offered to you by one who has loved you from the hour of your birth; and it shall have the concurrent sanction of Mrs. Hastings, who loves you at least as much as I do; or I will not send it. She is well, and knowing that I was going to write to you, charged me to assure you of her affection. We have heard lately from Ireland, and that all there were well; your excellent and virtuous father strenuously persevering in an occupation which many consider as a degradation. In some sort I think it one, and honour him the more for it for that very reason, deeming it a sacrifice of his pride, and his personal ease, to the welfare of his children.

Adieu, my dear Charles. May heaven bless and prosper you. Your truly affectionate friend.

P.S. I add what follows, as dictated by Mrs. Hastings. She authorizes me to say, that she approves most heartily of every syllable that I have written, and joins her recommendation to it. She rejoices to hear that you were so well, and is impatient for the letter which you have promised to write to her. She regrets exceedingly that it was not in her power to see dear Miss Greer before she embarked—her health and other causes not permitting her to go to London; but her best wishes and prayers will attend her. We shall long, not without much apprehension, to see our dear Marian; but fear we must wait many months first. When you write to either of us, it will give us a pleasure to know what station you occupy in the service: in short, there is nothing which can interest you that we shall not have an interest in. You will hear that we are under recent apprehensions of another war. There seems to be but too much reason to believe them to be well grounded.

To David Anderson, Esq., acknowledging the receipt of a Copy of one of Sir Walter Scott's Volunteering Songs.

Daylesford House, 13th September, 1803.

My dear Anderson,—I heartily thank you for your letter, short as it is. I thank you too for the beautiful verses that it enclosed. Beautiful they are indeed, and though consisting entirely of a trite image, perfectly original. They possess all the graces of poetry, with what the critics I believe call a complete whole, *i. e.* one single subject completely finished. I wish I had free access to the author. The only use that I should make of it, would be to persuade him if I could, to write his own acts, and turn them to poetry: such at least as concerned the part that all men are to take in the defence of the country, and such of course as all men ought to understand. It is not indeed necessary that an Act of Parliament should possess genius or elegance; but it should be intelligible, and it should be what I have praised in the poem, a whole. The late defence bills are terribly deficient in these qualities, though they are strongly marked with that sublimity which Mr. Burke says is displayed in an artificial combination of words, which have no meaning of their own, but are at the mercy of their readers or hearers to ascribe to them any meaning that they please. See his Sublime and Beautiful, with his exemplification of the doctrine in Virgil's receipt for making thunder: "Tres imbris torti radios," &c.

In obedience to the Parliamentary receipt, and applying my own meaning to the most sublime, or most mysterious part of it, I called out the youth of Daylesford, and with the very able instruction of Colonel Imhoff, my old porter called from Chelsea College for that purpose, and myself, looking on, taught them to march, and to carry themselves erect like soldiers, when a circular letter from the war minister to the Lord Lieutenant induced me to disband them, lest I should be thought guilty of disaffection, by teaching men the use of arms which they might possibly turn against their country, as they were precluded from the defence of it. In serious truth, I am sorry that the spirit of the people was not more effectually excited to action, and that when it had manifested itself, it was not encouraged, instead of being checked as it has been: but though checked, not (I trust) damped. I should have been pleased if an abridgment of the numbers who offered to serve as volunteers in each county, in the event of an invasion, had been published, for the honour of the country, and to undeceive our enemies. I am persuaded that the sum total would greatly exceed a million.

As we are not always conscious of the motives of our own actions, I am not sure that mine, when I began this letter, were not to save you half the postage of it by consigning it to the charge of Mrs. Hastings as far as London. She leaves me to-day with her venerable mother, who purposes, as soon as she can get passports, and a conveyance, to return to her own very distant home. This will be to both a most afflicting period. I remain only for another sorrowful office, to receive and lodge our poor friend, Sir John D'Oyley, and his mournful family, and shall then follow to town. Our stay there will be short, if we find no difficulty or delay in obtaining passports for Madame Chapusetin. If you should have occasion to write to me in the course of this month (but do not because of this supposition), direct to me at Colonel Imhoff, No. 6, Portugal Street, where we shall sojourn. I think I shall have occasion to write to you before I leave town.

Poor Lady D'Oyley died on the 6th of this month. Sir John had ventured over to Daylesford but a few days before, encouraged by her apparent amendment, which was such as to indicate every symptom of returning health. I have lately received a letter from our excellent friend Colonel Toone, expressive of similar hopes, I fear as delusive, of his daughter, who has lingered under excruciating pains for many months past. His letter is dated the 7th, and I am sure I should have heard from him again, if his hopes had been confirmed by a continuance of the same favourable appearances. There are not two better beings on earth than Toone and his wife: yet he sinks under his affliction; and she, with as sensible a heart as his own, sustains her health and strength unimpaired, though she is never absent from her child, by the force of religion. Adieu, my valued friend. Accept, and present to Mrs. Anderson, and to your sister, our united best regards, and every wish for your health and happiness. Yours affectionately.

P.S. Mrs. Sands left us on the 8th in apparently good health, but much regretting her departure, and as much regretted. I will give your thanks to Mr. Osborne. His direction is Melchet Park, Rumsay, Hants.

To Sir JOHN D'OYLEY, whom reverses of fortune had compelled to return to India.

London, 19th August, 1806.

My dear Sir John,—I closed a letter to you on the 11th of this month, and sent it the next day to be put into one of the packets, which I know it was, though I know not which. In that letter I told you that I had, in concert with Mr. and Mrs. Henry Grant, engaged to place your son, having previously removed him from Twyford, with Mr. Lendon, a teacher of twelve pupils at Pentonville, near Islington. I sent you, not knowing it, the wrong card, describing the branches of education taught at the school, and the terms of it; Mr. Lendon having added to the latter, since it was printed, five guineas entrance; as you will see by the right card enclosed. On the 14th I attended good Mrs. Grant, with John, to Mr. Lendon's, and delivered the dear boy to his charge, with a particular recommendation of him to Mrs. Lendon. We left him cheerful, well pleased, and in good apparent health. As he is yet, and perhaps by nature, delicate, I wrote to Sir Walter Farquhar, and desired him to permit me to call upon him, when he could spare me a few minutes of leisure, expressing my object, which was to consult him upon this subject. I had yesterday the pleasure of a visit from him, in which in the most kind and the heartiest manner, he anticipated my wishes; promising to see the little boy from time to time; to keep a constant watch on his health; to give proper instructions concerning the treatment of him to Mrs. Lendon; and to concert besides with Mr. Partington what might become necessary, in the event of his not being able himself to visit him, if his assistance should be occasionally wanted. He assured me that he would begin these benevolent offices by calling at Mr. Lendon's this morning. He said he would do his duty to his young relation; and I am sure he will do it.

I have already acquainted you with the letter which I had received from Mrs. Close in her husband's name, in consequence of one which you had written to him, and with the substance of my answer, in which I had detailed to him all that I had done, and purposed doing for John. To this I have received a reply from the same hand, "assuring me that Mr. Close is perfectly satisfied with my plan for little D'Oyley; that he wished long ago to have removed him from Twyford, but indisposition for several months prevented either his doing himself any thing, or giving any direction concerning him, or any other business." I add what follows in the first person of the letter, though what I have written is almost literal.

"He is now, thank God, so much better, that though he cannot read or write, he can converse, without much difficulty, and begged me to inform you, it gave him great pleasure to have met with a gentleman, who is well acquainted with Mr. Lendon, and who is a near neighbour to him, and I think he will be glad to show little John any kindnesses, if you, my dear friend, should approve of his now and then (at proper hours) paying him a visit. Mr. Lendon frequently associates with this gentleman." This is a kind of constructive testimony in favour of Mr. Lendon. I hope we shall have a better in John's improvement. Mrs. Close has also informed me of the power which you have given to Mr. Close to withdraw your pecuniary concerns from Mrs. Williams's hands, and offered "to remit to me, or any one whom I should think proper to appoint, any expense that has been incurred for dear little John." If they receive any money, and have no other call for it, I will charge them for Mr. Lendon's demands, which are yet very distant, meaning to make this the limit of my own responsibility.

Now, my dear Sir John, I must tell you, that though I have taken upon me to remove your son from one school where you yourself had placed him, under a real or supposed superintendency of many of your other friends, whom I have totally excluded from all participation both in that, and all other acts relating to him; and transferred him to another at a cost exceeding both your original instructions, and probably the amount of the funds appropriated to this portion of his expenses; and though I am determined to resist all efforts that may be made to take the boy from my jurisdiction, till you have given your sanction to it; yet I am fully aware that I have exceeded the letter of the authority with which you have invested me, nay, even your own expectations. You have expressed indeed a wish to charge me with the whole power over your child; you have declared, that among your numerous friends, I was the only one to whom you could delegate that important trust; yet, from a delicacy, which I can only regret, you assign to me only a general control. I have taken an absolute one, and the whole active management; for if I had waited to conciliate every person to whom you had given a right of interference, our poor child must have returned to Twyford; and if his health has suffered, and his understanding has been uncultivated in all the time that he was there before, the mischief would have been aggravated, and its effects more difficult of retrieval. I do not know that I have given offence to any; but I should, if I had consulted them, and decided upon my own judgment. You will, at least, have the satisfaction of knowing how your beloved child is disposed of, and occasionally of hearing what progress he makes, during an interval of a little less than two years. The sequel will depend upon yourself. If you approve of my plan, and choose to depute to me the care of him, I should have no objection to hold it in participation with Mr. and Mrs. Harry Grant. Otherwise it must be absolute; and to whomsoever you may consign that trust, it should be, to render it effectual, to that one alone, and be a delegation express, and such as may be shown as authentic. In making this provision, you will bear in mind that I am marching fast to my 74th year, and have no rational ground to expect the extension of my life beyond that term, though I feel no actual symptoms of mortality.

The commission which you gave me in one of your letters (I cannot now turn to it) I have not yet been able to accomplish, though it has pressed incessantly on my mind. I will write to you upon this subject hereafter.

Have I thanked you for your present of the Persian seal? I received it with pleasure, with a double pleasure, as a pledge of the distinction which you allow me in your friendship, and a precious memorial of a dear friend, whom I shall ever regret, and cherish in my most affectionate remembrance.

This is the 20th. Yesterday the nomination of Sir George Barlow to be Governor-general, and of Lord Lake, Messrs. Udney and Lumsdaine to the Council, passed the Court of Directors unanimously. So far I am pleased, but not satisfied. I dare not mention my reason, lest by the chance of war my letter should be intercepted.

I can impart nothing of news that you will not receive from the papers. I stand, like Addison's man of virtue, unmoved by the crush of falling worlds, and if I am not a gainer by any of the late convulsions, (for the most dreadful evils produce good to some men,) I am not a sufferer by them. I am in tolerable health, though I have resided seven weeks in London, and have been absent almost ten from Daylesford; and I have the happiness of seeing Mrs. Hastings in better health and looks, than she has appeared for many years past. I could add more, but I suspect her friends of flattery, and my own eyes of that fallacy which prepossession may impose on visual decay. She equally partakes in my cares and affection for our dear John, and in fervent wishes for your happiness, and the happiness and prosperity of all your children, to whom, and to their new relations, we desire to be jointly remembered with sincere expressions of affection, and equal claims to theirs. Adieu, my beloved friend, yours ever most truly.

To Mr. Thompson, on the rise in the value of Land.

Daylesford House, 2nd April, 1808.

My dear Thompson,—I thank you for your attention to my question concerning the estimate of my farm. I put it so abruptly, and in such concise terms, that I was afraid you would have considered it as the suggestion of the moment, and of no permanent consequence. The truth is, that my only tenant has always held his lease from year to year, without any condition but his rent. I want to make a new distribution of the lands; to give him a long lease of the portion allotted to him; for that purpose to ascertain their value; and also to make a provision for its future depreciation. The opinion given by Dr. Sheppard, though doubtless very accurate, will not serve for my purpose. It respects only the quality of the land. That I can well ascertain, and am almost qualified to estimate it myself. I am willing to give my tenant the advantage of his improvements, with one exception, but to make him pay me an increase in their valuation, proportioned to the diminution of the value of money.' For example, I find that in the year 1792, the average price of wheat was five shillings a bushel; it is now ten. This is independent of the variations of seasons, or culture; but has arisen from the progressive accumulation of our national debt, which has added so much more money, however unsubstantial, to our circulation. If the increase has been equally progressive, the common term of difference for each year has been 3¾d., and the rate of 1798, when my lands were valued, was by that mode of computation 6*s*. 10½*d*. I am therefore disposed to raise my rents by the rule of three for every £100, thus:—to 6*s*. 10½*d*.: 10*s*. :: £100: £145. 10*s*. But I am so shortsighted in these matters, that I am sure I am wrong in my application of my principle, though I am sure the principle itself is right. I, therefore, in my statement of the question meant to exclude the quality of the land altogether, and to say, suppose a field in a course of husbandry to have been worth 20*s*. an acre in 1798, and to have retained its quality unchanged, what is it worth now? To be sure the best mode of solving this question would be the practical one, of competition: but I cannot invite other bidders; for I cannot part with my farmer.

I beg your pardon for not answering the question which you put to me by the return of the post, because I am sure you had a good reason for obviating the delay; but unfortunately I had so wearied myself with other business begun before the post came in, that when I came to apply myself to your letter, I grew lazy and procrastinating, and either forgot your question, or that it might be answered in one word, "No;" and forgot again that Saturday being a non-conductor in matters of post, I should consequently lose two; and shall lose another, if I proceed in this waste of words. I answer then, "No." I never received from the Company, or from the nation (the nation!) any allowance of money for my own passage, or that of my fellow passengers from Bengal to England. The Directors generously allowed Mrs. Hastings a remission of the duties on her things; but made me pay an enormous sum—she says £1,000, I have forgot the precise amount—for mine, and permitted their officers to defraud me. I believe that, to be correct, I should say officer; for my memory fixes that charge on only one.

I did not know that Mrs. Harvey was a neighbour of mine; but I will avail myself of your information, and devise some decent mode of imparting to her the object of it.

Mrs. Hastings sends you one of her best compliments. You are always in our remembrance, always mentally, and often nominally in our cups. Your affectionate.

To the same, thanking him for the present of a Horse.

Daylesford House, 19th May, 1808.

My dear Friend,—I accept your present thankfully, but with remorse and regret: with remorse, because it originated with a commission; with regret, because I shall never dare again to desire you to procure for me anything which I cannot obtain by my own means, lest I shall appear to solicit a gift. But I repeat, that I accept, and thank you for it, and heartily. I had determined that I would leave off riding during the remainder of my life. I shall now make a point of conscience to ride constantly during the summer and autumn; and if it shall add (as it may) a year to my life, I will accept that too as your gift, and thank you for it.

My man will go off this evening, and find his way to Ilsley by to-morrow evening. I thank you for this accommodation. On all occasions of this nature you know there is a perquisite due to the groom, and (as I have no other way of conforming to it) I shall take the liberty to enclose a one pound note in this, and beg of you to pay it to the man whom you have employed to bring the pony to Ilsley. I am pleased to think that I shall be able to make trial of my new steed before I commence my excursion from Daylesford, which is fixed for the 24th.

I read in your disappointment, and friend Baber's, my own; but am consoled for it by the assurance that I must have been a gainer by it in the kind of revenge which you both took of me for it.

We desire you to present our affectionate regards to dear Mrs. Thompson, and to Miss Thompson, and accept our blessing on all your children. Remember us kindly to Mr. and Mrs. White. I am ever, my dear Thompson, your truly affectionate friend.

To the same, on the same subject.

Daylesford House, 2nd November, 1808.

My dear Thompson,—I receive so much pleasure from the sight of your handwriting, that I should feel myself inexcusable for not soliciting a more frequent repetition of your letters by the claim which I should give myself to it by my own if I had anything new to write to you, or even nothing, if I had a nothing that I could make pleasing; but for that I am grievously deficient both in imagination and self-satisfaction. I hope you blame yourself unjustly, for I keep an orderly list of all the letters that I write; and, unless I neglected to enter a letter, which I hope I did, my last entry in your name is dated the 19th of May last; so that I not only have not told you how I liked your pony, but I have not even acknowledged that I received him. I could justify myself, but it would be by telling a long story, and long stories are unfit for an unfranked letter. I will afford you, however, the satisfaction of knowing that he has proved to me an invaluable acquisition; for he is not only my favourite, but Mrs. Hastings's also, and therefore more mine. If Brewer had had eyes, or memory, he might have informed you that he met Mrs. Hastings on his back; for when she is in health (and the pony has much contributed to it) she rides him daily, often before breakfast, and sometimes repeatedly in the course of the morning; but you have excited our suspicion that he is not the identical horse which you intended to send us; for you call him a bay; Mrs. Hastings says he is a black; and to my senses he appears to be a dark roan. He cannot, however, be a changeling, for the genuine could not have been a better. I must add, that you have been the means of prolonging one amusement, and probable source of health, to both Mrs. Hastings and myself; for I had almost resolved, and Mrs. Hastings absolutely, to renounce riding during the remainder of our lives; and, with some days of exception, she is evidently in better health since she renewed that exercise, and evidently in better spirits by the means of it. In how many ways may the affection of a friend extend its effects beyond that of its professed act!

Mr. Forster shall have a supply of my barley wheat with all the information that I can give him concerning the manner of cultivating it. I will write to him myself. I will deal the same to you. I am glad that you are disposed to renew the trial of it. I suspect that the former failure of it was not caused by the sterility of the soil in which it was planted, but by the carelessness or ill-will of the people who planted it. It will thrive wherever barley will. I will send you what I can spare in the month of February or beginning of March, as I make it a rule to thrash only for immediate use, whether for sowing or malting, and never to take a stack either of wheat, barley wheat, or barley, to pieces, without thrashing it from day to day till it is finished. And you too shall obtain with a supply all the instruction and information relating to it that I am competent to give you. I can only say of its produce, that every body is pleas'd with'n that ha drunken en; which is saying a great deal.

I read with a pleasure that will last, the account

which you give me of your family. I have only had a glimpse of your eldest daughter since she was approaching to womanhood, but that glimpse was sufficient for my attestation of the truth of your report of her. Her form and features were excellent, both as conveying the impressions of beauty, and as indicative of the internal graces, and to these were added, when I saw her, the superior charms of external beauty, a glow of health almost unequalled. It was the fault of the churlish servants where she lodged that I saw her only once. My memory at least retains only one occasion of it. May the Almighty long bestow to her, to her dear mother, to all her brothers and sisters, and to yourself, that inestimable blessing! I am glad that you have relinquished your project, because it was right to do so, whatever its result may prove to others. Whatever errors you may commit, it will be a source of comfort to you now that you cannot be called over the coals for them.

We have not heard from Jersey a long time past, near ten days. They were well, and have promised us a long enjoyment of their society this winter, a portion of which we purpose to pass at their house in town, if my dear wife's agricultural duties will permit her to withdraw herself from her hitherto unremitted attention to them; for these are now exclusively hers; and if she derives no other emolument from it, her health, though with a late, but short interruption, is already improved by it. My own deposal I dignify by high examples, and call it abdication. Somehow or other I do not find my own occupation much diminished by this assumption of it.

If I had written to you last Friday, I should have told you that Mrs. Hastings was in better health than she had possessed for a twelvemonth back. What she has suffered since did not arise so much from any defect of her constitution as from a neglect of its peculiar wants; and she is sensible of it; and she is, just now, thank God! pretty well again. She herself does not yet know how necessary her health is to mine. Yet it will be a shameful inconsistency of confession, after such an observation, that I am, and have been, in better and more equable health than perhaps five men in a hundred at my time of life, fast approaching its 76th year, can boast of, if that be a subject for exultation. Though reluctant to send for my horse, I mount him (thanks to you for it) when he comes with pleasure. I sleep well; my hand is as steady as a human hand can be; and my spirits only disturbed, perhaps not so much as they ought, with my own prospect before me; add to this a promptness to lassitude with short and not violent exertions. I thank God that the best part of me, my affections, remains uninjured by wear; nay, I sometimes think them stronger than they were. It is on these, and on their moral principles of attraction, that I depend for the accomplishment of my best hopes of happiness hereafter—the perfected society of those whom I loved in this life. To this hope, my dear Thompson, you contribute largely; and the duration of the similar sentiment which I with pleasure hailed near the beginning of your letter, short as the letter was, will conduce to realize it.

I have suffered this letter to run into length, because by keeping it back another day, I hope to send it under the cover of a frank. It would have been closed within a much smaller compass yesterday, had I not been interrupted by a visit from young Scott Waring, the most wonderfully improved man in understanding and acquired endowments in the short interval since I thought him a little better than a blockhead that I ever knew. He was almost a dwarf when he went to

India. He is now about the stature of George Powney, only twice his bulk. He could not gratify my inquiries after my friends in Bengal, not having been there these three years; but his knowledge of Bombay is intimate, and, as far as I am interested in it, which is in a very confined degree, very gratifying to me. You desired me to be very communicative of everything which can interest you. I think I have complied with your request most biographically. But I have almost forgot to mention Mrs. Hastings's request to be informed whether you have had any late letters from Ireland, which enable you to ascertain whether there is any, and what, deficiency in the payment of Sir J. D'Oyley's interest. We both desire to be affectionately remembered to Mrs. Thompson, and that you will accept the same token of our affection to yourself.

To the same, on the death of his Daughter.

Daylesford House, 23rd November, 1809.

My very dear Friend,—I have been restrained from writing to you by the fear of irritating the sufferings of your mind by any allusion to them; and I have felt it as a seasonable relief, that my dear Mrs. Hastings has afforded me a plea to yield, for the time past, to that reluctance, by conveying in her letters the expression of my sympathetic feelings for you and your dear lady, with her own. All that your best friends (and I rate myself high in that relation) can effect in this case is to remind you, that there are those who do sympathize with you. All other consolations must spring up from your own breast: its recesses alone can attemper your grief. I would not wish, if I had the power, to cure it. Sorrow for those we love is the link that extends and binds the affinities of this world to the next, and is the pledge of our reunion with the objects of it. This is not a doctrine of the moment;

it is the result of the meditations of many past years. I have often, and intensely, dwelt upon it—I have written upon it—I have devised objections to it and refuted them—and I have imprinted it upon my heart with a holy conviction which is blended with my hopes of eternal felicity.

May heaven bless and preserve to you both, for all your years to come, all the present objects of your affection! Mrs. Hastings unites with me in kindest remembrances of Mrs. Thompson and yourself. I am, my dear friend, ever most affectionately yours.

To Mr. JOHN D'OYLEY, a son of Sir John, just entered at Heylibury College.

Daylesford House, 31st January, 1810.

My dear John,—I received your letter this morning, and answer it immediately, because I am much pleased with it. I am happy to hear that the professor, by whom you passed your examination, said he was very well satisfied with you. I am much pleased with your description of the college; an architect could not in the same compass of writing have expressed it more intelligibly. It is also my wish, as well as you express it to be yours, that you may pass as much of the next vacation as you can at Daylesford; but Mrs. Sperling will expect you to afford her a part of it, and I dare say you will think her claim but reasonable. So far as this regards Mrs. Grant, she has given her consent to it. But there is ample time between this and June to form this arrangement.

It was my wish, and at one time my intention, to go to town, for the purpose of assisting you in all the acts which were necessary for accomplishing your admission into the college; but the friendship and activity of Colonel Toone rendered it unnecessary, and did the business more effectually than I could have done it if I had taken it all upon myself; and I am the better pleased with having left it to him, because it has given him an opportunity of knowing your character, and that knowledge has made him your friend. Such friends are worth cultivating.

This suggests to me a subject on which I have had it some time in my mind to write to you. I believe I have not troubled you much (did I ever?) with advice. In the first place, I have thought you possessed so correct a mind as to be able to direct and control your own actions; and in the second, I have observed, that at your age advice is not always welcome, even when given with the kindest intentions and from the most experienced judgment. Mine is directed more to the place where you are than to yourself. I have heard of parties having been formed in the college against the authority of the masters, and that they have even proceeded to open violence. Upon such occasions it is a common trick of the leaders to preach to their followers the doctrine of public spirit, and to brand with meanness every one who will not join them and go the lengths that they do. As you value your future character and hopes of success in life, my dear Johnny, shun all such detestable cabals, and repel with firmness every advance made to you to poison your mind with their corrupt principles. In the service to which you are destined, you may hope to rise to situations of the highest authority. Begin early, by the practice of obedience where it is now due, to qualify and entitle yourself to the obedience of others, whose services may be necessary hereafter to your prosperity. Mr. Lendon delighted me in one of his letters, by telling me, that "*his boys looked up to you.*" Be looked up to where you now are and wherever you are hereafter. Disdain to be the tool of any one: be not a follower even of the wisest and the best: but do what is right from the impulse of your own judgment, not the example of others. In a word, maintain the character given of you by Mr. Lendon. *Be looked up to,* and acquire that eminent distinction by example and conciliation. This is a word not commonly addressed to a boy of fifteen; but you have been in the practice of the sense which it implies, and I trust therefore that you will thoroughly comprehend it.

As this is the first and will probably be the last moral advice that I shall offer to you, I beg that you will imprint it on your mind; and I desire, that you will write to me again very soon, to assure me of it. I am, my dear Johnny, your truly affectionate friend.

P.S. Mrs. Hastings gives her love to you. She is happy to hear that you have got so well through all your difficulties, and looks with pleasure to see you here in the summer. She desires me to say, that she feels the same interest for your good conduct that I do, as her affection for you is equal to mine.

To Mr. THOMPSON, on the death of a second Child.

Daylesford House, 21st August, 1812.

My dear Friend,—"The letter which communicated to us the tidings of your sad loss caused us, as you may well imagine, the deepest affliction. We will not attempt to say anything to assuage your grief, as that belongs solely to a higher power. Your consolation can only arise from that source, and the assurance of her perfect happiness. You have employed much of our anxious thoughts; and their result is, that if you feel yourself equal to undertake the journey, and will come under our roof with your son George, it will highly gratify us. You shall be under no restraint, see no one whom you will not wish to see, and indulge your own feelings, in which we shall participate rather than endeavour to repress them."

These, my dearest friend, are the words of my beloved wife, taken down with scarcely any alloy of my own; and it was principally for the want of an interval of leisure to interchange our thoughts upon this painful subject before answering your letter, that we have from day to day postponed it; for it seemed to prescribe a duty to us, at the same time that we were aware that anything we could do or say, under that impression, would be unavailing. For my part, I call God to witness, that if the temper of mind under which your letter was written could be changed by the suggestion of any sentiment that I might urge, I would suppress it. In my eyes you are yet a happy man; happy in the contemplation of the blessings which you still possess, and happy in that of the perfected virtues of her whom it has pleased God to remove from you for a few years of separation, to be followed by a certain reunion with her for ever. How rarely does it happen, that in a calamity of this kind our affections are not clouded by the recollection of some shade in the character of the lamented object, or by some compunctious feelings of our own past conduct towards it. You are conscious of having acquitted yourself of your duty; and of her you can say, in the sentiment of the Duke of Ormond, that you would not exchange your departed child, and lose your sorrow with it, to be the father, and to possess all the affections of a father, of any other daughter out of your own family, that could be given you in compensation.

We read the letter addressed to you by your divine daughter as a composition of inspiration. How indicative of a pure and spotless life, and how apt a close of it!

We pray you to present our most affectionate regards to dear Mrs. Thompson: may heaven bless you both! Your affectionate friend.

CHAPTER XIII.

Renewed embarrassments of Mr. Hastings—Correspondence with the Court of Directors—Conference with Mr. Addington—Negociation with the Prince of Wales—Return to Private Life—Correspondence.

FROM the tone of the preceding letters, the reader might find it difficult to collect, that he who wrote them was otherwise than at peace with the whole world; that his fortune was abundant, his condition in life in unison with his wishes, and his mind altogether at ease in reference both to the past and the future. Far be it from me to insinuate that Mr. Hastings ever gave way to a temper so unprofitable in itself,—so little worthy of a great man,—be his situation and prospects what they may, as querulous discontent. Mr. Hastings had been trained in a school which taught him to master his own feelings; yet were the difficulties which surrounded him, from first to last, trying enough. The arrangement which the Court of Directors had made for relieving him from the pressure of his pecuniary embarrassments proved quite inadequate. In spite of a rigid economy, for which his early habits peculiarly unfitted him, Mr. Hastings fell sadly into debt, and the idea of owing money seems to have been one of the most horrible that could be presented to his imagination. He appears to have suffered long, and in silence, ere he could make up his mind to assume again the character of a petitioner before the East India Company; yet a sense of what was due both to himself and to others, at length overcame his scruples. On the 16th of June, 1799, he accordingly wrote to Sir Stephen Lushington, who at that time filled the chair, enclosing a letter for the Court of Directors, which he wished the chairman to present. Both documents are so characteristic of the man, that I should not feel justified were I to withhold them.

To Sir Stephen Lushington.

Daylesford House, 16th June, 1799.

Dear Sir,—I do not apologise to you for the liberty which I take in troubling you with the enclosed, because I should think myself wanting in the respect which was due to your office, and the generous sentiments which your former conduct has taught me to believe that you entertain for me, if I were to transmit it through any other channel. Yet I must accompany it with a request which I cannot add without bespeaking your excuse for it. It is this, that if you should disapprove of the letter, or not choose yourself to present it to the Court, you will not insist on my recalling it; but you will either have the goodness to deliver it to the secretary, or that you will return it to me, that I may send it to him for presentation.

The purpose of the letter has dwelt upon my mind for more than three months past, with so many painful reflections, and a daily augmented remorse for having so long withheld it, that no reception which it could meet with would hurt me so much, as the consciousness of having neglected to try the only means which I can allowably use, to ward off the ruin which must inevitably fall upon me, or rather on others through me, if the Court of Directors should refuse me the relief which I have solicited; and which it was assuredly their original intention to afford.

Let it, my dear Sir, take its chance, and let me, at least, have the satisfaction of knowing the worst, with that of having done my duty so far, and have recourse to such other means as it may then become necessary and incumbent on me to take, to alleviate the consequences which I dread.

I beg you will permit me to address this to you, merely as a private letter; and that you will have the goodness to present mine, with Mrs. Hastings's respectful compliments to Lady Lushington. I am, dear Sir, your much obliged and obedient servant.

The letter enclosed ran as follows :—

To the COURT of DIRECTORS.

Daylesford House, 16th June, 1799.

Honourable Sirs,—A sense of duty, superior to every consideration of what may be termed delicacy, though long restrained by it, impels me to address your Honourable Court once more upon the subjects of my own concerns.

When a trial of nine years, instituted on charges preferred against me in the name of my country, had left me, though acquitted, exhausted of my whole fortune, and sinking under a load of debt, which had been contracted by it, your Honourable Court, acting on the declared wishes of the proprietors of the East India Company, my honourable employers, and participating in the same spirit of generosity, stood forth for my relief: and for this purpose, on the 20th of February, 1796, you passed two resolutions in my favour, one to grant me an annuity of 4000*l*. for the period of twenty-eight years and a half, commencing from the 21st of June, 1785; and the other to lend me the sum of £50,000, without any interest, for the term of eighteen years, upon my giving security to your satisfaction, for the repayment thereof. Both grants were declared to be intended for the purpose of relieving my present embarrassments, and the first to be made in consideration of important services rendered to the East India Company by me whilst I was Governor-general of India, and particularly in the increase of the revenues of the Company.

In consequence of the first of these resolutions, on the 3rd of March following, I received from your treasury the aggregate amount of the annuity due by the terms of the grant, to the end of the last half yearly period, being £42,000; but the second remained in suspense till the 22nd of the same month, when it obtained the final ratification of your Honourable Court, by a resolution, of which, as it essentially constitutes the plea and justification of my present petition, I beg leave to subjoin a literal copy.

"At a Court of Directors, held on the 29th of March, 1796, 'Resolved, that this Court do confirm their resolution of the 26th of February last, whereby they agreed to a loan of £50,000 to Mr. Hastings without interest, on condition that Mr. Hastings do give security to the satisfaction of the Court, for the repayment of the said sum of £50,000, by instalments of not less than £2000 per annum; and provided that the balances due, be all paid at the expiration of eighteen years from the time when the money shall be advanced, and that the said sum of £50,000 be a charge upon the territorial revenue of India.'"

By a subsequent order grounded on this resolution, I was required to deliver, and did deliver, separate assignments of £1000 out of each of the half-yearly payments of my annuity, for the payment of £36,000 of the loan of £50,000; and of my estate of Daylesford, rated at £14,000 for the remainder. These assignments were dated, I believe, the 8th of April, 1796.

To this arrangement I submitted with great, though silent regret, and some mortification. I considered it a direct contradiction to the declared terms of the loan; for instead of being exempted from the payment of interest, I was charged by it with an interest of four per cent., only one per cent. being remitted of the rate which might have been legally taken. It defeated, in a great measure, the beneficent purpose of the loan, by leaving me nearly as much encumbered with debt as I was before, transferring what I owed, rather than extinguishing it. To those who were only acquainted with the reiterated and confirmed resolutions of your Honourable Court, as they were publicly reported, I was held out as a man of superfluous opulence; but to others who better knew what had been bestowed, and what was withheld, the reduction of one moiety of a recompense so honourably made for acknowledged services, would suggest the idea of a too precipitate liberality, exceeding desert, and in part retracted, to apportion the one to the measure of the other.

Yet as I had no claim to what was thus resumed, nor yet to what remained, but that which I derived from your spontaneous bounty, I acquiesced, as I ought, in your determination, happy in obtaining an effectual deliverance from instant and extreme distress; and hoping by the observance of a line of strict economy, both to confine my expenses within the bounds of the means which I possessed to defray them, and if I could not lay up a provision for the destined hour of insolvency, at least not to aggravate its difficulties; and trusting to, I know not what remote contingency, for their prevention or removal. Three years afforded me for more temperate reflection have since dissipated that illusion.

If it had been left to my option, as the words of your resolution seem to imply, to offer such security as might be satisfactory to your Honourable Court, (which I have no doubt I could have done,) I should, by the same appropriation of three-fourths from my income, which I now make from it, have provided for the complete liquidation of the debt which I originally owed, with the interest accruing on it, and for the accumulation of something more than £36,000 by the expiration of the period when the repayment of your loan would become due; and I should then have only a deficiency of £14,000, for which the mortgage of my estate now in your hands is an ample security, to make up the full sum of your loan. But by the mode which your Honourable Court has prescribed for the repayment of your loan, though that will indeed be completely discharged, yet I shall still remain a debtor of £20,000, with the loss besides of the only productive property which I possess, my estate of Daylesford, which I shall have no means of redeeming.

I again repeat, that I have no claim upon your Court. Their bounty, and your direction of it, have already preserved me from the immediate and decided ruin to which the justice of my country, if I may not be allowed to give it any other appellation, had implacably devoted me, and which, though protracted, still hangs over me. From that source of relief, I do not ask for more, I ask only that you will render that relief effectual to the purposes for which it was granted, and according to the terms in which it was successively ordered and declared to be confirmed, by permitting me to hold without interest the loan which you were generously pleased to grant me without interest, that is to say, that you will be pleased to order an account to be made out, and annually renewed and kept. of the accumulated sums withheld from my annuity, and the growing interest, so that I may still reap the full benefit of it, in the same manner that I might have done had the whole been paid into my hands; but that it remain a deposit in yours, for the repayment of your loan when that shall finally become due, as far as its accumulation shall suffice for that end; and that credit be then given me for the amount, set in opposition to that of the amount of loan, and the balance only charged on my estate for the remaining payment.

It would be ungracious in me to distrust your liberality to me, after having so amply received the proofs of it; but it would also argue a presumption as culpable to infer your assent to my request, as a necessary conclusion from my own opinion of the reasonableness of it. You may possibly think otherwise of it. In that event, that I may not again obtrude myself upon your attention, may I request that you will have the goodness to permit this letter to be inscribed into your records, and that I may be apprized of your final determination upon it. I have the honour to be, &c.

There was no reluctance on the part of Sir Stephen Lushington to receive and lay before the Directors the preceding letter; neither were the Directors inclined to deal with it otherwise than in a spirit of perfect liberality. The Court met, took Mr. Hastings's proposition into consideration, and promptly and unanimously acceded to it. The following from the chairman, dated the 15th of

July, reached Daylesford on the 17th, and for the time being, at least, set the mind of its owner at rest.

East India House.

Sir,—I have great pleasure in forwarding to you the resolution of the Court of Directors, upon your late application. I am Sir, your very obedient servant.

S. Lushington.

At a Court of Directors, held on Tuesday the 9th of July, 1799, resolved, that in order to comply with the spirit and real intent of this Court's resolution, of the 26th February, 1796, to lend to Warren Hastings, Esq., the sum of £50,000, without interest; which resolution is defeated by the mode of stopping £2000 annually from the annuity, likewise granted to him; the said sum of £2000, so withheld at half yearly periods, be invested in the Company's bonds, and that the interest thereon accumulate till such time as the amount of the bonds, in principal and interest, shall liquidate the loan of £50,000; after which period Mr. Hastings or his heirs shall enter into the full receipt of the annuity of £4000 for the remainder of the term; and that the Company's treasurer and accountant be directed to carry the above resolution into effect.

The single subject on which Mr. Hastings appears never to have used aright his powers of discrimination and judgment was that of accounts. He invariably miscalculated the chances against himself, and the results on the present occasion were not different from what they had formerly been. The new resolution of the Court of Directors afforded him no relief from immediate difficulties; so that his embarrassments, instead of diminishing, increased from day to day. He never could bring the year's income to cover the year's expenditure; and he was once more driven by stern necessity to lay his case before his indulgent masters. It is an act of justice to all parties, that the form of this second application should be given, as well as that the measures adopted in consequence of it should be explained. The following speaks for itself.

To the Honourable Court of Directors, &c., &c., &c.

London, 30th May, 1804.

Honourable Sirs,—I once more submit to the necessity of exposing my personal wants to your Honourable Court, in the hope, and with the assurance (without which I should not venture to obtrude myself in the character of a suppliant on your attention), that my application, whatever may be its final result, will be received with your accustomed indulgence.

My case is briefly told. Your former beneficence, in the two instances of an annuity for my permanent subsistence, and of a loan for the discharge of my debts contracted by my impeachment, had the effect of a present and continued relief; yet it was not adequate to all its destined purposes. Other debts, derived from the same cause, still remained. The interest of these, added to the growing taxes, which I pay at a rate much exceeding the proportional value of my real income, and the resumption of one moiety of my annuity for the gradual liquidation of my debt to the Honourable Company, have left me a provision so unequal to my yearly expenses, that I have been under the necessity of borrowing £5000 on the mortgage of all my landed property; the interest of which is a further charge upon my income.

My expenses are none of them such as deserve the character of extravagance; yet I cannot conform to that strict line of economy which another might, who possessed by inheritance an income of the same measure as mine, and had formed the habits of his whole life to it. This was not to be expected from a man who had passed all the active part of his in the hourly discharge of public duties, which allowed him little leisure or thought to attend to his own affairs, or to care about them.

I have now no other resource left me, but in your liberality, and my confident belief that your Honourable Court will not suffer me to descend to the grave with my last moments embittered with the prospective horrors of an insolvent debtor.

I have served the Company long; they have approved of my services, and have amply rewarded them. I have suffered much, and (permit me to say) for acts which have originated in my zeal for their interests, and from which they enjoy many acknowledged benefits. It was not from them that I was entitled to expect a compensation for wrongs which they had not inflicted; yet to their benevolence I owe all of compensation that has been bestowed upon me. More I shall not urge in my own behalf; nor do I assert this as a claim to your generosity, but as a plea for so unprecedented an appeal to it.

In the consideration of the subject of this petition, (if you shall deem it deserving of that notice,) I request that you will not suffer the intended donation of the Nabob of Oude to mix itself with it. Doubts have been suggested to me relative to that donation, which make it an object of my duty to relinquish all pretension to it; and I request your Honourable Court to accept my absolute and unqualified renunciation of it. The sacrifice of a monthly pension, which is to cease with a life already approaching its seventy-second year, and which depends for its commencement upon a remote and uncertain contingency, will not be imputed to me as an affectation of disinterestedness. In truth I am interested in the privation of it. It has already interfered with a wish, which a very different sentiment prompted me to express in a letter addressed many years ago to your Honourable Court, and which has never quitted its place in my mind, "that I might owe my fortune wholly to your bounty;" and I shall rejoice to be disencumbered of the weight of a foreign obligation. I have the honour to be, &c.

There is nothing in the tone of this letter which can with the smallest truth be said, to derogate from the high and manly character of the writer. It is the appeal, doubtless, of one who is in great pecuniary distress, to parties whom he is conscious of having long and faithfully served, and on whose generosity he feels that he has strong claims, if not in law, at all events in moral equity; but it is nothing more. Let me not, however, withhold either from the Court or from the King's ministers, the credit which is, in like manner, their due. Before Mr. Hastings took courage to make known the necessities of his case, he communicated in the first instance with Mr. Addington, now the venerable and venerated Lord Sidmouth, who, as I need scarcely observe, held office, at this time, as First Lord of the Treasury. He was received by Mr. Addington, as he always had been, not merely with kindness, but with the consideration due to his merits; and both by him, and by Lord

Castlereagh, then President of the Board of Control, the best assurances of support were given. Thus fortified, and relying something on the good offices of those among his personal friends who were either in the Direction themselves, or had interest with the Directors, Mr. Hastings presented his petition. It was at once, and in the best possible temper, considered, and after some delay a resolution passed, granting him, for the remainder of the appointed term, the full amount of his annuity. Nor did the liberality of the Court end there: though they were prevented, I believe, by the interference of the Board of Control, from supplying out of their own treasury the sum requisite for the redemption of the mortgage on Daylesford, they relieved Mr. Hastings from all serious anxiety on that head, by antedating the annuity one whole year. From that day forth, Mr. Hastings, though never wealthy, was, at least for a season, delivered from the dread which had so much disturbed him heretofore. His means were, with economy, rendered equal to his wants; and economy, to a well regulated mind like his, presents no repulsive features, so long as it may be practised without absolutely trenching on the common courtesies and kindnesses of life.

It was at this stage in Mr. Hastings's career that an event befel, of which, because it is highly honourable to both parties, I feel myself called upon to take notice. Mr. Addington, now Lord Sidmouth, was then, as I have already stated, at the head of the King's Government. Against Mr. Addington, however, intrigues had been long carried on, which about the period of Mr. Hastings's second application to the East India Company attained their height; and he felt that it would not conduce either to the welfare of the country or to his own personal honour, were he, in defiance of an alienated House of Commons, to retain his place in the King's councils. Mr. Addington, accordingly, determined to resign; very much to the mortification of his royal master, and in decided opposition to the wishes of a large and influential portion of the community. Among those who deprecated the threatened resignation, Mr. Hastings was one, and though no farther connected with the minister, than that he had uniformly received at his hands marks of the most distinguished respect, he resolved to try the effect of a personal remonstrance, and to urge at least the suspension of the measure. With this view he waited upon Mr. Addington at his official apartments in Downing Street, and was immediately admitted to an audience. "I knew," said Lord Sidmouth, to whom I am indebted for this anecdote, "that Hastings was no common man, and even when he began to speak to me on a subject so delicate, I encouraged him to go on. After concluding his address, he was about to withdraw, but I would not permit it. I begged of him to keep his seat, that I might lay before him a candid statement of the situation in which I found myself, and then, continued I, you shall be the judge, whether or not I can, with propriety, remain in office. Hastings heard me with great attention, and when I ceased to speak, rose up and said, 'Sir, I came here determined, if possible, to convince you that you ought not to resign. You have satisfied me that the view which I took of the case was erroneous. I am now as thoroughly persuaded as you can be, that there is but one course open to you, consistent with your honour and your duty,—you must resign.' He then left me; and I do not hesitate to confess that I was better satisfied with myself, as well as with the decision at which I had arrived, after I found that the latter carried with it the approval of a man so competent in every respect to try the question, as Warren Hastings."

It might offend the good taste of the pure-minded and venerable statesman, to whom I am indebted for this anecdote, were I to describe the effect which, when orally delivered, it produced on myself. Let me therefore turn the reader's attention, at once, to Mr. Hastings's Diary, where I find the occurrence carefully noted down, with such observations on the conduct and bearing of the prime minister, as testify to the respect and esteem in which he was held by the journalist. Moreover, as Mr. Hastings appears to have carefully considered the line of argument which he was about to adopt, it may not be amiss if I transcribe his appeal at length. The entry runs thus:—

"On the 5th May, 1804, I waited on Mr. Addington by appointment, and spoke to him, after a short preface, as follows:—

"I have heard with sorrow, in which I can safely declare that no thought of my own interests has any share, that you are on the point of relinquishing your office. An unimportant individual, such as I am, whom no man fears to offend by the disclosure of his political opinions, and to whom no one can have an inducement to pay an interested court, may possess more authentic means than either yourself, or your personal friends, of knowing the sentiments of the people respecting your character, and the character and effect of your administration. Believe me, Sir, the voice of the House of Commons is not the voice of the people. This is very generally in your favour, and every day increases the number of your adherents. During the course of the last week I have scarce seen a man or woman (for all feel an interest in the present scene) that did not execrate the confederacy that has been formed against you; that did not express himself disgusted with the effrontery of so unnatural a combination of discordant interests, connexions, and opinions, and indignant at the savage attack, made at such a time, on the feelings, the peace, the health, and perhaps the life of the King.

"The people see and know that an ample, sufficient, and well distributed provision has been made for their defence against the threatened invasion; they see resources called forth, for which no one gave this country credit; they are pleased with the economy of the public expenditure; they have proclaimed a spirit of zeal and unanimity, which they certainly neither showed nor felt during the last war, nor during the late administration; they have not been intimidated by the power of arbitrary arrests and endless imprisonments; and even your enemies admit your integrity, while they profligately sneer at it. These are the characters of your administration, and in what is it deficient? I borrow the language of others, when I answer,—in oratory, that is, in that waste of words and time, which is the invariable substitute for useful matter and progressive action. Yet they see you prompt in reply, candid in explanation, and your mind stored with all the knowledge that can qualify you to discharge the arduous duties of your station.

"This remonstrance may be too late; Certainly not if his Majesty's consent has not yet been decidedly given to your resignation. His opposition to it will justify you to all the world in retracing whatever steps you have taken, and in maintaining the post which he has assigned you. Nay I know that it will be expected,—because you were called to this great trust by His Majesty's own selection; you are the minister of his choice and peculiar confidence.

"This, Sir, is the crisis which will determine the credit, importance, and all the colour of your future life. If you persevere and succeed, you will rise in the public estimation, and in your own. If you fail, you will be but where you would have been by your own self dismission, and you will retire compelled by necessity, and with the conscious rectitude of not having deserted your country, nor deceived the confidence of your sovereign."

Mr. Hastings then goes on to describe in detail,

what I have already recorded in substance, and adds :—

"At the close (of the conference) he requested, as a favour, that I would put down in writing what I had said. He gave me pens, ink, &c., and left me. I wrote the above, omitting the parenthetical sentence in the first and second lines.

"I think it proper to add, that I began my address, by desiring him not to judge of what I should take the liberty to say to him by my present humble rank in life (to which he replied with great courtesy), but hear me patiently without interruption, and permit me to depart without a reply. He heard me most attentively, and in silence. I left the writing, sealed, on his desk, and the following note enclosed with it.

"Sir,—As you have been pleased to stamp a degree of importance on what I took the great freedom to represent to you, by desiring me to leave it in writing, it may be necessary, though certainly implied, while I have the honour of presenting to you the transcript of it, to say, that it is with the full permission to apply it to whatever use you may think proper, though I know of none but one, which respects myself only ; that it may remain a memorial of the zeal, attachment, and reverence with which I have the honour to be, more than ever, your most devoted humble servant."

Having concluded these affairs, Mr. Hastings returned to the quiet of his home at Daylesford, and the society of the friends whom he there admitted to his intimacy. His correspondence, likewise, resumes, for a while, its strictly private nature ; and if here and there I discover in it traces of aspirations after a more busy career, these are invariably inscribed in colours which mark the total absence, on his part, of hope that the wheel of his fortune would ever again make such a revolution as might lead to the accomplishment of his wishes. I subjoin the following letters as specimens of the sort of feeling which I have endeavoured to describe, as at this time exercising some influence over him. They are both excellent in themselves, and every way characteristic of the writer.

To Sir John D'Oyley.

Daylesford House, 5th February, 1805.

My dear Sir John,—A letter from me is only a pledge of my affectionate remembrance; for I am so completely shut out from the world, and the knowledge of all that passes in it, that I am not able so much as to tell you what has been the cause of the late change which has been decreed in the government of India; whether Lord Wellesley has solicited his recall, or is to relinquish his office by compulsion. It has been sudden, and I believe occasioned much surprise. It has been reported to me, but I have forgot my authority, that Lord Castlereagh and the present Earl of Buckinghamshire were candidates for the succession, but that Mr. Pitt, to prevent the disagreements to which such a competition might give occasion, fixed his choice at once on Lord Cornwallis, without any solicitation from his Lordship, but rather soliciting his acceptance of the appointment. I have a great respect for Marquis Wellesley, and a high opinion of his talents; and I am sorry for the loss which you and Charles will sustain by his departure; but you are not unknown to Lord Cornwallis, and, from the coldness which is imputed to his character, I infer that he is not so partial to his immediate dependents as to be insensible to the merits, or useful qualities of others. Other news you will hear from better informed correspondents, and the public papers, which contain much more than I read. Among the late changes in the administration, there is only one that I take an interest in, and that is Mr. Addington's acceptance of the dignity of President of the Council. I am persuaded, that in this departure from his avowed purpose, he has yielded to the personal instances of the King, and to the necessity of adding strength, which his popularity would give, to the new administration. He is a good man, and I am almost sorry to make my eulogium of him suspicious by acknowledging personal obligations to him. Yet I think even these are proofs of the goodness of his motives; for what interest could prompt him to serve one so utterly incapable of making any return?

I wrote a short letter to you, and sent it to take its chance of an overland despatch, a few weeks after your departure; and on the 29th of October last I closed a long letter to you, comprising the history in detail of my own affairs. From an official timidity, and that indecision which seems peculiar to the Direction, and which I can well account for by their dependence on a superior authority, their resolution to allow the full sum of my annuity, though passed on the 25th of July, was not notified to me till the 21st of December; and the first payments to which it entitled me, were not made till the 29th of that month. Yet what has been done has been done with so much kindness and good-will, that I am perfectly satisfied, and as contented as a man can be that is in debt almost to the extent of his whole property.

On the 14th of August I received a fresh cause of rejoicing, in the dismission of Nubkishen's bill, which was decreed by the Master of the Rolls, to whom the

Chancellor (during the course of the process one of my advocates in the cause) relinquished the decision.

I returned on the 29th of July to Daylesford, after an absence of more than seven months, and brought back with me a cold of as long a standing, which I continued to nurse, and to increase it, till I was weary both of the cold and the nursing, and have since lost the former by neglect. My deafness in part remains, and I have felt the cold of the present winter more sensibly than I ever felt that of any which I have spent in England.

To Mr. Thompson.

Daylesford House, 3rd May, 1805.

My very dear Friend,—I feel the kindness of your self reproaches; but how much severer are those which they have awakened in my breast! for, I believe, few men live who have this sin so largely to answer for, and none that atone for it more by their regrets and repentance.

Your reflections on the detection of Lord Melville's corruptions are just. I should not have passed so severe a judgment on them when the public was first in possession of them as I do now, when I see them not only countenanced, but defended by the first servant of the kingdom, and an attempt made by the same man and his dependents to blacken the character of Lord St. Vincent, one of the first, if not the first, naval commander of this, or of any other country and age, in his zeal for his avowed friend. It may and will lower the character of Mr. Pitt; but it will not affect his stability. For this he has the effectual support both of his friends and of his most decided enemies. In this business I see many things that disgust and alarm me; but two which afflict me. You have mentioned one; the other I shall leave to your conjectures. I could talk to you for three hours upon this subject, and not exhaust it. I cannot expend my thoughts in writing; nor do I feel an inclination for it. Why, for instance, should I tell the father of eight children, that as our taxes multiply, as the value of money daily declines, and the public debt, and the increasing necessities of war multiply the bounties in the disposal of the minister, every family in England must in time, and not a distant one, be reduced to an absolute dependence on him, or at least to a choice between their duty to provide a subsistence for their children, and an adherence to their integrity?

Mr. Powney is very good. He has represented me as he wished me to be. I have regained as much of my hearing as belongs to my time of life, but I have not had much cause to boast of my health during this last winter, the cold of which I have felt more than that of any other; but my occasional visits to town after long absences ought to make me thankful that I am as I am; for I see many who are younger than myself much further advanced in their journey, and bearing heavier loads of age and infirmity than I do. Mrs. Hastings, whose health is of much more consequence to me than my own, was remarkably well, stout, and of course in great spirits, during all the last year, and till within about six weeks past. She is yet but an invalid, and I am sure that she does not deserve it; for she is temperance itself, and her exercises such as are most likely to give and to confirm health. In a month's period of my absence from home she has made such improvements in our garden, our lawn, our shrubberies, and even in the farm, as I could not have accomplished in six, if I had even had taste and judgment to design them. I hope you will afford me the pleasure, some time or other, of showing them to you in detail. You ought to be partial in your judgment of them; for, excepting myself, you have not a warmer friend out of your own family than she is.

I have not been fortunate in my stud. My old Arabian died of old age on the 23rd of January. His son, Prince, one of the best horses I ever had, has been long affected with an unknown complaint in his near fore foot, which caused him to fall with me one day in a half-speed gallop down hill; and that I might not trust him again, he has now an incurable cough. My grey mare, Ann, has disappointed me two years successively, and she is lame. So I seldom ride now, but about my own grounds, and that commonly on one of Mrs. Hastings's ponies.

Colonel and Mrs. Imhoff were so kind and considerate as to give me their company in my return from town, though they could only stay with us just a week. They left us both in perfect health, and were evidently the better for even so short an enjoyment of our pure atmosphere, good hours, and quiet. They, too, are among those whom you ought to believe love you on the credit of your own sentiments for them. This I take to be the meaning of one of Solomon's proverbs, which Bishop Louth in his Lectures professes not to understand. As I have begun a new sheet without matter left to occupy it, I will give you my version of the text. I have forgot the chapter :—

Seek you another's thoughts to trace?
Your own with calm reflection scan.
As in the pool face answers face,
So doth the heart of man to man.

Mrs. Hastings charges me to assure you and Mrs. Thompson of her truly affectionate regards and fervent wishes for both, and for your beloved children, and to her assurances and wishes I beg leave to add mine. I am ever, my dear Thompson, your affectionate.

Remember me kindly to your friend, Harry Vansittart. I am glad that he is so laudably employed, and am not sure that I regret his having totally quitted Oxford, if he has quitted it. I shall tell you in my next what I have—that is, what I shall have—done in the affairs of Mr. Warre.

So passed the time, both with Mr. Hastings and the nation at large, till the death of Mr. Pitt broke down the Tory Cabinet; and the Whigs, calling to their aid the large and influential section of the Grenvilleites, forced themselves into the Councils of their Sovereign. Mr. Hastings had never taken any decided part in the questions which kept the Whigs and Tories asunder. His leaning certainly was to the side of what would nowadays be termed liberal views in politics; that is to say, he was friendly to the removal of the Roman Catholic disabilities, and he lamented the precipitancy with which Europe had combined to force upon the French nation a government to which they had declared their abhorrence. But he was neither a leveller in reference to the constitution of his own country, nor yet an advocate for peace with France upon other than the most honourable terms. Mr. Hastings seems indeed to have been what the Whigs once were, and what they professed still to be in 1806; and having received marks of attention from several of the most distinguished leaders, among whom the Prince of Wales was at that time willing to be numbered, he conceived that the moment was favourable for making one more effort to emerge from obscurity. He accordingly wrote to Colonel McMahon on the 13th of March, requesting an audience of his royal master whenever it might suit the Prince's convenience to see him; and he received an answer by his messenger, appointing two o'clock on the following day for the interview. At the hour specified, Mr. Hastings repaired to Carlton-house. He was received with all the urbanity and kindness which gave their peculiar charm to the manners of George IV.; and at his Royal Highness's desire proceeded at once to unfold his business. For the account of what followed I shall again use the freedom of referring to Mr. Hastings's Diary. The following is the entry which I find there under the head 14th of March, 1806.

After describing the manner of his reception, and his own expressions of gratitude, the writer gives the substance of a short speech, as spoken by himself, to this effect.

"Since the great changes which have taken place in the administration of this country, I have purposely forborne to obtrude myself on your Royal Highness's notice, fearing to appear importunate and mistrustful of your Royal Highness's remembrance of me. But it has been suggested to me, that this caution, if extended too far, would render me liable to the imputation of disrespect, by marking a seeming indifference to your Royal Highness's intentions towards me. Under this influence. but not quite satisfied that I have done right in yielding to it, I have ventured to solicit the honour of presenting myself to your Royal Highness, but claiming nothing, and expecting nothing, till your Royal Highness, in your own time, shall do me the honour to make me the subject of your direct and effectual consideration.

"To the Prince's question," continues the Diary, "what were the specific objects that I looked to, I answered my first object has been employment, (i. e. as explained by his Royal Highness himself,) either the Board of Control or the Government of India. but of this I now relinquished all thoughts, perhaps I ought not to have entertained them. My next view was to obtain a reparation from the House of Commons for the injuries which I had sustained from their impeachment of me. Though acquitted, I yet stand branded on their records as a traitor to my country and false to my trust: (this point I left unconcluded.) The third point principally regards the expectations which your Royal Highness has yourself excited in the breast of the person in the world, whose wishes I have ever preferred to my own. Though the best, the most amiable of women, (the Prince said, courteously, 'she is so,') she is still a woman, and would prefer her participation in a title to any benefit that could be bestowed upon me, (these last were not the words, I have forgotten them.) The Prince cordially assenting, but (I thought) not as a thing to be done, but to be tried, said, I must employ Lord Grenville and Lord Moira to effect it; and on my expressing a wish to owe the execution of it to Lord Moira, after some further discussion, he desired me to go immediately to his Lordship, and tell him that he desired me. The Prince took my hand and professed his regard for me with so much fervour, that I could not help exclaiming impulsively, 'Sir, I know not how it is, but I have never yet parted from your Royal Highness, without added sentiments of gratitude and attachment.'"

I do not know how far it may be necessary for me to explain, that, from a very early stage in the impeachment, the Prince of Wales, and indeed the royal princes in general, ranged themselves warmly on the side of the accused. This personal friendship for Mr. Hastings never afterwards wore itself out; yet in the case of the Prince of Wales, at least, it certainly brought forth no substantial fruits. On the present occasion, for example, whatever his Royal Highness's wishes may have been, he did not succeed in accomplishing those of his illustrious suitor. On the contrary, the fears of some, and the old grudges of others among those who had succeeded Mr. Pitt and his friends in the Cabinet, effectually barred the avenue either to honours or employment, against Mr. Hastings; and to Lord Moira, his attached and zealous friend, was committed the ungracious task of making Mr. Hastings acquainted with the results of the negociation. They met at the Earl's residence by appointment on the 29th, against which date I find in the Diary already quoted the following entry.

"I expressed my regret and compunction at the part which I had been imperceptibly led to take in my conversations with his Lordship and the Prince of Wales on the 14th."—"When his Royal Highness drew from me the exposition of the specific point which I wished to obtain, I thought only of receiving it from his unparticipated bounty. Neither had I any other conception during my subsequent conversation with your Lordship. I was indeed a little startled, and ought to have been awakened to a sense of the danger into which I was precipitating myself, by an allusion of your Lordship. You expressed a doubt whether some of the members of the Cabinet would be brought to give their assent to any public act in my favour, which might imply a condemnation of their former behaviour towards me. It is evident that, as the concurrence offered is necessary, they cannot yield it, even to his Royal Highness's injunctions, without a sacrifice of their sentiments respecting me, nor, in short, without conferring a favour on me, though yielding only to the request of his Royal Highness. Notwithstanding this obvious conclusion, I still recurred to my former deception, and thought no more of these persons than as the instruments of his Royal Highness's purpose, not of mine. But I now see my error. My Lord, I never will receive a favour without an acknowledgment, much less will I accept a favour from men who have done me great personal wrongs, though the act so construed should be the result of their submission to a different consideration.

"I beg, my Lord, that the affair may go no farther. I am content to go down to the grave with the plain name of Warren Hastings, and should be made miserable by a title obtained by such means as should sink me in my own estimation." (This is the substance, and nearly, though not quite literal, of what I said.) His Lordship replied, that he perfectly conceived my feelings, but begged that I would not give up the point, but confide in him: and he promised that he would take care that nothing should pass that could reflect the smallest discredit on me, or wound my feelings, either in the way which I had mentioned, or in any other."

"In the conversation, Lord Moira interrupted me and said, he did not know that these gentlemen retained their prejudices against me. He had only supposed it as an effect of the human passions; they might cheerfully give their assent, which would be an indication that they no longer considered me in the light they had formerly done. I answered, this made no difference; I should still, in the case supposed, accept an obligation from men who had grossly wronged me; and added, in allusion to something more said by his Lordship, which I have forgotten, that the atonement ought to precede my acceptance of any thing like a favour from them, if in any case it could be justified. I expressed, at parting, my gratitude to him for the sincerity of which he had given me credit, after the manner in which I had expressed my objection to acknowledgments made, in which my heart did not participate."

Such were the results of the first and last attempt which Mr. Hastings ever made to introduce himself into public life, after he had withdrawn from the great field of his labours in India, and resumed his place among the untitled gentlemen of England. I offer no insult to his memory when I venture to assume, that they both mortified and disappointed him; because no man, conscious of the powers which he possessed, has ever yet been excluded from the means of exercising them, without experiencing mortification. Yet I cannot discover, either in his diary or in his correspondence, one sentence, or the clause of a sentence, which the most fastidious may with propriety interpret as expressive of disgust. On the contrary, the same cheerful and contented spirit which pervades the selection from his letters introduced into a former chapter, breathes through every line which his hand appears to have subsequently traced; indeed his very difficulties in money matters—and they came again—wrung from him no complaint, even while they compelled him to become once more a suitor for the bounty of the Company. I have nothing, therefore, to record of Mr. Hastings throughout the space of seven years, except that he spent his days in a dignified retirement, and found happiness himself in dispensing happiness throughout the circle which enjoyed the high privilege of being admitted to a share of his confidence and his esteem.

I subjoin a very few of the private letters which were written by Mr. Hastings between the years 1805 and 1813, rather as specimens of the bent of his well-regulated mind, than as containing any important or solid information. They seem to me very satisfactory.

To Sir John D'Oyley.

London, 1st February, 1806.

My dear Friend,—I have before me your letters of the 13th to the 16th of May; one of the 14th May by an overland despatch, of the 3d to the 9th of August, of the 6th to the 13th of October, and of the 22d to the 24th of October, 1805. The two last, with one from my dear Charles, came in the Medusa packet.

You have gratified me beyond my powers of expression, and my sense of it as an obligation is equal, by the very luminous and circumstantial detail which you have given me of the state of your family, your own situation and prospects, and the series of political events which had passed before your notice. All these I have read with an interest which has imprinted them deeply, but with very different characters, on my mind. What relates personally to yourself is the only portion of this communication from which I have derived any degree of satisfaction. From the rest, combining it with the miserable politics of this country, and the selfishness on which they are all grounded, I anticipate the most disastrous consequences. May God in his great mercy avert them!

If I answer your letters in detail, I may lose the opportunity and leisure afforded me to write on subjects of a more interesting nature.

In the first place I have the pleasure to tell you, that I have at length seen your son John. I was agreeably surprised to find him, though thin, in health; and though not advanced in instruction, improved in intelligence. The first I ascribe to Mrs. Grant; the second to nature: for I do not think that justice has been done him. It ought, however, to be a consolation to you, that, if he has lost two years of his life, if in that period his constitution has been neglected (I do not say that it was; upon this point Mrs. Grant and Sir

Walter Farquhar will probably give you their opinions, and they are better authorities), and his mind has stood still, there is a radical firmness in both, which will soon retrieve the past. He is gentle, pliant to authority (and that of Mrs. Grant is well adapted to an ingenuous mind), good tempered, and intelligent. Of the retentiveness of his memory he gave me the following proof. I asked him, if he had forgot the verses which I had given him to get by heart at Daylesford. "O no," said he, "I can repeat them." Being pressed by Mrs. Grant to repeat them, I objected, that it was not fair to take him by surprise. In truth, if I had expected the answer which he had given me, I should not have asked the question, at least not before a third person. But he immediately replied with so much confidence, that I acquiesced, and he recited the whole without a moment of recollection, or the slightest hesitation. To any one but yourself, this detail would appear frivolous. You will draw good conclusions from it. I communicated to Mr. and Mrs. Grant the right of control which you have given me, and the first use that I made of it was to advise them not to send the little fellow any more to the school where he has profited so little. There is a preparatory school intended for youths destined for the college at Hartford, but I cannot learn on what authority that title is given to it, for it is neither endowed, nor acknowledged by the Court of Directors; neither is it yet (if my information is correct) completely established. But Mrs. Grant has heard of a small seminary at Pentonville, near Islington, the master of which is a young man, about thirty years of age, who confines his instruction to twelve scholars, who live with him as his children, and eat at the same table with him and his wife, and on the same fare. Young Cockrell, the son of Pepys Cockrell, from whom I have this relation, passed through his hands in his way to Westminster school. He was ten years of age when he went to Mr. Lendon, and was ignorant of the first rudiments of education. He remained with him three years, was then transferred to Westminster, and was thought qualified, after a due examination, for the upper fifth form, into which he was placed. This is an instance of rapid tuition, exceeding anything that I ever heard of; for if he had been entered at first in the petty form, which is the lowest, and risen through all the regular gradations, he would not have attained the fifth in less than six years and a half. Here I shall close this subject, as I hope to tell you before I close my letter, either that your friends have made their final election of this school, or a better. I forgot to mention that in answer to my inquiries, which were very particular, concerning the mistress of the school, for Mr. Lendon is a married man, Mr. Cockrell said, she was very kind and attentive to all her husband's pupils.

I wish I had known your intention of leaving John subject to my general superintendency. I assure you that I was wholly ignorant of it, and that it was by inquiry only that I learnt the name of the place where he was at school. If ever you intimated that purpose to me, it must have been when I was affected with the infirmity of deafness; for I could not have been inattentive to such a charge.

10th February.—I am just returned from a visit which I have made with Mr. and Mrs. Grant to Mr. Lendon, the result of which was, that we have settled to place your son under his charge, and to carry the boy thither on Friday next, if his equipment can be ready by that day, if not, on Monday; that is, either on the 14th or 17th of this month. We were all pleased with the appearance and conversation of both the man and his wife. He seems about the age I mentioned, thirty; rather comely in his person, and his manners gentlemanlike. Mrs. Lendon, a pretty, good-humoured, little woman. I will enclose a card which specifies the terms, and other particulars of his school. The first are high. If this, with Johnny's other expenses, should chance to exceed the fund which you have provided for them, you shall be my debtor for the deficiency. Mr. Lendon has as yet only nine boys, which are three less than his complement.

I was mistaken in what I stated to you about the preparatory school. It is established. Its situation is about three or four miles from Hartford, at a place with a name like Halibury. The master's name is Luscombe: he bears a good character, and his wife an excellent one, and his terms are only sixty guineas a year, and fifty for entrance. Though not appointed by the Court of Directors, this school is considered as under their patronge. Against all these advantages we have agreed to prefer a school, which we know to be good, to one only reported to be so; an establishment of twelve boys to one unlimited in number; and a situation so near to Sir Walter Farquhar, Mrs. Grant, and Mrs. Partington, if (which God forbid) he should require either medical advice, or a temporary removal, to one, not perhaps more salubrious, at the distance of thirty miles from the reach of his friends.

While I am writing this, I have received a letter from Mrs. Close, written by her husband's desire, he himself being unable to write, desiring my opinion concerning the destination of your son, in consequence of a letter which he had received from you. In my answer I have detailed all that we have done, and our reasons for it. If he has disappointed the hopes which you had built on his neighbourhood to Twyford, impute it not to him. He has been long and dangerously ill, and too much reduced, I fear, to allow of the hope of his regaining the activity of body and mind which he once had.

Interesting, and most highly so, as your letters have been to me, I must forbear to make any comments upon them. One observation only will I permit myself to suggest upon the conduct of Lord Cornwallis, and the possibility of its being adopted by his successor, or successors, towards you, in opposition to the principles of the law from which you derive your appointment. I should be sorry that you made any appeal from them to the Court of Directors. From them you would get no redress; and if they were to take up your cause, it could hardly fail to excite enmity to you where you are. Perhaps the best service that could be done for you would be for the Court, in their next re-appointment of an old servant under the Act, to state his rights, and their expectations, as derived from the Act. I will endeavour to secure information of the next instances, and privately to excite the Court to adopt the sentiment in support of their authority, and the authority of the Company. In the mean time, you have sufficiently experienced the mutability of fortune, and the chances of life and death, to guard your mind against despondency. What one man will not do, another may; perhaps from principle; perhaps from favour; and the precedent once established will at least operate as a removal of the fundamental obstacle to your promotion.

It is not yet determined who shall succeed Lord Cornwallis; for as to Sir George Barlow, nobody seems to consider him as holding the Government. I wish they may send out a better man; but I much doubt it, if it is true that Mr. Francis and Lord Minto have been candidates for it, and had powerful friends to support them. The latter has received the actual appointment of President of the Board of Commissioners;

still I think he may renew his pretensions (God knows how founded) to the Government of India. This is not a time to entrust such a stake to such a man, nor to substitute party claims to knowledge and integrity in such a selection. A powerful administration has been formed; but I should doubt of Lord Sidmouth's being permitted to remain a member of it longer than while his influence, name, and interest are wanted to constitute the strength of it. You know how high he stands in my estimation. Of the rest I shall say nothing; for I know nothing of them.

I have recently been gratified by a fresh instance of the partial good-will of the Court of Directors towards me, in an unanimous resolution to suspend the operation of a law, by which all foreigners are disqualified to be admitted into their military service, to enable my excellent friend, Colonel Toone, to give his nomination of a cadetship of cavalry to a nephew of Mrs. Hastings. He is preparing to go out with the first fleet now under despatch. He is nineteen years of age, upwards of six feet high, and is in body and mind all military. I shall request you to present him to your acquaintance as my relation, and for his aunt's sake, a dear one. This is all that I have at present to say on that subject.

I shall close this letter now, that I may be sure of the packet. Give my love to all your dear children. Adieu, my beloved friend. Your ever affectionate.

11th Feb.—P. S. I have totally forgot whether my last letter to you went by the Belle packet. Mrs. Hastings is certain that it did. I remember that I said in it, I would write to Charles by the next packet. If you have received no letter from me with that intimation, that will be an evidence of my having written by that despatch; and I shall expect to receive a mutilated translation of the translation of it in a book of intercepted correspondence.

To the same.

Daylesford House, 30th December, 1806.

My dear Friend,—The letters which I received from you of this year's date are of the 26th of January, by Mr. Farquhar; 29th of January, 5th of February, by a land despatch; 8th of February and 1st of May. I believe I have already acknowledged all but the last. Mine of this year bear the following dates:—20th February, 25th February, 26th March, 29th July, and 1st August, besides three introductory, of Charles Chapuset, young Pfeiffer, and Mr. Whalley.

I have blamed myself for not writing to you more frequently; but I do not mend by self-reproach, and am not sure that it is just; for if any event occurred that interested you, or could be turned to your interest, I should assuredly neither neglect to apprize you of it, nor to avail myself of it. I am sick of looking to India, because I see nothing done for the advancement or preservation of our property in it that I like; nothing, indeed, but what I do not like. I was pleased with the resistance which was made by the Court of Directors to Mr. Fox's persevering attempts to force upon them their appointment of Francis and Lord Lauderdale to the Government of India. Such an effort of public spirit was too great a strain on their natural dependency of character to last, and they yielded to the prescription of a more unfit man than either, without a struggle or murmur, as if they had been contending only for the applause of virtue, without caring for the substance of it, or for the result. I should have thought that his administration of Corsica had made his talents sufficiently known to be dreaded. I feel for you; for his active malignity, which will never forgive the injuries which he has already done me, will too soon discover the concern which I have in your welfare, and do all he can to thwart it. But whatever part he assumes towards you or whatever may be your disappointments from other, and whatever sources, bear with them; do the best for yourself, console yourself in the good that your family has derived from your restoration to the service, and wait for better days. Neither are men immortal, nor the power of ministers everlasting. Even in the worst result, your patient perseverance will reward you with your own approbation, in the reflection that you have done your duty, and have not merited the evil that has been your portion. If you sink under the contest, and fly back to England, vexation and remorse will embitter the remainder of your days and accelerate the close of them.

I have been disappointed in the hopes which Mr. Farquhar gave me of a visit from Cheltenham as soon as he had completed his prescribed term of drinking the waters. I have written to him since, about five weeks ago, but whether he had then left Cheltenham, or whether he has written to me and his letter has miscarried, I have not heard from him since. So we are yet strangers, but I trust we shall not remain so. I have two strong inducements to make acquaintance with him,—he is your friend, and his character respectable.

I have told you what passed between Sir Francis Baring and myself respecting his son's marriage with your Harriet, and I sent you a copy of his letter to me, in answer to one from me which first announced it to him. I have neither seen him nor heard from him since. I am anxious to hear how they are since situated. With some apprehensions arising from the necessity imposed upon them of a frequent separation, I am yet upon the whole well pleased with your daughter's choice. The blood of the Barings is so intrinsically good, that I will not suppose that there can be one exception to it, and that the degenerate branch should have fallen to your lot.

I again recur to your desperate suggestion of returning to England. For God's sake repel with horror every idea of the kind. Suffer the extremes of sickness and want sooner than submit to so dreadful an alternative. Sickness may be alleviated (I know that the severest may) by abstinence, and the extremity of want by voluntary privations. But solitude, a voluntary banishment from all your children, the disappointment of every hope with which your imagination deluded you into so fatal and irretrievable a resolution, and the inseparable attendant of your latter days —remorse; lastly, to expire without one child, or even friend, to close your eyes, and receive your last injunctions;—what are poverty, sickness, and disappointment to miseries like these, and even those dreaded evils increased by the means so taken to escape from them?

I have taken no steps to amend your situation, or to obtain a redress of your grievances, except in what I have written to Colonel Toone. I could do no good by writing to any one else, not even to Sir Francis; and if you have made any public remonstrance, I fear it will only aggravate the injustice by which you have already suffered. I purpose being in town next month (I am writing in January), and my first object shall be to consult Sir Francis Baring, though I doubt his ability to do you service, unless Lord Minto should find out that Sir Francis can be of service to him, and that he may please him by serving you.

I come now to a subject of a more pleasing nature. Your son John is with us for the holidays. Though not so much advanced for his age, he is improved very far beyond my expectation; is master of his grammar to the syntax, which is a part of his exercise for the holidays, with sixty lines of Ovid's Epistles. These he began two months ago, and recited to me a part of what he had learnt very readily the other morning in a carriage. He is very fond of reading, and repeated to me, at the time that I have been speaking of, the substance of a combination of long stories from the Arabian Nights' Entertainment, with an accuracy that shows that he reads with a good attention, I should say with an attention exceeding his time of life. Of the solidity of his grammatical knowledge he offered an extraordinary proof the other evening. We were reading in company Walpole's Historical Doubts, and came to a quotation in Latin, which had in it the word "*contingerat*," evidently a blunder; but whether intended for contingeret, or contigerat, I could not immediately tell. Either would suit the text, but give a different sense to it. Mrs. Hastings playfully appealed to John, who answered at once,—it should be contigerat, because the *n* is lost in the perfect tense; and he was right. He is the most easy-tempered boy I ever knew; I will not except even my friend Charles.

Of our political situation you will know as much from the public papers as I can tell you. You may think Napoleon a wonderful man, but do not say so. As we cannot cope with him, it is the fashion to scold at him, and call him opprobrious names. I think we begin to drop the invectives of contempt. He is at present well employed in the subjugation of Poland, that is, in delivering it from its imperial and royal depredators. Surely the hand of God is in his present project. I am pleased with it, because it is a retribution of justice; and I am the more pleased with it, because it employs his strength, and may employ it for a length of time to come, on objects in which his success cannot prove hurtful to us, and at a distance which ensures our safety for a twelvemonth at least to come. I do not yet see any means provided at home to repel the dangers which such a foe may meditate against us. We have means, and they are equal to the emergency, but they yet lie, as my impeachment did once, in abeyance.

Mrs. Hastings is well, better, indeed, I thank God, than she has been in many preceding years. We are happy in the society of her son and daughter, who were our companions (did I not tell you so?) in our late visit to our friend David Anderson. Colonel Imhoff has repeatedly solicited employment, but hitherto without success.

I am writing in the beginning of the year. May it prove a fortunate one to you and yours! Adieu, my dearest friend. Mrs. Hastings charges me to assure you of her affectionate remembrance and good wishes. Assure your dear daughters of the same from us both. Yours ever.

To Mr. Thompson.

Daylesford House, 15th March, 1808.

My dear Thompson,—I thank you heartily for your very kind letter. I will first give you the information in which you have the principal interest, by telling you that I think Mrs. Hastings much better, and she thinks so too, for the medicines which I brought with me for her use from Dr. Vaughan, to whom she desired me to apply for advice as I was leaving town—a circumstance which proves that she was seriously ill; for I believe you know that she holds the whole science of medicine in too low estimation, except when she feels herself painfully ill. I am, as I have been ever since the last solstice, equably well. Do you know that, when chilled with cold, to enter at once a warm room, and much more to run to the fire, or to eat or drink anything warm and comfortable, are infallible causes of indisposition, and generally of painful and acute disease? I knew it not till I learned it by severe experience, a little before the period from which I have dated my recovered health, and I believe you are the only friend to whom I have not divulged the discovery. I soon after met with it in the shape of a maxim, in an excellent treatise upon colds, by a Mr. White. I fear, my friend, you will not readily find a purchaser for your estate, even though you could submit to a great loss in the sale of it. I have just read in a letter, that Lord Selkirk has bought a house, furnished, in Portland-place, for 5,000*l*. The depreciation of money affects only the cost of the minute wants of life. Perhaps you might succeed better in offering it for a lease, if you could get a safe and cleanly tenant for it.

There is certainly some mysterious spell put upon me, for I can no otherwise account for the utter neglect of me even by those who proclaim their belief of my past services and subsequent retention of what talents I formerly possessed. My opinions upon matters that come more within the cognizance of my experience than that of any man living have never been asked, but upon personal occasions, in which it was hazardous to give them. It is now too late to look for a change. Yet such a change may come, with others which are mortally to be deprecated. If it should, you, my friend, should be the first individual, after Charles, that should participate in its influence. This profession is like the courtesy of the dying courtier, "If where I am going I could serve you, Sir."

It is long since we have heard from Jersey; so long, that we were forced to apply to Lady Blunt for information; and from her Ladyship we learn by this day's post, that her last letter from Lady Imhoff, dated the 27th ultimo, reported them both well; Lady Imhoff only recovered from a severe illness, and comfortably lodged in one of the best houses in the island, of which they were then but taking possession.

I should have too much to say if I were to enter

upon political subjects. I have read much, and recommend to you of what I have read, Spence on Commerce, Malthus on Population, Lord Selkirk on Emigration, and Scott Waring's two pamphlets on Indian Missionaries. Malthus's appears to me to be one of the most enlightened publications of this and the last age. You have excited my curiosity to read Baring's pamphlet. The name alone would have proved a sufficient incitement, had I seen it so associated. But, if you can borrow it, read, above all things, Walter Scott's new poem of Marmion—not for political worth.

I had the pleasure of seeing Mrs. Thompson and your wonderfully improved and interesting daughter once when I was in town. I strove to see them a second time, but could get no one to announce me, and left my name only on the mantelpiece of the vestibule. I pray you to present, with Mrs. Hastings's, my best regards to both, and accept them cordially transmitted from Mrs. Hastings.

I had forgot my commission and your promise, and had recently formed the resolution of giving up riding during the remainder of my life. But you have revived my inclination for it, and I shall be thankful for the pony which you have provided for me. I rather say, I *am* thankful for it. Let me know what I am indebted to you for it, including in the cost the charge of its conveyance. My horse Prince caught a fever, which terminated in a great swelling in his hind-leg, with a gangrene of so foul and acrimonious a nature, that on the assurance of a surgeon that the bone was tainted by it, and that every day of the poor animal's life would be an accession of misery, I ordered him in pity to be shot. I had the consolation of knowing that he received the stroke of death without either the apprehension or sensation of it. He was the best of all the breed; but they were all defective, because they were all the progeny of old age. Such will almost always be the effect of such a cause. So affirms Plato in his ideal Commonwealth, and such is the more peremptory doctrine of Sarah Webb in her superintendency of our poultry yard, than whom I know not better authorities.

I think you have a neighbour, of whose knowledge in all affairs of husbandry you have a good opinion. I shall be obliged to you if you will ask him at what proportional rate he would estimate a farm beyond that which was put upon it by a professed surveyor in 1798; and I should like to have your opinion, too, upon it, if you are competent (as I dare say you are) to form one. It is a question of some consequence to me at this time. Yours affectionately.

To Mr. Charles D'Oyley.

Daylesford House, 6th January, 1809.

My dear Charles,—I thank you for the information contained in your letter of the 9th of February last, of your appointment to the collectorship of Dacca; and I heartily congratulate you upon it. Estimating its emoluments by its public importance, I conclude them to be equal to any that you can expect to attain for many years to come; and it is always prudent to adjust our conduct to our present station, as if it was the permanent provision for life, making the most of it, and rejecting all dependence on future, though more flattering prospects. I understand you have contracted debts. Let the discharge of these be your first concern. Appropriate a monthly saving for this purpose, and resolve, firmly resolve, to confine your monthly disbursements to the residue. By adhering to this rule, you will possess a mind at ease, a clear conscience, and acquire the habits of frugality, which few Indians practise on their return to their country, which they call home; and almost all wish, for that reason and its consequences, to return to their service, if they could obtain it. This is the second time that I have offered you my advice, the most ungracious of all gifts, and have at the same time prescribed the practice of it. Do not treat it as advice is commonly treated; but reflect that it comes from one who has loved you from your birth, and whom the course of a few years, or more probably a few months, may separate for ever from the only communication you can hold with him in this life. I had not the benefit of such advisers.

Your letter having lain by me some time, I had forgot that you mention in it the emoluments of your office, and estimate them at twenty-eight or thirty thousand rupees a-year, "trusting that you shall be able to lay by sixteen or twenty thousand rupees out of it every year." God bestow upon you the virtue to persevere in this resolution!

I regret that the new regulations of the service, which, in my opinion improvidently, prefer a tedious scholastic discipline in England, to the official completion of education in India, will put it out of your brother's power to visit his father and his family till four years more are past; but his health is good, his manners naturally those of a gentleman, and gentle in the primitive sense of the word, and he improves faster than could have been expected, after two years lost both to the cultivation of his body and mind. It has occurred to me, that John will enter on service at the period destined for the close of the Company's charter, and the commencement of a new political system, in which, I greatly fear, their interests will form an inconsiderable and degraded part. Bear this in mind, and watch the measures and events which may appear to lead to this consummation, that you may avail yourself of the knowledge (if well founded) for the application of it to your own prospects; and reserve it to your own breast.

I can give you no public news which you will not receive from the magazines, if you read them, for you will hardly waste your time in reading newspapers: but I fear I may anticipate what may not come so soon to your knowledge, the total subjugation of Spain by the French ruler before you receive this letter.

Mrs. Hastings sends her love to you, and we both desire you to present our affectionate regards to your amiable lady. Heaven bless and prosper you, my dear Charles. I am ever, most affectionately yours.

To Sir JOHN D'OYLEY.

Daylesford House, 4th October, 1811.

My dear Sir John,—I have received your letter of the 21st of April last, and read with great concern, that you have been, and were likely to continue a sufferer, by what appears to me to be the prevailing vice of your government and time,—the application of the authorities of office to the gratification of private vengeance, and the cover of corruption. As far as I am enabled, by your epitome of your case, to pass a judgment upon it, I entirely approve of your conduct, and most of all of your resolution to appeal, in the last resort, to the Court of Directors. But I hesitate to give an opinion on the concomitant step which you propose, of resigning all employment. If you should be driven to that necessity, I mean of appealing, no one that I know has a better narrative style than you are master of: but while you refer to documents in evidence of facts, you should be careful to confine them to that purpose, and not leave them to be necessary for explanation. Consult brevity by a punctual observance of order and connexion in the construction, but make your appeal complete in itself (though it should be a departure from that rule) by a concise explanation in the context, of every technical term which you may introduce, and of every official rule and practice that you allude to, as if you were writing to a man who had never before read a page upon the concerns of the East India Company. Constitute some active and attached agent, such as I suppose G. Baring to be, if he continues in England, and engage (if you can) some person in the Direction so far to patronize your cause, as to see that you are not injured by the patronage of others unfairly employed to injure you. On good Colonel Toone you cannot long rely. His constitution is so shaken, that, with the additional shock which it has recently received, I fear he has very little left—I will not say of life, but of the active powers of life. I have not heard from him, (indeed your letter announcing his son's death has been in my hands but two days,) and I shall not for some time to come have the heart to write to him: and what use I can make of the materials which you have afforded me I cannot yet devise. All affairs of the Company which are left to the Directors are wholly conducted by the chairman and deputy, and by them with such a spirit of procrastination, that very little is done out of the ordinary routine of current business; so that an appeal to them is too much like the filing of a Chancery suit; only that the approaching expiration of their charter may offer some chances of an intermediate amendment; and for the future, no one I believe knows, not even those by whom the next arrangement will be made, what that arrangement may be. While I live, and possess my faculties, those, in whatever way they can be employed, shall be at your service, and at the service of any one who may be better able to serve you, and shall be accredited by you. But I know not what my means, situation, or local residence may be a year hence, if life is granted to me so long.

I have no great opinion either of the views or animus of Lord Minto; but I regret his absence from Calcutta, as it must be productive of all the evils of an inefficient and unresponsible government. The frequent recurrences to this measure have totally deprived the governor in being, whoever he may be, of all his superintendency, and must (as it appears to me) have the effect of converting all the offices into so many independent authorities, besides the opportunities afforded for new interests to establish themselves, or rather *a* new interest to raise itself by superior talents, and the energies of intrigue. I am not afraid of saying, that no future Governor-general will discharge his duty properly that does not do as I did—inspect the weekly or monthly details of every department, and give his instructions as often to the head of it. This duty he can only perform by being constantly on the spot: it cannot be done by delegation. All the current business stood still while I was at Lucknow in 1784.

Mark, in the course of your present business, every gross violation of justice, and secure and fix the evidences of it. One example from your letter may suffice. You write, that " you were required to communicate the mode by which the money was accumulated, together with the intended appropriation of it." This was the requisition of a court of inquisition, not of a civil office, nor could a court of justice demand of any man what passed in the heart of another, though it might extract the truth from the corresponding testimonies of men who were privy to the facts relating to it. Such demands can only be construed artifices to ensnare innocence, to throw upon the person on whom they are made, the imputation of an informer, for an act of indispensable obligation. You had no alternative but to appropriate the money to your own use, which would have been fraudulent, or to carry it to the credit of the Company. The latter act being indispensable, rendered it incumbent upon you at the same time to declare how it came into your possession, and what information concerning it you could legally obtain from others. The Board of Trade, as I suppose it was to them that you were amenable, should have appointed a committee of inquiry, if more was necessary. This, or whatever equivalent mode the rules of government have appointed for such cases, should have been done, and they were guilty of a neglect of duty who did not do it. I do not understand what you write concerning the securities, and the charge intended to be drawn against you, nor by whom, for exacting them; nor can I apply the term of duplicity in any sense of the act, to it. It appears to me to have been not merely correct, but necessary; nor could the neglect of taking securities from the Amla be imputed to you, if (as I take it for granted) they were not of your appointment, nor appointed during your time. I will inquire whether any notice is taken of these transactions; and you may depend upon it, that I will not be wanting in anything that may be necessary to guard your character against any misconstruction or misrepresentation of them.

I have not heard lately from John, nor of him: I am satisfied that he is going on well. I pray to God that you may live to see him. He will be a blessing to you. If he goes out next spring, I shall not want Mr. Partington's assistance in defraying his further expenses, unless they exceed my estimate of them.

Give my love to my dear friend Charles, with that with which I am charged from his godmother; we both unite in affection and every good wish for you and all your family.

I must not omit to inform you of a very interesting

event which has taken place in our family, which is, the marriage of my nephew Woodman to Mrs. Hastings's niece, Miss Louise Chapuset, an amiable young woman, and so great a favourite of us both, that no other cause could have reconciled us to her separation from us.

We are both, for the present, well. Adieu, my dear friend. I am ever, yours with true affection.

To Mrs. Hastings.

Brackley, 29th October, 1809.

My beloved wife,—Neither I, when I promised to write to you from this place, nor you, when you exacted my promise, reflected, that Saturday was not a post day, and that a letter written on this day, Sunday, must go first to London, and would arrive at Daylesford, but a few hours before me; for the purpose of giving you, at the expense of double postage, information which I could deliver more amply and satisfactorily, and free of cost, if withheld till I came home. Yet I am bound by my promise; I love to converse with you, in whatever way I can; and my letter will at least answer one good purpose,—it will spare you the pain of doubtful expectation. On Tuesday, the day appointed for my return, I shall return; but as I propose to stop at Banbury for an hour, I shall not reach my beloved home till near five. I shall certainly be there (if it please God) not later than five. Thomas Woodman has done much to the parsonage, in which he has completed two good rooms below, and two above stairs; and the whole will in another year be a comfortable and hospitable mansion. He invited two neighbouring families yesterday to dine with us, decent and evidently good tempered people. One lady recommended herself to me by praising our friend Mrs. Sampson, who is of her acquaintance. He expatiates largely, and warmly, on the friendly dispositions of his townfolks; from which I infer that they think as kindly of his. The town is a handsome town, and reputed healthy. Old Woodman is as well, and looks as well, as I remember him forty years ago. I too am as well, and look as well, as I did four days ago. The road from Chipping Norton to Banbury is not bad, and from Banbury hither good.

T. Woodman was much delighted with your accumulated bounty, at which I was equally surprised, and had half a mind to be offended. He will thank you, and answer your letter himself, and write for both purposes by me, charging me in the mean time to say much that is handsome for him.

Adieu, my beloved. May the Almighty bless and protect you! This is my morning and nightly prayer, and the wish ever present in my heart.

To Mr. Thompson.

Daylesford House, 17th November.

My dear Thompson,—I can scarce tell you why I did not answer your letter when I received it, for I never had less leisure or less inclination to write than now.

I do not know whether Phipps was in my debt or not. If he was, his bond, with every other, for debts contracted in India, was left in Calcutta, and is there still.

I saw Mrs. Phipps when I was in town. She said, she wished *to go to service*, or do any anything for bread—Poor creature! that she had paid all her debts to a farthing, and was literally pennyless. When I return to town, and I ought to be there by next Monday, I will exert myself for her. At present, I am sufficiently occupied with cares of my own. In the mean time she is not in actual want, nor, I hope, in fear of it.

If you think fit to administer, and wish me to join you in it, you may. Offer our kindest remembrances to your dear lady, who has at present much the largest share of our good wishes, but can we divide them? I thank you most heartily for your game. It came most opportunely when it was most wanted, and was not to be had but through your bounty. Adieu, my dear friend, your affectionate.

CHAPTER XIV.

Mr. Hastings examined before the Houses of Parliament—Degree conferred upon him by the University of Oxford—Created a Privy Councillor—Introduced to the Emperor of Russia and King of Prussia—Dinner to the Duke of Wellington—Returns into Private Life.

FROM the year 1806, when he made his first and last attempt to take some share in the management of public affairs at home, Mr. Hastings spent his days in comparative obscurity. Contented he doubtless was; for the consciousness of deserving well of the country which neglected him continued present to his mind throughout, and in the pursuits of agriculture, and the indulgence of a pure and classical taste, he found ample occupation as well as great enjoyment. Moreover, his home was to him what it had ever been, a scene of the purest happiness, while his benevolence, the prominent feature in his character, was never at a loss for objects on which to exercise itself. There is a large portion of his correspondence now before me, which, for obvious reasons, I feel myself prohibited from making public, but of which I am free to state, that in every line it bears testimony to his excellency of heart and the strength and clearness of his judgment. Were any of his more distant friends anxious about the education or the general welfare of their children? They seem invariably to have thrown themselves upon Mr. Hastings for counsel, which, as well as more active assistance, was in no single instance refused. Did domestic differences arise, even between man and wife? Mr. Hastings was appealed to as the individual, among all their acquaintances, the best fitted either to bring the estranged parties together, or to arrange, in a manner satisfactory to all concerned, the terms of an amicable separation. As to applications for aid, either in launching young men into the world, or relieving widows and orphans from the pressure of pecuniary distress, there is really no end to them. And finally, his letters to the youth of both sexes, especially to boys, whether at school or college, or preparing themselves for the service of the East India Company, are all models of gentleness, and wisdom, and high principle. In a word, the years which Mr. Hastings spent apart from the busy world, and, as far as the world's observations went, in total neglect, were not only not passed in indolence and uselessness, but were devoted to the well-being of his fellow men in all ranks, and ages, and conditions. I question, indeed, whether even he ever did more good—I mean individual good—at any interval in his career, than during the season, when to society at large he appeared to have laid aside all active interest in the sayings and doings of its members.

It was not, however, in the arrangements of God's providence that Mr. Hastings should quit for ever the stage of life without having his wisdom appealed to, and his merits acknowledged, in quarters where both had been so long and so unaccountably neglected. When Parliament proceeded, in 1813, to inquire into the working of the revenue and judicial systems, and to make other preparations for the renewal of the Company's charter, Mr. Hastings was called from his retirement in the country to give evidence before both Houses. He obeyed the summons, cheerfully, preferring then, as on all former occasions, public duty to private ease; and, at the age of eighty-one, found himself, for the second time, ushered into the presence, first of the assembled Commons, and by and bye of the Lords. How different was his reception then from what it had been seven-and-twenty years previously! At the former of these periods he stood at the bar of both houses a prisoner, charged with heavy offences, and arraigned for his trial: now his entrance within their doors was greeted by the Commons of England with marks of respect, such as they have rarely bestowed upon a subject. The members, rising as if by common consent, stood with their heads uncovered, and so continued till he had assumed the seat which was placed for him within the bar. In like manner, after his evidence had been given, and he prepared to depart, the members rose again, thus demonstrating the total absence of sympathy which was between them and their predecessors in that place a quarter of a century before. Neither were the Lords behind hand with the Commons in paying respect to the venerable man who came to give them light on the subject of Indian politics. They, too, afforded him the accommodation of a seat; and, from the beginning to the close of the examination, heard him with a silence which was well nigh reverential. But he shall describe for himself, and his friend, Mr. Thompson, shall describe with him, both the scenes as they passed before their own eyes, and the feelings which they stirred up in Mr. Hastings's bosom. The following letters refer almost entirely to this subject.

To Mr. CHARLES D'OYLEY.

London, 15th April, 1813.

My dear Charles,—Though I date this from London, from which place I shall despatch it, I write it at a distance from it, and have not your letters by me. I think I have two acknowledged; but it is a long time since I wrote to you, and am glad of an interval which I have at my sure command to resume that office. By a late despatch I wrote to your father, and related to him all that was in my mind, and that bore a common interest to us both. The two subjects of this letter will be of that relation, and you will both equally partake of them.

Though my acquaintance with Lord Moira is but distant, at least more so on my side than his, it has obtained for me his spontaneous permission to recommend to him any special friends under his immediate government, a privilege, of which I have made but a scanty use. Your father's name and yours I have given in memorandum, as those of friends that were dear to me. Of John I have said nothing, because a considerable time must elapse before he will stand in need of that patronage that will lead to emolument. In the mean time his father will be his best patron, and if John through him is made known to the Governor-general it will be sufficient. His own conduct, and the growing interest of his father and brother, will entitle him, as I trust, to future favour. I have already written thus much to your father, and this must serve as a duplicate, and a provision against accidents.

I have lately received two most convincing and affecting proofs of my having outlived all the prejudices which have, during so many past years, prevailed against me. I have been called before both Houses of Parliament, and questioned at large concerning the points that bore a principal relation to the conditions proposed by the administration for the new charter of the East India Company. By the Commons I was under examination between three and four hours, and when I was ordered to withdraw, and was retiring, all the members, by one simultaneous impulse, rose with their heads uncovered, and stood in silence, till I passed the door of their chamber. The House was unusually crowded. The same honour was paid me, though, of course, with a more direct intention, by the

Lords. I consider it, in both instances, as bestowed on character, not on the worth of any information which they had drawn from me; for your father knows that I am in a singular degree deficient in the powers of utterance. To the same predilection I attribute it, that what I said on both occasions gave unanimous satisfaction. The Duke of Gloucester, with his accustomed goodness, took me with him in his carriage, calling upon me for the purpose, to the House of Lords, sat with me in the outer room till I was called in, conducted me to the chamber, where the Lords sat in full committee, afterwards reconducted me to his carriage, which reconveyed me home by his orders; and when the House broke up, he himself came to make his report of what had passed to Mrs. Hastings, with the same kind of glee that you, or your dear father, would have expressed upon the same occasion. And I bless him for it.

I believe I wrote to Sir John, that I had been visited by a first fit of the gout. It was not violent, but continued long, and kept me sedentary while it lasted. I am now quite free from it, and well: My dear Mrs. Hastings is uncommonly so, and affords me the delight to witness the influence which the happy exuberance of her spirits produces on those of every society in which she mixes. We meditate to return to Daylesford before the end of this month; but I believe I shall soon come back to town, as I feel too great an anxiety to see the progress of the present discussion of the affairs of India in Parliament, to bear that I should remain at a distance from the field of action. How it is likely to terminate I cannot yet form a conjecture; but I fear the worst, from the more than political animosity which has marked the proceedings against the Company. The party in opposition to the government is in this contest united with it.

I shall close my letter here, and write again to Sir John on my return to town. With Mrs. Hastings's kind regards and my own to you both, and to Mrs. D'Oyley, I remain, my dear Charles, yours most faithfully.

From Mr. Thompson to Sir John D'Oyley.

London, 17th May, 1813.

My dear Sir John,—Mr. Hastings has already sent you his evidence before the House of Commons on the India question. By his desire I have now the pleasure to forward to you that which he delivered before a committee of the House of Lords. I wish you were now in England for many reasons, but particularly that you might participate in the triumph which our great friend has obtained over all his enemies. He has not, I believe, one remaining. Those whom death has spared, remorse has converted into friends, and I am most perfectly convinced there is not at this moment a man in England, the worth of whose private and public character is more universally and indisputably admitted than his is. I accompanied him to the House of Commons when he went to give his evidence. Whilst we were sitting in the Speaker's room preparatory to his examination, Sir Thomas Plumer came to us, and I congratulated him on the very different auspices under which we now assembled from those which formerly brought us there. He heartily participated in this feeling, and earnestly said, "Did you not hear just now a great noise in the House?" upon our answering in the negative, he added, "I made sure you must, for when Mr. Hastings's name was mentioned, and a motion made that he might be offered a chair, a louder acclamation followed than I ever remember to have heard within its walls." At the close of his evidence the members, influenced by one common feeling of respect, rose spontaneously, and taking off their hats, stood whilst he retired. You who know the warmth and generosity of his heart will readily conceive how forcibly it was touched, and how delightfully affected by so unequivocal, unlooked for, and rare a testimony of public esteem. His reception before the Lords was hardly less flattering. The Duke of Gloucester, at his own request, called upon him and took him in his chariot to the House, waited with him in one of the chambers till he was summoned, accompanied him into the committee room, attended whilst he gave his evidence, and at its close conducted him back again to his Royal Highness's chariot. Whilst before the Lords he was accommodated with a seat, an honour which I am told is almost unprecedented. Throughout the whole investigation the most marked attention has been paid, both to his person and his opinions. The very officers of both houses, even to the printers of their proceedings, as well as the persons employed by the Company, seem to have vied with each other in manifesting their respect for him. You will not fail to observe that he gave his testimony under disadvantages not felt by the other witnesses. Being the person who was first examined in both houses, he was in some measure a guide and pioneer to his followers, showing and clearing the way, not merely for those who were to answer the questions, but for those who were to ask them. Neither the Commons, nor the Lords, nor even the Council seemed at first distinctly to see their course, and when you shall compare the direct, luminous, and copious answers which he gave to questions frequently indistinct and irrelevant, you will, I think, perceive that at the very outset of the inquiry he enlarged and liberalized its scope and tendency, confirmed the succeeding witnesses, and gave to their evidence that firmness, decision, expansion, and consistency by which it is upon the whole so remarkably and so honourably distinguished.

As I know Mr. Hastings has lately written to you I shall say nothing of his situation or views. He intended to have left town last Tuesday, but he was on the preceding day attacked by a fever, the consequence of a cold, and was obliged to delay his departure till Friday, when he set out for Daylesford in a state of convalescence, and with the prospect of a speedy and complete recovery. Mrs. Hastings was in high health.

I formerly wrote to you concerning your pecuniary transactions with Mrs. Hastings. I now enclose for your information the copy of a letter which I lately addressed to your respective agents, Messrs. Butler and Burrowes, on the same subject. I earnestly wish that the two policies of insurance may be found in the possession of Mr. Edmund Grange; but I have the pleasure of informing you that, even if they should be lost, we may recover their amount upon giving to the office a bond of indemnity against their future production.

I was sorry to hear from Mr. Hastings that you had lately suffered much indisposition. Sincerely wishing you a return of health, and the long enjoyment of that and every other earthly blessing, I remain, dear Sir John, very truly yours.

If you should be disposed to favour me with a letter, direct it to the care of Messrs. Edmund Boehm and John Tayler, London.

From Mr. Hastings to Mr. Thompson.

Daylesford House, 23rd May, 1813.

My dear Thompson,—I wrote to you a feeble letter on Friday, and am going to write another. Mrs. Hastings was so pleased with your letter, that she had a copy taken of it, which she keeps as a memorial; and has desired me to return the original. I read it with as much pleasure as she did. In the choice of sentiments which might give a name to what I felt on my reception from the two houses of Parliament, it was consistent with your accustomed partiality to prefer the best. I certainly felt a "warmth" of some kind; but whether of "generosity," pride, or vanity, I am not able myself to distinguish. It is neither pride, nor vanity, in the common acceptation of those words, to delight in the good opinion of my fellow countrymen, to see such a sanction afforded to my friends for their predilection of me, and to be the means of reflecting my own credit on the person whose happiness so many years past have bound to my own. The suffrage of my masters, conveyed to me through their chairman, has consummated my exultation. After all these demonstrations of self-satisfaction, it is but fair that I should proceed to its counterpoise. I was employed during the greatest part of my sitting hours yesterday in correcting the manuscript copy of my evidence in the House of Lords by your errata, and was mortified at meeting with errors, incongruities, and unfinished paragraphs, which were all my own, and incorrigible. I have given (that is, I have lent) David Anderson my printed evidence, and I want one now sadly to correct it.

In my answer to the eleventh question, instead of "pensioners left upon the *country* of government," read "*bounty* of government." There are other errors of the manuscript, such as, in the first answer, $\frac{39}{135}$ (*i.e.* 39th line, the paragraph consisting of 135 lines), "possessors" stands for "professors"; $\frac{43}{135}$, "successively" for "successfully;" $\frac{67}{135}$, "trait of their character, their temperance is," &c. for "trait of their character, their temperance, which is," &c. But I will not proceed, as I suspect that this may have mistakes which are not in the print. I meet with one, a sad one, which I cannot correct.

I mend slowly, am very weak, and have left off animal food and wine. If that won't save me, brandy won't. Adieu! Your affectionate friend.

P. S. Mrs. Hastings desires me to give her thanks for the copy of your letter to Sir John D'Oyley.—Have I not? She is just returned half starved from church.

Among other mistakes, it might have been a curious one for the next century to have discovered among the Daylesford archives, an envelope superscribed a letter from the Chairman of the East India Company, the address of which was, *Ma bien aimée Madame.*

I do not know how far the proceedings of Parliament may have drawn the attention of the University of Oxford to the slighted merits of Mr. Hastings, but this much I am enabled to state—that he was scarcely returned to his seclusion at Daylesford, ere he received from the Vice-chancellor an announcement that it was intended to confer upon him, at the ensuing commemoration, the honorary degree of Doctor of Laws. To the compliment thus offered, as well as to the flattering manner in which it was carried out, I find a pleasant reference made in Mr. Hastings's diary; where he likewise speaks of Dr. Phillimore's Latin oration in terms of high praise, though not more highly than the elegance of its composition deserved. Yet of one fact, which appears to me to mark more conspicuously than all the rest the triumph of his good name over prejudice, the journalist has omitted to take notice. As the Commons had done in the house, so the junior members of the University of Oxford did in their theatre; they rose to a man when the illustrious octogenarian appeared, and greeted him, both in coming and going, with reiterated shouts. I need not inform those to whom the customs of the university are familiar, that the season of the commemoration is to the under graduates a sort of Saturnalia, during which they bestow, with unsparing lungs, tokens either of respect or its opposite upon the several public men who come under their notice. On this occasion Warren Hastings was, above all the different candidates for university honours, the decided favourite; and it is but just to add, that in his case the young men exhibited the same good sense and perfect impartiality that they are accustomed to do on all similar occasions. The following letters refer, in part, to this transaction, and therefore demand insertion.

To Elijah Impey, Esq.

Daylesford House, 11th August, 1813.

My dear Elijah,—I availed myself of your kind permission to draw upon your bookseller for three copies of your poem,* which I have duly received, and thank you for them most heartily. How much I was pleased with the poem I cannot tell you; but I have a greater pleasure in conveying to you the sentiments and words of my dear Mrs. Hastings. "Tell him," she said, "that I am delighted with it. It is excellent, charming, and has nothing of sickness in the compo-

* Addressed to Dr. Phillimore on his Latin speech presenting Mr. Hastings to the degree of LL.D. at Oxford.

sition of it; nor is it possible to be better." Similar is the judgment of all our present household, who are all good judges, and have delivered their opinions in terms that marked the feelings of the heart in full accordance with the discrimination of the mind. I have just now read it over anew, for the purpose of selecting such passages as were praiseworthy above the rest; but I like the whole so much, that I should appear to myself to depreciate what I omitted in particularising. Yet I may, without the invidiousness of comparison, notice some peculiar excellences which have struck me as such. Lamenting as I do the cause which drew from you the emphatical allusion to your state of health, I must agree with Mrs. Hastings, that the poem has no intuitive symptoms of a mind enfeebled by sickness; and even those six lines possess a beauty, which in a body at ease mere inspiration could not have given. The whole of the address to Dr. Phillimore possesses at once the merit of harmony with that, in the high degree, of compression; and, if I may (after what I have declared against selection) fix upon one part that rises high above the rest, though high, it is the following couplet, which closes the enumeration:—

> "The deep, well-omen'd voice of thunder, given
> To speak and ratify the will of Heaven."

But I may pronounce my praises of the four lines in the tenth page, which allude to my domestic felicity, without scruple; for my judgment has no share in them; and yet my approbation of them (of the sentiment I mean) is boundless, and another person feels the same kind of partiality to them.

The tardy utterance of the evidence delivered at the bar of the House of Commons is most happily, and richly, *transmuted;* and the line describing the rising of the members ("How the mute Board," &c.), is certainly not inferior to the original, if the well appropriated epithet does not give it a superiority. You already know my opinion of the passages which relate to Lord Nelson and Lord Wellington. They are fine, as the principle on which they are founded is just, and well applied.

After having disclaimed all intention of separate encomium, I have bestowed it separative on all inclusively, and after all, am compelled conscientiously to lament, that the whole is a beautiful exaggeration. But proceed with truth, or fiction, I defy you to exceed its intrinsic worth.

Mrs. Hastings desires me to assure you of her kind and grateful regards, and unites with mine to dear Lady Impey and our dear Marian. Adieu, my friend, yours most affectionately.

To Mr. Thompson.

Daylesford House, 15th September, 1813.

My dear Friend,—I am ashamed to have let a letter of yours remain an age unacknowledged; and it was one of all others, the neglect of which would have added remorse to shame, had not my own self-love been at the same time a sufferer by it; for I certainly should have indulged that infirmity, had I written to you, by accepting, with a much stronger complacency than I now feel, your congratulations on the honours bestowed upon me by the University of Oxford. Of these you have your share, and, with the addition of one or two more select names, this was a predominant sentiment in my mind when I received them. Mrs. Hastings and I thank you for your reflection on the forbearance of the mad dog, and both agree, that independently of the affectionate interest which excited it, it was the best thing that any dog, mad or sane, ever gave occasion to be said of him.

Since the receipt of your letter, and for some time before, I have not seen Mr. Leigh, nor can I learn when he may be expected at Adlestrop. I do not like to write to him, because I should fear that the formality of it would frustrate my intention; but if I must, I must write before he loses the remembrance of my claim on him as an old neighbour.

Where are you? To tell you the truth, to ask this question was the prime motive of my writing this letter, as Mrs. Motte (God bless her!) is to leave us to-morrow, and has undertaken to find you out and convey it. My dear Mrs. Hastings is well, and desires me to assure you of her affection. I am well, but suffer under something like an anniversary languor, to the first occasion of which you were a witness in the year 1781. Perhaps there is no great necessity for an octogenarian to seek for adscititious reasons for not feeling himself in such spirits as when the Lords and Commons of the realm bestowed so much pains to keep them in action twenty years preceding. I am ever, my dear Thompson, your truly affectionate friend.

Mr. Hastings was exceedingly delighted, as indeed he had the best reason to be, with the evidence thus afforded to the triumph of truth over prejudice; and to the estimate in which, after long years of persecution and neglect, his own merits as a faithful servant to the public were beginning to be held. Yet was his situation at the moment as embarrassing as can well be conceived, and particularly to one who, like himself, both dreaded, with an almost superstitious dread, the accumulation of debts, and shrank from the only means by which its accumulation could be avoided. Mr.

Hastings had by this time outlived the period for which his annuity from the East India Company was granted, and found himself in the eighty-second year of his age on the very verge of pauperism. There is something so unbecoming the rightful position of the preserver of British India in these repeated exhibitions of his pecuniary distresses, and of the course which he was driven to adopt for the purpose of relieving them, that I may well be excused if I pass, with a rapid pen, over the transactions of this particular epoch. Enough is done when I state, that he appeared again before the Court of Directors as a suitor; and that the Court, after some delay, came to the resolution of continuing his annuity for the term of his natural life. To a proposition, which was hazarded, of increasing the pension to five thousand pounds, and including the name of Mrs. Hastings with that of her husband in the grant, the Court would not however listen; and it would be idle to deny that Mr. Hastings experienced both disappointment and mortification at the refusal.

Meanwhile, the affairs of Europe had taken that mighty turn, which led first to the loss of the French army in Russia, and ultimately to the abdication of Napoleon, and the re-settlement of the grandson of Louis the Sixteenth on the throne of his ancestors. It was a period in our history when the hearts of all men, from the Prince Regent down to the beggar by the highway side, appeared mad with joy. The triumph of England was indeed complete, and, as if to mark the sense which they entertained of her unwavering constancy and stubborn valour during a war of unexampled duration, emperors, and kings, and warriors, and statesmen, from all the European nations, whom her example had finally roused, flocked over in crowds, and took up their residence in her capital. It is no business of mine to describe the succession of fetes and public entertainments which kept London, for a brief space, in a state of violent excitement. By all orders and degrees of its inhabitants they were freely shared, and upon the good feelings of all they produced their customary effects, by calling them strongly into action.

I am not prepared to say that Mr. Hastings owed anything to the operation of this common principle of human nature in the highest quarter, yet the fact is beyond dispute, that on the 5th of May, 1814, he received, to his extreme surprise, an official intimation that the Prince Regent having been graciously pleased to add his name to the list of privy councillors, his presence at the next meeting of Council was desired, in order that he might be sworn in. Mr. Hastings obeyed the summons, as a matter of course, accepted the honour so handsomely bestowed upon him, was admitted to a lengthened audience by his royal master soon afterwards, and returned home highly gratified by the whole proceeding. Not however within these limits was the favour personally shown to him circumscribed. When the allied sovereigns repaired to Oxford, Mr. Hastings was especially invited to meet them there, and again received, in their presence, marks of unqualified respect from the senate, and of ardent and not less sincere admiration from the under graduates in the theatre. Again, he was not only present at the magnificent entertainment given at Guildhall, on the 18th of June, but the Prince Regent embraced that opportunity of presenting him to the Emperor of Russia, and the King of Prussia, as the most deserving, and at the same time one of the worst used men in the empire. "But I have made a beginning," continued his Royal Highness, "and shall certainly not stop there. He has been created a Privy Councillor, which he is to regard as nothing more than an earnest of the esteem in which I hold him; he shall yet be honoured as he deserves." Flattering words, no doubt, to fall from the lips of a prince, and doubly grateful when spoken by one who knew so well as George the Fourth how to give to them their full effect; yet were they followed by no results favourable to the fortunes of him who was their object. Mr. Hastings played his part in all the pageants which cast their halo over that brief season of national joy. He even presided at a dinner given by the gentlemen connected with India to the Duke of Wellington, on the 11th of July, and proposed the illustrious duke's health, in a speech remarkable for its neatness and good taste. Yet he returned, when all was done, to his seclusion at Daylesford, and for purposes of further advancement was never heard of more. The following letters, which I have taken at random out of a number written at this period, will best explain his own movements in the throng, and the feelings which were called forth by the sort of reception which everywhere attended him.

To David Anderson, Esq.

London, 20th June, 1814: 6, Portugal-street.

My dear Friend,—When I write to you, my mind forcibly recurs to your sorrow, yet (I fear) but little abated; for you have more than your own to compel its duration, and I feel, as if every endeavour to draw your attention from it, was a painful intrusion. Yet it is from the interchange of friendly communications alone, that you can obtain that effectual composure, for which your own strength of understanding will have laid the foundation. But of this perhaps I repeat too much, and shall proceed to subjects of inferior interest.

I have received your affectionate letter, and one which has interested me much from my young friend David, with an elegant testimony of his regard for the friend of his father. I allude exclusively to the short, but very comprehensive, and (if I may say it) appropriate address prefixed to his judicial disputation;

which, as far as it falls within the compass of my general knowledge, I am much pleased with, particularly with its conciseness of connexion and perspicuity, which accommodates a subject of a nature so new and technical to my own comprehension. In whatever way he may apply his chosen profession, I have no fears for his success in it.

I shall now say something of myself. You would have been the first to whom I should have imparted the late honour conferred upon me, if it had happened at another time. You will be pleased to hear, that it was unsolicited, and, except by an indefinite hint, unknown and unsuspected. It was accompanied, and followed in a private audience, by the most gracious expressions of benevolence, from the Prince Regent. The same indications I have repeatedly received on other occasions, which have brought me to his Royal Highness's notice, and most conspicuously at the late magnificent festival at Guildhall, where he did me the honour to present me to the Emperor, the King of Prussia, and the Duke of Oldenburgh, in a manner too flattering to be written, and more audible than was merely necessary for the great personages to whom it was addressed. I have a freer and purer sensation of satisfaction in informing you, that I have borne my part in all the late ceremonials and festivals at Oxford, a scene of incessant fatigue during three complete days, without the least injury to my health, and since my return, the dinner at Guildhall, with a cold caught on the journey of my return to town, and not increased by this last and severe trial of my constitution. From these proofs of what I can endure, I think I shall last through another winter, and but for one consideration alone, I think I am pre-reconciled to what may be my destiny beyond it. In the mean time I have the happiness of seeing Mrs. Hastings improve in health, even in the tumult of this town, and though she has not yet received any accession to it by the gratification of those incitements of curiosity, which prevail to a degree approaching to madness in all the world around her. We often talk of you, and dear Mrs. Anderson, and always with fervent wishes for your present tranquillity, and yet reserved happiness. To these we join our most affectionate regards. Pray remember me, with Mrs. Hastings's commissioned affections, to both your sons. I will write to my friend David, with one of the first intervals of leisure that are afforded me, which are not many. Adieu, my most dear friend.

We shall not leave London very soon, nor without apprising you of it.

To the same.

London, 12th July, 1814.

My dear Friend,—Some time before I received your last kind letter, I heard, by two indirect channels, of the loss of your brother John. I grieve for it on your account, and much on my own; for I am much indebted to him for a series of personal kindnesses; and at this time feel my concern for this event aggravated by the regret, that I had never testified to him the sense which I really entertained of the obligation. I believe, too, that it was some addition, that he seemed to have undergone so little change in his person, as to have justified the expectation of a life of extended duration; but I have lived to a strangely checkered period of my own; interested, and not without a degree of compunction, in the daily occurring diversity of passing satisfaction, and its intermixture with the severe domestic distresses of one friend, and the past and impending afflictions of others. In these you have a fellow share; for most of my friends are in the same degree yours; but hopeless as the cases are, I will not anticipate them. Let me turn to myself, a subject at this moment not unpleasing. In the first place, I have the great satisfaction of seeing Mrs. Hastings, who came in a sick state to London, at once improved to a state of unmixed health and exuberant spirits, and looks, if not of youth, of something full as good. I, on my part, have undergone various scenes of fatigue, to which I should have thought myself unequal some years ago, and have not suffered from any, except going to the thanksgiving at St. Paul's, which almost put a period to my career of exertions; for I had a sharp, but temporary fever that night. By a day's abstinence, and a little quiet, I have been since enabled to go through the office which had been assigned me of presiding at the dinner given by the Indian gentlemen to the Duke of Wellington; and I accomplished it with more success than the past, having (in spite of my natural impediments, both in voice, utterance and recollection) prefaced the health of the Duke with an address which was well received. If I can get a frank, I will send you a copy of it, with a continuation of my reflections on the combination of past events, from which much of what I said was taken. I cannot proceed in that work. I live too much in the world, to be able to *think* of what passes in it; and the time approaches, when I shall be too little in the world to *know* what passes in it. I believe we shall return into the country next Monday, the 18th.

I shall be anxious to hear how David has acquitted himself of his first essay in his profession.

I am not surprised that Mrs. Anderson had not recovered sufficient composure of mind to admit the return of society. I am convinced, that it must have cost her much to see her friends and relations the first time. Time and society in grief are more likely than satiety to temper it.

Since I wrote a little more than the first sheet of this letter, I have been at my friend Toone's door. He was not at home; from which I draw a bad omen, as his youngest daughter, of whom, till very lately, they had begun to entertain more sanguine expectations than of the elder, was expected in town two days ago, if she was able to bear the journey. Desiring to ask the servant some questions, I found myself deprived of the power of utterance. This infirmity, of which I do not know whether I have yet informed you, recurs without pain, affecting at the same time the muscles of one hand (not always the same hand) and of the mouth. It seldom lasts more than ten minutes; but its inferior effects upon my hand are almost perpetual, weakening my hold of my pen, and causing me to make continual blunders. This you must have noticed, and therefore I have mentioned it, and accounted for it. How fortunate that I escaped this visitation on the 11th of the month; that, on the contrary, my voice was clear, and audible, and my mind collected! I now bid you farewell. Mrs. Hastings unites with me in kindest regards and fervent wishes, and I hope dear Mrs. Anderson will bear these remembrances from two persons who love her as dearly as any out of the circle of her own family. Remember us affectionately to David and Hastings and to your sister, and your brother James and his lady. Your affectionate friend.

To the same.

London, 20th July, 1814.

My dear Friend,—I have suffered my vanity to be too much gratified by the applauses bestowed on my address to the Duke of Wellington at the dinner given to him, at which I presided, and have been punished for it in a way that has already almost effaced its first impression by my conviction that I have deserved it.

The managers of the subscription sent a copy of the speech to the newspapers, which they (or one of them) inserted, with the following addition:—"The Chairman's speech, from his feeble voice, could only be heard by those who were near the chair; but it was received with much satisfaction," &c. It is not true that my voice was "feeble;" and it was ludicrous, that what I had said should be "received with much satisfaction" by those who did not hear it. Its design, however, was evidently to cast a doubt upon its authenticity. This conclusion I have since drawn from the following circumstances. At a dinner given on the 16th to the Duke of Wellington by the Court of Directors, the following healths were drunk by the Chairman, in the following order:—"Mr. Hastings, and the Governments of India." Then followed, "The Marquis Wellesley, with thanks to him for his distinguished services in India." I am told, that in all the papers (I know it is in one of them), the toasts are thus delivered:—"Marquis Wellesley, with thanks to him for his distinguished services in India." "Lord Teignmouth, Sir George Barlow, Sir John Macpherson, the Right Hon. Warren Hastings, who have served the East India Company with distinguished honour to themselves, and advantage to the Company." All this is a fabrication, arising from a purpose unknown to myself till yesterday, in which some of my most warm friends, and other persons of high respectability, are concerned, and Sir George Dallas the mover of it. It was a proposal to erect my statue in the India House; which was opposed by the friends of Lord Wellesley, unless a similar honour was paid to him, and preceded mine. This was compromised by joining us together, my name being allowed the precedence, and a petition of nine proprietors has been actually prepared (as I have said), requesting a Court of Proprietors to be summoned; but not yet presented, on account, I believe, of the lateness of the season. You may wonder, that I should be all this time in ignorance of all this; but so it was; yet something had imperfectly transpired, and not attributing it to any but the Court of Directors themselves, and not suspecting any competition or compromise, I purposely sought to elude any further or direct knowledge of it. Yesterday Sir George imparted it to Mrs. Hastings, and I called upon him this morning, to thank him for his zealous intention, but peremptorily refusing my assent to it, and to every attempt of the kind whatever, except what should arise from the Court of Directors themselves, and from their own mere motion. On his giving me an assurance, that "nothing should be done that should hurt my feelings," I replied, "No, nothing whatever; let the whole business be put an end to all together." I will not trouble you with another long story; but I have been influenced principally by a similar affair which happened in May last; for which I have since reproached myself. Now I will announce the copy of my address, which I will enclose, regretting only that I could not get a frank for it. It is true, I am aware of the incongruity of your existing state of mind with a subject of so worldly a connexion; but I have reflected, that you cannot have an easier to assist in drawing you back to the habits and to a participation in the intercourse of social life; and you owe yourself to society.

We had made progress in packing up all our furniture, and destined yesterday morning for our final departure, when on Monday we received an invitation to the Prince Regent's fète on Thursday next, to-morrow. We now *hope*, for I will never again say, *will*, to leave the town on Saturday, I trust, not worse in health than I came, and Mrs. Hastings, I thank God, much better.

We desire to be remembered by you and your dear lady with your usual affection, and pray for the perfect restoration of your tranquillity; and we offer our affectionate regards to all your family. I am ever your true and affectionate friend.

I subjoin a copy of the address, to which so much allusion is made; not without a persuasion on my own mind, that it will be read with general interest.

Address to the Duke of WELLINGTON at Burlington House on Monday the 11th of July, 1814.

The gentlemen of this assembly, who formerly held occupations in the various departments of the East India Company's service in India, have solicited the honour of your Grace's presence in this day's festival, to congratulate your Grace on your happy return to the bosom of your country, and to testify in this manner their admiration of your great and eminent services.

In offering this tribute they are animated with the same sense of gratitude which glows in every British heart; but they claim to feel it, if not in a superior degree, in a peculiar manner, from having been, some of them, the associates of your early warfare, many near witnesses of it, and all possessing a common interest in the train of victories by which you supported and extended the power of the British Empire in India; thus uniting at the same time a brother's glory with your own. They have seen the same spirit displayed in the plains of Berar, as hath since been shown on the heights of Vittoria; but the course of your latter achievements has been distinguished by a much more elevated character, in which you have appeared as the delegated champion of the most sacred relations of human society. Let the following facts be taken in proof of this assertion. Whoever looks back upon the wonderful series and termination of events in the Christian world, and traces them through all their combinations, must be convinced, that in the wanton and perfidious aggression at Bayonne, the late ruler of France riveted the first link of that moral chain of retribution, which, closing at Bourdeaux, dissolved, as by a talismanic explosion, the whole frame of his usurped dominion; involving in the same simultaneous catastrophe the restoration of the House of Bourbon, till then unheeded in the general contest, though here, and here only, cherished and befriended; and its rights, which appeared annihilated for ever, to their primitive state, rank and integrity in the system of nations, as if they had never been suspended.

It was the Duke of Wellington, who, himself led by an unseen hand, conducted the movements of this awful scheme of overruling justice. It was at Bourdeaux where his arms were arrested in their prescribed course, not by resistance, but by the digressive offer of submission to the legitimate heir of the French monarchy, from the unanimous voice of the inhabitants of that city, composing a population sufficiently numerous to extend its influence, as it did, to all the departments around it.

This was the consummated work of our most noble guest, under the auspices of that Being, who, whatever means he may employ for the chastisement of offending nations, invariably makes choice of the best moral characters, as his fittest instruments, for the dispensation of his blessings and his mercies to mankind.

From this time forth the tenor of Mr. Hastings's

existence became as calm and even and undisturbed as if he had never filled in the eye of the world a wider space than appertains, as a matter of right, to the well-educated country gentleman. His intimacies continued, indeed, to be as extensive and as highly valued as ever, for I find letters written to him in the most affectionate strain, not by the friends of his early youth alone, but by many of the most distinguished men of the day. But his name, if mentioned at all within the precincts of Carlton House, called forth no especial expressions of favour. No titles were bestowed upon him, no pensions nor employments offered. He sank once more into the obscurity of private life, which the honours attached to the dignity of a Privy Councillor were not of a nature to disturb.

I subjoin the following letters, not because the information which they contain is either extensive or important, but because they seem to me to describe, in a very interesting manner, the state of the writer's mind at a season when its vigour is just beginning to decay. They are the productions of a noble spirit conscious of its growing infirmities, yet nowise cast down by the anticipations excited by that consciousness. Mr. Hastings had completed his eighty-third year when the last of them was written.

To David Anderson, Esq.

Daylesford House, 6th October, 1814.

My dear Friend,—I seize the early opportunity afforded me of acknowledging with thanks the receipt of your affectionate letter; but I regret at the same time the unpleasant tidings which it conveys of my dear godson's late indisposition. Though past, I regret that it has come. I wish I could impress on the minds of all in whose welfare my own interest is concerned, one concomitant rule of health which I myself acquired late, but which I verily believe to be a better preservative of it than the whole pharmacopeia, namely, to avoid the cold air, when the body is heated with exercise, or more especially, with the sun; and to avoid equally the warm air, and warm nourishment, under the opposite extreme of cold.

I shall expect with an attentive remembrance the introduction of your young friends, Lord Elcho and Mr. Charteris; and we shall be opportunely at home so long after the expected period of their coming to Christ Church, as to afford us a reasonable hope of it. I regret that I knew not before that the former was already a member of the university. I do not know—O yes, you must, that I am myself a member of the university, and adopted under circumstances which have endeared it to me.

I wish I could have accompanied you in your late tour. Every inch that has fallen within the touch of Walter Scott is to me as consecrated ground. I have been retracing your letter, but with a too cursory, and unsatisfactory, haste to decide, whether that, or some inferior authority, has induced me to hope for another composition from his fertile and wonderful mind.

I write with my watch before me, to measure the time which is allowed me for this letter, having a long journey to make, to participate in an entertainment made for our late most benevolent guest, the Duke of Gloucester, who did us the honour (a term for which I rather substitute pleasure, from the interest he seemed to take, and manifestly did take in it), made by our good neighbours, Sir Charles and Lady Cockerell. Mrs. Hastings goes with me, but returns. I continue till Saturday by his own desire—almost past the season of such kinds of excursion, being liable to frequent recurrences of what my physicians are shy of calling a paralytic affection, which, without any attendant pain, deprives at the same instant my fingers (of one hand only) of motion and almost of sensation, and my speech of articulation; but seldom lasting more than half an hour.

Sir Charles and Lady Imhoff are returned to England, and we hope for the long interdicted pleasure of seeing both next Tuesday.

I must now conclude—and indeed my pen begins to fail me. I dread the arrival of every post from our valuable friend, Toone.

We have had, and enjoyed, the same delightful weather that has accompanied you in your journey; and to-day, for the first change, it has rained; but I venture to foretell a return of fair weather after a short respite. Mrs. Hastings seems to have anticipated change of weather in its approach; so as to make me almost regret that she is to be my companion in this day's entertainment, though no one can derive more benefit than she does in her health from the cheerful intercourse of society, or contribute more to it. To you and yours we unite in cordial affection, and in prayers for your health and prosperity. Adieu, my dear friend. I am ever, most truly, yours.

To the same.

Daylesford House, 12th February, 1815.

My dear Friend,—If I had not laid an obligation upon myself to write to you to-day by engaging a frank, I should still leave your letter of the 7th of last month unacknowledged, from the consciousness that my mind wanted those powers of perception which were necessary for the interchange of the most ordinary communications, when instead of pursuing the context, the train of connexion is broken by a perpetual call upon the attention to preserve every word in its place, and to prevent even syllables and letters from encroaching on each other. Such I am, and I think it more kind, and more creditable to tell you so, than to leave the detection of my blunders, but not the cause of them, to your own discovery. I am tempted to mention two inconsistencies in my case, (as they appear to me,) because I cannot help viewing them in the light of physical curiosities. I did once possess the faculty which you give me credit for, of amusing myself, when I could not sleep, by pursuing a train of thoughts, retentively, and unbroken, through a long period of the night. Last night, by way of experiment, I got by heart six lines of Walter Scott, on going to bed, and forgot them, without the power of recovering them, before I had composed myself. But of this enough. Apropos of Walter Scott, I have read him through twice, once with Mrs. Hastings, who is disposed to read him once more, and I am as much pleased with the congeniality of her taste, as with the work itself. I am pleased with the correctness of the versification, the variety of character, its unvaried consistency, the perfect dignity of Robert Bruce, his other appropriate endowments, and the beautiful manner in which he has worked out the completion of his character by incidental traits of it; but, far above all the rest, I am struck with the anathema of the monk, and its sublime contrast with the parody of the prophecy of Balaam. I have not seen or heard of my friend and namesake, and have been afraid of noticing his visit to London, lest it should draw him from his better pursuits. I admire in all that he does his uncommon energy of mind. We are at home, and whenever he comes we shall be gladder to see him than any southron of his acquaintance.

I have hardly dared to name to you the name of our friend Toone; but I must. He is released; but his wonderful wife, after yielding to little more than a day of sorrow, has resumed all her wonted domestic employments, "meets all her family at breakfast and dinner, and is now employed in the melancholy office of preparing her son's things for his return to China." It is among my regrets, that you and your dear lady live at such a distance from us. Present, with Mrs. Hastings's affectionate regards to dear Mrs. Anderson, to all your family, mine also, and accept the same, and believe me ever most truly, my dearest friend, yours most affectionately.

It is not quite with my own consent that I yield to Mrs. Hastings's desire to make known to you, that Mrs. Harvey's friends have set on foot a subscription for her relief.

To the same.

Daylesford House, 14th April, 1815.

My dear Friend,—The event which you dreaded in your brother James's family has, I find, since come to pass, and I most sincerely grieve to hear it. For any of the other casualties of life, I should give him credit for the power of bearing them with greater fortitude than any man that I ever knew; but I fear, this will prove a severe trial.

To you, my dear friend, whatever I write must bespeak your kind indulgence by the affection which dictates it; but the report which I have made of myself has been proved but too true in the necessity which it has imposed upon me to suspend the use of my pen since I began this letter; which I had rendered compulsory by the means which you recommended in the commencement of your last; but I will not again allude to it; nor is it to complain, but to apologize, that I now do. I rejoice that, with the first information of dear Mrs. Anderson's cold and cough, I received the news of her amendment, and that she was so much better since, as to yield to the solicitations of her family, and to participate in their recreations. Pray assure her of the interest which Mrs. Hastings and I never cease to take in her health, and may heaven support and bless her!

I do not like to give an opinion respecting the conduct of health, especially in a delicate frame, except to *pro*, not to *pre*scribe; but whatever may be said of invitations, of this I am certain, from long and confirmed experience, that *crowded* dinners, long sitting at table, and, above all, *crowded* drawing-rooms, are invariably injurious to health; but I confine my observation to the last exclusively, I dare recommend this negative rule to my godson.

Mistaking your letter in the first hasty perusal of it, and having long wished to recover a paper (to which you allude) upon the subject of a bank for the use of the poor, which I had sent to Mr. Whitbread, I wrote to him for it. His answer, followed by a polite search for it, led to the proof, that it had been intercepted and destroyed in the way, for the sake of the money paid for the carriage; and I am afraid, this will prove one frequent effect of the new India post bill. Your plan is much better than mine, and, I conceive, easy of application. It is much wanted, wherever it can be adopted.

Have you ever been able to reduce your thoughts to any consistent state upon the subject of the late revolution in France? Two things are presented by it; one of which absolutely does, and the other may, falsify Solomon's declaration,—nothing is, or can happen, new under the sun; for the imagination of man never conceived the invasion of a great empire by a mere adventurer, at the head of 600 men, and succeeding in it without a blow; or that a foreign confederacy should force upon a whole people, against their declared choice, a sovereign ruler, and that ruler the untainted blood of their own hereditary monarchs. The present appearances seem to promise this last result. If it fails, I contemplate its possible failure in one moral cause, from which the opposite conclusion might be, with the best reason of things, deduced. If I can, I will tell you why in another letter. Mrs. Hastings and I are going to London in the middle of the week after next, projected only for a fortnight; but who will answer for its duration?

Mrs. Hastings offers her affectionate regards, as I do mine, to yourself, David, Hastings, and all within your reach of your family. You can have no conception of the real length of this letter. Adieu, my dear friend, yours ever.

To the same.

Daylesford House, 10th September, 1815.

My dear Friend,—Your letter of the 2nd, short as it was, afforded me the most satisfactory intelligence that you could give me, and conveyed in terms the most delightful; that "Mrs. Anderson and your two sons were well, and that you were all enjoying a great deal of happiness." May this blessed state continue to be your lot through many succeeding years, and theirs through as many generations!

For myself I can only say, that I am comparatively much better than I have been for many months past, happy in witnessing the good health, good spirits, and good looks of Mrs. Hastings (though with some alloy of transitory ailment) still unabated; and my own, of each kind, perfect in all points, but memory of the past, and of present recollection.

I do not like the aspect of public affairs, but derive more than adequate compensation from the vast superiority of comparative credit which the French themselves attribute to our countrymen, in the sufferings entailed upon them by the sovereigns and soldiers of the combined armies. I view with the same sensations as you do, the miraculous transformation of the beautiful island of St. Helena, which used to afford us so much enjoyment, converted into a state prison of a deposed emperor. I am sorry for its degradation, and more so to contemplate the British nation in the character of the jailer of Europe, which is established by this, her second appearance in that relation. By what means, in the latent operations of God's providence, the deliverance of Bonaparte from this sequestration is to be effected, I have not the slightest conception.

In the war with Nepaul, I have no fear but of its conclusion in a treaty of peace, which, after our past defeats, would lower the credit of our arms even more than it would raise that of our enemies; besides that it would be an abandonment of the principle to which, in our steady perseverance in it, we owe all our present greatness in India. The war with Ceylon was, I am afraid, unjust in its commencement, now seven or eight years past; but if terms of peace were repeatedly offered to the Rajah (as is asserted) and rejected, the general detestation of his character will justify his punishment, and legalize our conquest; at least, if we pay a due regard to the rights of the ancient inhabitants. The undivided possession of the island must in any case be advantageous, and, let the odium fall where it will, the Company will bear no share of it.

I sincerely sympathized with your brother James, for his late severe loss, but I could not condole with him. had not the heart to touch the sore of affliction, where no human means, and least of all such as I could apply, could avail to allay it. When you see or write to him, I pray you to assure him of my affectionate remembrance.

I have extended this letter far beyond my usual ability, and have just power left for the following recollection. It will be in the memory of my old associates at Chunar, in 1783, that I drew out two march-routes for the two parties that were detached to the attack of the fort of Sutteef-poor. They marched by *prescribed* stages, and arrived almost at the same instant, at the same point of attack. This will not justify a similar operation of three detachments sent by three *undefined* lines, through *an unknown* labyrinth of thickets and rocks, with a plan for their converging in the same point of attack, as was done at, I forget the name of the place, in the first operations against the Goorcallies. It was impossible that the event should have turned out otherwise than it did. Our ill success in this campaign was not owing to the superior skill or courage of our enemies, beyond what we have experienced of those qualities in the natives of India; but to the want of local knowledge of the same species of warfare, and of the means of availing ourselves of the advantage which our nation possesses in its discipline against mere numbers acting without it.

Mrs. Hastings joins me in every sentiment of affection to you, dear Mrs. Anderson, and your excellent sons. We wish also to be kindly remembered to your sister. I am charged by Sir Charles and Lady Imhoff to present to you all the same regards. I am ever, my dear friend, yours.

CHAPTER XV.

Last days of Mr. Hastings—Rebuilding of Daylesford Church—Illness, Death, and Character.

I HAVE now approached that stage in my narrative beyond which lies little else than the record of events that sadden;—the history of a great mind slowly but surely becoming subject to the universal law of decay, and of a constitution, always feeble, sustaining shock after shock, till it is finally overthrown. Mr. Hastings lived, after the date of the last of the letters introduced into the previous chapter, a space of three years, lacking eighteen days. During the whole of that period he retained the use of his faculties to a very remarkable degree, enjoying the society of his friends, taking a lively interest in their welfare, and occupying himself, as he had previously done, with his farm, with his garden, with his household, with his books, and with his pen. Yet he was not the man that he had once been. Riding became too violent an exercise for him, and he laid it aside; he then took his airings in the carriage; and from the entries in his Diary, I find that he paid two separate visits to London; during one of which, by the bye, the following testimonial to a green old age is given. In 1817, he writes thus:—"March 13. I visited the Marquis of Hastings at Camden Hill Club. My health drunk with marks of the most expressive kindness. Thirty-nine members present." Nor does the exertion appear to have broken him down, for against the following day there is inserted this statement: "I wrote my name at the Dukes of York and Clarence, and made twenty-one visits." But the spirit, in this case, seems to have been willing, when the flesh was weak, for the termination of the memorandum is sufficiently melancholy. "I came home with a cold and cough, which troubled me all night. Commencement of my confinement almost entirely to my bed."

Mr. Hastings's constitution had been delicate from his infancy. Nothing, indeed, except the extreme temperance of his habits could have carried him through a long life of constant exertion. Yet was he subject from first to last to frequent attacks of illness, from which he did not often recover without a good deal of suffering. Still, if we except the fever from which in 1783 he suffered so severely, none of these appear to have been of such a nature as to threaten the extinction of life; but the case was different now. So early as the year 1813, he was seized with a numbness in the right side, which he himself attributed to a paralytic affection, and though he ultimately shook the weakness off, it is probable that it left some traces of its influence behind. Not that his spirits were ever in the most remote degree weighed down by them. On the contrary, his cheerfulness never left him; and often when others appeared anxious and uneasy on his account, he cheated them of their fears by turning them into ridicule. But I find in his Diary frequent allusions to the circumstance, in terms which seem to indicate something like an expectation, that his death, come when it might, would be sudden. All these, however, indicate a temper composed, tranquil, and sustained by a deep religious feeling; a sentiment which seems to have been with him a portion of his nature; so pure it was, so constantly present, yet so unobtrusive. Moreover, Mr. Hastings never, to the last, permitted the mind to prey upon itself for want of occupation. The parish church of Daylesford, which stood upon his own land, and was frequented, almost exclusively, by his own tenants and dependants, had, through the neglect of former lords of the manor, become grievously dilapidated. He determined to restore it; and making choice of his own architect, and in a great measure supplying his own plans, he began what was to him a labour truly of love, in the month of July, 1816. It afforded him pleasant occupation for three whole months, and pleasant materials for the memory to work upon when they were ended. And as to the rest, literature, and the act of replying to the letters of such of his friends as happened to be far off, and delighted to remind him of their existence, filled up many an hour, and seem uniformly to have done so to his own satisfaction. Let the reader judge of the tone of his noble mind, noble even in its decay, by the following specimens of his familiar correspondence.

To DAVID ANDERSON, Esq.

Daylesford House, 19th October, 1816.

My dear Friend,—You will have learnt as much as was interesting of this family to the 10th of last month, from your excellent son, my godson, who left us on that day, to enter on the commencement of his travels. I have been much pleased to find both him and his brother engaged in so useful an occupation. I am glad that they have chosen to follow their separate researches, that each may profit by the improvement of the knowledge of which they have already laid the foundation, and of the diversity of their natural talents; and I am not sorry to perceive in Hastings a disposition to seek his train of adventures without the embarrassment of a companion. One requisite, I am sure, they both possess, that they may be safely trusted with the care of themselves. Heaven prosper and protect them!

Hastings has told you, that he found me very busy in the rebuilding of our parish church. I feel a little spice of vanity in relating, that I began the demolition of the old fabric on the 8th of July, and completed the whole of the renewed building on the 14th of September, in exactly sixty days, deducting the intervening Sundays. To this account must be added windows, pavement, and doors; against which I set the cove of a ceiling nearly finished, but not a part of the old church. This, with the delay of a month for two coats of plaster already laid, and some ornamental additions, will about close the work, so as to admit of divine service being performed in it on Sunday, the 6th of November, just four months from the dilapidation. But I am afraid I must be content with the admission; as the popular objection to the effluvia of new mortar will deprive me of the essential part of my first congregation, and the rector has an object nearer his heart and home in daily expectation of the birth of a child.

I scarcely know what passes in town, and of the best news that I hear, my approbation is much qualified. I rejoice at the additional splendour which the African campaign has bestowed on our naval fame; but grieve at the fruitless expenditure of so much of the best blood of our country. I am pleased at the bountiful legacy which the Bhow Begum has bequeathed to the Company, if it is true that she has done it; but am ashamed of the duplicity of our laws, and the iniquity of our Government, if they ratify the acceptance of it. I am delighted even to enthusiasm, that our military glory has been pitted in a fair trial with our great rival, the nation of France, with our superiority acknowledged and adjudged; but I am grieved to see a suffering people rescued from the most atrocious oppression, and made by their own voluntary surrender an integral part of our own empire, without a record of its achievement, although obtained without one British life lost in the acquisition; and I very much fear, for the sole want of that sanction to its celebrity.

Adieu, my dear friend. Accept from Mrs. Hastings and myself our fervent and united wishes, and most affectionate regards to yourself, to dear Mrs. Anderson, and all your relatives and connexions. I am ever, most truly yours.

To E. B. Impey, Esq.

Daylesford House, 19th November, 1816.

My dear Elijah,—I had been long in expectation of a letter from you, and as long in the daily exercise of self-reproach for not having in all that time written to you. Both of us have claims to large allowances, but very different even in the similarity of the causes from which they originate. You suffer only from the temporary depression of those energies which you inherently possess; and wait only the revolutionary change which every constitution, both of body and mind, possesses for their complete reproduction. That mine have passed that period, this laboured, and scarce intelligible, if intelligible, attempt to convey my meaning too plainly demonstrates.

I am beyond measure pleased with your meditated removal to a cottage residence, and assure myself that it will be the means of ameliorating your time, health, and mind, in their united occupations. I received the first intelligence of the sum generally awarded you from your portion of the funds in France, with a distrust that scarce allowed me to rejoice at it, and am happy to receive your confirmation of it, scanty as the amount now appears. I hope the tenant will not find means in the tricks to which our law, pure and sure as it is in comparison with its practice in another part of the united kingdom, to defeat your right of speedy possession; and shall anxiously wait for the news of your confirmed investiture.

In addition to my other disabilities, I am exposed to the lengthened interruptions of visitors, which has been the case since I had proceeded through the greater part of this letter, and have now scarce time to give you, and through you, the commissioned regards of Mrs. Hastings, with my own, to your dear mother and sister; and to tell you that we are all well, myself particularly so, notwithstanding the difficulty of keeping the separate powers of my appetite, and its forbearance, in good mutual understanding. I use no exercise, and find that I am in best health without it. I have almost exhausted the sources of amusement which my church for the last five months (nearly) has afforded me, but dwell upon them still, and shall continue to do so by reflection.

I have reprinted a little tract, which you will remember, upon the means of guarding houses from fires, and shall order an impression, amicitiæ gratiâ, to be sent to you. Pray send me at your next leisure your verses on Halhed's, or rather your composition on his recompositions. Adieu.

My dinner (for I dine alone) is on the table; and you must excuse my correcting the faults of this uninteresting letter. I am, my dear Elijah, ever yours.

Sir Charles and Lady Imhoff desire their kind remembrance.

To David Anderson, Esq.

Daylesford House, 9th December, 1816.

My dear Friend,—I have been gratified beyond measure by a long and interesting letter from your son, my excellent godson. Two requisites for a young traveller he possesses in an eminent degree; an eagerness for the acquisition of those substances of knowledge which travelling can give, and a determination to be pleased. This last qualification indeed he had no need of this species of instruction to bestow; for if it was ever inherent in any human being, it has been his property coeval with the first perception of his reason, and always equally accompanied with the faculty of repaying in full the pleasure he received. Heaven bless, and grant him the continuance of that protection which it has already afforded him! I am happy to hear that you were so soon in the expectation of the return of my friend David, and hope you will allow me to share with you in that pleasure, whenever it comes to pass.

You will have known how much I have interested myself in the rebuilding of our parish church, and will be pleased to hear that we had divine service performed in it for the first time yesterday, to as full a congregation as it would hold. I was unexpectedly gratified by an appropriate sermon, with a prefatory prayer, both, in my judgment, of the first merit. This work undertaken from necessity, but attributed by my neighbours to a much more laudable motive, has afforded me five months of constant recreation, both of body and mind; and I verily believe that it has been the means of suspending the decay of both. What has given me most cause for regret is my inability to walk to the distance of the village; and the difference which it has more strongly impressed upon my mind than I ever felt it before, between executing a purpose from the instant of its impulse, and giving orders for many consecutive operations, and waiting for their tardy execution, with an equal chance of its being defeated at last by the coming (I love my neighbours too well to call it intrusion) of a long seated country visit. It just occurs to me to observe, that the kind of amusement to which I have been alluding is the most conformable of any to the last stage of mental infirmity, by engaging the attention upon corporeal objects, (like those of idolatrous worship,) which my day-labourers and I alike comprehend without effort, and like the better for that poor facility.

When you next indulge me with a letter, I shall be obliged to you, if you will let me know whether you are acquainted with Robert Owen, and his establishment of cotton, and the machinery of moral character, at New Lanark; because our fireside has been very much amused and edified by two small publications bearing his name, and asserting pretensions, which we should have deemed incredible, if he did not appeal to the people of his own institution, and to many of the first characters of both kingdoms for the truth of them.

Mrs. Hastings is variably, but generally well, and joins with me in affectionate regards to Mrs. Anderson and yourself, and kind remembrances to your brother and sister.

I do not think that the late attempt to excite seditious disturbances in London yield, much cause for alarm. It seems to have been, both in design and execution, well calculated to discourage any better concerted purpose, and is therefore so far good.

You will grieve for the loss of our dear friend, General Palmer. I have some time expected it, and long relinquished the hope of seeing him again. These considerations allay, but cannot totally extinguish the regret of the last, I had almost said eternal, separation; for it is not easy to discriminate our sense of that separation from a better expectation suggested by reason, and confirmed by revelation. Adieu, my dear friend. Yours most affectionately.

To E. B. Impey, Esq.

Daylesford House, 19th December, 1816.

My dear Elijah,—Yesterday was my eighty-fourth birth-day, and I actually had my pen in my hand, prepared to congratulate you on the occasion, perhaps in anticipation of your congratulation, the sentiment of which I know to be always present in your breast, whether obtruded or not into formal expression; but I had suffered other occupations to precede it, and I had neither time, mind, nor strength left for all the employment which I had designed for the subject of my letter, and I therefore adjourned it to this morning.

I could account in a similar manner for not executing the purpose to which I was strongly impelled on the receipt of your poetry on Halhed's luted tea-cups. It was not, however, for want of a due impulse to blazon its worth; for I put it to a test which would have marred nine at least out of ten compositions of accidental merit that had been submitted to it. I read the lines to our family party, prefacing the lecture with the praises due to it, and an assurance that they would lose nothing of the promised admiration, but receive it improved by the prepossession; and they all assured me that it was so. One of the most conspicuous excellencies of your poetry consists, in my attribution of it, in the harmony of its numbers. This I think observable in an uncommon degree on that of the present subject, to which you have given a new beauty of a very different, and certainly very difficult, kind; that is, if I can make my own ideas intelligible, a three-fold metaphor carried on through a collected series of opposite allusions, to the powers of original composition, mechanic skill, and those powers of criticism, all united in their common relation to the reparation of broken china, with the coalition of all with two subjects as opposite as excellence and inanity can make them, our friend Halhed and Vancouvre. A small portion of the same judgment and imagination, well distributed, would go a great way towards the creation of an epic poem.

Mrs. Hastings desires me to inquire how Lady Impey, dear Marian, and yourself are, and when you leave Brighton; with her affectionate regards, and the added, and best wishes of the season to those always extant. I pray you also to present and accept of mine, and by their especial commission, of Sir Charles and Lady Imhoff's.

I must not conclude my letter without announcing

the restoration of divine service to the renovated church of Daylesford, under every auspicious circumstance, from which the blessing of God could be inferred on the past work and its consummation. I shall be gratified by the opportunity, whenever you can give it to me, of showing it to you. God bless you, my dear friend, ever yours.

To DAVID ANDERSON, Esq.

Daylesford House, February, 1817.

My dear Friend,—My last letter to you was dated the 10th of December, and your last to me the 8th of the same month. I congratulate you, though late, on David's safe return, and on the best proof which he could produce of the profitable employment of his travels—your attestation of it. Not biassed by a sense of paternal privation, my wishes for the return of my godson will be gratified by a later accomplishment of them. In the mean time, if you can tell me by what direction a letter from me may have a chance of reaching his hands, I should like to avail myself of it to write to him. His delicacy has made him (purposely I know) withhold from me that information. I am particularly pleased with his episodical excursion to Tangiers, as it afforded him a new view of men and manners, which he could not have acquired from the information of other adventurers, and which their separation into parts would deprive them of, the aggregate sense produced by their united comprehension. If I live, I will lay claim to the privilege of seeing his journal.

I will not affect to receive unexpectedly your approbation of my little tract. Was it not for the obloquy which Mr. Nash has cast on the name of the Prince Regent, I would solicit his royal highness's patronage of the general design: but the buildings now rearing their fine shapes in the very face of Carlton House would make any attempt of that kind a reflection on my own loyalty; and besides my reverence for the principle, the personal attachment which I bear to him is equal to that of the most favoured of his subjects.

I am afraid we have not yet seen the worst of our public distresses. There is an axiom in political economy which will work its own effect with a certain consummation, in defiance of all reasoning and legislation; and it is this: every year adds to the past debt, and to the necessity of its annual augmentation. It is, therefore, in a rapid course of approximation to that point at which the national disbursements shall be equal to the national income; at which it seems demonstrative, that neither will the debt be susceptible of payment, nor the public creditors of the means which the public interest yielded of subsistence, nor the Government of its powers of motion. I suppose we are not far from that period; and whenever we are so near to it as to feel it a subject of general belief, that very belief will render the final ruin unavoidable. This brings us precisely to the point of "your round game at cards," in which we shall be in debt to each other, and having neither money to pay, nor counters to play, break up by mutual necessity and mutual consent.

In a former letter (I believe the last) I mentioned that our literary circle had been much entertained by a book written by Robert Owen of New Lanark. Can you give me any account of him?

We purpose going to town in a few days; that is, if we can, to be present at the Court on the Queen's birth-day; and, without any reason which I could satisfactorily explain, I think I ought to show myself in town; as at sea in a tempest, I could not keep my cabin, though I did no good, and was in the officers' way.

We neither of us ever lose you and your dear lady out of our remembrance, and recommend ourselves to yours with every kind regard and good wishes to yourselves, to Miss Anderson, David, and your brother James. I am, my dear friend, most truly and affectionately yours.

To George Nesbitt Thompson, Esq.

Daylesford House, 22d February, 1817.

My dear Thompson,—I answer your kind letter today, though a Saturday, because I may not be able to-morrow. My first and best news is, that Mrs. Hastings is free from what I may assuredly call her rheumatic complaint, and I look to the symptoms of her health only as the indications of her probable ability, or not, to perform our journey to town, now meditated for the 1st of March, to give to our friends time to complete their preparations to receive us.

I shall take my memoir to town and will reprint it, if there is no claim of copyright in my way. My bookseller writes that it is out of print, *i.e.*, forgotten. I intend to apply to the Chairman for leave to take a copy of my original salt minute. This is now become necessary in my own defence; for Sir Thomas Barnard, after desiring me to send him immediately the corrections of his postscript, and receiving them by the returning post, published his own erroneous state of the transaction, just as it stood in the draft which you saw of his intended publication. This conduct surprises me; for in my answer I almost in terms protested against what he had proposed to write, as it represented Mr. Vansittart as the inventor of the design, and hardly left me, or, as he calls it, "my genius," a share in the execution. My words are concise, and I will copy them :—

"The first conception, as well as the essay, on which the first and partial trial of the new mode was made, was entirely my own. It was not till the commencement of the next season that the entire plan was adopted and carried into action, with all its subordinate parts; and then it was that Mr. H. Vansittart was selected for nomination, if not (as I believe he was) actually nominated by myself, to be placed at the head of the department," &c. I added afterwards:—"It is the only instance, in the course of a government of thirteen years, in which a great and lasting measure of finance was devised by myself, and carried into execution by my own separate and pledged responsibility." I am angry; but I shall cool before I get to town. In the mean time I will suppose some possible mistake to have happened; but it has confirmed me in the resolution to bring the original project, unconnected with its debatable matter, before the public.

I am tempted to acquaint you with a more pleasing, though less interesting discovery. On Tuesday last I ordered Dadge to take out the frame of freestone which closes the east termination of the ventilator of the ceiling, or cove, between the roof and body of the church, in order to see whether the rain had penetrated the slates, or the mildew or dry rot infected the timbers. Dadge entered the passage; found all dry, sound, and clean, and a torrent of air that no candle could have withstood if he had carried one. This was the object that I had most at heart, speculating that every sunshine would rarify and blow out the air within, and every cold blast compress it, so as to keep it in a perpetual state of alternation and refreshment.

I offer you, on trust, Mrs. Hastings's best regards, and am myself, my dear Thompson, ever affectionately.

To David Anderson, Esq.

Daylesford House, 17th May, 1817.

My dear Friend,—I hasten to answer your kind

letter, though this is not a post day; but the earnest solicitude which you express to know the present state of my health demands this return of attention from me; and I am so easily put out of my way, that I cannot answer for my actions beyond the present moment.

I have had a long confinement from sickness, not, I think, of that kind that can be attributed to the habit. The immediate cause was the rupture of an artery with the extraction of a large tooth, and a hæmorrhage which followed it of several hours' duration, though its effect in the final debility produced by it did not manifest itself till the second day after the accident. Since that time I have been rapidly advancing in strength, and am not conscious that my health during the whole process has undergone any derangement. I have made trial of my strength since my return, by two excursions in my garden, and am convinced that I am as stout at least as I was before my departure from home on the 1st of March. We returned to this place on the 8th of this month. I reckon it among the memorable incidents of this period, that on the 13th of March, being the only day that I had been able to attend our club of Indians, every member of it that could did give his attendance, for the assigned purpose of marking their personal regard, to the number of thirty-nine in the company, with every demonstration of it that such an occasion admitted. I can neither describe the manner of it, nor (yet much less) its effects on my sensations. These are the honours after which my soul has aspired; viz., the testimony of those, with whom I have participated in so many modes and degrees, the different relations of society, and implicating the corresponding sentiments of many besides to whom I am personally unknown.

I am ashamed to have occupied so large a portion of

my letter about myself, but the nature of your inquiry naturally led me so near to this digression, that I fell into it before I was aware of the transition. There was a time, and that not very distant, when a flight of this kind, if the close of my letter was protracted to another day, would have cost me the abolition of all that I had previously written; but I can no longer afford to waste time and my scanty means in correction.

It is a great consolation to Mrs. Hastings and myself, that your first intimation of Mrs. Anderson's late illness was accompanied with the assurance of her convalescence, which we hope will be followed, if it has not already attained it, by her perfect restoration, and that you will have the goodness to announce it to us.

I expect much from the continuation of Hastings's travels. I should not say to his father that I should be pleased with his extending them to the full attainment of as much knowledge as may be reasonably hoped from that species of discipline, because I am persuaded that his stamina will acquire enduration from that exercise of them at the same time.

Mrs. Hastings is, I flatter myself, much improved by our visit to London, though she alarmed us much one night by a sudden and violent attack of the pleurisy; but it lasted only a few days, and passed without any durable consequence.

I unite with my dear Mrs. Hastings in the truest sentiments of friendship for Mrs. Anderson, yourself, your sister, and my friend, who (I am glad to find, or please myself with that construction of the sentence in which you mention him) is become a fixed inmate in the house of his father. Heaven bless you all, my dear friend! Yours most affectionately ever.

Sunday, 18th May. Before the ink was quite dry on the letters of my name, the postman brought me a letter from my godson, dated from Naples. I am pleased with the coincidence, and happy to learn that he was well, though I gather that information by inference from the manner in which he speaks of the plan of his subsequent line of progress rather than from direct expression. My blessing attends him.

To E. B. Impey, Esq.

Daylesford House, May, 1817.

My dear Elijah,—You have employed me on an ungrateful service, in which I have succeeded accordingly, that is, not at all. Perhaps it was not to be expected, that a spirit employed in the contemplation of the finest feelings of moral and physical reality should descend to seek for their likenesses in a forced application of them to the gross instruments of "love and murder." But the answer made to my reference was in pretty plain terms, that the much superior powers of the English poet were unworthily wasted on a translation of a German original,* of which she had declared her dislike while it retained its first form and composition. As to myself I recognize the melody which distinguishes all your poetry, and forms the best character of this; and there my criticism necessarily stops.

I am sorry for the report of Lord Liverpool's intended resignation; because I always approved of his conduct as a minister, and still more as a Parliamentary orator; and I am glad that this was my opinion of him before it was biassed by any prejudice of my own concern; for I learned at the time, from a noble friend, who might, by suppression only, have let it pass for his own act, that the intention of giving me a seat in the Privy Council arose from his said Lordship's recommendation. I add with pleasure, and as his due,

* Theodore Körner's celebrated song of the Sword.

the name of that friend;—it was Lord Sidmouth. A peculiar fatality seems to have been attached to my political fortune; that every effort of my own to promote it has invariably failed, and sometimes with discredit; but where it has succeeded, the success has been derived from causes unforeseen by myself, like "Malvolio's greatness, thrust upon him." I dare not trust my self-love to enumerate the instances. Though I have feebly answered to your appeal on one critical question, I am strongly tempted to propose one to you, of a very different nature, namely, by what appellation a husband ought to designate his wife in an address to a very superior authority. Is there any decent word in our language that can be substituted for the word, "*my wife?*" You will guess at the nature of this inquiry, and its allusion.*

I have accomplished a short—a very short—noon's walk, and am delighted with the warmth of it. It ought to be remembered, that we are not yet advanced beyond the 18th of our poetical May.

Continue at your leisure to write to me, and dispense with regular answers. You can interest on any subject; but your dear mother's health, your sister's health, and your own, will never fail. Present and accept the affectionate remembrances of our family; and be you all blest.

To David Anderson, Esq.

Daylesford House, 22d December, 1817.

My dear and respectable Friend,—My dear godson, for whose return, as connected with his personal safety, I have for some time since felt an increasing anxiety proportionate to the increased duration of his absence, is happily returned to the bosom of his family, pos-

* This was answered on the high authority of Shakspeare, by quoting the passage where Othello demands from the Venetian Senate "fit exhibition for his wife."

sessed of health, the well-employed exercise of his intellectual faculties, and an enlargement of his knowledge of mankind. This is the tenth or eleventh day since your letter has apprised me of his arrival without having yet drawn from me the expression of that mutual gratulation which it might have been expected to excite. This instance may serve more than the most minute detail of my way of life, to show of how many impediments, internal and external, it consists, to the correct intercourse of my duties with society. I heartily congratulate you, and dear Mrs. Anderson, on this event, and on the possession of two such sons, to bless and cheer the long, I hope, remainder of your united lives; and not to bless and cheer alone, but to add to the length of them. May the Almighty grant it; and may the approaching festival of this closing year, and the progress of the next, afford an earnest of those that are to come!

Perhaps at some not very remote period of time (for I have not much to spare), some friend coming for a temporary purpose from your son Hastings's neighbourhood to London, may afford him a safe opportunity of entrusting him with the conveyance of his journal for my perusal—for *ours,* I should say;—in that case I promise as quick a despatch and return of it, by the same, or any other means, that may be enjoined. It will not hurt him to be read by his warmest admirers.

The account which your last letter gives of Mrs. Anderson's health, though concise, encourages our hope that it was in a state of amelioration. Of your own health you say nothing, and I trust from presumptive evidence of not inconsiderable weight that it is at least not bad.

I believe the hand of Government, opportunely lent to the aid of husbandry, might in all seasons prove o essential benefit to it; but it is at all times so implicated with the superior claims of finance, that these will for ever interfere with the equitable application of the measures professedly advanced for that purpose. My chilleys, which are the only remaining branch of my charge in the farm or garden, furnish me with a good analogical criterion of the productive powers of the land in other more important articles of cultivation. I used to raise them, till the fruit was set, in common frames, and afterwards transplanted them into the open air. The last year my crop totally failed, except a few which were raised in the hot-house, so called, but not heated. This year all my out-door plants failed; those under glass, which were very numerous, have yielded abundantly, but ripened about six weeks of computation later.

I myself am almost as much debarred from the sources of the knowledge of Indian affairs as you describe yourself to be; but from the little that has transpired, so as to come within my reach, I think the Mahrattas no longer possess their ancient constitutional union, which recurred on every recurrence of common danger, though ready to dissolve on its removal, and thus leave them at liberty to adopt the principles of independent policy. But I ground my hopes of an exemption from a near state of warfare, from the operation of a better principle; which I will endeavour to explain, though at the expense of a double postage, because I think that, in the course of my argument, I shall find you prepossessed with my opinion.

Nobody knows better than you do, how assiduous the people of India are in studying the characters of others with whom they have any concerns, their skill in detecting the talents, weaknesses, designs and propensities of their opponents, and in concealing their own; having less recourse to general policy than to encounter errors in the conduct opposed to them. The most notorious instance of this practice that I ever knew was that which was observed by Hyder in, I think, his first war with the Government of Fort St. George. Our defence consisted of two unconnected armies, one commanded by an able officer, General Smith; the other by Colonel Wood, one very deficient. Hyder avoided General Smith, and eluded all his attempts to bring him to an action, while he acted on the weak understanding of Colonel Wood by feints and shows of attack, by appearances of forces in different quarters, but never proceeding to a direct attack but when he was sure of his advantage. By this time the character of Lord Hastings must be well known, and duly appreciated. They will know him to be a man of superior talents, steady of purpose, and determined; for these he is. They will therefore have no inducement to commence an unprovoked attack upon him, and much to dread the consequences, if they did. I believe, too, that he has hitherto manifested rather a desire of contracting the limits of our territorial possessions than of enlarging them: they have nothing of course to fear from his ambition; and they who have ambitious designs of their own will wait till they have a shabby Governor-general to cope with. These are my reasons for believing, that we shall have peace *in his time.* [I hope I am not liable to the sin of parody.] In the mean time I hear that the Court of Directors are pleased with the Marquis. This, too, will be known, and will help to raise his diplomatic interest. You will recollect that I profess to write from conjecture and deduction, not knowledge.

My time, though continued to a second day of writing, is almost at the post hour, and I must hasten to the close of my letter. Mrs. Hastings desires me to say everything that is kind on her behalf, to you, Mr. Anderson, and your sons, adding to Hastings: "He must let us see his journal." I am sorry to say, that she has not been well since the death of our beloved and lamented princess. In truth it has sickened us all. Sir Charles and Lady Imhoff desire to add their kind remembrances. I, mine, of course, with prayers for your happiness, and all our appropriate wishes of the season. I pray you also to offer my most friendly regards to your brother James. I wish you, when you see Lord Haddington, to assure his Lordship, with my respects, that I receive with more than common pleasure the frequent notices of his remembrance. I am ever, my very dear friend, yours most affectionately.

I have spoken of the last two years of Mr. Hastings's life, as if to describe their tenor in detail would affect the reader with melancholy only; and I have assigned as my reason the fact, that they furnish evidence of little else than the gradual decay of the powers of a great mind, and the breaking up of the frame in which, for fourscore and six years, it had been lodged. I think that I am bound to modify, if I do not retract these assertions. There is nothing to sadden in the contemplation of a noble spirit struggling to the last against the infirmities of the flesh; and preparing to go back, disciplined even by suffering, to Him who gave it. Neither am I justified in drawing conspicuously into view, the evidences, comparatively slight and of rare occurrence, of the havoc which old age was making in its faculties. The following letter to Mr. Impey, written but a few months previous to his demise, exhibits Mr. Hastings in a light entirely distinct from that of the dotard. It is worthy of the best days of his manhood; and shows that, when roused by circumstances, the mind could still, despite of the body's weakness, both feel and reason as it used to do a quarter of a century previously.

To E. B. Impey, Esq.

Daylesford House, 19th April, 1818.

My dear Elijah,—I will not affect to regret the trouble which I have given you; for I know that you not unreluctantly submitted to it, and I have gained by it both useful and profitable knowledge. You have taught me one truth, not professedly intending it; that the only materials of authentic history are those which have been compiled by writers who have written so long after the events which they relate as to have had no interest in them. I think, I know two exceptions, viz., Coxe's histories of the lives of Lord Orford and Lord Walpole; for both contain copious evidences of the facts which establish them. But even this author allows himself the privilege of exercising his own judgment under so fair a sanction that his opinion may pass for a verification. By your account of Dr. Aikin, he delivers a false or imperfect impression of facts without falsifying the facts themselves, as in an special instance where, alluding to my reception of Cheyt Sing at Buxar, he negatively says: "of which different accounts have been given." This is candour and impartiality with a vengeance. I cannot pursue the observations of your letter, because there are days in which my sight, and the memory of connected sentences, both together fail me; but I think that an historian that neglects to develop the truth from a well attested anecdote, like the following, corroborated by personal character, and the combinations of concurrent acts and declarations, is unfit to be trusted as one. Previous to the day on which the article of Benares was debated, the ministerial members had received instructions to give their votes against it. At an early hour of that morning, Mr. Dundas called on Mr. Pitt, awoke him from his sleep, and engaged him in a contest of three hours' duration, which ended in an inversion of the ministerial question; of which it was my chance to be apprised the same morning. The fact has appeared in print, the change of votes is an attestation of it, one member only, Lord Mulgrave, refusing to submit to so base a prostitution of his word. But I must stop; for my mind forsakes me. I thank you for your beneficial exertion; and shall concern myself no more with contemporaneous history.

God bless you, my dear friend. Add my blessing of your dear mother, and the dear Marian, with Mrs. Hastings's, to mine. Your affectionate.

At the moment when the preceding letter was written, the hand of death had already fallen upon Mr. Hastings. I do not think, from what I find in his Diary, that either to himself, or to the affectionate group which surrounded him, this truth was fully known, yet a comparison between the entry for the 19th of January, and the nature of the disease which ultimately carried him off, leaves no reason to doubt that the case was so. The memorandum in question runs thus:—"I have laboured for near a fortnight, with an inflammation in the roof of my mouth, and an inability to eat solids." There is no further notice taken of this malady, except to describe the means which were from time to time applied, for the purpose of removing it; but I cannot discover that they proved efficacious. On the contrary, other infirmities, arising out of it, seem to have grown upon him from day to day; and as they are faithfully set down, though without one word of bitterness or even of complaint, I should scarce do justice to his memory, were I to pass them by. How touching, I had almost said how full of poetry, are the following:—

"May 21st. Heated, and my nerves shaken by walking. This is the third day that I have been affected with the confused sounds, as of distant multitudes.

"22nd. I have been visited by confused and indistinct sensations, as of the sounds of distant multitudes. I date their first perception from the 20th,—at times resembling slow music—but its effect!!!

"23rd. The same, whether sensible or imaginary, not distinguishable."

How mysterious this communion of unearthly voices, with the spirit hovering, as it were, on the brink of the great gulf,—how sublime the idea, that they should have spoken to the soul of the righteous man, in the tones 'of low music!'

From the date of this entry, Mr. Hastings continued gradually to sink, though not without frequent efforts of the constitution to rally. I find him, for example, on the 31st, so far improved that he is able to attend divine service in the parish church; while on the 13th of July he took an airing in the carriage. But the fiat had gone forth which told out the number of his days, and all the care of his friends, and the skill of his physicians, availed not to counteract it. There is something, to my taste, touching, yet sacred in the extreme, in the tone of the great man's Diary, as it is thenceforth kept—a mere record of bodily sufferings,—inscribed too in characters which sufficiently indicate the approach of the moment which should arrest their progress for ever. Take, as a specimen, the following extracts, beginning with that which describes the occurrences of the 13th :—

"I took an airing after dinner in the coach, with Mrs. Hastings. In leaving it I was seized with staggering, I sent for Mr. Haynes, who took from me about seven ounces of blood. The bandage loosening, I lost much more. After the operation I slept a little, and awoke in great and universal agitation, which ceased with the second discharge of blood. I slept well, and awoke as usual, but with additional weakness.

"14th. Mrs. H. wrote an excuse to the Duke of Gloucester, who was engaged to come on Thursday, and sent Robert with the letter.

"15th. Robert returned early with an answer, written after a music meeting at Gloucester. I have passed this day unexpectedly and regretfully well.

"16th. I passed an unquiet night, and arose with my limbs weak and shaken.

"19th. My health better, but strength much diminished. I dined alone. I sat in the great chair much of the middle of the night, and afterwards in the bed; lay till late.

"20th. I awoke with my throat much swelled, and a difficulty of swallowing; at breakfast, continued unabated, which I took alone, but without pain, and my appetite the same as it has been, unchanged through all other variations. At night I took ten grains of magnesia, with rhubarb. I cannot recollect the loss of time, but ascribe the past events of this day to weakness.

"21st. ——"

Alas!! there is no entry on the 21st. The figures stand there on the margin of the leaf, but the leaf itself is a blank. Mr. Hastings's Diary was never afterwards resumed. It is well, perhaps, under these circumstances, that I am still enabled to carry on my story in the words of one who witnessed the sufferings of the illustrious patient, and did his best to lessen them. The following is from Sir Charles Imhoff to Mr. David Anderson, of St. Germain's, and I would not substitute for its unaffected statement of facts, any narrative of my own.

To David Anderson, Esq.

Daylesford House, Chipping Norton, 12th August, 1818.

My dear Sir,—I grieve to tell you that our valuable friend Mr. Hastings has been very ill, and is still suffering much by a complaint that has affected the throat, and almost entirely prevented the power of deglutition. This disease has been attended occasionally by fever, and we have been in a state of great uneasiness and suspense; however, I think I may venture to add that I perceive a considerable amendment. He took his breakfast yesterday with some little degree of comfort, and to-day he has repeated the same, with additional ease therefore I pray that I may have it in my power to write you more favourable accounts in the course of a few days. Our dear friend talked much of you yesterday, and of Mrs. Anderson, and expressed his joy that your son Hastings was recovered from so severe an indisposition. I beg you to be assured of the pleasure we derive from this circumstance, and we will thank you to remember us kindly to him, as likewise to Mr. David Anderson.

We hope Mrs. Anderson is recovered from her late severe illness; assure her, I pray you, of our kindest remembrance. Accept the best affection of Mr. Hastings, and distribute the best regard to all your circle. I am, my dear Sir, yours faithfully.

C. IMHOFF.

The hopes held out by Sir Charles Imhoff, and greedily welcomed by the gentleman to whom they were offered, were not destined to receive their accomplishment. Mr. Hastings grew perceptibly worse from hour to hour, till in the end all power of deglutition failed him. I cannot describe, with the fidelity of those who witnessed it, the extent of his patience under such a load of suffering, or the gentleness with which he smiled upon the anxious faces that were gathered round his couch, bidding them look up to the God in whom he trusted. But one remarkable trait of the tenderness and undying nature of his love for the wife of his bosom, and his friend and companion through so many years of vicissitudes, it would ill become me to omit. On the 3rd of August, just nineteen days previous to his decease, when the malady which preyed upon his vitals had attained its height, and the certainty of a speedy deliverance was strong upon him, he dictated the following letter to his old and faithful friend Mr. Toone. The Court of Directors did not feel themselves called upon to attend to the dying request of the most illustrious man whom their service had ever produced, but that is a matter with which I, as his biographer, have no concern. His letter to Mr. Toone ran thus :—

To S. Toone, Esq.

Daylesford House, 3d August, 1818.

My dearest Friend,—I impose upon myself the last office of communication between you and me, to inform you that a few hours remain which are to separate us from each other for ever, and I was willing to perform it with my own hand; but on a slight trial I have found it beyond my remaining powers, and the hand that writes this is as authentic and equally dear to me as my own. The infliction that must end me is a total privation of the function of deglutition, which is equivalent to the extremity of hunger by the inability to take nourishment. I have called you by the only appellation that language can express, my "yar wooffadar," my profitable friend; for such, with every other quality of friendship, I have ever experienced yours to be in all our mutual intercourse, and my heart has returned it (unprofitably I own) but with equal sentiments of the purest affection. In the approaching hour I feel but one mixed interest, I mean the loss of the annuity which I derive from my benefactors the East India Company, which must cease with my life, and leave the dearest object of all my mortal concerns in a state of more than comparative indigence. This is not one to which she ought to be reduced, for she has been the virtual means of supporting the powers of life and action by which in so long an interval (I think thirteen years) I was enabled to maintain their affairs in vigour, strength, credit, and respect; and in one instance especially, when she was in the city of Patna, and I in a seat of greater danger, she proved the personal means of guarding one province of their Indian dominion from impending ruin by her own independent fortitude and presence of mind, varying with equal effect as every variation of event called upon her for fresh exertions of it. My own conscience assuredly attests that I myself have not been wanting in my duty to my respectable employers, and I require no further return than the continuance of that reward which they have thought proper equally to confer on my services and sufferings; the latter have been great, but not without their reward from my country. I allude to them only, though I feel them with the deepest gratitude. Whatever causes may have occasionally, and in the midst of contending opinions, partially drawn their benevolence from me, I quit the world and their service, to which I shall conceive myself to the latest moment that I draw my breath still devotedly attached, in the firm belief that in the efficient body of the Court of Directors I leave not an individual ill affected towards me. I do not express my full feelings. I believe them all to be kindly, generously disposed towards me; and to the larger and constituent body, I can only express a hope that, if there are any of a different sentiment, the number is but few, for they have supported me when I thought myself abandoned by all the other powers from whom I ever thought myself entitled to that benefit.

The appeal which I now make I could not deliver without a sense of presumption to the Court of Directors themselves. I hope I do not carry that presumption too far in approaching them through you, my declared and beloved friend, into whose hands I commit it, without further expression,—indeed I have already exhausted its last powers. My latest prayers shall be offered for their service; for the welfare of my beloved country; and for that also of the land whose interests were so long committed to my partial guardianship, and for which I feel a sentiment in my departing hours not alien from that which is due from every subject to his own. To you, my friend, I close with my grateful thanks for the many proofs I have received of your friendship, and my prayers for every individual of your blessed family. Adieu.

Having read over and signed this letter, Mr. Hastings felt that his business with the world was ended. He turned his attention, therefore, exclusively, as far as extreme bodily suffering would allow, to other and holier concerns; and, surrounded by a group of true and mourning friends, by Mrs. Hastings, Sir Charles and Lady Imhoff, his nephew; Mr. Woodman and Mrs. Woodman, Mrs. Hastings's niece, he received, at the hands of the clergyman of the parish, the sacrament of the Lord's Supper. But why continue these details? Let two of those who were present when the event occurred describe how this great and good man gave up the ghost. Of the following letters, one is from the pen of Mrs. Barton, a lady to whom Mr. Hastings had stood godfather, and from whom he never, throughout many vicissitudes of fortune, withdrew his regard. The other, blistered with the tears which she shed while she was writing, came from Mr. Hastings's beloved daughter-in-law, the present Lady Imhoff. I trust she will pardon me for having put upon record a document which does so much honour to her true and gentle heart.

To David Anderson, Esq.

Daylesford, 23d August, 1818.

My dear Sir,—Sir C. Imhoff's letter will have prepared you for the heart-rending intelligence I have now the pain to comumnicate to you, of the death of the most perfect of human beings (the indulgent friend and parent of my life), our beloved and most dear Mr. Hastings!

He had been ill nearly six weeks; and from its first approach, his illness bore an alarming aspect, and his sufferings were very great indeed—borne with uncomplaining fortitude, the most touching meekness of temper, and pious resignation to the will of God. But his last moments, we have the consolation to know, were, by the skill and attention of Sir H. Halford, rendered easy; and his pure and gentle spirit quitted its earthly abode yesterday evening at seven, without a struggle or even a sigh.

Sir C. Imhoff would, I am sure, have performed this melancholy task of writing to you, but he is much indisposed, and unable to exert himself; and to me it is a particular and soothing satisfaction to pay respectful attention to the feelings of those who were so dear as you were to the heart and esteem of my ever dear and beloved Mr. Hastings.

Your last letter was read to him, and he expressed the most affectionate interest in the welfare of you and yours. I am, my dear Sir, in the deepest affliction for the dreadful, dreadful loss I have sustained, yours very truly and sincerely,

MARIAN BARTON.

From Lady Imhoff to the same.

Daylesford House, 26th August, 1818.

My dear Sir,—Sir Charles has just received your letter, so full of feeling and anxious inquiries after our adored friend. You will have learnt the sad, sad news from the pen of Mrs. Barton. But to *such* friends of our blessed saint's, as you and yours ever were, I cannot resist taking up my pen to explain to you why you did not have the most painful tidings either from Imhoff or myself, rather than from a common acquaintance. Mrs. Barton had written the letter before I had gained composure enough for the purpose; and Imhoff was so much indisposed in body, as well as afflicted in mind, that he was confined to his bed. I thank you, my dear Sir, for asking so particularly after me, because, knowing the attachment that my heart and soul bore to that heavenly being, I am sure you would well say, "Where was Lady Imhoff?" Thank heaven! I was for the last month close to his bed and couch side, with his adored hand in mine, and to my lips; and often has he waved it over my head, and said, "God bless you, my dear Charlotte"—which blessings have rooted deep in my sorrowing heart; for as his sad sufferings ended, mine and ours began, to last as long as we have breath. Oh, such sweetness! such kindness! such patience! such affectionate thanks for little kindnesses and attentions, that our hearts ever prompted, was enough to break them before they had finished their duty. I gave the adored and patient sufferer the last thing he took, a mouthful of cold water, and for which he put his blessed hand on mine, for he could not then speak, and in one hour after, his pure spirit was taken to heaven, without our knowing exactly when it fled, for it left his beloved, benign countenance without a *trace* of pain or suffering upon it; and it is still the feast of my eyes (if such an expression can be understood as I feel it), and the exact counterpart of the marble bust in the library. Dearest Mrs. Hastings, and Imhoff, and Mrs. and Miss Barton were around him. Not one impatient expression ever escaped him. Never did he ask or wish for medical advice; he always said, "Surely at my age it is time to go;" and he all along said, "God only can do me good;" and to our anxious hope of his being better, he would say, "My dear, why wish me to live to suffer thus? none of you know what I suffer." It was the vitals that were attacked; and the heat within his throat and left side was, I am convinced, dreadful. Nothing gave him any satisfaction (and that was momentary) but the coldest water in his mouth, for the power of deglutition having long failed, nothing went into the stomach; and when Sir Henry Halford saw this sad, emaciated, patient sufferer, he said, that he had, ever since the attack in the throat, *lived on his own substance.* He gave us the only consolation in his power, which was, that everything had been done that could be done. One of the latest *true* pleasures he had, was hearing me read to him your letter to my husband; and in my hearing he blest you all. Our poor dear Mrs. Hastings, deeply as she is, and must long be, affected, bears up as well as we could possibly expect. Oh, my dear Sir, you who knew him, can feel for us in the ever-to-be-deplored, irreparable loss we have had in such a sincere, angelic friend; but God has, I am sure, placed him in the best of his house, where "he has many mansions;" and perhaps he is now our guardian angel, as I told him I hoped he would be, if the Almighty judged fit to rob us of our treasure in this world. Farewell, my dear Sir; my love to dear Mrs. Anderson, and kindest compliments to Miss Anderson, and kindest regards to your sons. Did poor dear Mrs. Hastings know I was writing, I should be charged with everything kind from her. Always your sincere, faithful, and obliged friend,

CHARLOTTE IMHOFF.

P. S. I fear you will scarcely be able to read what I have with much difficulty seen to write. Imhoff charges me to give his affectionate regards to you and yours.

Thus died, in the eighty-sixth year of his age, the Right Honourable Warren Hastings, of whom it may with truth be affirmed, that, whether we look to his public or his private career,—to the eminent services which he rendered to his country, or to the many graces and virtues which adorned his individual character,—neither his own nor any other age has produced a man more entitled to a nation's gratitude, more deserving of the love and reverence of all who enjoyed the privilege of his familiar acquaintance. Of the public character of that great and good man, I do not think that I am here required to say one word. The unvarnished record of his proceedings is now before the public; and if it fail to establish his claim to be accounted both an upright and a sagacious statesman, everything like panegyric, whether proceeding from me or from others better qualified to speak his praise, must fall pointless to the ground. For Mr. Hastings's merits are not like those of men less severely tried, to be set forth by an array of generalities however skilfully put together. It would but insult his memory were I to describe him, for example, as brave, patient, persevering, long-sighted, and industrious. He was all this, and a great deal more; he belonged to that class, limited in point of numbers, in extent of moral influence on their own and succeeding generations defying all our powers of computation, who win empires or preserve them, in despite of difficulties and discouragements such as men of a grasp of mind less comprehensive by a single hair's-breadth, would have refused to encounter. Mr. Hastings's claim to the admiration of the wise and the good must therefore be judged of by the history of his whole life. It would be worse than idle, were I, at the close of a narrative like the present, to seek, in a few well-turned and laboured sentences, to set them forth.

But while I thus express myself, let me not forget to remind the reader that Mr. Hastings was not only great in his public capacity, but good. As the individual appointed to preserve and consolidate the British empire in Asia, he never, indeed, permitted his energies to slumber. He restored order, in times of peace, to provinces which were in absolute confusion when he received them; and established a system of administration, under which, had it been acted upon perseveringly, the resources of the country would have been, even in his own day, fully developed. So also when war came, he met it boldly; and in spite of the ceaseless opposition of those with whom it was appointed him to consult, he brought it to a triumphant conclusion. But this is not all. Mr. Hastings, against whom the Commons of England brought the charge, among others, that he cruelly oppressed the natives of India, and laid their country waste, was, by these natives of every rank and class, looked up to as a father; and is still spoken of by their descendants as the greatest benefactor to their race of all whom their European masters ever set over them. I cannot think of referring the reader, while discussing such a subject, to the addresses and testimonials which, during the progress of his trial, poured in upon Mr. Hastings from all parts of India. These are not, indeed, without their value, and might, if they stood alone, be appealed to as affording abundant proof that his humanity was equal to his vigour. But tradition is, in cases of this sort, of much more value than contemporary evidence; and tradition, both local and general, as well in retired villages as at the seat of government, is all in Mr. Hastings's favour. There are three portraits suspended in the town hall of Calcutta, which no native from the interior ever approaches without doing homage to them, and one of these is the likeness of Warren Hastings.

I believe that they who most delight in comparing illustrious men together have instituted no parallel between Mr. Hastings and any other Governor of British India than Lord Clive. "Lord Clive," it is said, "acquired for England her empire in the East; Mr. Hastings saved it. They were equally instruments adapted to the necessities of the times in which they lived, and equally deserve to be held in grateful remembrance by their country." Far be it from me to detract from the merits, or undervalue the services, of Lord Clive. The former were worthy of all honour, the latter were bravely and perseveringly carried through. Yet as the difficulties of his situation are not for a moment to be compared with those which Mr. Hastings was required to surmount, so I am quite sure that the debt of gratitude due at this hour to the memory of the great statesman is a thousandfold more pressing than that which England owes to her great warrior. For, in the first place, if Clive conquered an empire, he did so in the common course of events. He had a feeble enemy to oppose him, and he carried the might of England in his train. Whereas Mr. Hastings saved the same empire when assailed from without by the most formidable combination that ever threatened its existence, and enlarged its bounds, and consolidated its strength, not only without support from those under which he acted, but in direct opposition to their wishes. And finally, supposing the merits of the two men to have been equal, how stands the balance of their rewards? Lord Clive returned to England enormously rich; he was raised to the peerage; and, though persecuted for a while by the violence of faction, left his titles and his wealth to his children. Mr. Hastings came back with a fortune barely adequate to place him in the rank of a private gentleman; he was immediately arraigned as a criminal before the highest tribunal in the land, and, after a trial which continued throughout nine whole years, obtained an acquittal, and was reduced to beggary. I need not pursue the subject further. To Lord Clive, in his lifetime, a grateful country offered, in defiance of faction, many palpable marks of its favour. The same country owes to the memory of Mr. Hastings, not only the recompense of valuable services bestowed, but compensation for heavy wrongs inflicted, and never to this hour atoned for.

When we turn again to contemplate the private character of Mr. Hastings, we find it so richly endowed with all that connects man with his Maker; so full of gentleness, patience, long suffering, meekness, temperance; so true, so just, so generous, so placable, that a disposition to paint in detail is restrained by the apprehension, groundless perhaps, yet not unnatural, lest the language of truth should be mistaken for that of prejudice, or, at all events, of exaggerated panegyric.

I cannot, however, after the full exposure which has been made to me of all Mr. Hastings's habits of thinking and of acting, speak of him in other terms than as the most amiable of his race. His genius, expansive as it was, and adapted to the highest place in the management of empires, seems to me to have been the attribute for which he least deserved the reverence of his fellow men. He was the tenderest and most affectionate of husbands; the kindest of masters; the truest and most disinterested of friends; charitable, giving to the term its just, because its most comprehensive meaning; liberal, high-minded, unselfish. He had no faults, even of temper, for that was calm and serene, and thoroughly disciplined; and to sum up all, his religion was at once deep, sincere, and unobtrusive. I repeat, that I have not been able, by all the researches which I have instituted, to discover in the character of Warren Hastings a single trait which I can venture to denounce as a fault, for his weaknesses, and weaknesses he doubtless had, were all of such a nature as to carry our best sympathies along with them, and enlist more and more our affections on the side of him whose greatness they shaded, only so far as they brought his amiable and gentle feelings prominently into view.

It is not, however, by dwelling upon topics so general as these, that I can hope to convey to the minds of such as knew him not, any just idea of the sort of place which Mr. Hastings filled in society, after the cares and anxieties of office had ceased to perplex him. Let me rather draw the reader's attention to one or two minute details, for my knowledge of which I am indebted to one of Mr. Hastings's most valued friends, who, being himself a frequent guest at Daylesford, had the best opportunity of judging, and whose modesty alone prevents me from recording his name in connexion with the debt of kindness which I owe him. The following is the substance of much that he was good enough to write for my information, and which, but for a prohibition to the contrary, I should have greatly preferred giving in his own words.

" From the period when my intimacy with Mr. Hastings began," says my correspondent, " that is to say, from 1799 to the date of his lamented death, he resided chiefly in the country, with intermissions occasioned solely by visits to his friends, and now and then a month, or a portion of a month, spent in London. From the latter he never returned without the strongest expressions of predilection for his own delightful home, where all his affections centered. Indeed, Mr. Hastings's tastes were essentially domestic ; for though he lived in the constant interchange of a liberal hospitality with a distinguished and admiring neighbourhood, it was among his own guests, at his own table, in his own study, and in the bosom of his own family, that he appeared ever most like himself, and therefore to the greatest advantage." Of his habit of early rising, as well as of the manner in which he was accustomed to comport himself during the progress of the general breakfast, in which he never joined, I have already given an account ; yet it was not on such occasions only that he ministered to their comforts, while he laboured to amuse, and to instruct both the guests of a day, and the members of his own household. Mr. Hastings was never at a loss for the most agreeable as well as edifying subjects of conversation ; for he was alive at once to all the events that were passing both at home and abroad, and conversant not less with the grave than with the lighter literature of the day. Moreover, his mind, though deeply stored with moral and philosophical thought, was tinctured to a remarkable extent with classical elegance. He made, indeed, no pretensions to scholastic learning, and had so far, during the more active season of his life, lost the habit of pursuing it, that when leisure came he never thought seriously of resuming his studies, yet nobody could fail to perceive that at one period he must have been familiar with the best Greek and Latin authors; and that on the model which they offered, his own views of excellence in literary composition were formed. At the same time there was a peculiarity about his taste in these matters, which deserves notice. While Mr. Hastings praised, as they deserved, the authors, both ancient and modern, whom the universal judgment of scholars has placed at the head of their respective departments; his quotations, strange to say, were more frequently taken from Lucan, for example, than from either Homer or Virgil; from Young, than from Shakspeare or Milton. This is curious enough, especially with reference to Young, whose images are invariably as sombre as his train of thought is melancholy. Yet the circumstance may be accounted for, when we bear in mind that sympathy of feeling exercises in such cases a greater influence over our memories, at least, than the dictates of judgment. Let me not, however, be misunderstood. Grave and even sombre thought was not distasteful to Mr. Hastings; indeed his writings prove that he frequently indulged in it. Nevertheless his mind and conversation were both essentially cheerful, without however descending, under any circumstances, to the tolerance of levity. Mr. Hastings, capable, in no ordinary degree, of the exercise of wit, was keenly alive to the perception of it in others. He laughed heartily, could trifle with the gayest, and thought it not beneath him to relish a pun; but the most remote approach to ribaldry offended his taste, and never failed of receiving from him an immediate check.

Of the absolute unselfishness of Mr. Hastings's nature the reader is by this time aware. He was the most benevolent of human beings; yet in all his tenderness for the feelings of others,—in all his disregard of his own, he never lost sight of the grand principle of justice, without which benevolence degenerates into weakness. His warmest personal predilections could not hinder him from rebuking in those whom he loved a deviation from integrity, however slight; and these rebukes were invariably given with a gravity of which the most inconsiderate failed not to acknowledge the force. In like manner there was no exertion which he was not ready to make, provided he saw before him the prospect of benefiting a fellow-creature, were it only by raising him in his own esteem, and winning for him the good opinion of others. Over the reputations of his youthful friends in particular, and they were both numerous and sincerely attached, he used to watch with more than parental anxiety; and he never omitted an opportunity of leading them on to increased exertion, by assigning a full measure of praise to exertions that were past. Take the following as a specimen of the delicacy and admirable taste with which he was accustomed to dispense these important favours.

When Mr. E. B. Impey, the son of Sir Elijah, and the elegant author of the Illustrations of German Poetry, was a student of Christ Church, Oxford, Mr. Hastings was accustomed, both for his own sake and for the sake of his father's memory, which he dearly loved, to have the young man very much about him. At the termination of one of these visits he presented the student with a beautiful Persian mare, of which, with the respect for order and nicety which distinguished all his proceedings, he drew up an elaborate pedigree. Mr. Impey rode the gentle creature back to college, and not long afterwards thanked the donor in a Latin epigram of great merit, to which a Sapphic ode was appended. The author of these elegant trifles thought no more about them, till one day the dean, the celebrated Cyril Jackson, came into his garret with some manuscripts in his hands, and, very much to Mr. Impey's astonishment, showed to him his own poems. The verses, it appeared, had been sent by Mr. Hastings to the dean. The dean was charmed with the good taste and scholarship which they displayed, and immediately formed, as in such cases he was apt to do, a cordial friendship for their author. "To that act of kindness on Mr. Hastings's part," writes Mr. Impey, "I owe in a very great degree my introduction to the notice of the late dean, and the favour and protection of that distinguished man, which, in after life, were on various occasions productive to me of essential benefit."

Another remarkable feature in the character of Mr. Hastings was the dignity with which he abstained from complaining of his own wrongs, far more of giving utterance to harsh or reproachful expressions, while alluding to the individuals who had been chiefly instrumental in producing them. Indeed his own career, and the recompense which it received, were topics of conversation which he never voluntarily introduced. Nevertheless the subject was one on which, when broached by others, he exhibited no disinclination to enter; and he always spoke of it with a degree of dignified reverence, which marked his consciousness, without any display of the merit that was attributed to him. At the same time, when reviewing, as he was sometimes induced to do, the circumstances of his trial—the bitterness and overwhelming talents of his accusers, and the establishment of his own innocence in despite of all,—he was never known to utter a sentence from which the listener would be able to collect that a feeling, in the most remote degree allied to the vindictive, cankered in his soul. On the contrary, his indignation would, for the most part, evaporate either in some devout expression of resignation to God's will, or by and bye in an expostulatory copy of verses, or a pointed epigram. It must not, however, be supposed that Mr. Hastings was ever otherwise than alive, either to the extent of his own wrongs or to the demerits of such as had inflicted them. The former he taught himself to bear with magnanimity; the latter he was prompt to forgive: but he could not forget either the one or the other. Nor was forgetfulness in his case to be expected; for Mr. Hastings had to lament not only the active malice of avowed enemies, but the unaccountable tardiness of professing friends to fulfil expectations which they had themselves excited. "I wish," said he, a few days previous to his death, when the subject of the Regent's behaviour at Guildhall chanced to come under discussion, "I wish the Prince, for his own sake, had abstained from making that display of his good intentions. I was a Privy Councillor at the moment; it was not worth while to speak of more, when more, as the event has shown, was not intended."

Another instance of the self-possession which never deserted him, as well as of the dignity which threw its halo over all his proceedings, I am enabled to give on the authority of an eye-witness.

It happened about the year 1810 that Mr. Hastings, being on a visit at Newark Park, the residence of Sir Elijah Impey, received an invitation from the Prince Regent, then at Brighton, to dine with his Royal Highness in the Pavilion. Mr. Hastings went, Sir Elijah and his son bearing him company; and all three were a good deal surprised to find that Mr. Sheridan had been especially brought thither to meet them. The object which the Prince had in view was, doubtless, laudable. He was anxious that between Mr. Hastings and Mr. Sheridan—not the least violent of the violent men who acted as managers during the impeachment—a good understanding should arise, and he brought them together under the idea that, through his personal influence, they might become reconciled. Mr. Sheridan accordingly advanced, at a given signal from his royal host, and in some well-turned sentences delivered himself of an apology, which amounted to this:—"that the part which he had taken in events long gone by must not be regarded as any test of his private opinions, because he was then a public pleader, whose duty it is, under all circumstances, to make good, if he can, the charges which he is commissioned to bring forward." Mr. Hastings retreated one step, looked Mr. Sheridan full in the face, made a low bow, but answered not a word. "Had Mr. Sheridan," said he, after the party returned to Newark

Park, "confessed as much twenty years ago, he might have done me some service." No further intercourse, however, took place between the parties, nor was the subject ever again by Mr. Hastings referred to.

I have spoken elsewhere of Mr. Hastings's skill both in horticulture and farming. I have nothing to add to that statement, except that he transacted business with his bailiff as regularly and with as much care as if the subsistence of himself and his family had depended on the management of his crops. The functionary in question, who is still, I believe, the principal tenant on the estate of Daylesford, was always addressed by him as "Farmer Bowles;" and Farmer Bowles, like the rest of his domestics and dependants, loved Mr. Hastings tenderly. Nor was this all. In the arrangement and decoration of his pleasure grounds, Mr. Hastings played the part not only of a scientific landscape gardener, but of a skilful artisan. The lakes, the waterfalls, the very groups of rockwork which are dispersed about the gardens and shrubberies of Daylesford, owe in some measure their forms to his manual exertions; for besides giving directions, it was his pride to take the lead in carrying out plans which his own ingenuity had devised. It is worthy of remark that the large stones which principally compose these grottoes were brought from a place in the vicinity of Daylesford, where for centuries they had lain, not without the distinction of having more than one wild legend attached to them. They are mentioned by Nash and other topographical writers as " the grey geese of Addlestrop."

Mr. Hastings's hospitality was on all occasions dispensed on the most liberal and considerate scale. When he first established himself at Daylesford, indeed, it was his custom to entertain not only his friends as often as they chose to visit him, but their horses and servants, without any other limits than the capacity of his stables, which were extensive. By and bye, however, he discovered that, with corn at the height of the war prices, such a practice was incompatible with a narrow income, and not without bitter expressions of regret, of which I find the record in his Diary, he followed the example of his neighbours and broke through it. Still his attention to his guests continued to be of the most gratifying as well as considerate kind. His own room lay contiguous to the large library, which at Daylesford was the place of common resort during the forenoon; and of his anxious care for their convenience, his friends were never long left without the most satisfactory proofs. When the pressure of business compelled him, as it often did, to absent himself for a few hours from the circle, he was sure to look in, from time to time, for the purpose of ascertaining whether any thing were needed which he could supply. And finally, he always found leisure to join in the out-door excursions or amusements which might be proposed. He rode or drove, or walked abroad every day, provided the state of the weather would permit; and he never took this exercise without carrying one or more delighted companions along with him.

I do not know how far it may be necessary to add, that Mr. Hastings was exceedingly temperate both in eating and drinking. His table, indeed, was always supplied with the most delicate viands, and in a very graceful manner, for he particularly shone by his urbanity as a host, and the manners of Mrs. Hastings were delightful; but his own diet was simple in the extreme. He was a great water-drinker, and so fastidious in the quality of the beverage, that he would send for it when in London from a considerable distance to the spring which rises near the barracks that adjoin to Kensington Gardens. But I must not continue these details any further. The bent of Mr. Hastings's disposition urged him unceasingly to the practice of benevolence in the most extended sense of the term. The temper of his mind and heart were in every respect noble, and lofty, and pure; and, above all, religion, a sacred and a vital principle, never seems with him to have slumbered;—whether he were occupied in doing good to his fellow creatures, or in conducting, as he regularly did, the morning and evening worship of his household before the throne of their common Creator. For among others of his remains, I find forms of prayer such as he was in the habit of using in the domestic circle, and I am bound to state that by the simple grandeur of the style, not less than by the purity of the sentiments expressed in them, they do equal honour to his literary taste and to the simplicity and the depth of his devotional feelings.

Mr. Hastings died, as I have already stated, on the 22nd of August, his last moments being strictly in keeping with the calm dignity and self composure which characterized the whole course of his active life. Of the nature of his malady, I have already made mention. It was such as to waste his bodily strength from hour to hour, and to subject his frame to great agony, without producing any debilitating effect upon his mind; and the consequence was that he was himself perfectly aware of the near approach of the crisis long before the most watchful of his kind and watchful attendants observed it. For many days he could receive no nutriment whatever. Water, taken from a particular spring, was indeed the only beverage which he would accept; and he held it in his mouth only till the fever which burned up his throat and pallet had deprived it of its extreme coldness. But even of that, not one drop passed into the stomach; for the organs of deglutition were paralyzed, and any attempt to swallow brought on convulsions. At length, however, nature gave way. "I am going at last, my Charlotte," said he to Lady Imhoff, whose hand was clasped in his, as she sat at the bed-side; "I feel that I am going at last; and, Oh, I am grateful."

"Your voice is strong, dear Mr. Hastings," was her reply; "God will not take you from us yet."

"You do not know what I suffer," was his answer; "God bless you, my children; I leave you to Marian's care, she will bless you when—"

As he said this, he loosened the hold of Lady Imhoff's hand, and, not without a visible effort, drew a cambric pocket handkerchief, which lay on the pillow beside him, over his own face. His weeping attendants neither restrained him, nor formed any augury from the proceeding. Wherefore their grief and horror may be imagined when, finding that he suffered it to lie there some time, they removed the covering, and beheld the features of a corpse. I do not know what the principle may have been which swayed him; whether an anxious desire to save the feelings of his friends, or that he wished to hide from all mortal eyes the last struggle while it was in progress, but however this was, the act of covering up his own face in the very moment of severance between soul and body has about it a character which I can describe as nothing short of sublime. Unless my memory deceive me, there are but three great men in history of whom a similar anecdote is related—Socrates after he had swallowed the hemlock, Pompey when the assassin's sword was bare, and Julius Cæsar composing himself to death in the Capitol. Doubtless the same lofty sense of self-respect which operated with them, operated with Warren Hastings also. They would not exhibit their weakness, even in death, to any other gaze than that of the Creator.

The funeral of Mr. Hastings, though meant to be strictly private, was attended by all the noblemen and gentlemen who resided in the neighbourhood of Daylesford. It took place on the 9th; and in a grave behind the chancel of the church, which is now railed round, and surmounted by an urn, all that was mortal of one of England's best and greatest sons went to its rest. His monument, likewise, which confronts you as you enter the sacred pile itself, is eminently characteristic both of the modesty and the worth of Mr. Hastings. It is a plain mural tablet of white marble, erected, I believe, at the expense of his widow, with a transcript from the legend of which I bring my labours to a close, not without a deep sense of their inadequacy to do justice to the great importance of my subject. The inscription runs thus:—

In a Vault,
Just beyond the Eastern extremity of this Church,
Lies the Body of the Right Honourable WARREN HASTINGS,
Of Daylesford House, in this Parish,
The first Governor-General of the British Territories in India,
A Member of His Majesty's Most Honourable Privy Council,
LL. D. and F. R. S.:
The last public effort of whose eminently virtuous and lengthened life was
the re-erection of this sacred edifice, which he superintended with
singular energy and interest to its completion;
And in which, alas!
The holy rites of Sepulture were very shortly afterwards performed
over his Mortal Remains.
He died on the 22d of August, 1818,
Aged 85 Years and 8 Months.
"Lord, lettest thou thy servant depart in peace."

THE END.

London: Printed by W. CLOWES and SONS, Stamford Street.